5000611847

KT-560-876

WITHDRAWN

Contemporary Debates in Cognitive Science

Contemporary Debates in Philosophy

In teaching and research, philosophy makes progress through argumentation and debate. *Contemporary Debates in Philosophy* presents a forum for students and their teachers to follow and participate in the debates that animate philosophy today in the western world. Each volume presents opposing viewpoints on contested themes and topics in the central subfields of philosophy, and is edited and introduced by an expert in the field. The opposing essays, commissioned especially for the volumes in the series, are thorough but accessible presentations of opposing points of view.

1. Contemporary Debates in Philosophy of Religion *edited by Michael L. Peterson and Raymond J. VanArragon*
2. Contemporary Debates in Philosophy of Science *edited by Christopher Hitchcock*
3. Contemporary Debates in Epistemology *edited by Matthias Steup and Ernest Sosa*
4. Contemporary Debates in Applied Ethics *edited by Andrew I. Cohen and Christopher Heath Wellman*
5. Contemporary Debates in Aesthetics and the Philosophy of Art *edited by Matthew Kieran*
6. Contemporary Debates in Moral Theory *edited by James Dreier*
7. Contemporary Debates in Cognitive Science *edited by Robert J. Stainton*

Forthcoming *Contemporary Debates* are in:

Metaphysics *edited by Ted Sider, Dean Zimmerman, and John Hawthorne*
Philosophy of Mind *edited by Brian McLaughlin and Jonathan Cohen*
Social Philosophy *edited by Laurence Thomas*
Political Philosophy *edited by Thomas Christiano*
Philosophy of Language *edited by Ernie Lepore*

Contemporary Debates in Cognitive Science

Edited by

Robert J. Stainton

Blackwell
Publishing

© 2006 by Blackwell Publishing Ltd
except for editorial material and organization © 2006 by Robert J. Stainton

BLACKWELL PUBLISHING
350 Main Street, Malden, MA 02148-5020, USA
9600 Garsington Road, Oxford OX4 2DQ, UK
550 Swanston Street, Carlton, Victoria 3053, Australia

The right of Robert J. Stainton to be identified as the Author of the Editorial
Material in this Work has been asserted in accordance with the UK Copyright,
Designs, and Patents Act 1988.

All rights reserved. No part of this publication may be reproduced, stored in a
retrieval system, or transmitted, in any form or by any means, electronic, mechanical,
photocopying, recording or otherwise, except as permitted by the UK Copyright,
Designs, and Patents Act 1988, without the prior permission of the publisher.

First published 2006 by Blackwell Publishing Ltd

1 2006

Library of Congress Cataloging-in-Publication Data

Contemporary debates in cognitive science / edited by Robert J. Stainton.
    p.   cm. – (Contemporary debates in philosophy ; 7)
    Includes bibliographical references and index.
    ISBN-13: 978-1-4051-1304-5 (hardback : alk. paper)
    ISBN-10: 1-4051-1304-9 (hardback : alk. paper)
    ISBN-13: 978-1-4051-1305-2 (pbk. : alk. paper)
    ISBN-10: 1-4051-1305-7 (pbk. : alk. paper)   1. Cognitive science–Philosophy.
  I. Stainton, Robert J.   II. Series.

    BF311.C659 2006
    153–dc22

                                                                          2005026948

A catalogue record for this title is available from the British Library.

Set in 10/12.5pt Rotis Serif
by Graphicraft Limited, Hong Kong
Printed and bound in the UK
by TJ International, Padstow, Cornwall

The publisher's policy is to use permanent paper from mills that operate a sustainable
forestry policy, and which has been manufactured from pulp processed using acid-free
and elementary chlorine-free practices. Furthermore, the publisher ensures that the text
paper and cover board used have met acceptable environmental accreditation standards.

For further information on
Blackwell Publishing, visit our website:
www.blackwellpublishing.com

Contents

Acknowledgments

A great number of people – too many to mention here – made suggestions of topics, authors, etc. as the volume took shape. I am grateful for their (sometimes anonymous) help. I am also grateful, of course, to the authors for their excellent contributions ... and for their patience while the book was completed. I would also like to thank the extremely helpful crew at Blackwell. Finally, I must acknowledge the Carleton University Doctoral Program in Cognitive Science. My sense of what cognitive science is, and my understanding of all the issues discussed in this volume, derive largely from a decade or so spent working with colleagues and students in that wonderful unit. Special thanks to Andy Brook, its founder. This book is dedicated to him.

Notes on Contributors

Adele Abrahamsen is Associate Project Scientist in the Center for Research in Language at the University of California, San Diego. Her research focuses on the onset and early development of symbolic gestures and words as well as foundational and theoretical issues in cognitive science. She is author of *Child Language: An Interdisciplinary Guide to Theory and Research* (1977) and coauthor, with William Bechtel, of *Connectionism and the Mind* (Blackwell, 2002).

William Bechtel is Professor in the Department of Philosophy and the interdisciplinary programs in Cognitive Science and Science Studies at the University of California, San Diego. Much of his recent research addresses the nature of mechanisms and mechanistic explanation as they figure in biology and cognitive science. He is author of *Discovering Cell Mechanisms* (forthcoming) and coauthor, with Robert Richardson, of *Discovering Complexity* (1993), and with Adele Abrahamsen, of *Connectionism and the Mind* (Blackwell, 2002). In addition, he is coeditor of *A Companion to Cognitive Science* (Blackwell, 1998) and *Philosophy and the Neurosciences* (Blackwell, 2001) as well as the journal *Philosophical Psychology*.

Peter Carruthers is Professor of Philosophy at the University of Maryland. His primary research interests for most of the last dozen years or so have been in the philosophy of psychology. He has worked especially on theories of consciousness and on the role of natural language in human cognition. But he has also published on such issues as: the nature and status of our folk psychology; nativism, and modularity; issues to do with evolutionary psychology and cognitive architecture; theories of intentional content; and defence of a notion of narrow content for psychological explanation. In a previous incarnation he trained as a Wittgensteinian, and published two monographs on Wittgenstein's *Tractatus*.

Brie Gertler is Associate Professor of Philosophy at the University of Virginia. She works on issues in the philosophy of mind, including the problem of self-knowledge, the status of physicalism, and the scope of mental content. Her papers have appeared in *Analysis, Noûs, Philosophical Studies, Philosophy and Phenomenological Research*, and other journals. She is editor of *Privileged Access: Philosophical Accounts of Self-Knowledge* (2003).

Gerd Gigerenzer is Director at the Max Planck Institute for Human Development, Berlin; former Professor of Psychology at the University of Chicago; and John M. Olin Distinguished Visiting Professor, School of Law, University of Virginia. His books include *Simple Heuristics that Make Us Smart* (with Peter Todd and the ABC Research Group, 1999), *Adaptive Thinking: Rationality in the Real World* (2000), *Bounded Rationality: The Adaptive Toolbox* (with Reinhard Selten, 2001), and *Reckoning with Risk* (2002, published in the US as *Calculated Risks*, 2002). He is the winner of the Association of American Publishers Prize for the best book in the Social and Behavioral Sciences, the American Association for the Advancement of Science (AAAS) Prize for Behavioral Science Research, and the 2002 German Science Book of the Year Prize.

Terence Horgan is Professor of Philosophy at the University of Arizona. He works, often collaboratively, in philosophy of mind, philosophy of cognitive science, epistemology, decision theory, metaphysics, metaethics, and philosophy of language. He and John Tienson coauthored *Connectionism and the Philosophy of Psychology* (1996). His recent articles include "Phenomenal intentionality and the brain in a vat" (with J. Tienson and G. Graham), in R. Schantz (ed.) *The Externalist Challenge* (2004), "Internal-world skepticism and the self-presentational character of phenomenal consciousness," in U. Kriegel and K. Williford (eds.) *Consciousness and Self-Reference* (forthcoming), and "Some ins and outs of transglobal reliabilism (with D. Henderson), in S. Goldberg (ed.) *The Externalism/Internalism Debate in Semantics and Epistemology* (forthcoming).

Ray Jackendoff is Professor of Philosophy and codirector of the Center for Cognitive Studies at Tufts University. He previously taught at Brandeis University. His research is centered on natural language semantics and its relation to human conceptualization, with major side interests in syntax, social cognition, consciousness, and musical cognition. He is a Fellow of the American Academy of Arts and Sciences and of the American Association for the Advancement of Science. He was President of the Linguistic Society of America in 2003 and of the Society for Philosophy and Psychology in 1991. His most recent books are *Foundations of Language* (2002) and, coauthored with Peter Culicover, *Simpler Syntax* (2005).

Kirk Ludwig is Professor of Philosophy at the University of Florida. He has published articles in the philosophy of language, mind, action, and epistemology. He is editor of *Donald Davidson* (2003) and coauthor with Ernie Lepore of *Donald Davidson: Meaning, Truth, Language and Reality* (2005), and the forthcoming *Donald Davidson: Truth-theoretic Semantics*.

William G. Lycan is William Rand Kenan, Jr. Professor of Philosophy at the University of North Carolina. He is author of *Logical Form in Natural Language* (1984), *Knowing Who* (with Steven Boër, 1985), *Consciousness* (1987), *Judgement and Justification* (1988), *Modality and Meaning* (1994), *Consciousness and Experience* (1996), *Philosophy of Language: A Contemporary Introduction* (2000), and *Real Conditionals* (2001). He has also edited an anthology, *Mind and Cognition* (Blackwell, 1990, 1999).

David Matheson completed his PhD in the Department of Philosophy at Brown University in 2003. His doctoral work, supervised by the prominent epistemologist Ernest Sosa, explored the relation between everyday knowledge commitments and epistemological theory. He is currently teaching in the Department of Philosophy at Carleton University (Ottawa, Canada), and is an executive committee member of the Canadian Society for Epistemology.

Robert J. Matthews is Professor of Philosophy, Rutgers University, and member of the Rutgers Center for Cognitive Science. His research is focused in the philosophy of mind and in the foundations of cognitive science, specifically computational psycholinguistics. He has particular interests both in propositional attitudes, propositional attitude ascriptions, and their role in cognitive scientific theorizing and in formal learning-theoretic models of first language acquisition and their import for linguistic nativism. He has just completed a book-length manuscript, *The Measure of Mind*, which argues for a measurement-theoretic account of the attitudes.

James McGilvray teaches philosophy of mind and philosophy of language at McGill University in Montreal; he is also coordinator for McGill's cognitive science program. His work in recent years has been strongly influenced by Chomsky's effort to construct a naturalistic science of language. Books include *Chomsky: Language, Mind, and Politics* (1999) and *The Cambridge Companion to Chomsky* (as editor and contributor, 2005).

Jesse J. Prinz is Associate Professor in the Department of Philosophy at the University of North Carolina at Chapel Hill. He taught previously in the Philosophy-Neuroscience-Psychology Program at Washington University in St Louis. He is the author of *Furnishing the Mind: Concepts and their Perceptual Basis* (2002), *Gut Reactions: A Perceptual Theory of Emotion* (2004), and two other forthcoming books. He is also the editor of the forthcoming *Handbook to the Philosophy of Psychology*. His areas of research include concepts, emotion, moral psychology, the nature/nurture debate, and the neural basis of consciousness.

Geoffrey K. Pullum is Professor of Linguistics and Distinguished Professor of Humanities at the University of California, Santa Cruz. In addition to many books and articles in theoretical linguistics, his publications include a book of humorous and satirical essays about the study of language called *The Great Eskimo Vocabulary Hoax* (1991), and *The Cambridge Grammar of the English Language* (with Rodney Huddleston and others, 2002), a descriptive grammar which was awarded the Leonard Bloomfield Book Award from the Linguistic Society of America in 2004. He

Notes on Contributors

was the Constance E. Smith Fellow at the Radcliffe Institute for Advanced Study at Harvard University in 2005–6, when his joint chapter with Barbara C. Scholz in this volume was completed.

Georges Rey completed his PhD in Philosophy at Harvard University in 1978. He works primarily on the foundations of cognitive science. He has published on issues of consciousness and qualia, concepts and intentionality, and the philosophy of linguistics. He is the author of *Contemporary Philosophy of Mind* (Blackwell, 1997), the editor (with Barry Loewer) of *Meaning in Mind: Fodor and His Critics* (Blackwell, 1991), and the section editor for cognitive science for the *Routledge Encyclopedia of Philosophy*. He has taught at SUNY Purchase, the University of Colorado, and has held visiting positions at MIT, CREA, the University of Split, the University of London, the Australian National University, and Stanford. He is presently Professor of Philosophy at the University of Maryland at College Park.

Richard Samuels is Lecturer in Philosophy at King's College, London. His research focuses primarily on issues in the philosophy of psychology and the foundations of cognitive science. He has published papers on nativism, cognitive architecture, evolutionary psychology and the implications of empirical psychology for our understanding of human rationality. He is currently completing a book on cognitive architecture.

Barbara C. Scholz lives in Santa Cruz, California, and held the Frieda L. Miller Fellowship at the Radcliffe Institute for Advanced Study at Harvard University during 2005–6, when her joint chapter with Geoffrey K. Pullum in this volume was completed. She publishes articles in journals of philosophy, psychology, linguistics, and psycholinguistics. Her particular interests lie in model-theoretic syntax and the philosophy of linguistic science.

John Tienson is Professor of Philosophy at the University of Memphis. He has published extensively on the foundations of cognitive science, including *Connectionism and the Philosophy of Psychology* (with Terence Horgan, 1996). He is currently working on a book in the philosophy of mind entitled *Phenomenal Intentionality*, with Terence Horgan and George Graham, Wake Forest University. He has recently published a dozen articles in the philosophy of mind related to the book, many with Horgan and Graham.

Christopher Viger has been assistant professor at the University of Western Ontario since 2002. He received his PhD in philosophy from McGill University in 1999 and has done postdoctoral work at Tufts University with Daniel Dennett; at the CUNY Graduate Center, with David Rosenthal; and at Rutgers University. His research areas are in philosophy of mind, philosophy of language, and cognitive science, with particular interest in the connection between language and thought in an attempt to find alternatives to the language of thought hypothesis. He has published in such journals as *Mind and Language*, *Synthese*, and *Philosophical Psychology*.

Ralph Wedgwood is a Lecturer in Philosophy at the University of Oxford and a Fellow of Merton College, Oxford. He has written several articles on metaethics and epistemology, and on related issues in metaphysics, philosophy of mind, and philosophy of language. He is currently finishing a book which gives a general theory of normative thought and discourse (that is, thought and discourse about what *ought* to be the case); this theory is based on the idea that "the intentional is normative" – that is, the idea that the nature of mental states that have "intentional content" can only be explained in partly normative terms.

Timothy Williamson is Wykeham Professor of Logic at Oxford University. He has also taught at Edinburgh University and Trinity College Dublin, and held visiting appointments at MIT, Princeton, ANU, and the University of Canterbury. He is the author of *Identity and Discrimination* (Blackwell, 1990), *Vagueness* (1994), and *Knowledge and its Limits* (2000), and of numerous articles in journals such as *Mind, Journal of Philosophy, Philosophical Review, Philosophy and Phenomenological Research, Mind and Language, Theory and Decision, Journal of Symbolic Logic, Journal of Philosophical Logic, Studia Logica,* and *Notre Dame Journal of Formal Logic.* He is a Fellow of the British Academy, the Royal Society of Edinburgh, and the Norwegian Academy of Science and Letters.

Notes on Contributors

Preface

Robert J. Stainton

This volume is about debates in cognitive science. Yet it is part of a series called *Contemporary Debates in Philosophy*. How can it be both?

Let's begin with what cognitive science is. It is the interdisciplinary attempt to understand the mind, most especially the human mind. More specifically, one can think of cognitive science as having four branches: there are the behavioral and brain sciences, like psycholinguistics, neuroscience, and cognitive psychology; there are those social sciences that more or less directly inform us about the mind, like anthropology and sociolinguistics; there are formal disciplines like logic, computer science, and especially Artificial Intelligence; and, finally, there are parts of philosophy, especially philosophy of mind and language. The hallmark of cognitive science, in brief, is that it draws on the methods and results of all these branches, to attempt to give a global understanding of the mind.

To anticipate a worry, the idea obviously is not that philosophy is wholly contained in cognitive science. To pick only two examples, history of philosophy and political philosophy clearly aren't parts of cognitive science. What's more, even some parts of, say, philosophy of mind don't fit easily within cognitive science, e.g., issues about personal identity and life after death. The intersection, rather, is between certain sub-areas of philosophy and the other three branches.

From this definition alone we can immediately see why a debate can be both part of cognitive science and part of philosophy – for there is overlap between the two overarching fields. Some of the debates in this volume exemplify overlap of that kind. Brie Gertler and William Lycan debate about the nature and source of consciousness. Peter Carruthers, Jesse Prinz, and Richard Samuels debate the variety and extent of modular specialization in the human mind. Geoffrey Pullum and Barbara Scholz debate with Robert Matthews and James McGilvray about how language develops in the mind, and specifically about the role that an innate endowment plays. Such questions are core parts of traditional philosophy of language and mind, but they are equally core parts of today's cognitive science. Thus there is an *intersection* of philosophy and cognitive science.

There is another way, however, in which a debate can be both philosophical and cognitive scientific. Many researchers accept that, though philosophy and empirical science are not the same thing, nevertheless the two are continuous. According to this view, called "naturalism," there is no sharp dividing line where philosophy stops and empirical science begins. This isn't merely the claim, just made, that a question can fall into both domains (e.g., the nature of space and time is among the oldest philosophical issues, but it is also pursued by experimental methods). The additional idea is that work which is straightforwardly empirical can bear on long-standing "properly philosophical" questions, and vice versa. Debates in this volume which exemplify empirical results informing philosophy include Kirk Ludwig and Chris Viger on the nature and function of perception. Recent research on how human thermoreceptors work, for instance, suggests that it is not their job to give an accurate representation of temperature to the agent. Instead, the job of a thermoreceptor is to bypass accuracy in favor of immediate, limb-saving reactions – like withdrawing a hand from something hot. This can seem to suggest that a very long tradition in philosophical thinking about perception misconceives the phenomenon from the get-go. (Ludwig firmly resists this inference.) Or again, what rationality is, is an extremely long-standing philosophical issue. The empirical research that Gerd Gigerenzer brings to bear in his debate with David Matheson again suggests that the philosophical tradition has deeply misunderstood rationality's fundamental nature. Going in the other direction, from philosophy to empirical science, Timothy Williamson urges that knowledge should be as central to the scientific understanding of the mind as it is to philosophical epistemology. Knowledge, insists Williamson, is a fundamental mental state with an importantly different behavioral profile than well-grounded belief. Thus the interdisciplinary attempt to understand the mind – cognitive science – cannot leave knowledge out. (This, in turn, means that cognitive science cannot ignore what is outside the mind, since a state counts as knowledge only insofar as it corresponds to what obtains "out there.") As another example, Ray Jackendoff and Georges Rey differ sharply about the implications for the science of language/mind of metaphysical worries about what "really exists" independently of the mind. These are all four of them *interactions* between philosophy and cognitive science.

So, how could a debate be both part of philosophy and part of cognitive science? In many ways, actually. There are various sorts of intersections and untold interactions. Speaking of "untold," let me end with this. Whether an investigation into x will yield evidence relevant to y cannot be known a priori: it depends upon whether x and y turn out to be linked in interesting ways. One just never knows for sure, then, which curious facts might turn out to be deeply evidentially relevant to a problem one is working on. To my mind, it is this aspect of the intersection and interaction between cognitive science and philosophy – never knowing where the next big lead may come from – that makes work in this area so challenging, but also so exciting.

Enjoy.

JUST HOW MODULAR IS THE MIND?

The Case for Massively Modular Models of Mind

Peter Carruthers

My charge in this chapter is to set out the positive case supporting massively modular models of the human mind.[1] Unfortunately, there is no generally accepted under-standing of what a massively modular model of the mind *is*. So at least some of our discussion will have to be terminological. I shall begin by laying out the range of things that can be meant by "modularity." I shall then adopt a pair of strategies. One will be to distinguish some things that "modularity" definitely *can't* mean, if the thesis of massive modularity is to be even remotely plausible. The other will be to look at some of the arguments that have been offered in support of massive modularity, discussing what notion of "module" they might warrant. It will turn out that there is, indeed, a strong case in support of massively modular models of the mind on *one* reasonably natural understanding of "module." But what really matters in the end, of course, is the substantive question of what sorts of structure are adequate to account for the organization and operations of the human mind, not whether or not the com-ponents appealed to in that account get described as "modules." So the more inter-esting question before us is what the arguments that have been offered in support of massive modularity can succeed in showing us about those structures, whatever they get called.

1 Introduction: On Modularity

In the weakest sense, a module can just be something like a dissociable functional component. This is pretty much the everyday sense in which one can speak of buy-ing a hi-fi system on a modular basis, for example. The hi-fi is modular if one can purchase the speakers independently of the tape-deck, say, or substitute one set of speakers for another for use with the same tape-deck. Moreover, it counts towards the modularity of the system if one doesn't have to buy a tape-deck at all – just purchasing a CD player along with the rest – or if the tape-deck can be broken while the remainder of the system continues to operate normally.

Understood in this weak way, the thesis of massive mental modularity would claim that the mind consists entirely of distinct components, each of which has some specific job to do in the functioning of the whole. It would predict that the properties of many of these components could vary independently of the properties of the others. (This would be consistent with the hypothesis of "special intelligences" – see Gardner, 1983.) And the theory would predict that it is possible for some of these components to be damaged or absent altogether, while leaving the functioning of the remainder at least partially intact.

Would a thesis of *massive* mental modularity of this sort be either interesting or controversial? That would depend upon whether the thesis in question were just that the mind consists entirely (or almost entirely) of modular components, on the one hand; or whether it is that the mind consists of *a great many* modular components, on the other. Read in the first way, then nearly everyone is a massive modularist, given the weak sense of "module" that is in play. For everyone will allow that the mind does consist of distinct components; and everyone will allow that at least some of these components can be damaged without destroying the functionality of the whole. The simple facts of blindness and deafness are enough to establish these weak claims.

Read in the second way, however, the thesis of massive modularity would be by no means anodyne – although obviously it would admit of a range of different strengths, depending upon *how many* components the mind is thought to contain. Certainly it isn't the case that everyone believes that the mind is composed of a great many distinct functional components. For example, those who (like Fodor, 1983) picture the mind as a big general-purpose computer with a limited number of distinct input and output links to the world (vision, audition, etc.) don't believe this.

It is clear, then, that a thesis of massive (in the sense of "multiple") modularity is a controversial one, even when the term "module" is taken in its weakest sense. So those evolutionary psychologists who have defended the claim that the mind consists of a great many modular components (Tooby and Cosmides, 1992; Sperber, 1996; Pinker, 1997) are defending a thesis of considerable interest, even if "module" just *means* "component."

At the other end of the spectrum of notions of modularity, and in the strongest sense, a module would have all of the properties of what is sometimes called a "Fodor-module" (Fodor, 1983). That is, it would be a domain-specific innately-specified processing system, with its own proprietary transducers, and delivering "shallow" (nonconceptual) outputs (e.g., in the case of the visual system, delivering a $2^1/_2$-D sketch; Marr, 1983). In addition, a module in this sense would be mandatory in its operations, swift in its processing, isolated from and inaccessible to the rest of cognition, associated with particular neural structures, liable to specific and characteristic patterns of breakdown, and would develop according to a paced and distinctively-arranged sequence of growth.

Let me comment briefly on the various different elements of this account. According to Fodor (1983) modules are domain-specific processing systems of the mind. Like most others who have written about modularity since, he understands this to mean that a module will be restricted in the kinds of content that it can take as

Peter Carruthers

input.[2] It is restricted to those contents that constitute its *domain*, indeed. So the visual system is restricted to visual inputs; the auditory system is restricted to auditory inputs; and so on. Furthermore, Fodor claims that each module should have its own transducers: the rods and cones of the retina for the visual system; the eardrum for the auditory system; and so forth.

According to Fodor, moreover, the outputs of a module are *shallow* in the sense of being nonconceptual. So modules generate *information* of various sorts, but they don't issue in *thoughts* or *beliefs*. On the contrary, belief-fixation is argued by Fodor to be the very archetype of a *non*modular (or holistic) process. Hence the visual module might deliver a representation of surfaces and edges in the perceived scene, say, but it wouldn't as such issue in *recognition* of the object as a chair, nor in the *belief* that a chair is present. This would require the cooperation of some other (nonmodular) system or systems.

Fodor-modules are supposed to be innate, in some sense of that term, and to be localized to specific structures in the brain (although these structures might not, themselves, be local ones, but could rather be distributed across a set of dispersed neural systems). Their growth and development would be under significant genetic control, therefore, and might be liable to distinctive patterns of breakdown, either genetic or developmental. And one would expect their growth to unfold according to a genetically guided developmental timetable, buffered against the vagaries of the environment and the individual's learning opportunities.

Fodor-modules are also supposed to be mandatory and swift in their processing. So their operations aren't under voluntary control (one can't turn them off), and they generate their outputs extremely quickly by comparison with other (nonmodular) systems. When we have our eyes open we can't help but see what is in front of us. And nor can our better judgment (e.g., about the equal lengths of the two lines in a Müller-Lyer illusion) override the operations of the visual system. Moreover, compare the speed with which vision is processed with the (much slower) speed of conscious decision making.

Finally, modules are supposed by Fodor to be both isolated from the remainder of cognition (i.e., encapsulated) and to have internal operations that are inaccessible elsewhere. These properties are often run together with each other (and also with domain specificity), but they are really quite distinct. To say that a processing system is *encapsulated* is to say that its internal operations can't draw on any information held outside of that system. (This isn't to say that the system can't access any stored information at all, of course, for it might have its own dedicated database that it consults during its operations.) In contrast, to say that a system is *inaccessible* is to say that other systems can have no access to its internal processing, but only to its outputs, or to the results of that processing.

Note that neither of these notions should be confused with that of *domain specificity*. The latter is about restrictions on the input to a system. To say that a system is domain specific is to say that it can only process inputs of a particular sort, concerning a certain kind subject-matter. Whereas to say that the processing of a system is encapsulated, on the one hand, or inaccessible, on the other, is to say something about the access-relations that obtain between the internal operations of that system and others. Hence one can easily envisage systems that might *lack* domain specificity, for example (being capable of receiving any sort of content as input), but whose internal operations are nevertheless encapsulated and inaccessible (Carruthers, 2002a; Sperber, 2002).

2 What Massive Modularity Could Not Be

It is obvious that by "module" we can't possibly mean "Fodor-module," if a thesis of massive mental modularity is to be even remotely plausible. In particular, some of the items in Fodor's list will need to get struck out as soon as we move to endorse any sort of central-systems modularity, let alone entertain the idea of *massive* modularity.[3] If there are to be conceptual modules – modules dealing with commonsense physics, say, or commonsense biology, or with cheater-detection, to name but a few examples that have been proposed by cognitive scientists in recent decades – then it is obvious that modules cannot have their own proprietary transducers. Nor can they have shallow outputs. On the contrary, their outputs will be fully-conceptual thoughts or beliefs.

Domain specificity also needs to go, or to be reconceptualized in terms of functional rather than content domains, in the context of a thesis of massive modularity. Although it may well be the case that *many* modules are domain specific, it can't be the case that *all* are, if the thesis that the mind is built exclusively or almost exclusively out of modules is to be at all believable.[4] Consider practical reasoning, for example. This is plausibly a distinct system of the mind, with a significant innate component, whose internal operations might be encapsulated from and inaccessible to the remainder of cognition (Carruthers, 2004a). And it is a system whose basic architecture is probably very ancient indeed, being common even to insects as well as to ourselves and other mammals (Carruthers, 2004b). But it plainly can't be domain specific, since in order to do its job it will have to be capable of receiving any belief, and any desire, as input.

Swiftness of processing also needs to go, in the context of massive modularity, except perhaps in comparison with the speed of *conscious* thought processes, if the latter are realized in cycles of modular activity, as Carruthers (2002a) has maintained. For if the mind is *massively* modular, then we will lack any significant comparison-class. Fodor-modules were characterized as swift in relation to *central* processes; but a massive modularist will maintain that the latter are modular too. However, it looks as if the claim of mandatory operation can be retained. Each component system of the mind can be such that it automatically processes any input that it receives. And certainly it seems that some of the alleged central modules, at least, have such a property. As Segal (1998) points out, we cannot help but see the actions of an actor on the stage as displaying anger, or jealousy, or whatever; despite our knowledge that he is thinking and feeling none of the things that he appears to be. So the operations of our mind-reading faculty would appear to be mandatory.

What of claims of innateness, and of neural specificity? Certainly one *could* maintain that the mind consists almost exclusively of innately channeled processing systems, realized in specific neural structures. This would be a highly controversial claim, but it wouldn't be immediately absurd. Whether this is the *best* way to develop

Peter Carruthers

and defend a thesis of massive modularity is moot. Certainly, innateness has been emphasized by evolutionary psychologists, who have argued that natural selection has led to the development of multiple innately channeled cognitive systems (Tooby and Cosmides, 1992). But others have argued that modularity is the product of learning and development (Karmiloff-Smith, 1992). Both sides in this debate agree, however, that modules will be realized in specific neural structures (not necessarily the same from individual to individual). And both sides are agreed, at least, that development begins with a set of innate attention biases and a variety of different innately-structured learning mechanisms.

My own sympathies in this debate are towards the nativist end of the spectrum. I suspect that much of the structure, and many of the contents, of the human mind are innate or innately channeled. But in the context of developing a thesis of *massive* modularity, it seems wisest to drop the innateness-constraint from our definition of what modules are. For one might want to allow that some aspects of the mature language faculty are modular, for example, even though it is saturated with acquired information about the lexicon of a specific natural language like English. And one might want to allow that modules can be constructed by over-learning, say, in such a way that it might be appropriate to describe someone's reading competence as modular.

Finally, we come to the properties of encapsulated and inaccessible processing. These are thought by many (including Fodor, 2000) to be the core properties of modular systems. And there seems to be no a priori reason why the mind shouldn't be composed exclusively out of such systems, and cycles of operation of such systems. At any rate, such claims have been defended by a number of those who describe themselves as massive modularists (Sperber, 1996, 2002, 2005; Carruthers, 2002a, 2003, 2004a). Accordingly, they will be left untouched for the moment, pending closer examination of the arguments in support of massive modularity.

What we have so far, then, is that if a thesis of massive mental modularity is to be remotely plausible, then by "module" we cannot mean "Fodor-module." In particular, the properties of having proprietary transducers, shallow outputs, domain specificity, comparatively fast processing, and significant innateness or innate channeling will have to be struck out. That leaves us with the idea that modules might be isolable function-specific processing systems, whose operations are mandatory, which are associated with specific neural structures, and whose internal operations may be both encapsulated from the remainder of cognition and inaccessible to it. Whether all of these properties should be retained in the most defensible version of a thesis of massive mental modularity will be the subject of the next two sections of this chapter.

3 Arguments for Massively Modular Minds

In this section I shall consider three of the main arguments that have been offered in support of a thesis of massively modular mental organization. I shall be simultaneously examining not only the strength of those arguments, but also the notion of "module" that they might warrant.

3.1 The argument from biology

The first argument derives from Simon (1962), and concerns the design of complex functional systems quite generally, and in biology in particular. According to this line of thought, we should expect such systems to be constructed hierarchically out of dissociable subsystems, in such a way that the whole assembly could be built up gradually, adding subsystem to subsystem; and in such a way that the functionality of the whole should be buffered, to some extent, from damage to the parts.

Simon (1962) uses the famous analogy of the two watch-makers to illustrate the point. One watch-maker assembles one watch at a time, adding micro-component to micro-component one at a time. This makes it easy for him to forget the proper ordering of parts, and if he is interrupted he may have to start again from the beginning. The second watch-maker first builds sets of subcomponents out of the given micro-component parts, and then combines those into larger subcomponents, until eventually the watches are complete. This helps organize and sequence the whole process, and makes it much less vulnerable to interruption.

Consistent with such an account, there is a very great deal of evidence from across many different levels in biology to the effect that complex functional systems are built up out of assemblies of subcomponents. Each of these components is constructed out of further subcomponents and has a distinctive role to play in the functioning of the whole, and many of them can be damaged or lost while leaving the functionality of the remainder at least partially intact. This is true for the operations of cells, of cellular assemblies, of whole organs, and of multi-organism units like a bee colony (Seeley, 1995). And by extension, we should expect it to be true of cognition also, provided that it is appropriate to think of cognitive systems as biological ones, which have been subject to natural selection. Accordingly, we will now spend some time examining this question.

What sorts of properties of organisms are apt to have fitness effects? These are many and various, ranging from gross anatomical features such as size, shape, and color of fur or skin, through the detailed functional organization of specific physical systems such as the eye or the liver, to behavioral tendencies such as the disposition that cuckoo chicks have to push other baby birds out of the nest. And for anyone who is neither an epiphenomenalist nor an eliminativist about the mind, it is manifest that the human mind is among those properties of the human organism that may have fitness effects. For it will be by virtue of the mind that almost all fitness-enhancing behaviors – such as running from a predator, taking resources from a competitor, or wooing a mate – are caused.

On any broadly realist construal of the mind and its states, then, the mind is at least a prime *candidate* to have been shaped by natural selection. How could such a possibility fail to have been realized? How could the mind be a major cause of fitness-enhancing behaviors without being a product of natural selection? One alternative would be a truly radical empiricist one. It might be said that not only most of the contents of the mind, but also its structure and organization, are acquired from the environment. Perhaps the only direct product of natural selection is some sort of extremely powerful learning algorithm, which could operate almost equally well in a wide range of different environments, both actual and non-actual. The fitness-enhancing

Peter Carruthers

properties that we observe in adult minds, then, aren't (except very indirectly) a product of natural selection, but are rather a result of learning from the environment within which fitness-enhancing behaviors will need to be manifested.

Such a proposal is an obvious non-starter, however. It is one thing to claim that all the *contents* of the mind are acquired from the environment using general learning principles, as empiricists have traditionally claimed. (This is implausible enough by itself; see section 3.2 below.) And it is quite another thing to claim that the structure and organization of the mind is similarly learned. How could the differences between, and characteristic causal roles of, beliefs, desires, emotions, and intentions be learned from experience?[5] For there is nothing corresponding to them in the world from which they could be learned; and in any case, any process of learning must surely presuppose that a basic mental architecture is already in place. Moreover, how could the differences between personal (or "episodic") memory, factual (or "semantic") memory, and short-term (or "working") memory be acquired from the environment? The idea seems barely coherent. And indeed, no empiricist has ever been foolish enough to suggest such things.

We have no other option, then, but to see the structure and organization of the mind as a product of the human genotype, in exactly the same sense as, and to the same extent that, the structure and organization of the human body is a product of our genotypes. But someone could still try to maintain that the mind isn't the result of any process of natural selection. Rather, it might be said, the structure of the mind might be the product of a single macro-mutation, which became general in the population through sheer chance, and which has remained thereafter through mere inertia. Or it might be the case that the organization in question was arrived at through random genetic drift – that is to say, a random walk through a whole series of minor genetic mutations, each of which just happened to become general in the population, and the sequence of which just happened to produce the structure of our mind as its end-point.

These possibilities are so immensely unlikely that they can effectively be dismissed out of hand. Evolution by natural selection remains the only explanation of organized functional complexity that we have (Dawkins, 1986). Any complex phenotypic structure, such as the human eye or the human mind, will require the cooperation of many thousands of genes to build it. And the possibility that all of these thousands of tiny genetic mutations might have occurred all at once by chance, or might have become established in sequence (again by chance), is unlikely in the extreme. The odds in favor of either thing happening are vanishingly small. (Throwing a six with a fair dice many thousands of times in a row would be much more likely.) We can be confident that each of the required small changes, initially occurring through chance mutation, conferred at least some minor fitness-benefit on its possessor, sufficient to stabilize it in the population, and thus providing a platform on which the next small change could occur.

The strength of this argument, in respect of any given biological system, is directly proportional to the degree of its organized functional complexity – the more complex the organization of the system, the more implausible it is that it might have arisen by chance macro-mutation or random genetic walk. Now, even from the perspective of commonsense psychology the mind is an immensely complex system, which seems to be organized in ways that are largely adaptive.[6] And the more we learn about the mind from a scientific perspective, the more it seems that it is even more complex than we might initially have been inclined to think. Systems such as vision, for example – that are treated as "simples" from the perspective of commonsense psychology – turn out to have a hugely complex internal structure.

The prediction of this line of reasoning, then, is that cognition will be structured out of dissociable systems, each of which has a distinctive function, or set of functions, to perform.[7] This gives us a notion of a cognitive "module" that is pretty close to the everyday sense in which one can talk about a hi-fi system as "modular" provided that the tape-deck can be purchased, and can function, independently of the CD player, and so forth. Roughly, a module is just a dissociable *component*.

Consistent with the above prediction, there is now a great deal of evidence of a neuropsychological sort that something like massive modularity (in the everyday sense of "module") is indeed true of the human mind. People can have their language system damaged while leaving much of the remainder of cognition intact (aphasia); people can lack the ability to reason about mental states while still being capable of much else (autism); people can lose their capacity to recognize just human faces; someone can lose the capacity to reason about cheating in a social exchange while retaining otherwise parallel capacities to reason about risks and dangers; and so on and so forth (Sachs, 1985; Shallice, 1988; Tager-Flusberg, 1999; Stone et al., 2002; Varley, 2002).

But just *how many* components does this argument suggest that the mind consists of? Simon's (1962) argument makes the case for hierarchical organization. At the top of the hierarchy will be the target system in question (a cell, a bodily organ, the human mind). And at the base will be the smallest micro-components of the system, bottoming out (in the case of the mind) in the detailed neural processes that realize cognitive ones. But it might seem that it is left entirely open how high or how low the pyramid is (i.e., how many "levels" the hierarchy consists of); how broad its base is; or whether the "pyramid" has concave or convex edges. If the pyramid is quite low with concave sides, then the mind might decompose at the first level of analysis into just a few constituents such as *perception*, *belief*, *desire*, and *the will*, much as traditional "faculty psychologies" have always assumed; and these might then get implemented quite rapidly in neural processes. In contrast, only if the pyramid is high with a broad base and convex sides should we expect the mind to decompose into *many* components, each of which in turn consists of many components, and so on.

There is more mileage to be derived from Simon's argument yet, however. For the complexity and range of functions that the overall system needs to execute will surely give us a direct measure of the manner in which the "pyramid" will slope. (The greater the complexity, the greater the number of subsystems into which the system will decompose.) This is because the hierarchical organization is there in the first place to ensure robustness of function. Evolution needs to be able to tinker with one function in response to selection pressures without necessarily impacting any of the others.[8] (So does learning, since once you have learned one skill, you need to be able to isolate and preserve it while you acquire others. See Manoel et al., 2002.)

Roughly speaking, then, we should expect there to be one distinct subsystem for each reliably recurring function that human minds are called upon to perform. And

Peter Carruthers

as evolutionary psychologists have often emphasized, these are *myriad* (Tooby and Cosmides, 1992; Pinker, 1997). Focusing just on the social domain, for example, humans need to: identify degrees of relatedness of kin, care for and assist kin, avoid incest, woo and select a mate, identify and care for offspring, make friends and build coalitions, enter into contracts, identify and punish those who are cheating on a contract, identify and acquire the norms of one's surrounding culture, identify the beliefs and goals of other agents, predict the behavior of other agents, and so on and so forth – plainly this is just the tip of a huge iceberg, even in this one domain. In which case the argument from biology enables us to conclude that the mind will consist in a *very great many* distinct components, which is a (weak) form of massive modularity thesis.

3.2 The argument from task specificity

A second line of reasoning supporting massive modularity derives from reflection on the differing task demands of the very different learning challenges that people and other animals must face, as well as the demands of generating appropriate fitness-enhancing intrinsic desires (Gallistel, 1990, 2000; Tooby and Cosmides, 1992, 2005). It is one sort of task to learn the sun's azimuth (its height in the sky at any given time of day and year) so as to provide a source of direction. It is quite another sort of task to perform the calculations required for dead reckoning, integrating distance traveled with the angle of each turn, so as to provide the direction and distance to home from one's current position. And it is quite another task again to learn the center of rotation of the night sky from observation of the stars, extracting from it the polar north. These are all learning problems that animals can solve. But they require quite different learning mechanisms to succeed (Gallistel, 2000).

When we widen our focus from navigation to other sorts of learning problem, the argument is further reinforced. Many such problems pose computational challenges – to extract the information required from the data provided – that are distinct from any others. From vision, to speech recognition, to mind-reading, to cheater-detection, to complex skill acquisition, the challenges posed are plainly quite distinct. So for each such problem, we should postulate the existence of a distinct learning mechanism, whose internal processes are computationally specialized in the way required to solve the task. It is very hard to believe that there could be any sort of *general* learning mechanism that could perform all of these different roles.

One might think that conditioning experiments fly in the face of these claims. But general-purpose conditioning is rare at best. Indeed, Gallistel (2000; Gallistel and Gibbon, 2001) has forcefully argued that *there is no such thing as* a general learning mechanism. Specifically, he argues that the results from conditioning experiments are best explained in terms of the computational operations of a specialized rate-estimation module, rather than some sort of generalized associative process. For example, it is well established that *delay* of reinforcement has no effect on rate of acquisition, so long as the intervals between trials are increased by the same proportions. And the number of reinforcements required for acquisition of a new behavior isn't affected by interspersing a significant number of unreinforced trials. These facts are hard to explain if the animals are supposed to be building associations, since the delays and unreinforced trials should surely *weaken* those associations. But they can be predicted if what the animals are doing is estimating relative rates of return. For the rate of reinforcement per stimulus presentation *relative to* the rate of reinforcement in background conditions remains the same, whether or not significant numbers of stimulus presentations remain unreinforced, for example.

What emerges from these considerations is a picture of the mind as containing a whole host of specialized learning systems (as well as systems charged with generating fitness-enhancing intrinsic desires). And this looks very much like *some* sort of thesis of massive modularity. Admittedly, it doesn't yet follow from the argument that the mind is composed *exclusively* of such systems. But when combined with the previous argument, outlined in section 3.1 above, the stronger conclusion would seem to be warranted.

There really is no reason to believe, however, that each processing system will employ a *unique* processing algorithm. On the contrary, consideration of how evolution generally operates suggests that the same or similar algorithms may be replicated many times over in the human mind/brain. (We could describe this by saying that the same module-*type* is tokened more than once in the human brain, with distinct input and output connections, and hence with a distinct functional role, in each case.) Marcus (2004) explains how evolution often operates by splicing and *copying*, followed by adaptation. First, the genes that result in a given micro-structure (a particular bank of neurons, say, with a given set of processing properties) are copied, yielding two or more instances of such structures. Then second, some of the copies can be adapted to novel tasks. *Sometimes* this will involve tweaking the processing algorithm that is implemented in one or more of the copies. But often it will just involve provision of novel input and/or output connections for the new system.

Samuels (1998) challenges the above line of argument for massive processing modularity, however, claiming that instead of a whole suite of specialized learning systems, there might be just a single general-learning/general-inferencing mechanism, but one operating on lots of organized bodies of innate information. (He calls this "informational modularity," contrasting it with the more familiar form of *computational* modularity.) However, this would surely create a serious processing bottleneck. If there were really just one (or even a few) inferential systems – generating beliefs about the likely movements of the surrounding mechanical objects; about the likely beliefs, goals, and actions of the surrounding agents; about who owes what to whom in a social exchange; and so on and so forth – then it looks as if there would be a kind of tractability problem here. It would be the problem of forming novel beliefs on all these different subject matters in real time (in seconds or fractions of a second), using a limited set of inferential resources. Indeed (and in contrast with Samuel's suggestion) surely *everyone* now thinks that the mind/brain is massively parallel in its organization. In which case we should expect there to be distinct systems that can process each of the different kinds of information at the same time.

Samuels might try claiming that there could be a whole suite of distinct domain-general processing systems, all running the same general-learning/general-inferencing algorithms, but each of which is attached to, and draws upon the resources of, a distinct domain-specific body of innate information. This would get him the computational advantages of *parallel* processing, but without commitment (allegedly) to any

Peter Carruthers

modular processing. But actually this is just a variant on the massive-computational-module hypothesis. For there is nothing in the nature of modularity per se that requires modules to be running algorithms that are distinct from those being run by other modules, as we have just seen. What matters is just that they should be isolable systems, performing some specific function, and that their internal operations should be computationally feasible (as we will see in section 3.3 below). So one way in which massive modularity could be realized is by having a whole suite of processors, each of which performs some specific function within the overall architecture of the mind, and each of which draws on its own distinctive body of innate information relevant to that function, but where the algorithms being computed by those processors are shared ones, replicated many times over in the various different processing systems.

Although possible in principle, however, this isn't a very *likely* form of massive modularity hypothesis. For it does come with severe computational costs. This is because the difference between this "informational module" hypothesis and the classic "computational module" hypothesis just concerns whether or not the innate information is explicitly represented. The classical idea is that there will be, within the mind-reading faculty for example, an algorithm that takes the system straight from, "x is seeing that P" to "probably x believes that P" (say). The information that people believe what they see is implicitly represented in the algorithm itself. Samuel's view, in contrast, will be that there is an intermediate step. Domain-general inference mechanisms will draw on the explicitly represented belief that people believe what they see, in order to mediate the inference from premise to conclusion. Imagine this multiplied again and again for all the different sorts of inferential transition that people regularly make in the domain of theory of mind, and it is plain that his proposal would come with serious computational costs. And it is equally clear that even if informational modules were the initial state of the ancestral mind/brain, over evolutionary time informational modules would be replaced by computational ones.

Combining the arguments of sections 3.1 and 3.2, then, we can predict that the mind should be composed entirely or almost entirely of modular components (in the everyday sense of "module"), many of which will be innate or innately channeled. All of these component systems should run task-specific processing algorithms, with distinct input and/or output connections to other systems, although some of them may replicate some of the same algorithm types in the service of distinct tasks. This looks like a thesis of massive modularity worth the name, even if there is nothing here yet to warrant the claims that the internal processing of the modules in question should be either encapsulated, on the one hand, or inaccessible, on the other.

3.3 The argument from computational tractability

Perhaps the best-known of the arguments for massive modularity, however – at least among philosophers – is the argument from computational tractability, which derives from Fodor (1983, 2000).[9] And it is generally thought that this argument, if it were successful, would license the claim that the mind is composed of *encapsulated* processing systems, thus supporting a far stronger form of massive modularity hypothesis than has been defended in this chapter so far (Carruthers, 2002a; Sperber, 2002).

The first premise of the argument is the claim that the mind is realized in processes that are computational in character. This claim is by no means uncontroversial, of course, although it is the guiding methodological assumption of much of cognitive science. Indeed, it is a claim that is denied by certain species of distributed connectionism. But in recent years arguments have emerged against these competitors that are decisive, in my view (Gallistel, 2000; Marcus, 2001). And what remains is that computational psychology represents easily our best – and perhaps our only – hope for fully understanding how mental processes can be realized in physical ones (Rey, 1997). In any case, I propose just to *assume* the truth of this first premise for the purposes of the discussion that follows.

The second premise of the argument is the claim that if cognitive processes are to be realized computationally, then those computations must be *tractable* ones. What does this amount to? First of all, it means that the computations must be such that they can *in principle* be carried out within finite time. But it isn't enough that the computations postulated to take place in the human brain should be tractable in principle, of course. It must also be feasible that those computations could be executed (perhaps in parallel) in a system with the properties of the human brain, within timescales characteristic of actual human performance. By this criterion, it seems likely that many computations that aren't strictly speaking intractable from the perspective of computer science, should nevertheless count as such for the purposes of cognitive science.

There is a whole branch of computer science devoted to the study of more-or-less intractable problems, known as "Complexity Theory." And one doesn't have to dig very deep into the issues to discover results that have important implications for cognitive science. For example, it has traditionally been assumed by philosophers that any candidate new belief should be checked for consistency with existing beliefs before being accepted. But in fact consistency-checking is demonstrably intractable, if attempted on an exhaustive basis. Consider how one might check the consistency of a set of beliefs via a truth-table. Even if each line could be checked in the time that it takes a photon of light to travel the diameter of a proton, then even after 20 billion years the truth-table for a set of just 138 beliefs (2^{138} lines) still wouldn't have been completed (Cherniak, 1986).

From the first two premises together, then, we can conclude that the human mind must be realized in a set of computational processes that are suitably tractable. This means that those processes will have to be *frugal*, both in the amount of information that they require for their normal operations, and in the complexity of the algorithms that they deploy when processing that information.

The third premise of the argument then claims that in order to be tractable, computations need to be encapsulated; for only encapsulated processes can be appropriately frugal in the informational and computational resources that they require. As Fodor (2000) explains it, the constraint here can be expressed as one of *locality*. Computationally tractable processes have to be *local*, in the sense of only consulting a limited database of information relevant to those computations, and ignoring all other information held in the mind. For if they attempted to consult all (or even a significant subset) of the total information available, they would be subject to combinatorial explosion, and hence would fail to be tractable after all.

Peter Carruthers

This third premise, in conjunction with the other two, would then (if it were acceptable) license the conclusion that the mind must be realized in a set of encapsulated computational processes. And when combined with the conclusions of the arguments of sections 3.1 and 3.2 above, this would give us the claim that the mind consists in a set of encapsulated computational systems whose operations are mandatory, each of which has its own function to perform, and many of which execute processing algorithms that aren't to be found elsewhere in the mind (although some re-use algorithms that are also found in other systems for novel functions). It is therefore crucial for our purposes to know whether the third premise is really warranted; and if not, what one might put in its stead. This will form the topic of the next section.

4 What Does Computational Frugality Really Require?

I have claimed that the first two premises in the Fodorian argument sketched in section 3.3 are acceptable. So we should believe that cognition must be organized into systems of computational processes that are appropriately *frugal*. The question is whether frugality requires encapsulation, in the way that is stated by the third premise of the argument. The idea has an obvious appeal. It is certainly true that *one* way to ensure the frugality of a set of computational systems, at least, would be to organize them into a network of encapsulated processors, each of which can look only at a limited database of information in executing its tasks. And it may well be the case that evolution has settled on this strategy in connection with many of the systems that constitute the human mind. It is doubtful, however, whether this is the *only* way of ensuring frugality.

The assumption of encapsulation (at least, as it is normally understood – see below) may derive from an older tradition in cognitive science and Artificial Intelligence (AI), in which information search had to be *exhaustive*, and in which algorithms were designed to be optimally reliable. But this tradition is now widely rejected. Most cognitive scientists now think that the processing rules deployed in the human mind have been designed to be *good enough*, not to be optimal. Given that speed of processing is always one constraint for organisms that may need to think and act swiftly in order to survive, evolution will have led to compromises on the question of reliability. Indeed, it will favor a *satisficing* strategy, rather than an optimal one. And likewise on information search: evolution will favor a variety of search heuristics that are good enough without being exhaustive.

These points are well illustrated by the research program pursued in recent years by Gigerenzer and colleagues (e.g., Gigerenzer et al., 1999). They have investigated the comparative reliability and frugality of a variety of rules for use in information search and decision making, with startling results. It turns out that even very simple heuristics can be remarkably successful – such as choosing the only one of two options that you recognize, when asked which of two cities is larger, or when asked to predict which of two companies will do best in the stock market. In some cases these simple heuristics will even out-perform much fancier and information-hungry algorithms, such as multiple regression. And a variety of simple heuristics for searching for information within a wider database, combined with stopping-rules if the search is unsuccessful within a specified time-frame, can also work remarkably well – such as accessing the information in the order in which it was last used, or accessing the information that is partially activated (and hence made salient) by the context.[10]

For a different sort of example, consider the simple practical reasoning system sketched in Carruthers (2002a). It takes as initial input whatever is currently the strongest desire, for P.[11] It then queries the various belief-generating modules, while also conducting a targeted search of long-term memory, looking for beliefs of the form $Q \supset P$. If it receives one as input, or if it finds one from its own search of memory, it consults a database of action schemata, to see if Q is something doable here and now. If it is, it goes ahead and does it. If it isn't, it initiates a further search for beliefs of the form $R \supset Q$, and so on. If it has gone more than n conditionals deep without success, or if it has searched for the right sort of conditional belief without finding one for more than some specified time t, then it stops and moves on to the next strongest desire.

Such a system would be frugal, both in the information that it uses, and in the complexity of its algorithms. But does it count as encapsulated? This isn't encapsulation as that notion would generally be understood, which requires there to be a limited module-specific database that gets consulted by the computational process in question. For here, on the contrary, the practical reasoning system can search within the total set of the organism's beliefs, using structure-sensitive search rules. But for all that, there is *a* sense in which the system is encapsulated that is worth noticing.

Put as neutrally as possible, we can say that the idea of an encapsulated system is the notion of a system whose internal operations *can't* be affected by *most or all* of the information held elsewhere in the mind. But there is a scope ambiguity here.[12] We can have the modal operator take narrow scope with respect to the quantifier, or we can have it take wide scope. In its narrow-scope form, an encapsulated system would be this: concerning most of the information held in the mind, the system in question *can't* be affected by *that* information in the course of its processing. Call this "narrow-scope encapsulation." In its wide-scope form, on the other hand, an encapsulated system would be this: the system is such that it *can't* be affected by *most* of the information held in the mind in the course of its processing. Call this "wide-scope encapsulation."

Narrow-scope encapsulation is the one that is taken for granted in the philosophical literature on modularity. We tend to think of encapsulation as requiring some determinate (and large) body of information, such that *that* information can't penetrate the module. However, it can be true that the operations of a module can't be affected by most of the information in a mind, without there being some determinate subdivision between the information that can affect the system and the information that can't. For as we have just seen, it can be the case that the system's algorithms are so set up that only a limited amount of information is ever consulted before the task is completed or aborted. Put it this way: a module can be a system that *must* only consider a small subset of the information available. Whether it does this via encapsulation as traditionally understood (the narrow-scope variety), or via frugal search heuristics and stopping rules (wide-scope encapsulation), is inessential. The important thing is that the system should be *frugal*, both in the information that it uses and in the resources that it requires for processing that information.

The argument from computational tractability, then, does warrant the claim that the mind should be constructed entirely out of systems that are *frugal*; but it doesn't warrant a claim of encapsulation, as traditionally understood (the narrow-scope variety). It does, however, warrant a non-standard encapsulation claim (the wide-scope version). In addition, it supports the claim that the processing systems in question should have internal operations that are *inaccessible* elsewhere. Or so I shall now briefly argue by *reductio*, and by induction across current practices in AI.

Consider what it would be like if the internal operations of each system were accessible to all other systems. (This would be *complete* accessibility. Of course the notions of *accessibility* and *inaccessibility*, just like the notions of *encapsulation* and *lack of encapsulation*, admit of degrees.) In order to make use of that information, those other systems would need to contain a model of those operations, or they would need to be capable of simulating or replicating them. In order to use the information that a given processing system is currently undertaking such-and-such computations, the other systems would need to contain a representation of the algorithms in question. This would defeat the purpose of dividing up processing into distinct subsystems running different algorithms for different purposes, and would likely result in some sort of combinatorial explosion. At the very least, we should expect that *most* of those processing systems should have internal operations that are inaccessible to all others; and that *all* of the processing systems that make up the mind should have internal operations that are inaccessible to *most* others.[13]

Such a conclusion is also supported inductively by current practices in AI, where researchers routinely assume that processing needs to be divided up among distinct systems running algorithms specialized for the particular tasks in question. These systems can talk to one another and query one another, but not access one another's internal operations. And yet they may be conducting guided searches over the same memory database. (Personal communication: Mike Anderson, John Horty, Aaron Sloman.) That researchers attempting to build working cognitive systems have converged on some such architecture is evidence of its inevitability, and hence evidence that the human mind will be similarly organized.

This last point is worth emphasizing further, since it suggests a distinct line of argument supporting the thesis of massive modularity in the sense that we are currently considering. Researchers charged with trying to build intelligent systems have increasingly converged on architectures in which the processing within the total system is divided up among a much wider set of task-specific processing mechanisms, which can query one another, and provide input to each other, and many of which can access shared databases. But many of these systems will deploy processing algorithms that aren't shared by the others. And most of them won't know or care about what is going on within the others.

Indeed, the convergence here is actually wider still, embracing computer science more generally and not just AI. Although the language of modularity isn't so often used by computer scientists, the same concept arguably gets deployed under the heading of "object-oriented programs." Many programming languages now enable a total processing system to treat some of its parts as "objects" which can be queried or informed, but where the processing that takes place within those objects isn't accessible elsewhere. This enables the code within the "objects" to be altered without having to make alterations in code elsewhere, with all the attendant risks that this would bring. And the resulting architecture is regarded as well nigh inevitable once a certain threshold in the overall degree of complexity of the system gets passed. (Note the parallel here with Simon's argument from complexity, discussed in section 3.1 above.)

5 Conclusion

What emerges, then, is that there is a strong case for saying that the mind is very likely to consist of a great many different processing systems, which exist and operate to some degree independently of one another. Each of these systems will have a distinctive function or set of functions; each will have a distinct neural realization; and many will be significantly innate, or genetically channeled. Many of them will deploy processing algorithms that are unique to them. And all of these systems will need to be *frugal* in their operations, hence being encapsulated in either the narrow-scope or the wide-scope sense. Moreover, the processing that takes place within each of these systems will generally be inaccessible elsewhere.[14] Only the results, or outputs, of that processing will be made available for use by other systems.

Does such a thesis deserve the title of "massive *modularity*"? It is certainly a form of massive modularity in the everyday sense that we distinguished at the outset. And it retains many of the important features of Fodor-modularity. Moreover, it does seem that this is the notion of "module" that is used pretty commonly in AI, if not so much in philosophy or psychology (McDermott, 2001). But however it is described, we have here a substantive and controversial claim about the basic architecture of the human mind; and it is one that is supported by powerful arguments.

In any complete defense of massively modular models of mind, so conceived, we would of course have to consider all the various arguments *against* such models, particularly those deriving from the holistic and creative character of much of human thinking. This is a task that I cannot undertake here, but that I have attempted elsewhere (Carruthers, 2002a, 2002b, 2003, 2004a). If those attempted rebuttals should prove to be successful, then we can conclude that the human mind will, indeed, be massively modular (in one good sense of the term "module").

Acknowledgments

Thanks to Mike Anderson, Clark Barrett, John Horty, Edouard Machery, Richard Samuels, Aaron Sloman, Robert Stainton, Stephen Stich, and Peter Todd for discussion and/or critical comments that helped me to get clearer about the topics covered by this chapter. Stich and Samuels, in particular, induced at least one substantial change of mind from my previously published views, in which I had defended the idea that modules must be encapsulated (as traditionally understood). See Carruthers, 2002a, 2003.

Notes

1 For the negative case, defending such models against the attacks of opponents, see Carruthers, 2002a, 2002b, 2003, 2004a.

2 Evolutionary psychologists may well understand domain specificity differently. They tend to understand the domain of a module to be its *function*. The domain of a module is what it is *supposed to do*, on this account, rather than the class of contents that it can receive as input. I shall follow the more common *content* reading of "domain" in the present chapter. See Carruthers, forthcoming, for further discussion.

3 This is no accident, since Fodor's analysis was explicitly designed to apply to modular input and output systems like color perception or face recognition. Fodor has consistently maintained that there is nothing modular about central cognitive processes of believing and reasoning. See Fodor, 1983, 2000.

4 Is this way of proceeding question-begging? Can one insist, on the contrary, that since modules *are* domain-specific systems, we can therefore see at a glance that the mind can't be massively modular in its organization? This would be fine if there were already a pre-existing agreed understanding of what modules are supposed to be. But there isn't. As stressed above, there are a *range* of different meanings of "module" available. So principles of charity of interpretation dictate that we should select the meaning that makes the best sense of the claims of massive modularists.

5 Note that we aren't asking how one could learn from experience *of* beliefs, desires, and the other mental states. Rather, we are asking how the differences between these states themselves could be learned. The point concerns our acquisition of the mind itself, not the acquisition of a *theory* of mind.

6 As evidence of the latter point, witness the success of our species as a whole, which has burgeoned in numbers and spread across the whole planet in the course of a mere 100,000 years.

7 We should expect many cognitive systems to have a *set* of functions, rather than a unique function, since multi-functionality is rife in the biological world. Once a component has been selected, it can be co-opted, and partly maintained and shaped, in the service of other tasks.

8 Human software engineers and artificial intelligence researchers have hit upon the same problem, and the same solution, which sometimes goes under the name "object-oriented programming." In order that one part of a program can be improved and updated without any danger of introducing errors elsewhere, engineers now routinely modularize their programs. See the discussion towards the end of section 4.

9 Fodor himself doesn't argue for *massive* modularity, of course. Rather, since he claims that we know that central processes of belief fixation and decision making *can't* be modular, he transforms what would otherwise be an argument for massive modularity into an argument for pessimism about the prospects for computational psychology. See Carruthers, 2002a, 2002b, 2003, 2004a for arguments that the knowledge-claim underlying such pessimism isn't warranted.

10 See Carruthers, forthcoming, for an extended discussion of the relationship between the massive modularity hypothesis and the simple heuristics movement, and for elaboration and defense of a number of the points made in the present section.

11 Note that *competition for resources* is another of the heuristics that may be widely used within our cognitive systems; see Sperber, 2005. In the present instance one might think of all activated desires as competing with one another for entry into the practical reasoning system.

12 Modal terms like "can" and "can't" have wide scope if they govern the whole sentence in which they occur; they have narrow scope if they govern only a part. Compare: "I can't kill everyone" (wide scope; equivalent to, "It is impossible that I kill everyone") with, "Everyone is such that I can't kill them" (narrow scope). The latter is equivalent to, "I can't kill anyone."

13 One important exception to this generalization is as follows. We should expect that many modules will be composed out of other modules as parts. Some of these component parts may feed their outputs directly to other systems. (Hence such components might be shared between two or more larger modules.) Or it might be the case that they can be queried independently by other systems. These would then be instances where some of the intermediate *stages* in the processing of the larger module would be available elsewhere, without the intermediate *processing* itself being so available.

14 As we already noted above, the notions of "encapsulation" and "inaccessibility" admit of degrees. The processing within a given system may be *more* or *less* encapsulated from and inaccessible to other systems.

References

Carruthers, P. (2002a). The cognitive functions of language. And author's response: modularity, language and the flexibility of thought. *Behavioral and Brain Sciences*, 25/6, 657–719.

— (2002b). Human creativity: its evolution, its cognitive basis, and its connections with childhood pretence. *British Journal for the Philosophy of Science*, 53, 1–25.

— (2003). On Fodor's Problem. *Mind and Language*, 18, 502–23.

— (2004a). Practical reasoning in a modular mind. *Mind and Language*, 19, 259–78.

— (2004b). On being simple minded. *American Philosophical Quarterly*, 41, 205–20.

— (forthcoming). Simple heuristics meet massive modularity. In P. Carruthers, S. Laurence, and S. Stich (eds.), *The Innate Mind: Culture and Cognition*. New York: Oxford University Press.

Cherniak, C. (1986). *Minimal Rationality*. Cambridge, MA: MIT Press.

Dawkins, R. (1986). *The Blind Watchmaker*. New York: Norton.

Fodor, J. (1983). *The Modularity of Mind*. Cambridge, MA: MIT Press.

— (2000). *The Mind doesn't Work that Way*. Cambridge, MA: MIT Press.

Gallistel, R. (1990). *The Organization of Learning*. Cambridge, MA: MIT Press.

— (2000). The replacement of general-purpose learning models with adaptively specialized learning modules. In M. Gazzaniga (ed.), *The New Cognitive Neurosciences* (2nd edn.). Cambridge, MA: MIT Press.

Gallistel, R. and Gibbon, J. (2001). Time, rate and conditioning. *Psychological Review*, 108, 289–344.

Gardner, H. (1983). *Frames of Mind: The Theory of Multiple Intelligences*. London: Heinemann.

Gigerenzer, G., Todd, P., and the ABC Research Group (1999). *Simple Heuristics that Make Us Smart*. New York: Oxford University Press.

Karmiloff-Smith, A. (1992). *Beyond Modularity*. Cambridge, MA: MIT Press.

Manoel, E., Basso, L., Correa, U., and Tani, G. (2002). Modularity and hierarchical organization of action programs in human acquisition of graphic skills. *Neuroscience Letters*, 335/2, 83–6.

Marcus, G. (2001). *The Algebraic Mind*. Cambridge, MA: MIT Press.

— (2004). *The Birth of the Mind: How a Tiny Number of Genes Creates the Complexities of Human Thought*. New York: Basic Books.

Marr, D. (1983). *Vision*. San Francisco, CA: Walter Freeman.

McDermott, D. (2001). *Mind and Mechanism*. Cambridge, MA: MIT Press.

Pinker, S. (1997). *How the Mind Works*. London: Penguin Books.

Rey, G. (1997). *Contemporary Philosophy of Mind*. Oxford: Blackwell.

Sachs, O. (1985). *The Man who Mistook his Wife for a Hat*. London: Picador.

Samuels, R. (1998). Evolutionary psychology and the massive modularity hypothesis. *British Journal for the Philosophy of Science*, 49, 575–602.

Seeley, T. (1995). *The Wisdom of the Hive: The Social Physiology of Honey Bee Colonies*. Cambridge, MA: Harvard University Press.

Segal, G. (1998). Representing representations. In P. Carruthers and J. Boucher (eds.), *Language and Thought*. New York: Cambridge University Press.

Shallice, T. (1988). *From Neuropsychology to Mental Structure*. New York: Cambridge University Press.

Simon, H. (1962). The architecture of complexity. *Proceedings of the American Philosophical Society*, 106, 467–82.

Sperber, D. (1996). *Explaining Culture: a Naturalistic Approach*. Oxford: Blackwell.

— (2002). In defense of massive modularity. In I. Dupoux (ed.), *Language, Brain and Cognitive Development*. Cambridge, MA: MIT Press.

— (2005). Massive modularity and the first principle of relevance. In P. Carruthers, S. Laurence, and S. Stich (eds.), *The Innate Mind: Structure and Contents*. New York: Oxford University Press.

Stone, V., Cosmides, L., Tooby, J., Kroll, N., and Knight, R. T. (2002). Selective impairment of reasoning about social exchange in a patient with bilateral limbic system damage. *Proceedings of the National Academy of Science*, 99, 11531–6.

Tager-Flusberg, H. (ed.) (1999). *Neurodevelopmental Disorders*. Cambridge, MA: MIT Press.

Tooby, J. and Cosmides, L. (1992). The psychological foundations of culture. In J. Barkow, L. Cosmides, and J. Tooby (eds.), *The Adapted Mind*. New York: Oxford University Press.

Tooby, J., Cosmides, L., and Barrett, C. (2005). Resolving the debate on innate ideas: learnability constraints and the evolved interpenetration of motivational and conceptual functions. In P. Carruthers, S. Laurence, and S. Stich (eds.), *The Innate Mind: Structure and Contents*. New York: Oxford University Press.

Varley, R. (2002). Science without grammar: scientific reasoning in severe agrammatic aphasia. In P. Carruthers, S. Stich, and M. Siegal (eds.), *The Cognitive Basis of Science*. New York: Cambridge University Press.

CHAPTER TWO

Is the Mind Really Modular?

Jesse J. Prinz

When Fodor titled his (1983) book the *Modularity of Mind*, he overstated his position. His actual view is that the mind divides into systems some of which are modular and others of which are not. The book would have been more aptly, if less provocatively, called *The Modularity of Low-Level Peripheral Systems*. High-level perception and cognitive systems are non-modular on Fodor's theory. In recent years, modularity has found more zealous defenders, who claim that the entire mind divides into highly specialized modules. This view has been especially popular among evolutionary psychologists. They claim that the mind is massively modular (Cosmides and Tooby, 1994; Sperber, 1994; Pinker, 1997; see also Samuels, 1998). Like a Swiss army knife, the mind is an assembly of specialized tools, each of which has been designed for some particular purpose. My goal here is to raise doubts about both peripheral modularity and massive modularity. To do that, I will rely on the criteria for modularity laid out by Fodor (1983). I will argue that neither input systems, nor central systems are modular on any of these criteria.

Some defenders of modularity have dropped parts of Fodor's definition and defined modularity with reference to a more restricted list of features. Carruthers (chapter 1, THE CASE FOR MASSIVELY MODULAR MODELS OF MIND) makes such a move. My arguments against modularity threaten these accounts as well. My claim is not just that Fodor's criteria are not jointly satisfied by subsystems within the mind, but they are rarely satisfied individually. When we draw boundaries around subsystems that satisfy any one of Fodor's criteria for modularity, we find, at best, scattered islands of modularity. If modules exist, they are few and far between. The kinds of systems that have been labeled modular by defenders of both peripheral and massive modularity probably don't qualify. Thus, modularity is not a very useful construct in doing mental cartography.

1 Fodor's Criteria

Modularity should be contrasted with the uncontroversial assumption of "functional decomposition": the mind contains systems that can be distinguished by the functions they carry out. The modularity hypothesis is a claim about what some of the systems underlying human competences are like. Fodor characterizes modularity by appeal to nine special properties. He says that modular systems are:

1 Localized: modules are realized in dedicated neural architecture;
2 Subject to characteristic breakdowns: modules can be selectively impaired;
3 Mandatory: modules operate in an automatic way;
4 Fast: modules generate outputs quickly;
5 Shallow: modules have relatively simple outputs (e.g., not judgments);
6 Ontogenetically determined: modules develop in a characteristic pace and sequence;
7 Domain specific: modules cope with a restricted class of inputs;
8 Inaccessible: higher levels of processing have limited access to the representations within a module;
9 Informationally encapsulated: modules cannot be guided by information at higher levels of processing.

Fodor's criteria can be interpreted in different ways. Perhaps a system is modular to the extent that it exhibits properties on the list. Alternatively, some of the properties may be essential, while others are merely diagnostic. In recent writings, Fodor (2000) has treated informational encapsulation as a *sine qua non* for modularity. Defenders of massive modality focus on domain specificity in ontogenetic determination (Cosmides and Tooby, 1994; Sperber, 1994). I will emphasize these properties in what follows, but I will also discuss the other properties on the list, because, even if they are not essential, Fodor implies that they cluster together. I am skeptical. I think the properties on Fodor's list can be used neither jointly nor individually to circumscribe an interesting class of systems.

2 Localization and Characteristic Breakdowns

The first two items in Fodor's account of modularity – localization and characteristic breakdowns – are closely related. The claim that mental faculties are localized is supported by the fact that focal brain lesions cause selective mental deficits. Further evidence for localization comes from neuroimaging studies, which purport to pinpoint the brain areas that are active when healthy individuals perform mental tasks.

The evidence for anatomical localization seems overwhelming at first, but problems appear on closer analysis. Uttal (2001) points out that there is considerable inconsistency across laboratories and studies. For example, there is little agreement about the precise location of Broca's area, the alleged center of language production (Poeppel, 1996). Indeed, aspects of language production have been located in every lobe of the brain (Pulvermüller, 1999). Or consider vision. There is considerable debate about the location of systems involved in processing things as fundamental as space and color. Uttal also points out that neuroimaging studies often implicate large-scale networks, rather than small regions, suggesting that vast expanses of cortex contribute to many fundamental tasks. Sometimes the size of these networks is underestimated. By focusing on hotspots, researchers often overlook regions of the brain that are moderately active during task performance.

Lesion studies are mired by similar problems. Well-known deficits, such as visual neglect, are associated with lesions in entirely different parts of the brain (e.g., frontal eye-fields and inferior parietal cortex). Sometimes, lesions in the same area have different effects in different people, and all too often neuropsychologists draw general conclusions from individual case studies. This assumes localization rather than providing evidence for it. Connectionist models have been used to show that focal lesions can lead to specific deficits even when there is no localization of functions: a massively distributed artificial neural network can exhibit a selective deficit after a few nodes are removed (simulating a focal lesion), even though those nodes were not the locus of the capacity that is lost (Plaut, 1995). More generally, when a lesion leads to an impairment of a capacity, we do not know if the locus of the lesion is the neural correlate of the capacity or the correlate of some ancillary prerequisite for the capacity.

I do not want to exaggerate the implications of these considerations. There is probably a fair degree of localization in the brain. No one is tempted to defend Lashley's (1950) equipotentiality hypothesis, according to which the brain is an undifferentiated mass. But the rejection of equipotentiality does not support modularity. Defenders of modularity combine localization with domain specificity: they assume that brain regions are exclusively dedicated to specific functions. Call this "strong localization." If, in reality, mental functions are located in large-scale overlapping networks, then it would be misleading to talk about anatomical regions as modules.

Evidence for strong localization is difficult to come by. Similar brain areas are active during multiple tasks, and focal brain lesions tend to produce multiple deficits. For example, aphasia patients regularly have impairments unrelated to language (Bates, 1994; Bates et al., 2000). Even genetic language disorders (specific language impairments) are co-morbid with nonlingusitic problems, such as impairments in rapid auditory processing or orofacial control (Bishop, 1992; Vargha-Khadem et al., 1995; Tallal et al., 1996).

To take another example, consider the discussion in Stone et al. (2002) of a patient who is said to have a selective deficit in reasoning about social exchanges. This patient is also impaired in recognizing *faux pas* and mental-state terms, so he does not support the existence of a social exchange module. Nor does this patient support the existence of a general social cognition module, because he performs other social tasks well.

In sum it is difficult to find cases where specific brain regions have truly specific functions. One could escape the localization criterion by defining modules as motley assortments of abilities (e.g., syntax plus orofacial control; social exchange plus *faux pas*), but this would trivialize the modularity hypothesis. There is little evidence that the capacities presumed to be modular by defenders of the modularity hypothesis are strongly localized.

Jesse J. Prinz

3 Mandatory, Fast, and Shallow

The next three items on Fodor's characterization of modules are supposed to capture a distinctive style of processing. Modules, he says, are mandatory, fast, and shallow. I don't think that these properties capture an interesting class of systems within the mind. There is little reason to think they are intimately related to each other. A system whose processes are mandatory (i.e., automatic) need not be fast. For example, consider the system underlying circadian rhythms, which regulate the sleep-wake cycle. Nor should we expect mandatory processes to be shallow. Semantic priming is mandatory, but it taps into conceptual knowledge. The three properties under consideration are more of a grab bag than a coherent constellation.

The three properties are uninteresting when considered in isolation. Consider automaticity. Everyone agrees that some mental processes are automatic, but most mental capacities seem to integrate automatic processes with processes that are controlled. For example, we form syntactic trees automatically, but sentence production can be controlled by deliberation. Likewise, we see colors automatically, but we can visually imagine colors at will. The automatic/controlled distinction cannot be used to distinguish systems in an interesting way.

Now consider speed. As remarked above, some capacities that look like plausible candidates for mental modules may be slow (e.g., those governing circadian rhythms). In addition, there are large variations in performance speed within any general system, such as vision or language. Verb conjugation, for example, may depend on whether the verb in question is regular or irregular, and whether the verb is frequent or infrequent. There is little inclination to say that verb conjugation is more modular when it is accomplished more quickly. In addition, some of the worst candidates for modular processes are relatively fast: priming is instantaneous but it can link elements in entirely different systems (the smell of coffee may evoke memories of a holiday in Rome).

Finally, consider the suggestion that modules have shallow outputs. Shallow outputs are outputs that do not require a lot of processing. As an example, Fodor suggests that it doesn't take the visual system much processing to output representations of basic categories (e.g., apple, chair, car). But how much processing is too much? There is a lot of processing between retinal stimulation and visual recognition, and far fewer steps in certain higher cognitive processes, which Fodor regards as nonmodular (e.g., it takes one step to infer "fiscal conservative" from "Republican"). To get around this difficulty, one might restrict "shallow outputs" to nonconceptual outputs. Carruthers (chapter 1) rightly complains that this would beg the question against defenders of massive modularity: they claim conceptual tasks are modular. Definitions of "shallowness" are either too inclusive or too exclusive. It is not a useful construct for dividing up the mind.

4 Ontogenetic Determinism

Fodor implies that modules are ontogentically determined: they develop in a predictable way in all healthy individuals. Modules emerge through the maturation, rather than learning and experience. In a word, they are innate. I am skeptical. I think many alleged modular systems are learned, at least in part.

Of all alleged modules, the senses have the best claim to being innate, but they actually depend essentially on experience. Within the neocortex of infants, there is considerably less differentiation between the senses than there is in adults. Cortical pathways seem to emerge through a course of environmentally stimulated strengthening of connections and pruning. One possibility is that low-level sensory mechanisms are innate (including sense organs, subcortical sensory hubs, and the cytoarchitecture of primary sensory cortices), while high-level sensory mechanisms are acquired through environmental interaction (Quartz and Sejnowski, 1997). This conjecture is supported by the plasticity of the senses (Chen et al., 2002). For example, amputees experience phantom limbs because unused limb-detectors get rewired to neighboring cells, and blind people use brain areas associated with vision to read Braille. In such cases, sensory wiring seems to be input driven. Thus, it is impossible to classify the senses as strictly innate or acquired.

Strong nativist claims are even harder to defend when we go outside the senses. Consider folk physics: our core knowledge of how medium-sized physical objects behave. It is sometimes suggested that folk physics is an innate module. For example, some developmental psychologists conjecture that infants innately recognize that objects move as bounded wholes, that objects cannot pass through each other, and that objects fall when dropped. I don't find these conjectures plausible (see Prinz, 2002). Newborns are not surprised by violations of boundedness (Slater et al., 1990), and five-month-olds are not surprised by violations of solidity and gravity (Needham and Baillargeon, 1993). Indeed, some tasks involving gravity and solidity even stump two-year-olds (Hood et al., 2000). My guess is that innate capacities to track movement through space combine with experience to derive the basic principles of folk physics (compare Scholl and Leslie, 1999). If so, folk physics is a learned byproduct of general tracking mechanisms.

Consider another example: massive modularists claim that we have an innate capacity for "mind-reading," i.e., attributing mental states (e.g., Leslie, 1994; Baron-Cohen, 1996). The innateness claim is supported by two facts: mind-reading emerges on a fixed schedule, and it is impaired in autism, which is a genetic disorder. Consider these in turn. The evidence for a fixed schedule comes from studies of healthy western children. Normally developing western children generally master mind-reading skills between the third and fourth birthdays. However, this pattern fails to hold up cross-culturally (Lillard, 1998; Vinden, 1999). For example, Quechua speakers of Peru don't master belief attribution until they are eight (Vinden, 1996). Moreover, individual differences in belief attribution are highly correlated with language skills and exposure to social interaction (Garfield et al., 2001). This suggests that mind-reading skills are acquired through social experience and language training.

What about autism? I don't think that the mind-reading deficit in autism is evidence for innateness. An alternative hypothesis is that mind-reading depends on a more general capacity which is compromised in autism. One suggestion is that autistic individuals' difficulty with mind-reading is a consequence of genetic abnormality in oxytocin transmission, which prevents them from forming social attachments, and thereby undermines learned social skills (Insel et al., 1999).

Jesse J. Prinz

As a final example, I want to consider language. I will keep my remarks brief, because I have criticized the evidence for an innate language faculty elsewhere (Prinz, 2002; see also Scholz and Pullum (chapter 4, IRRATIONAL NATIVIST EXUBERANCE). I restrict myself to a brief comment on the allegation that language emerges on a fixed schedule. It seems, for example, that children reliably begin to learn words between 8 and 10 months, and they begin to combine words around 18 months. These numbers do not support innateness. They are statistical averages that belie enormous variation. Bates et al. (1995) found that, in early word comprehension, age accounted for only 36 percent of the variance, and individual differences were huge. In a sample of 10-month-olds, the reported number of words known ranged from 0 to 144. Among 18-month-olds, Bates et al. found that 46 percent combined words sometimes, and 11 percent did so frequently. The rate of learning may depend on factors such as general cognitive development and working memory span (e.g., Seung and Chapman, 2000). If the rate of language acquisition is variable and correlated with nonlinguistic factors, then it is bad evidence for innateness.

In presenting these examples, I have been trying to show that the evidence for innateness has been exaggerated. The developmental trajectory of many mental capacities is consistent with a learning story. I don't mean to suggest that we lack specialized capacities. Specialized capacities can be learned. This has been demonstrated by recent work on computational modeling (Jacobs, 1999). For example, one class of connectionist models works on the principle that inputs will be processed in the portion of the network that makes fewest errors when processing the training data. Using such a model, Thomas and Karmiloff-Smith (2002) demonstrate that a network trained to form past-tense verbs from their present-tense forms will spontaneously produce a subcomponent that handles regular verbs and another subcomponent that handles irregulars. Their network has one pathway with three layers of units and another pathway with two. The two-layer pathway is better with regulars and the three-layer pathway is better with irregulars, because irregular endings are not linearly separable. These two pathways are not task specific before training, but they end up being task specific afterwards. Such toy examples show that we can easily acquire specialized subsystems through learning. That means there is no reason to expect an intimate link between innateness and specialization. Once that link is broken, the role of innateness in defending modularity is cast into doubt.

5 Domain Specificity

Domain specificity is closely related to innateness. To say that a capacity is innate is to say that we are biologically prepared with that specific capacity. Innate entails domain specific. But, as we have just seen, domain specific does not entail innate. Therefore, in arguing against the innateness criterion of modularity, I have not undermined the domain specificity criterion. Domain specificity is regarded by some as the essence of modularity, and it deserves careful consideration.

It is difficult to assess the claim that some mental systems are domain specific without clarifying definitions. What exactly is a "domain"? What is "specificity"? On some interpretations, domain specificity is a trivial property. "Domain" can be interpreted as a synonym for "subject matter." To say that a cognitive system concerns a domain, on this reading, is to say that the system has a subject matter. The subject matter might be a class of objects in the world, a class of related behaviors, a skill, or any other coherent category. On the weak reading, just about anything can qualify as a domain. Consider an individual concept, such as the concept "camel." A mental representation used to categorize camels is specific to a domain, since camels are a coherent subject matter. Likewise for every concept.

"Specificity" also has a weak reading. In saying that a mental resource is domain specific, we may be saying no more than that is it is used to process information underlying our aptitude for that domain. In other words, domain specificity would not require exclusivity. Consider the capacity to throw crumpled paper into a wastebasket. Presumably, the mental resources underlying that ability overlap with resources used in throwing basketballs in hoops or throwing tin cans into recycle bins. On the weak definition of "specificity," we have a domain specific capacity for throwing paper into wastebaskets simply in virtue of having mental resources underlying that capacity, regardless of the fact that those resources are not dedicated exclusively to that capacity.

Clearly defenders of domain specificity want something more. On a stronger reading, "domain" refers, not to any subject matter, but to matters that are relatively encompassing. Camels are too specific. The class of animals might qualify as a domain, because it is more inclusive. Psychologists have this kind of category in mind when they talk about "basic ontological domains." But notice that the stronger definition is hopelessly vague. What does it mean to say domains are relatively encompassing? Relative to what? "Camel" is an encompassing concept relative to the concept: "the particular animal used by Lawrence to cross the Arabian desert." Moreover, it is common in cognitive science to refer to language, mind-reading, and social exhange as domains. Are these things encompassing in the same sense and to the same degree as "animal"? In response to these difficulties, some researchers define domains as sets of principles. This won't help. We have principles underlying our knowledge of camels, as well as principles underlying our knowledge of animals. I see no escape. If we drop the weak definition of "domain" (domain = subject matter), we still find ourselves with definitions that are vague or insufficiently restrictive.

Things are slightly better with "specificity." On a strong reading, "specific" means "exclusively dedicated." To say that modules are domain specific is to say that they are exclusively dedicated to their subject matter. This is a useful explanatory construct, and it may be applicable to certain mental systems. Consider the columns of cells in primary visual cortex that are used to detect edges. These cells may be dedicated to that function and nothing else. Perhaps modules are supposed to be like that.

There is still some risk of triviality here. We can show that any collection of rules and representations in the mind-brain is dedicated by simply listing an exhaustive disjunction of everything that those rules and representations do. To escape triviality, we want to rule out disjunctive lists of functions. We say that systems are domain specific when the domain can be specified in intuitively coherent way. Let's assume for the sake of argument that this requirement can be made more precise. The problem is that alleged examples of modules probably aren't domain specific in this strong sense.

Jesse J. Prinz

Consider vision. Edge detectors may be domain specific, but other resources used for processing visual information may be more general. For example, the visual system can be recruited in problem solving, as when one uses imagery to estimate where a carton of milk can squeeze into a crammed refrigerator. Some of our conceptual knowledge may be stored in the form of visual records. We know that damage to visual areas can disrupt conceptual competence (Martin and Chao, 2001). I have also noted that, when people lose their sense of sight, areas once used for vision get used for touch. Visually perceived stimuli also generate activity in cells that are bimodal. The very same cells are used by the touch system and the auditory system. If we excluded rules and representations that can be used for something other than deriving information from light, the boundaries of the "visual system" would shrink considerably. At the neural level of description, it is possible that only isolated islands of cells would remain. This would be a strange way to carve up the mind. One of the important things about our senses is that they can moonlight. They can help each other out and they can play a central role in the performance of cognitive tasks. Vision, taken as a coherent whole, is not domain specific in the strong sense, even if it contains some rules and representations that are.

Similar conclusions can be drawn for language. I have said that language may share resources with systems that serve other functions: pattern recognition, muscle control, and so on. Broca's area seems to contain mirror neurons, which play a role in the recognition of manual actions, such as pinching and grasping (Heiser et al., 2003). Wernicke's area seems to contain cells that are used in the categorization of nonlinguistic sounds (Saygin et al., 2003). Of course, there may be some language-specific rules and representation *within* the systems that contribute to language. Perhaps the neurons dedicated to conjugating the verb "to be" have no nonlinguistic function. Such highly localized instances of domain specificity will offer little comfort to the defender of modularity. They are too specific to correspond to modules that have been proposed. Should we conclude that there is a module dedicated to the conjugation of each irregular verb?

There is relatively little evidence for large-scale modules, if we use domain specificity as the criterion. It is hard to find systems that are exclusively dedicated to broad domains. Vision and language systems are not dedicated in the strong sense, and the same is true for other alleged modules. Consider mind-reading, which clearly exploits domain general capacities. I noted above that mind-reading is correlated with language skills. Hale and Tager-Flusberg (2003) found that preschoolers who failed the false belief task were more likely to succeed after receiving training in sentential complement clauses. They went from 20 percent correct in attribute false beliefs to over 75 percent correct. Mind-reading also depends on working memory. Performance in attributing false beliefs is impaired in healthy subjects when they are given an unrelated working memory task (McKinnon and Moscovitch, unpublished). In neuroimaging studies, mind-reading is shown to recruit language centers in left frontal cortex, visuospatial areas in right temporal-parietal regions, the amygdala, which mediates emotional responses, and the precuneus, which is involved in mental image inspection and task switching. In short, mind-reading seems to exploit a large network of structures all of which contribute to many other capacities.

This seems to be the general pattern for alleged modules. The brain structures involved in mathematical cognition are also involved in language, spatial processing, and attention (Dehaene, 1997; Simon, 1997). Folk physics seems to rely on multi-object attention mechanisms (Scholl and Leslie, 1999). Moral judgment recruits ordinary emotion centers (Greene and Haidt, 2002).

For all I have said, alleged modules may have domain specific *components*. Perhaps these systems use some proprietary rules and representations. But they don't seem to be proprietary throughout. Therefore, domain specificity cannot be used to trace the boundaries around the kinds of systems that modularists have traditionally discussed.

6 Inaccessibility and Encapsulation

The final two properties on Fodor's list are closely linked. Modules are said to be inaccessible and encapsulated. That means, they don't let much information out and they don't let much information in. Fodor thinks the latter property is especially important. Carruthers places emphasis on both encapsulation and inaccessibility. I think neither property is especially useful in carving up the mind.

Let's begin with inaccessibility. Fodor claims that systems outside a module have no access to the internal operations within that module. This seems plausible introspectively. I have no introspective access to how my visual system achieved color constancy or how my syntax system parses sentences. Nisbett and Wilson (1977) have shown that human judgment is often driven by processes that operate below the level of consciousness. Does this confirm that operations within modules are inaccessible? No: it shows only that we lack conscious access. It tells us nothing about whether operations within unconscious mental systems are accessible to other unconscious systems. For all we know, there may be extensive accessibility below the level of awareness.

This is where Carruthers comes in. He has a principled argument for the conclusion that mental systems are by and large inaccessible. He says that, in order for one system to access information in another, the first system would need to represent how the other system works. But that means it would need to represent all the rules and representations of that other system. This would defeat the purpose of dividing the mind into separate systems, and it would lead to a combinatorial explosion. Therefore, most systems must be inaccessible to each other.

I am not persuaded by this argument. It rules out the view that all systems are *completely* accessible to all others, but it does nothing to refute the possibility that *some* systems have *some* access to others. For example, conceptual systems might have access to syntactic trees, but lack access to subtle transformation rules used in deriving those trees. Limited accessibility would not lead to a combinatorial explosion, and it might be useful for some systems to have an idea what other systems are doing. By analogy, the President cannot attend every cabinet meeting, but it would help him to have some idea of how cabinet members reached any given decision.

Let me turn from inaccessibility to encapsulation – the final item on Fodor's list and, for him, the most important. Fodor tries to prove that perceptual systems are

Jesse J. Prinz

modular by appealing to perceptual illusions. The interesting thing about illusions is that they persist even when we know that we are being deceived. The two lines in the Müller-Lyre illusion appear different in length even though we know they are they same. If perception were not encapsulated, then the illusion would go away as soon as the corrective judgment is formed. Belief would correct experience.

Fodor's argument is flawed. There are competing explanations for why illusions persist. One possibility is that perception always trumps belief when the two come into conflict. Such a trumping mechanism would be advantageous, because, otherwise, we could not use experience to correct our beliefs. The trumping mechanism is consistent with the hypothesis that perception is not encapsulated. Beliefs may be able to affect perception when the two are not in conflict. To test between trumping and encapsulation, we need to consider such cases. Consider ambiguous figures. Verbal cueing can lead people to alter their experience of the duck-rabbit. Likewise, we can electively experience a Necker cube as facing right, facing left, or as a gemstone facing directly forward. In paintings that covey depth by scale, we can see figures in the distance as far away or we can see them as tiny people floating in the foreground.

There are many other examples of top-down effects (i.e., cases in which systems at a relatively advanced stage of processing exert influence on systems that are involved in earlier stages of processing). For example, expectations can lead us to experience things that aren't there. If you are waiting for a visitor, every little sound may be mistaken for a knock on the door. Or consider visual search: when looking for a Kodak film carton, small yellow objects pop out in that visual field. The most obvious case of top-down influence is mental imagery. Cognitive states can be used to actively construct perceptual representations (Kosslyn et al., 1995). This makes sense of the neuroanatomy: there are dense neural pathways from centers of higher brain function into perception centers.

There is also evidence for top down-effects in language processing. Defenders of modularity would have us believe that language divides into a number of modular subsystems, including syntax, semantics, and phonology. These subsystems are alleged to be impervious to each other, but there is empirical evidence to the contrary. For example, in the phenomenon of phoneme restoration, subjects are presented with sentences containing deleted phonemes, but, rather than hearing an acoustic gap, the missing phoneme is filled in. Importantly, the phoneme that is heard is determined by the semantic interpretation of the sentence (Warren and Warren, 1970). If subjects hear, "The _eel is on the axel," they experience a "w" sound in the gap. If they hear, "The _eel is on the orange," they experience a "p" sound.

There is also evidence that syntax can be affected by conceptual knowledge. Marslen-Wilson and Tyler (1987) showed that conceptual factors exert highly specific influences on sentence completion, and they do so at the same speed as lexical factors. In one experiment, subjects are given the following story: "As Philip was walking back from the shop he saw an old woman trip and fall flat on her face in the street. She seemed unable to get up again." The story then continues with one of two sentence fragments: either "He ran toward . . ." or "Running towards . . ." In both fragments, the appropriate next word is "her," but in the first case that choice in determined *lexically* by the prior pronoun in the sentence ("he") and in the second case that choice is determined *conceptually* (we know that people cannot run when they are lying down). Remarkably, subjects are primed to use the word "her" equally fast in both conditions. If lexical processing were encapsulated from conceptual processing, one would expect lexically determined word choices to arise faster. These results imply that formal aspects of language are under immediate and constant influence of general world knowledge.

Thus far, I have been talking about top-down influences on input systems. There is also evidence that input systems can speak to each other. This is incompatible with encapsulation, because a truly encapsulated system would be insulated from *any* external influence. Consider some examples. First, when subjects hear speech sounds that are inconsistent with observed mouth movements, the visual experience systematically distorts the auditory experience of the speech sounds (McGurk and MacDonald, 1976). Second, Ramachandran has developed a therapeutic technique for treating phantom limb pain, in which amputees use a mirror reflection to visually relocate an intact limb in the location of a missing limb; if they scratch or sooth the intact limb, the discomfort in the phantom subsides (Ramachandran et al., 1995). Third, sound can give rise to touch illusions: hearing multiple tones can make people feel multiple taps, when there has been only one (Hötting and Röder, 2004). Finally, people with synesthesia experience sensations in one modality when they are stimulated in another; for example, some people see colors when they hear sounds, and others experience shapes when they taste certain flavors. All these examples show that there can be direct and content-specific cross-talk between the senses.

The empirical evidence suggests that mental systems are not encapsulated. But the story cannot end here. There is also a principled argument for encapsulation, which is nicely presented by Carruthers. It goes like this: mental processes must be computationally tractable, because the mind is a computer, and mental processes are carried out successfully in a finite amount of time; if mental processes had access to all the information stored in the mind (i.e., if they were not encapsulated), they would not be tractable (merely checking consistency against a couple hundred beliefs would take billions of years); therefore, mental processes are encapsulated.

Carruthers recognizes that there is a major flaw in this argument. According to the second premise, mental processes would be intractable if they had access to all the information stored in the mind. This is actually false. Computational systems can sort through stupendously large databases at breakneck speed. The trick is to use "frugal" search rules. Frugal rules are ones that radically reduce processing load by exploiting simple procedures for selecting relevant items in the database. Once the most relevant items are selected, more thorough processing of those items can begin. Psychologists call such simple rules "heuristics" (Kahneman et al., 1982). There is overwhelming evidence that we make regular use of heuristics in performing cognitive tasks. For example, suppose you want to guess which of two cities is larger, Hamburg or Mainz. You could try to collect some population statistics (which would take a long time), or you could just pick the city name that is most familiar. This Take the Best strategy is extremely easy and very effective; it is even a good way to choose stocks that will perform well in the market (Gigerenzer et al., 1999). With heuristics, we can avoid exhaustive database searches even when a complete database is at our disposal. There are also ways to search through a colossal database without much

Jesse J. Prinz

cost. Internet search engines provide an existence proof (Clark, 2002). Consider Google. A Google search on the word "heuristic" sorts through over a billion web pages in 0.18 seconds, and the most useful results appear in the first few hits. Search engines look for keywords and for web-pages that have been frequently linked or accessed. If we perform the mental equivalent of a Google search on our mental files, we should be able to call up relevant information relatively quickly. The upshot is that encapsulation is not needed for computationally tractability.

At this point, one might expect Carruthers to abandon the assumption that mental systems are encapsulated. Instead, he draws a distinction between two kinds of encapsulation. Narrow-scope encapsulation occurs when most of the information held in the mind is such that a system can't be affected by that information in the course of processing. This is the kind of encapsulation that Fodor attributes to modules, and it is what Carruthers rejects when he appeals to heuristics. It is possible that any item of information is such that a system could be affected by it. But Carruthers endorses wide-scope encapsulation: systems are such that they can't be affected by most of the information held in the mind at the time of processing. This seems reasonable enough. If every item in the mind sent inputs to a given system simultaneously, that system would be overwhelmed. So, I accept "wide-scope encapsulation." But "wide-scope encapsulation" is not really encapsulation at all. "Encapsulation" implies that one system cannot be accessed by another. "Wide-scope encapsulation" says that all systems are accessible; they just aren't accessed all at once. Carruthers terminological move cannot be used to save the hypothesis that mental systems are encapsulated. In recognizing the power of heuristic search, he tacitly concedes that the primary argument for encapsulation is unsuccessful.

I do not want to claim that there is *no* encapsulation in the mind. It is possible that some subsystems are impervious to external inputs. I want to claim only that there is a lot of cross-talk between mental systems. If we try to do mental cartography by drawing lines around the few subsystems that are encapsulated, we will end up with borders that are not especially helpful. Encapsulation it is not sufficiently widespread to be an interesting organizing principle.

7 Conclusion: Decomposing Modularity

Throughout this discussion, I have argued that Fodor's criteria for modularity do not carve out interesting divisions in the mind. Systems that have been alleged to be modular cannot be characterized by the properties on Fodor's list. At best, these systems have *components* that satisfy some of Fodor's criteria. There is little reason to think that these criteria hang together, and, when considered individually, they apply to a scattered and sundry assortment of subsystems. It is grossly misleading to say that the mind is modular. At best, the mind has a smattering of modular parts.

That does not mean that the mind is a disorganized mash. At the outset, I said that modularity is not equivalent to functional decomposition. The mind can be described as a network of interconnected systems and subsystems. We can represent the mental division of labor using flowcharts whose units correspond to functionally distinguished components that carry out subroutines and contribute, in their limited way, to the greater whole. My goal has been to criticize a specific account of what the functional units in the mind are like. The functional units need not be fast, automatic, innate, shallow, or encapsulated. Some of the components may be dedicated to a single mental capacity, but others may serve a variety of different capacities. It is possible that no component in the mind exhibits the preponderance of properties on Fodor's list.

Some defenders of modularity are committed to nothing more than functional decomposition. They reject Fodor's list and adopt the simple view that the mind is a machine with component parts. *That* view is uncontroversial. Massive modularity sounds like a radical thesis, but, when the notion of modularity is denatured, it turns into a platitude. Of course central cognition has a variety of different rules and representations. Of course we bring different knowledge and skills to bear when we reason about the social world as opposed to the world of concrete objects. Of course it is possible for someone to lose a specific cognitive capacity without losing every other cognitive capacity. Controversy arises only when functional components are presumed to have properties on Fodor's list.

I think the term "modularity" should be dropped because it implies that many mental systems are modular in Fodor's sense, and that thesis lacks support. Cognitive scientists should continue to engage in functional decomposition, but we should resist the temptation to postulate and proliferate modules.

References and further reading

Baillargeon, R., Kotovsky, L., and Needham, A. (1995). The acquisition of physical knowledge in infancy. In D. Sperber, D. Premack, and A. J. Premack (eds.), *Causal Cognition: A Multidisciplinary Debate*. New York: Oxford University Press.

Baron-Cohen, S. (1996). *Mindblindness: An Essay on Autism and Theory of Mind*. Cambridge, MA: MIT Press.

Bates, E. (1994). Modularity, domain specificity and the development of language. In D. C. Gajdusek, G. M. McKhann, and C. L. Bolis (eds.), *Evolution and Neurology of Language: Discussions in Neuroscience*, 10, 136–49.

Bates, E., Dale, P., and Thal, D. (1995). Individual differences and their implications for theories of language development. In P. Fletcher and B. MacWhinney (eds.), *Handbook of Child Language*. Oxford: Blackwell.

Bates, E., Marangolo, P., Pizzamiglio, L., Devescovi, A., Ciurli, P., and Dick, F. (2000). Linguistic and nonlinguistic priming in aphasia. *Brain and Language*, 76, 62–9.

Bishop, D. V. (1992). The underlying nature of specific language impairment. *Journal of Child Psychology and Psychiatry*, 33, 3–66.

Caramazza, A. and Mahon, B. Z. (2003). The organization of conceptual knowledge: The evidence from category-specific semantic deficits. *Trends in Cognitive Science*, 7, 354–61.

Chen, R., Cohen, L. G., and Hallett, M. (2002). Nervous system reorganization following injury. *Neuroscience*, 111, 761–73.

Clark, A. (2002). Local associations and global reason: Fodor's frame problem and second-order search. *Cognitive Science Quarterly*, 2, 115–40.

Cosmides, L. and Tooby, J. (1994). Origins of domain specificity: the evolution of functional organization. In L. A. Hirschfeld and S. A. Gelman (eds.), *Mapping the Mind: Domain Specificity in Cognition and Culture*. New York: Cambridge University Press, 85–116.

Dehaene, S. (1997). *The Number Sense*. New York: Oxford University Press.

Fodor, J. (1983). *The Modularity of Mind*. Cambridge, MA: MIT Press.

— (2000). *The Mind Doesn't Work That Way: The Scope and Limits of Computational Psychology*. Cambridge, MA: MIT Press.

Garfield, J. L., Peterson, C. C., and Perry, T. (2001). Social cognition, language acquisition and the development of the theory of mind. *Mind and Language*, 16, 494–541.

Gigerenzer, G., Todd, P. M., and the ABC Research Group (1999). *Simple Heuristics that Make Us Smart*. New York: Oxford University Press.

Greene, J. and Haidt, J. (2002). How (and where) does moral judgment work? *Trends in Cognitive Science*, 6, 517–23.

Hale, C. M. and Tager–Flusberg, H. (2003). The influence of language on theory of mind: a training study. *Developmental Science*, 6, 346–59.

Heiser, M., Iacoboni, M., Maeda, F., Marcus, J., and Mazziotta, J. C. (2003). The essential role of Broca's area in imitation. *European Journal of Neuroscience*, 17, 1123–8.

Hood, B., Carey, S., and Prasada, S. (2000). Predicting the outcomes of physical events: two-year-olds fail to reveal knowledge of solidity and support. *Child Development*, 71, 1540–54.

Hötting, K. and Röder, B. (2004). Hearing cheats touch, but less in congenitally blind than in sighted individuals. *Psychological Science*, 15, 60–4.

Insel, T. R., O'Brien, D. J., and Leckman, J. F. (1999). Oxytocin, vasopressin, and autism: is there a connection? *Biological Psychiatry*, 45, 145–57.

Jacobs, R. A. (1999). Computational studies of the development of functionally specialized neural modules. *Trends in Cognitive Science*, 3, 31–8.

Kahneman, D., Slovic, P., and Tversky, A. (eds.) (1982). *Judgment Under Uncertainty: Heuristics and Biases*. New York: Cambridge University Press.

Kosslyn, S. M., Thompson, W. L., Kim, I. J., and Alpert, N. M. (1995). Topographical representations of mental images in primary visual cortex. *Nature*, 378, 496–8.

Lashley, K. (1950). In search of the engram. *Symposia of the Society for Experimental Biology*, 4, 454–82.

Leslie, A. M. (1994). ToMM, ToBy, and Agency: core architecture and domain specificity. In L. Hirschfeld and S. Gelman (eds.), *Mapping the Mind: Domain Specificity in Cognition and Culture*. New York: Cambridge University Press.

Lillard, A. (1998). Ethnopsychologies: cultural variations in theories of mind. *Psychological Bulletin*, 123, 3–32.

Marslen-Wilson, W. and Tyler, L. (1987). Against modularity. In J. L. Garfield (ed.), *Modularity in Knowledge Representation and Natural-Language Understanding*. Cambridge, MA: MIT Press.

Martin, A. and Chao, L. (2001). Semantic memory and the brain: structure and processes. *Current Opinion in Neurobiology*, 11, 194–201.

McGurk, H. and MacDonald, J. (1976). Hearing lips and seeing voices. *Nature*, 264, 746–8.

McKinnon, M. and Moscovitch, M. (unpublished). Domain-general contributions to social reasoning: perspectives from aging and the dual-task method. Manuscript, University of Toronto.

Needham, A. and Baillargeon, R. (1993) Intuitions about support in 4.5-month-old infants. *Cognition*, 47, 121–48.

Nisbett, R. and Wilson, T. (1977). Telling more than we can know: verbal reports on mental processes. *Psychological Review*, 84, 231–59.

Pinker, S. (1997). *How the Mind Works*. New York: Norton.

Plaut, D. C. (1995). Double dissociation without modularity: evidence from connectionist neuropsychology. *Journal of Clinical and Experimental Neuropsychology*, 17, 291–321.

Poeppel, D. (1996). A critical review of PET studies of phonological processing. *Brain and Language*, 55, 317–51.

Prinz, J. J. (2002). *Furnishing the Mind: Concepts and their Perceptual Basis*. Cambridge, MA: MIT Press.

Pulvermüller, F. (1999). Words in the brain's language. *Behavioral and Brain Sciences*, 22, 253–336.

Quartz, S. R. and Sejnowski, T. J. (1997). The neural basis of cognitive development: a constructivist manifesto. *Behavioural and Brain Sciences*, 20, 537–96.

Ramachandran, V. S., Rogers-Ramachandran, D., and Cobb, S. (1995). Touching the phantom limb. *Nature*, 377, 489–90.

Samuels, R. (1998). Evolutionary psychology and the massive modularity hypothesis. *British Journal for the Philosophy of Science*, 49, 575–602.

Saygin, A. P., Dick, F., Wilson, S. M., Dronkers, N. F., and Bates, E. (2003). Neural resources for processing language and environmental sounds: evidence from aphasia. *Brain*, 126/4, 928–45.

Scholl, B. J. and Leslie, A. M. (1999). Explaining the infant's object concept: beyond the perception/cognition dichotomy. In E. Lepore and Z. Pylyshyn (eds.), *What is Cognitive Science?* Oxford: Blackwell.

Seung, H.-K. and Chapman, R. S. (2000). Digit span in individuals with Down's syndrome and typically developing children: temporal aspects. *Journal of Speech, Language, and Hearing Research*, 43, 609–20.

Simon, T. J. (1997). Reconceptualizing the origins of number knowledge: a non-numerical account. *Cognitive Development*, 12, 349–72.

Slater, A., Morison, V., Somers, M., Mattock, A., Brown, E., and Taylor, D. (1990). Newborn and older infants' perception of partly occluded objects. *Infant Behavior and Development*, 13, 33–49.

Sperber, D. (1994). The modularity of thought and the epidemiology of representations. In L. A. Hirschfeld and S. A. Gelman (eds.), *Mapping the Mind: Domain Specificity in Cognition and Culture*. New York: Cambridge University Press.

Stone, V. E., Cosmides, L., Tooby, J., Kroll, N., and Knight, R. T. (2002). Selective impairment of reasoning about social exchange in a patient with bilateral limbic system damage. *Proceedings of the National Academy of Sciences*, 99, 11531–6.

Tallal, P., Miller, S. L., Bedi, G., et al. (1996). Language comprehension in language-learning impaired children improved with acoustically modified speech. *Science*, 271, 81–4.

Thomas, M. S. C. and Karmiloff-Smith, A. (2002). Are developmental disorders like cases of adult brain damage? Implications from connectionist modelling. *Behavioural and Brain Sciences*, 25/6, 727–88.

Uttal, W. R. (2001). *The New Phrenology: The Limits of Localizing Cognitive Processes in the Brain*. Cambridge, MA: MIT Press.

Van Giffen, K. and Haith, M. M. (1984). Infant response to Gestalt geometric forms. *Infant Behavioral Development*, 7, 335–46.

Vargha-Khadem, F., Watkins, K., Alcock, K., Fletcher, P., and Passingham, R. (1995). Praxic and nonverbal cognitive deficits in a large family with a genetically transmitted speech and language disorder. *Proceedings of the National Academy of Science*, 92, 930–3.

Vinden, P. G. (1996). Junin Quechua children's understanding of mind. *Child Development*, 67, 1701–16.

—— (1999). Children's understanding of mind and emotion: A multi-culture study. *Cognition and Emotion*, 13, 19–48.

Warren, R. M. and Warren, R. P. (1970). Auditory illusions and confusions. *Scientific American*, 223, 30–6.

Is the Human Mind Massively Modular?

Richard Samuels

Introduction: Minds as Mechanisms

Among the most pervasive and fundamental assumptions in cognitive science is that the human mind (or mind-brain) is a *mechanism* of some sort: a physical device composed of functionally specifiable subsystems. On this view, *functional decomposition* – the analysis of the overall system into functionally specifiable parts – becomes a central project for a science of the mind, and the resulting theories of *cognitive architecture* essential to our understanding of human psychology.

None of this is, of course, in any way distinctive of massive modularity (MM). On the contrary, these commitments have very wide acceptance among cognitive scientists and have done so since the inception of the discipline. If MM is of value, then, it is not merely because it advocates a mechanistic conception of minds; it must also embody a distinctive, interesting, and plausible hypothesis about our cognitive architecture.

The central aim of this chapter is to argue that, as things stand, there is little reason to suppose advocates of MM have succeeded in articulating such a hypothesis. On some readings, the MM hypothesis is plausible but banal. On other readings, it is radical but wholly lacking in plausibility. And on still further (more moderate but still interesting) interpretations, it remains largely unsupported by the available arguments since there is little reason to suppose that *central systems* – such as those for reasoning and decision making – are modular in character. Contrary to what Peter Carruthers and others maintain, then, the case for MM is not strong. But it would be wrong to conclude, as Jesse Prinz and others have done, that the mind is not modular to any interesting degree (Prinz, chapter 2, IS THE MIND REALLY MODULAR?). This is because it is very plausible that relatively peripheral regions of cognition – especially for low-level perception – are modular in character. I thus advocate a middle way between those who endorse a thoroughgoing massive modularity and those who reject modularity altogether.

Here's how I'll proceed. In section 1, I clarify the main commitments of MM and the attendant notion(s) of a module. In section 2, I sketch some of the main theoretical arguments for MM and highlight their deficiencies. In section 3, I very briefly discuss some problems with the experimental case for MM. In section 4, I outline some reasons for finding MM at least in radical form implausible. Finally in section 5, I argue against those who not merely reject MM but deny minds are modular to any interesting degree.

1 What's at Issue?

To a first approximation, MM is the hypothesis that the human mind is largely or entirely composed from a great many modules. Slightly more precisely, MM can be formulated as the conjunction of three claims:

> *Composition Thesis*: The human mind is largely or entirely composed from *modules*.
> *Plurality Thesis*: The human mind contains a great many modules.
> *Central Modularity*: Modularity is found not merely at the periphery of the mind but also in those *central* regions responsible for reasoning and decision-making.

In what follows I assume advocates of MM are committed to the conjunction of these claims. Even so, each is amenable to a variety of different interpretations that vary considerably in interest and plausibility. More needs to be said if we are to get clearer on what's at issue.

1.1 Composition Thesis

MM is in large measure a claim about the kinds of mechanisms from which our minds are composed – viz., it is largely or even entirely composed from *modules*.[1] As stated, this is vague in at least two respects. First, it leaves unspecified the precise extent to which minds are composed from modules. In particular, this way of formulating the proposal accommodates two different positions, which I call *strong* and *weak* massive modularity. According to strong MM *all* cognitive mechanisms are modules. Such a view would be undermined if we were to discover that any cognitive mechanism was nonmodular in character. By contrast, weak MM maintains only that the human mind – including those parts responsible for central processing – are *largely* modular in structure. In contrast to strong MM, such a view is clearly compatible with the claim that there are some nonmodular mechanisms. So, for example, the proponent of weak MM is able to posit the existence of some nonmodular devices for reasoning and learning.

A second respect in which the above Composition Thesis is vague is that it leaves unspecified what modules *are*. For present purposes, this an important matter since the interest and plausibility of the thesis turns crucially on what one takes modules to be.[2]

Minimal processing modules

At one extreme, modules are just distinct, functionally characterized cognitive mechanisms of the sort that correspond to boxes in a cognitive psychologist's flow diagram

(Fodor, 2000). This *minimal* conception of modules is one some advocates of MM really appear to adopt. So, for example, Tooby and Cosmides (1992) characterize modules as "complex structures that are functionally organized for processing information" (Tooby and Comsides, 1992; see also Pinker, 2005). Even so, it is too weak for an interesting and distinctive Composition Thesis since almost all cognitive scientists agree that minds are composed from such mechanisms. But it does not follow from this alone that a distinctive version of MM cannot be formulated in terms of this anodyne notion (Fodor, 2005; Prinz, chapter 2). In particular, some have suggested that an MM formulated with this notion is interesting not because it claims minds are composed of minimal modules but because it claims there are a *large number* of such mechanisms (Carruthers, chapter 1, THE CASE FOR MASSIVELY MODULAR MODELS OF MIND). I consider this suggestion in section 1.2.

Robust modules

So, the minimal notion of a module won't suffice for an interesting Composition Thesis. But debate in cognitive science frequently assumes some more robust conception of modularity; of which the most well known and most demanding is the one developed in Fodor (1983). On this view, modules are functionally characterizable cognitive mechanisms which are (at least paradigmatically) domain specific, informationally encapsulated, innate, mandatory, fast relative to central processes, shallow, neurally localized, exhibit characteristic breakdown patterns, are inaccessible, and have characteristic ontogenetic timetables (Fodor, 1983).[3]

Though the full-fledged Fodorian notion has been highly influential in many areas of cognitive science (Garfield, 1987), it has not played much role in debate over MM,[4] and for good reason. The thesis that minds are largely or entirely composed of Fodorian modules is obviously implausible. Indeed, some of the entries on Fodor's list – relative speed and shallowness, for example – make little sense when applied to central systems (Carruthers, chapter 1; Sperber, forthcoming). And even where Fodor's properties can be sensibly ascribed – as in the case of innateness – they carry a heavy justificatory burden that few seem much inclined to shoulder (Baron-Cohen, 1995; Sperber, 1996).

In any case, there is a broad consensus that not all the characteristics on Fodor's original list are of equal theoretical import. Rather, domain specificity and informational encapsulation are widely regarded as most central. Both these properties concern the architecturally imposed[5] informational restrictions to which cognitive mechanisms are subject – the range of representations they can access – though the kinds of restriction involved are different.

Domain specificity is a restriction on the representations a cognitive mechanism can take as *input* – that "trigger" it or "turn it on." Roughly, a mechanism is domain specific (as opposed to domain general) to the extent that it can only take as input a highly restricted range of representations.[6] Standard candidates include mechanisms for low-level visual perception, face recognition, and arithmetic.

Informational encapsulation is a restriction on the kinds of information a mechanism can use as a *resource* once so activated – paradigmatically, though not essentially, information stored in memory. Slightly more precisely, a cognitive mechanism is encapsulated to the extent it can access, in the course of its computations, less than all of the information available to the organism as a whole (Fodor, 1983). Standard candidates include mechanisms, such as those for low-level visual perception and phonology, which do not draw on the full range of an organism's beliefs and goals.

To be sure, there are many characteristics other than domain specificity and encapsulation that have been ascribed to modules. But if one uses "module" as more than a mere terminological expedient – as more than just a nice way of saying "cognitive mechanism" – yet deny they possess either of these properties, then one could with some justification be accused of changing the subject. In view of this, I will tend when discussing more robust conceptions of modularity to assume that modules must be domain specific and/or encapsulated. This has a number of virtues. First, these properties clearly figure prominently in dispute over MM. Moreover – and in contrast to the minimal module version of the Composition Thesis discussed earlier – the claim that minds are largely or entirely composed of domain specific and/or encapsulated mechanisms is a genuinely interesting one. Not only does it go beyond the banal claim that our minds are comprised from functionally characterizable cognitive mechanisms; but it is also a claim that opponents of MM almost invariably deny. In later sections I will consider the plausibility of this thesis; but first I need to discuss the other two theses associated with MM.

1.2 Plurality Thesis

Advocates of MM sometimes suggest their position is distinctive and interesting in part because it countenances a large number of cognitive mechanisms. In spelling out their position, for example, Tooby and Cosmides maintain: "our cognitive architecture resembles a confederation of hundreds or thousands of functionally dedicated computers (often called modules)" (Tooby and Cosmides, 1995, p. xiv).

This suggests a commitment to what I earlier called the Plurality Thesis: i.e., that the human mind contains a great many modules.

How interesting and distinctive is this thesis? If formulated in terms of a robust notion of modularity, it appears quite radical. After all, there are many who deny that domain specific and/or encapsulated devices have a substantial role to play in our cognitive economy. But what if the Plurality Thesis is formulated using the minimal notion of a module? Would this be an interesting and distinctive claim? Certainly, advocates of MM sometimes appear to suggest that it is. For example Carruthers claims: "those evolutionary psychologists who have defended the claim that the mind consists of a great many modular components (Tooby and Cosmides, 1992; Sperber, 1996; Pinker, 1997) are defending a thesis of considerable interest, even if 'module' just means 'component'" (Carruthers, chapter 1).

The idea seems to be that while virtually all cognitive scientists think minds are composed from distinct, functionally characterizable devices, many reject the claim that there are *lots* of such devices. According to Carruthers, for example, it is a claim rejected by "those who ... picture the mind as a big general-purpose computer with a limited number of distinct input and output links to the world" (Carruthers, chapter 1, p. 4). In which case, it may seem that MM is an interesting thesis even when formulated in terms of the minimal notion of a module.

Richard Samuels

On reflection, however, it's hard to see how this could be right: how a mere plurality of functionally specifiable mechanisms could make for an interesting and distinctive MM. This is because even radical opponents of MM endorse the view that minds contain a great many such components. So, for instance, the picture of the mind as a big general-purpose, "classical" computer – roughly, the sort of general-purpose device that manipulates symbols according to algorithmically specifiable rules – is often (and rightly) characterized as being firmly at odds with MM. Yet big general-purpose computers are not simple entities. On the contrary, they are almost invariably decomposable into a huge number of functionally characterizable submechanisms.[7] So, for example, a standard von Neumann-type architecture decomposes into a calculating unit, a control unit, a fast-to-access memory, a slow-to-access memory, and so on; and each of these decomposes further into smaller functional units, which are themselves decomposable into submechanisms, and so on. As a consequence, a standard von Neumann machine will typically have hundreds or even thousands of subcomponents.[8] Call this a version of massive modularity if you like. But it surely isn't an interesting or distinctive one.

1.3 Central Modularity

So far we have discussed the Composition and Plurality theses and seen that both are interesting on a robust construal of modules, but that neither seems interesting or distinctive on the minimal conception. But there is another thesis that requires our attention, the thesis of Central Modularity, which states that modules are found not merely at the periphery of the mind but also in those *central* regions responsible for reasoning and decision making.

This does not strictly follow from any of the claims discussed so far since one might deny there are any central systems for reasoning and decision making. But this is *not* the view that advocates of MM seek to defend. Indeed, a large part of what distinguishes MM from the earlier, well-known modularity hypothesis defended by Fodor (1983) and others is that the modular structure of the mind is not restricted to input systems (those responsible for perception, including language perception) and output systems (those responsible for producing behavior). Advocates of MM accept the Fodorian thesis that such peripheral systems are modular. But *pace* Fodor, they maintain that the *central* systems responsible for reasoning and decision making are largely or entirely modular as well (Jackendoff, 1992). So, for example, it has been suggested that there are modules for such central processes as social reasoning (Cosmides and Tooby, 1992), biological categorization (Pinker, 1994), and probabilistic inference (Gigerenzer, 1994 and 1996). In what follows, then, I assume MM is committed to some version of Central Modularity.

Again, how interesting a thesis is this? If formulated in terms of the minimal notion, it's hard to see how Central Modularity could be an interesting and distinctive one. After all, even those who endorse paradigmatically nonmodular views of central cognition can readily accept the claim. For example, advocates of the "Big Computer" view of central systems can accept the claim that central cognition is entirely subserved by a great many minimal modules since big computers are themselves composed of a great many such entities. All this is, of course, wholly compatible with there being some suitable modification that makes for an interesting version of Central Modularity. But the point I want to insist on here is that if one's arguments succeed only in supporting this version of the thesis, then they fail to support a distinctive and interesting version of MM.

Things look rather different if a robust conception of modules is adopted. Here, the degree to which one's version of Central Modularity is interesting will depend on (a) the extent to which central cognition is subserved by domain specific and/or encapsulated mechanisms and (b) how many such modules there are. Both these questions could be answered in a variety of different ways. At one extreme, for example, one might adopt the following view:

> *Strong Central Modularity*: All central systems are domain specific and/or encapsulated, and there are a great many of them.

That would be a genuinely radical position since it implies that there are no domain general, informationally unencapsulated central systems. But this Strong Central Modularity is very implausible. For as we will see in later sections, there are no good reasons to accept it, and some reason to think it is false. At the other extreme, one might maintain that:

> *Weak Central Modularity*: There are a number of domain specific and/or encapsulated central systems, but there are also nonmodular – domain general and unencapsulated – central systems as well.

Such a proposal is not without interest. But it is not especially radical in that it does not stray far from the old-fashioned peripheral modularity advocated by Fodor. Nor is it implausible in the way that Strong Central Modularity is. Nonetheless, as we will see, there is at present little reason to accept it. The general arguments for MM don't support this view; and the empirical case for even this version of Central Modularity is surprisingly weak.

2 The Allure of Massive Modularity

Though MM is an empirical hypothesis, many claim it is plausible in the light of quite general, theoretical arguments about the nature of evolution, cognition and computation. But even the most prominent and plausible of these arguments are unsatisfactory since they fail to discriminate between interesting versions of MM – such as those that imply Strong or Weak Central Modularity – and other widespread views.[9]

2.1 Evolvability

A discussion of evolutionary stability in Simon (1962) is sometimes invoked as an argument for MM (Carston, 1996; Carruthers, chapter 1). According to Simon, for an evolutionary process to reliably assemble complex functional systems – biological systems in particular – the overall system needs to be *semi-decomposable*: hierarchically organized from components with relatively limited connections to each other. Simon illustrates the point with a parable of two watchmakers – Hora and Tempus

Richard Samuels

– both highly regarded for their fine watches. But while Hora prospered, Tempus became poorer and poorer and finally lost his shop. The reason:

> The watches the men made consisted of about 1000 parts each. Tempus had so constructed his that if he had one partially assembled and had to put it down – to answer the phone, say – it immediately fell to pieces and had to be reassembled from the elements . . . The watches Hora handled were no less complex . . . but he had designed them so that he could put together sub-assemblies of about ten elements each. Ten of these sub-assemblies, again, could be put together into a larger sub-assembly and a system of ten of the latter constituted the whole watch. Hence, when Hora had to put down a partly assembled watch in order to answer the phone, he lost only a small part of his work, and he assembled his watches in only a fraction of the man-hours it took Tempus. (Simon, 1962)

The obvious moral – and the one Simon invites us to accept – is that evolutionary stability requires that complex systems be hierarchically organized from dissociable subsystems; and according to Carruthers and Carston, this militates in favor of MM (Carston, 1996, p. 75).

Response. Though evolutionary stability may initially appear to militate in favor of MM, it is in fact only an argument for the familiar mechanistic thesis that complex machines are hierarchically assembled from (and decomposable into) many subcomponents. But this clearly falls short of the claim that all (or even any) are domain specific or encapsulated. Rather it supports at most the sort of banal Plurality Thesis discussed earlier; one that is wholly compatible with even a Big Computer view of central processes. All it implies is that if there are such complex central systems, they will need to be hierarchically organized into dissociable subsystems – which incidentally, was the view Simon and his main collaborators endorsed all along (Simon, 1962; Newell, 1990).

2.2 Analogy with other biological systems

Throughout the biological world – from cells to cellular assemblies, whole organs, and so on – one finds hierarchical organization into semi-decomposable components. We should expect the same to be true of cognition (Chomsky, 1980; Carruthers, chapter 1).

Response. Same problem as the previous argument. Though all this is correct, it is at most an argument for the claim that our minds are semi-decomposable systems – hierarchically organized into dissociable subsystems – a conclusion that is in no way incompatible with even the most radically nonmodular accounts of central systems.

2.3 Task specificity

There are a great many cognitive tasks whose solutions impose quite different demands. So, for example, the demands on vision are distinct from those of speech recognition, of mind-reading, cheater-detection, probabilistic judgment, grammar induction, and so on. Moreover, since it is very hard to believe there could be a single general inferencing mechanism for all of them, for each such task we should postulate the existence of a distinct mechanism, whose internal processes are computationally specialized for processing different sorts of information in the way required to solve the task (Carruthers, chapter 1; Cosmides and Tooby, 1992, 1994).

Response. Two points. First, if the alternatives were MM or a view of minds as comprised of just a single general-purpose cognitive device, then I too would opt for MM. But these are clearly not the only options. On the contrary, one can readily deny that central systems are modular while still insisting there are plenty of modules for perception, motor control, selective attention, and so on. In other words, the issue is, not merely whether some cognitive tasks require specialized modules but whether the sorts of tasks associated with central cognition – paradigmatically, reasoning and decision making – typically require a proliferation of such mechanisms.

Second, it's important to see that the addition of functionally dedicated mechanisms is not the only way of enabling a complex system to address multiple tasks. An alternative is to provide some relatively functionally inspecific mechanism with requisite bodies of information for solving the tasks it confronts. This is a familiar proposal among those who advocate nonmodular accounts of central processes. Indeed, advocates of nonmodular reasoning architectures routinely assume that reasoning devices have access to a *huge* amount of specialized information on a great many topics, much of which will be learned but some of which may be innately specified (Anderson, 1990; Newell, 1990). Moreover, it is one that plausibly explains much of the proliferation of cognitive competences that humans exhibit throughout their lives – e.g., the ability to reason about historical issues as opposed to politics or gene splicing or restaurants. To be sure, it *might* be that each such task requires a distinct mechanism, but such a conclusion does not flow from general argument alone. For all we know, the same is true of the sorts of tasks advocates of MM discuss. It may be that the capacity to perform certain tasks is explained by the existence of specialized mechanisms. But how often this is the case for central cognition is an almost entirely open question that is not adjudicated by the argument from task specificity.

2.4 Bottleneck argument

If central processing were subserved by only a small number of general-purpose mechanisms as opposed to a multiplicity of modules, there would be a kind of tractability problem: a serious *processing bottleneck* that would prohibit the formation of beliefs on different topics in real time (Carruthers, chapter 1).

Response. For this to be an objection to the claim that we possess only a small number of central systems it would need to be that, as a matter of fact, central cognition is *not* subject to such bottlenecks. But it's far from clear this is true. Second, even if we assume for the sake of argument that there are few such bottlenecks, it's utterly unclear MM is the only way to avoid them. What MM permits is the *parallel* operation of multiple mechanisms. But it's not the only way to exact this benefit since there are at least two other (not mutually exclusive) ways that parallelism can increase the speed of processing. First, at the level of cognitive architecture, it may be that the component cognitive parts of a given non-modular mechanism operate at the same time. Second, there may be (and surely is) parallelism at the level of *implementation* so that individual, non-modular cognitive mechanisms have a parallel implementation within the circuits of the brain.

Richard Samuels

2.5 Computational tractability

It is common to argue for MM on the grounds that the alternatives are computationally intractable. In brief, the argument is as follows: Human cognitive processes are realized by computational mechanisms. But for this to be the case, our cognitive mechanisms would need to be computationally tractable; and this in turn requires that they be informationally encapsulated – that they have access to less than all the information available to the mind as a whole. Hence, the mind is composed of informationally encapsulated cognitive mechanisms.

Response. If one is disinclined to accept a computational account of cognitive processes, this is not an argument one is likely to take seriously. But even if one endorses a computational account of the mind, the argument still doesn't work. There is a long story about what's wrong (see Samuels, 2005). But the short version is that computational tractability does not require informational encapsulation in any standard sense of that expression; and the claim that some *other* kind of "encapsulation" is involved is tantamount to relabeling. As ordinarily construed, a mechanism is encapsulated only if – by virtue of architectural constraints – there is some relatively determinate class of informational states that it cannot access. (For example, the paradigmatic cases of encapsulated devices – low-level perceptual devices – cannot access the agent's beliefs or desires in the course of their computations.) While such an architectural constraint may be one way to engender tractability, it is clearly not the only way. Rather, what's required is that the mechanism be *frugal* in its use of information: that it not engage in exhaustive search but only use a restricted amount of the available information. Moreover, this might be achieved in a variety of ways, most obviously by heuristic and approximation techniques of the sort familiar from computer science and Artificial Intelligence.

So, it would seem that the tractability argument fails: frugality, not encapsulation, is what's required. Carruthers has responded to this, however, by drawing a distinction between two notions of encapsulation: the standard notion, which he calls "narrow-scope encapsulation" and another notion, "wide-scope encapsulation," on which the "operations of a module can't be affected by most of the information in a mind, without there being some determinate subdivision between the information that can affect the system and the information that can't" (Carruthers, chapter 1, p. 16). But this really isn't an interesting notion of encapsulation. For not only is it different from what most theorists mean by "encapsulation," but it's simply what you get by denying exhaustive search; and since virtually no one thinks exhaustive search is characteristic of human cognition, the present kind of "encapsulation" is neither distinctive nor interesting.

3 The Empirical Case for Massive Modularity

So far I have focused on the theoretical arguments for MM and found them wanting. But what of the empirical evidence? Many have claimed MM is plausible in light of the available experimental data (Sperber, 1996; Pinker, 1997, 2005). I am unconvinced. Although there is considerable evidence for relatively low-level modular mechanisms

– a point I return to in section 5 – the experimental case for *central* modularity is not strong (Samuels, 1998; Fodor, 2000). To the extent things seem otherwise, I suspect it is because the interpretation of data is heavily driven by a prior acceptance of the general theoretical arguments for MM – arguments which as we have seen there is little reason to endorse.[10]

In some cases, the reliance on general theoretical considerations in the absence of convincing data is egregious. (My current favorite example is the "homicide module" hypothesis advocated by Buss and his collaborators; see Buss and Duntley, 2005.) But even in cases where the influence of such considerations is less obvious, the data for Central Modularity are uncompelling. Often the problem is that the putative evidence for specialized modules can be better explained in terms of other, less specific processes. This is well illustrated by arguably the flagship case of a putative reasoning module: a dedicated mechanism for social contract reasoning (Comsides and Tooby, 1992; Gigerenzer and Hug, 1992). Advocates of this hypothesis sometimes represent it as a kind of modularist assault on the "doctrinal 'citadel' of . . . general-purpose processes": human reasoning (Cosmides and Tooby, 1992). But the main experimental support for the hypothesis – evidence of so-called content effects in Wason's Selection Task – can be very plausibly explained in terms of quite general features of language comprehension and, hence, provides no support for a dedicated social contract reasoning mechanism (Sperber et al., 1995; Fodor, 2000; Sperber and Girotto, 2003).

Another problem with the experimental case for Central Modularity is that even where the data suggest some kind of specialized cognitive structure for a given domain, it seldom adjudicates clearly between claims about the existence of specialized *mechanisms* and claims about the existence of specialized bodies of *knowledge*, such as a mentally represented theory. The former are modularity theses in the relevant sense while the latter are wholly compatible with a highly nonmodular account of central processing on which different bodies of knowledge are used by a small set of non-modular mechanisms (Newell, 1990; Gopnik and Meltzoff, 1997; Fodor, 2000). This point is well illustrated by the debate over folk biology. Many have proposed the existence of specialized cognitive structures for folk biology. But while some maintain it is subserved by a dedicated module (Pinker, 1994; Atran, 1998, 2001), others claim merely that we posses a body of information – a theory – that is deployed by relatively inspecific inferential devices (Carey, 1995). The problem is that the main available evidence regarding folk biology – e.g., cross-cultural evidence for universality, developmental evidence of precocity, anthropological evidence for rapid cultural transmission, and so on – fails to adjudicate between these options. What they suggest is that folk biology involves some dedicated – and perhaps innate – cognitive structure. But once the general arguments for MM are rejected, there is little reason to interpret it as favoring a *modular* account of folk biology.

Finally, even where the evidence for previously unrecognized modules is strong, it seldom turns out to be clear evidence for *central* modularity. Consider, for example, the "geometric module" hypothesis advocated by Cheng, Gallistel, and others (Gallistel, 1990; Hermer-Vazquez et al., 1999). Though contentious, the evidence for such a device is quite compelling. But this does not support a modular view of *central* processes since the geometric module is most plausibly construed as part of vision or visuomotor control (Pylyshyn, 1999). Perhaps surprisingly, a similar point applies to

Richard Samuels

what is widely regarded as among the strongest candidates for Central Modularity: the theory of mind module (ToMM) hypothesized by Alan Leslie and his collaborators (Leslie et al., 2004). The ToMM hypothesis is not without problems (see Nicholls and Stich, 2002). But even if we put these to one side, the existence of ToMM would do little to strengthen the case for Central Modularity since in its most recent and plausible incarnations, ToMM is characterized as a relatively low-level device for selective attention; and moreover one which relies heavily on decidedly nonmodular executive systems – most notably the "selection processor" – in order to perform its characteristic function (Leslie et al., 2004). Thus what is widely viewed as a strong candidate for Central Modularity both fails to be a clear example of a central system, and also presupposes the existence of nonmodular systems.

4 Some Reasons to Doubt Massive Modularity

So, the experimental evidence for Central Modularity is rather less strong than one would expect if MM were true. But there are also familiar – and in my view very plausible – claims about human thought which collectively suggest the existence of paradigmatically nonmodular central systems. In particular:

Conceptual integration. We are capable of freely combining concepts across different subject matters or content domains (Carruthers, 2003). So, for example, it's not merely that I can think about colors, about numbers, about shapes, about food, and so on. Rather I can have thoughts that concern all these things – e.g., that I had two roughly round, red steaks for lunch.

Generality of thought capacities. Not only can we freely combine concepts, we can also deploy the resulting representations in our theoretical and practical deliberations – to assess their truth or plausibility, but also to assess their impact on our plans and projects.

Inferential holism. Given surrounding conditions – especially, background beliefs – the *relevance* of a representation to the theoretical or practical tasks in which one engages can change dramatically.[11] Indeed, it would seem that given appropriate background assumptions, almost any belief can be relevant to the task in which one engages (Copeland, 1993).

Task range. We are capable of performing an *exceedingly wide* – perhaps unbounded – range of cognitive tasks of both a practical and theoretical nature (Newell, 1990).

Between task correlations. There is a huge amount of empirical evidence that performance on many central cognitive tasks *co-varies*. Thus psychometric studies appear to show that performance in any single task (e.g., arithmetic) is a reliable predictor of performance in a wide range of other cognitive tasks (e.g., spatial reasoning, deductive reasoning, spelling, reading, and so on) (Anderson, 1992).

The existence of general mental retardation. There are various organic disorders – most notably Down's syndrome – which produce across the board deficits in the performance of such highly correlated intellectual tasks (Anderson, 1998).

Taken individually, none of these phenomena mandates the existence of nonmodular central systems; and nor collectively do they preclude the existence of modular ones. In other words, the above are clearly compatible with what I called Weak Central

Modularity. Nevertheless, taken together, they do strongly suggest the existence of nonmodular – domain general and unencapsulated – mechanisms for thought and, hence, that Strong Central Modularity is false. This is because the assumption there are such mechanisms goes some way to help explain the above facts.

In contrast, if one rejects nonmodular mechanisms altogether, the prospects of accommodating these phenomena appear bleak; and to date, efforts to do so have been deeply unsatisfactory. Some strongly modular architectures – such as those embodied in Brook's animats – are precisely specified computational proposals but clearly inadequate to explaining the above phenomena (Kirsh, 1991; Bryson, 2000). In contrast, other modular proposals are so vague as to be almost wholly lacking in content. So, for example, it is common for advocates of MM to claim that the above kinds of phenomena can be largely explained by the fact that minds contain *so many* modules: "a network of subsystems that feed each other in criss-crossing but intelligible ways" (Pinker, 2005; see also Pinker, 1994; Buss, 2000). But these are not explanations so much as statements of the problem given a commitment to MM. The challenge is to sketch the *right sort* of plurality and "criss-crossing" between mechanisms – one that could plausibly exhibit the above sorts of phenomena. Finally, even those proposals that avoid vacuity or obvious inadequacy only seem to accommodate the above phenomena to the extent that they smuggle nonmodular mechanisms back in. So, for example, Carruthers has sketched what purports to be an MM account of practical and theoretical reasoning that seeks to accommodate the above sorts of phenomena (Carruthers, 2003, 2004). But the proposal fails since it posits various mechanisms – specifically, a "relevance module" and a practical reasoning system – which are domain general and, despite Carruthers' claims to the contrary, unencapsulated as well.[12] So, the prospects of accommodating the above phenomena without positing nonmodular mechanisms appear bleak; and in view of the lack of argument or evidence for MM, I'm inclined to think the effort of trying to do so is, in any case, wasted.

5 Whither Modularity?

The main burden of this chapter has been to argue that the case for an interesting and distinctive version of MM is not strong because there is little reason to suppose *central* processes are modular. In this section I conclude with some comments on a more radical view: that little or none of cognition – including peripheral systems for low-level perception – are modular in character. In my view, this claim goes too far since there are strong empirical grounds for positing a wide array of non-central modules. Efforts to draw grand conclusions about the irrelevance of modularity thus strike me as, at best, premature and, at worst, a serious distortion of our current, best picture of the cognitive mind.

5.1 Evidence for modularity

As with almost any scientific hypothesis, the empirical case for peripheral modularity is not so strong as to exclude all competitors. But what matters is the relative

Richard Samuels

plausibility of competing hypotheses; and on balance I'm inclined to think the evidence – convergent evidence from neuroanatomy, psychophysics, computational modeling, developmental psychology, and so on – supports the existence of modules for many non-central cognitive processes.

The case is most plausible for low-level (or "early") visual processes – for example, those involved in the perception of color, shape from motion, and depth from disparity. In such cases one finds illusions strongly suggestive of mechanisms encapsulated from belief (Fodor, 1983; Pylyshyn, 1999). Moreover, in contrast to central processes, we possess quite detailed and plausible computational models of these perceptual processes: models which suggest the kinds of computations involved are highly specialized for very specific sorts of input and draw on very restricted kinds of information (Palmer, 1999). So, for example, the computations involved in computing depth from disparity are quite different from those involved in computing lightness; and the sorts of information relevant to one are irrelevant to the other. Finally, and again in contrast to central processes, a fair amount is known about the neural basis of such processes; and again what we know suggests that the modular picture is very plausible (Zeki and Bartels, 1998).

Nor is the case for modularity only plausible for low-level perceptual mechanisms. Though perhaps less compelling, there is still a good case to be made elsewhere, including: face recognition (McKone and Kanwisher, 2005), place-specific visual processing (Epstein et al., 1999), approximate arithmetic (Butterworth, 1999; Feigenson et al., 2004), and grammar-specific processing (van der Lely et al., 2004). In each such case, one finds a pattern of results strongly suggestive of modularity: evidence of dissociations, evidence for idiosyncratic styles of processing or distinctive representational formats, and ERP and imaging studies suggestive of distinctive neural responses. All this is, I suppose, good evidence for modularity. Not beyond dispute, but strong nonetheless.

Why, then, do so many reject the modularity of such processes? Since the empirical literature on such matters is enormous, it will not be possible to address much of what has been said here. But fortunately, Prinz (chapter 2) provides an excellent (and brief) presentation of the case against peripheral modularity: one that draws together many familiar strands of argument, but also exhibits many of the problems found in other critiques. In what follows, then, I focus primarily on Prinz's arguments, though many of my comments apply more broadly than this.

5.2 Arguments against domain specificity

According to Prinz, "alleged modules may have domain-specific components" – e.g., proprietary rules and representations – but they "don't seem to be proprietary throughout." Prinz's argument for this conclusion divides in two. First, he distinguishes between some different senses of "specificity" and "domain" and argues that for a mechanism to be interestingly domain specific it should be *exclusively* dedicated to processing some *relatively inclusive* subject matter. Next, Prinz argues that the main alleged examples of modules – vision, language, mathematics, folk physics, etc. – are not domain specific in this sense. Neither part of the argument strikes me as convincing.

Characterizing domain specificity

I see no reason to assume that for a mechanism to be interestingly domain specific, its domain must be inclusive – as broad as language, vision or theory of mind, for example. First, the assumption fits poorly with how the notion of domain specificity in fact gets used in cognitive science. Many of the most prominent advocates of modularity – Fodor and Sperber, for example – explicitly deny that domains must be broad in this way (Fodor, 1983; Sperber, 1994); and many of the most carefully studied examples of domain-specific mechanisms – depth from disparity, for example – are not all that inclusive.

Second, contrary to what Prinz appears to suggest, the admittance of fine-grained domains need not trivialize claims about domain specificity. There is nothing trivial, for example, in claiming we possess mechanisms exclusively dedicated for edge detection, scene geometry, or approximate arithmetic. Of course, if one insisted on treating just *any* entity for which some subject matter could be specified as a *bona fide* domain-specific mechanism, then triviality threatens. Therein lies the route to mechanisms for, say, reasoning about camels in London on Tuesdays, or planning wheat-free picnics in 2005. But this is not a problem with a fine-grained notion of domain specificity, or indeed with the notion of domain specificity at all. Rather, it's a problem that arises when one adopts a silly attitude towards the individuation of cognitive mechanisms. The main problem with a distinct "mechanism" for reasoning exclusively about camels in London on Tuesdays is not that its domain is too fine-grained, but that *there is no such mechanism.* To be sure, there are genuine issues about what the criteria for individuating cognitive mechanisms ought to be. But the present discussion highlights that silliness ensues if one individuates by domain alone. My suggestion: Don't do it.

Evidence against domain specificity?

Even laying aside the above concern, Prinz's argument still fails since the main kind of evidence he cites is largely *irrelevant* to the domain specificity of cognitive mechanisms. Prinz objects to many alleged cases of domain specificity on the grounds that the processes involved in one kind of task share cognitive/neural resources with processes of other sorts. So, for example: language processing shares resources with nonlinguistic pattern recognition; mind-reading shares resources with language processing and also uses working memory; arithmetic shares resources with language and spatial processing, and so on. On the basis of such considerations, Prinz concludes that there are unlikely to be domain-specific mechanisms of the sort that modularists posit.

What are we to make of this argument? The logic is rather murky. In particular, it is very unclear how one gets from claims about resource sharing to conclusions about the absence of domain-specific mechanisms. That said, the general idea appears to be that since domain-specific mechanisms are *exclusively dedicated* to processing a given domain of information, there cannot be domain-specific devices for processes that depend on resources recruited for many *different* domains. On reflection, however, this argument turns on a shift between two different senses in which a domain specific mechanism might be exclusively dedicated:

Richard Samuels

- The mechanism only processes information in a given domain, D;
- The mechanism only processes – and, moreover, is the *only* mechanism that processes – information in D.

The former is one to which advocates of domain-specific modules are plausibly committed; but it is not one on which resource sharing counts as evidence against domain specificity. Thus the existence of mechanisms which are exclusively dedicated in this sense is perfectly compatible with the very familiar position – one endorsed by many modularists – on which cognitive processes depend on both domain-specific *and* domain-general mechanisms. For example: Leslie and his collaborators claim mind-reading depends on both a domain-specific theory of mind module and domain-general executive systems (Leslie, 2003). In contrast, the second notion of exclusive dedication does license inferences from resource sharing to a failure of domain specificity and, hence, precludes precisely such cases. But the problem for Prinz is that advocates of domain specific mechanisms are clearly not committed to mechanisms which are exclusively dedicated in this way.

5.3 Evidence against informational encapsulation

Let's turn to the case against encapsulated mechanisms. Prinz's strategy is to try to undermine what is widely regarded as the most plausible case for encapsulation: perceptual illusions which modularists claim result from the operation of low-level perceptual mechanisms. But *pace* Fodor, Pylyshyn, and others, Prinz maintains illusions are not good evidence for encapsulation because there is a competing hypothesis – what he calls the "trumping hypothesis" – which explains the existence of illusions and, moreover, does a better job of accommodating evidence of top-down effects on perception. Again, I am unconvinced.

First, the trumping hypothesis itself is hard to make sense of. The rough idea is simple enough: though belief is trumped by perception when the two are in conflict, it can influence perception when no conflict exists. But how exactly is this to occur? On the most natural interpretation, what's required is some kind of consistency check between belief (e.g., that the lines in the Müller-Lyer illusion are of equal length) and a representation produced by some perceptual process (e.g., that the lines are of different length). But if the trumping hypothesis were correct, such a checking process would *presuppose* the existence of encapsulated perceptual mechanisms. After all, for a consistency check to occur at all, there must be a *perceptual* representation – i.e., the output of some perceptual device – that can be checked against belief. And since, according to the trumping hypothesis, beliefs only influence perceptual processing when no conflict exists, it cannot be that beliefs are implicated in producing the output of *this* perceptual device.

In any case, the data cited by Prinz do not merit the rejection of encapsulated low-level perceptual mechanisms. Following a long tradition, Prinz argues that top-down effects on perception are incompatible with encapsulation. But the argument turns on the assumption that a "truly encapsulated system would be insulated from *any* external influence"; and this is simply false. On the contrary, advocates of encapsulation agree with their opponents that there are top-down influences on perception.

What's at issue is the character and extent of this influence. Specifically, what advocates of encapsulated early perception are most concerned to reject is a picture – widely associated with Bruner's New Look psychology – on which early perceptual mechanisms have something approximating an unlimited access to one's beliefs and desires in the course of their online processing (Fodor, 1983, p. 60; Pylyshyn, 1999). But this rejection is wholly compatible with many sorts of external cognitive influence on perception, including:

- Shifts in loci of focal attention brought about by clues, instructions, or preferences about where to look;
- Top-down processing *within* a perceptual modality;
- Cross-talk between perceptual systems;
- Diachronic or developmental effects in which one's beliefs and goals influence the development of perceptual systems – e.g., via training effects;
- Beliefs and desires influencing late perceptual processes, such as perceptual categorization.[13]

As far as I can tell, all the putative objections to encapsulation Prinz cites fall into one or other of these categories. For example, it is very plausible that the influence of verbal cues and decisions on our experience of ambiguous figures consists in the production of shifts in the locus of focal attention (Peterson and Gibson, 1991; Pylyshyn, 1999). Similarly, the role of expectations – e.g., in producing non-veridical experiences – is plausibly viewed as an influence on late perceptual processes. And so on. In view of this, I see no reason here to deny the modularity of early perception.

Conclusion

We started by clarifying the sort of view that advocates of MM seek to defend. We then saw that the main theoretical arguments for views of this sort fail to provide reason to prefer them over other competing proposals, such as those on which much of cognition depends on nonmodular mechanisms with access to bodies of specialized information. Next, we saw that the available experimental case for MM is not strong because there is little evidence for the existence of modular central systems. Moreover, we saw that there is some reason to reject a strong MM which claims that all central systems are domain specific and/or encapsulated. Finally, we saw that while MM is not well supported by the arguments and evidence, it would be wrong to maintain that minds are not modular to any interesting degree since there are good reasons to suppose that more peripheral regions of the mind – especially for low-level perception – are modular in character. Where does this leave us? If our assessment of the evidence is correct, then the most plausible position to adopt is one that takes a middle way between those, such as Carruthers, who endorse a thoroughgoing massive modularity and those, such as Prinz, who reject modularity altogether. The situation is, in other words, much as Fodor advocated over two decades ago (Fodor, 1983).

Richard Samuels

Acknowledgments

I would like to thank Guy Longworth, David Papineau, Gabe Segal, Rob Stainton, and Mark Textor for helpful comments on earlier drafts of this chapter. I would also like to thank Brian Scholl for helpful discussion of the material in section 5.

Notes

1 There is a familiar notion of modularity, sometimes called Chomskian modules, on which modules are not mechanisms but systems of mental representation – bodies of mentally represented knowledge or information – such as a grammar or a theory (Segal, 1996; Samuels, 2000; Fodor, 2000). Paradigmatically, such structures are truth-evaluable in that it makes sense to ask of the representations if they are true or false. Moreover, they are often assumed to be innate and/or subject to informational constraints (e.g., inaccessible to consciousness). Although Chomskian modules are an important sort of cognitive structure, they are not the ones most relevant to the sort of position advocated by massive modularists. This is because advocates of MM appear to assume that modules are a species of cognitive *mechanism*. I say this for two main reasons. First, it is very plausible on the basis of their explicit comments about what modules are. Dan Sperber, for example, characterizes modules as a species of "autonomous mental mechanism" (Sperber, 2002; Sperber and Hirschfeld, 2004), while Cosmides and Tooby characterize them as "functionally dedicated computers"; all of which indicates a conception of modules as cognitive mechanisms. Moreover, if modules are construed as Chomskian modules, it's hard to make sense of what advocates of MM say about the relationship between their position and other views. So, for example, MM is routinely (and correctly) presented as being in opposition to views on which central cognition depends on the activity of one (or a few) general-purpose computers (Cosmides and Tooby, 1992; Carruthers, chapter 1). But if modules are construed as systems of mental representations, it's unclear why any opposition should exist. After all, the claim that central cognition depends on, say, a single universal Turing machine is wholly compatible with the existence of a great many Chomskian modules – bodies of information deployed by the mechanism. This is, however, surely *not* the sort of view advocates of MM seek to defend. Indeed Carruthers (chapter 1) says as much when explicitly contrasting this sort of "informational modularity" with the "computational modularity" he seeks to defend.

2 The following discussion is by no means exhaustive. For more detailed discussions of different notions of modularity see Segal, 1996, and Samuels, 2000.

3 This list is sometimes construed as a *definition* of modularity (Karmiloff-Smith, 1992). But Fodor rejects this in favor of the idea that modularity admits of degree and that cognitive mechanisms are modular to the extent that they possess all or most of the features on this list to some interested degree (Fodor, 1983, p. 37; Coltheart, 1999).

4 Incidentally, not even Fodor adopts it in his recent discussions of MM (Fodor, 2000, 2005).

5 To claim that a property of a cognitive mechanism is *architecturally* imposed, minimally implies the following. First, they are relatively enduring characteristics of the device. Second, they are not mere products of *performance* factors, such as fatigue or lapses in attention. Finally, they are supposed to be *cognitively impenetrable* (Pylyshyn, 1984). To a first approximation: they are not properties of the mechanism that can be changed as a result of alterations in the beliefs, goals and other representational states of the organism.

6   It should go without saying – though I'll say it anyway – that the notion of domain specificity *admits of degree* and that researchers who use the notion are interested in whether we possess mechanisms that are domain specific to some *interesting* extent. The same points also apply to the notion of informational encapsulation.

7   Indeed this is more-or-less guaranteed by the widespread assumption that the functional decomposition of a "large" system will typically have many levels of aggregation (Simon, 1962). I return to this point in section 2.1.

8   A similar point applies to the sort of radical connectionism on which the mind is characterized as one huge undifferentiated neural network. This is often – and rightly – seen as the antithesis of MM (Pinker, 1997); and yet it is committed to a vast plurality of mechanisms. After all, each node in a neural network is a mechanism; and on any version of the connectionist story, there will a great many such nodes.

9   There are other less plausible arguments for MM, which due to space limitations I will not consider here. For further discussion of other arguments for MM see Tooby and Cosmides, 1992; Sperber, 1994; and Samuels, 2000.

10 See Prinz (chapter 2, IS THE MIND REALLY MODULAR?) for complementary criticisms of the experimental case for MM.

11 The same would also appear to be true of many of a representation's epistemic properties – e.g., simplicity and conservativism.

12 They are "wide-scope encapsulated." But as already noted, this is not encapsulation as ordinarily construed.

13 Indeed, given that encapsulation admits of degree, an input system might be encapsulated to some interesting degree and yet still have access to some beliefs and goals in the course of its operations.

References and further reading

Anderson, J. R. (1990). *The Adaptive Character of Thought.* Hillsdale, NJ: Erlbaum.

Anderson, M. (1992). *Intelligence and Development: A Cognitive Theory.* Oxford: Blackwell.

— (1998). Mental retardation, general intelligence and modularity. *Learning and Individual Differences,* 10/3, 159–78.

Atran, S. (1998). Folk biology and the anthropology of science: Cognitive universals and cultural particulars. *Behavioral and Brain Sciences,* 21, 547–609.

— (2001). The case for modularity: Sin or salvation? *Evolution and Cognition,* 7, 46–55.

Baron-Cohen, S. (1995). *Mindblindness: An Essay on Autism and Theory of Mind.* Cambridge, MA: MIT Press.

Bryson, J. J. (2000). Cross-paradigm analysis of autonomous agent architecture. *Journal of Experimental and Theoretical Artificial Intelligence,* 12/2, 165–90.

Buss, D. (2000). *Evolutionary Psychology.* New York: Allyn & Bacon.

Buss, D. and Duntley, J. (2005). On the plausibility of adaptations for homicide. In P. Carruthers, S. Laurence, and S. Stich (eds.), *The Innate Mind: Structure and Contents.* New York: Oxford University Press.

Butterworth, B. (1999). *The Mathematical Brain.* London: Macmillan.

Carey, S. (1995). On the origins of causal understanding. In S. Sperber, D. Premack, and A. Premack (eds.), *Causal Cognition.* Oxford: Clarendon Press.

Carruthers, P. (2003). On Fodor's problem. *Mind and Language,* 18, 502–23.

— (2004). Practical reasoning in a modular mind. *Mind and Language,* 19, 259–78.

Carston, R. (1996). The architecture of the mind: modularity and modularization. In D. Green (ed.), *Cognitive Science.* Oxford: Blackwell.

Chomsky, N. (1980). *Rules and Representations*. New York: Columbia University Press.

Coltheart, M. (1999). Modularity and cognition. *Trends in Cognitive Sciences*, 3/3, 115–20.

Copeland, J. (1993). *Artificial Intelligence: A Philosophical Introduction*. Oxford: Blackwell.

Cosmides, L. (1989). The logic of social exchange: has natural selection shaped how humans reason? Studies with Wason Selection Task. *Cognition*, 31, 187–276.

Cosmides, L. and Tooby, J. (1992). Cognitive adaptations for social exchange. In J. Barkow, L. Cosmides, and J. Tooby (eds.), *The Adapted Mind*. New York: Oxford University Press.

— and — (1994). Origins of domain specificity: the evolution of functional organization. In L. Hirschfeld and S. Gelman (eds.), *Mapping the Mind*. Cambridge: Cambridge University Press.

Epstein, R., Harris, A., Stanley, D., and Kanwisher, N. (1999). The parahippocampal place area: recognition, navigation, or encoding? *Neuron*, 23, 115–25.

Feigenson, L., Dehaene, S., and Spelke, E. (2004). Core systems of number. *Trends in Cognitive Sciences*, 8/7, 307–14.

Fodor, J. (1983). *The Modularity of Mind*. Cambridge, MA: MIT Press.

— (2000). *The Mind doesn't Work that Way*. Cambridge, MA: MIT Press.

— (2005). Reply to Steven Pinker: "So how does the mind work?" *Mind and Language*, 20/1, 25–32.

Gallistel, R. (1990). *The Organization of Learning*. Cambridge, MA: MIT Press.

— (2000). The replacement of general-purpose learning models with adaptively specialized learning modules. In M. Gazzaniga (ed.), *The New Cognitive Neurosciences* (2nd edn.). Cambridge, MA: MIT Press.

Garfield, J. (ed.) (1987). *Modularity in Knowledge Representation and Natural-Language Understanding*. Cambridge, MA: MIT Press.

Gigerenzer, G. (1994). Why the distinction between single-event probabilities and frequencies is important for psychology (and vice versa). In G. Wright and P. Ayton (eds.), *Subjective Probability*. New York: Wiley.

Gigerenzer, G. and Hug, K. (1992). Reasoning about social contracts: Cheating and perspective change. *Cognition*, 43, 127–71.

Gopnik, A. and Meltzoff, A. (1997). *Words, Thoughts and Theories*. Cambridge, MA: MIT Press.

Hermer-Vazquez, L., Spelke, E., and Katsnelson, A. (1999). Sources of flexibility in human cognition: Dual-task studies of space and language. *Cognitive Psychology* 39, 3–36.

Jackendoff, R. (1992). Is there a faculty of social cognition? In R. Jackendoff, *Languages of the Mind*. Cambridge, MA: MIT Press.

Karmiloff-Smith, A. (1992). *Beyond Modularity*. Cambridge, MA: MIT Press.

Kirsh, D. (1991). Today the earwig, tomorrow man. *Artificial Intelligence*, 47, 161–84.

Leslie, A. M., Friedman, O., and German, T. P. (2004). Core mechanisms in "theory of mind." *Trends in Cognitive Sciences*, 8, 528–33.

McKone, E. and Kanwisher, N. (2005). Does the human brain process objects of expertise like faces? A review of the evidence. In S. Dehaene, J. R. Duhamel, M. Hauser, and G. Rizzolatti (eds.), *From Monkey Brain to Human Brain*. Cambridge, MA: MIT Press.

Newell, A. (1990). *Unified Theories of Cognition*. Cambridge, MA: Harvard University Press.

Nicholls, S. and Stich, S. (2002). *Mindreading*. New York: Oxford University Press.

Palmer, S. (1999). *Vision Science: Photons to Phenomenology*. Cambridge, MA: MIT Press.

Peterson, M. A. and Gibson, B. S. (1991). Directing spatial attention within an object: altering the functional equivalence of shape descriptions. *Journal of Experimental Psychology: Human Perception and Performance* 17, 170–82.

Pinker, S. (1994). *The Language Instinct*. New York: William Morrow.

— (1997). *How the Mind Works*. New York: Norton.

Is the Human Mind Massively Modular?

— (2005). So how does the mind work? *Mind and Language*, 20/1, 1–24.

Pylyshyn, Z. (1984). *Computation and Cognition*. Cambridge, MA: MIT Press.

— (1999). Is vision continuous with cognition? The case for cognitive impenetrability of visual perception. *Behavioral and Brain Sciences*, 22, 341–423.

Samuels, R. (1998). Evolutionary psychology and the massive modularity hypothesis. *British Journal for the Philosophy of Science*, 49, 575–602.

— (2000). Massively modular minds: Evolutionary psychology and cognitive architecture. In P. Carruthers and A. Chamberlain (eds.), *Evolution and the Human Mind: Modularity, Language and Meta-Cognition*. Cambridge: Cambridge University Press.

— (2005). The complexity of cognition: tractability arguments for massive modularity. In P. Carruthers, S. Laurence, and S. Stich (eds.), *The Innate Mind: Structure and Contents*. New York: Oxford University Press.

Segal, G. (1996). The modularity of theory of mind. In P. Carruthers and P. Smith (eds.), *Theories of Theory of Mind*. Cambridge: Cambridge University Press.

Simon, H. (1962). The architecture of complexity. *Proceedings of the American Philosophical Society*, 106, 467–82.

Sperber, D. (1994). The modularity of thought and the epidemiology of representations. In Hirschfeld, L. and Gelman, S. (eds.), *Mapping the Mind*. Cambridge: Cambridge University Press.

— (1996). *Explaining Culture: A Naturalistic Approach*. Oxford: Blackwell.

— (2002). In defense of massive modularity. In I. Dupoux (ed.), *Language, Brain and Cognitive Development*. Cambridge, MA: MIT Press.

— (2005). Massive modularity and the first principle of relevance. In P. Carruthers, S. Laurence, and S. Stich (eds.), *The Innate Mind: Structure and Contents*. Oxford: Oxford University Press.

Sperber, D. and Girotto, V. (2003). Does the selection task detect cheater detection? In K. Sterelny and J. Fitness (eds.), *From Mating to Mentality: Evaluating Evolutionary Psychology*. New York: Psychology Press.

Sperber, D. and Hirschfeld, L. (2004). The cognitive foundations of cultural stability and diversity. *Trends in Cognitive Science*, 8/1, 40–6.

Sperber, D., Cara, F., and Girotto, V. (1995). Relevance theory explains the selection task. *Cognition*, 52, 3–39.

Tooby, J. and Cosmides, L. (1992). The psychological foundations of culture. In J. Barkow, L. Cosmides, and J. Tooby (eds.), *The Adapted Mind*. New York: Oxford University Press.

Van der Lely, H. K. J., Rosen, S., and Adlard, A. (2004). Grammatical language impairment and the specificity of cognitive domains: Relations between auditory and language abilities. *Cognition*, 94, 167–83.

Varley, R. (2002). Science without grammar: Scientific reasoning in severe agrammatic aphasia. In P. Carruthers, S. Stich, and M. Siegal (eds.), *The Cognitive Basis of Science*. Cambridge: Cambridge University Press.

Varley, R. A., Siegal, M., and Want, S. (2001). Severe impairment in grammar does not preclude theory of mind. *Neurocase*, 7, 489–93.

Zeki, S. and Bartels, A. (1998). The autonomy of the visual systems and the modularity of conscious vision, *Philosophical Transactions of the Royal Society London*, 353, 1911–14.

HOW MUCH KNOWLEDGE OF LANGUAGE IS INNATE?

CHAPTER FOUR

Irrational Nativist Exuberance

Barbara C. Scholz and Geoffrey K. Pullum

The protracted dispute over the degree of independence of language acquisition from sensory experience often degenerates into an unsavory cavalcade of exaggerated claims, tendentious rhetoric, and absurd parodies of opposing views.[1] In this chapter we try to distinguish between partisan polemics and research programs. If either side of the partisan dispute about the acquisition of syntax were as stupid as the opposing side alleges, the free-for-all would not be worthy of serious attention; but in fact we think there are two important complementary research programs for syntax acquisition involved here.

We are skeptical about recent triumphalist claims for linguistic nativism, and this may lead to us being mistaken for defenders of some sort of "empiricism."[2] But touting empiricist stock is not our project. Curbing the excesses of irrational nativist exuberance is more like it. We argue that it is premature to celebrate nativist victory (as Laurence and Margolis, 2001, seem to be doing, for instance),[3] for at least two reasons. First, the partisan dispute is too ill-delineated to reach a resolution at all, because of a persistent tendency to conflate non-nativism with reductive empiricism, and because of equivocations rooted in the polysemy of the word "innate" (section 2). And second, linguistic nativist research programs need theories of learning – exactly what non-nativist research programs aim to develop (section 3).

Although we use "linguistic nativism" throughout this paper to denote a number of contemporary views about the acquisition of syntax, the reader will note that we tend to avoid using "innate." We try instead to address the specifics that the term "innate" often seems to occlude rather than illumine: the extent to which the acquisition of syntax proceeds independently of the senses, for example, and the extent to which it depends on generally applicable human cognitive capacities. The traditional "empiricist" claim is that the syntactic structure of languages (like everything else) is learned from sensory input. This could be false in at least two ways: it could be that the syntactic aspects of language are not acquired at all, but are antecedently known or available; or it could be that the influence of sensory input is not anything that could be described as "learning" in any normal sense. This distinction will be important below when we consider a debate about whether the products of "triggering" count as being innate.

Linguistic nativists refer to the constraints they posit on language acquisition as "linguistic knowledge" or "Universal Grammar" (abbreviated "UG"). We are going to assume they mean the following conjunction: (i) language acquisition is constrained by either *universal linguistic principles* or *biases due to language-specialized cognitive mechanisms*, and (ii) these are either *unacquired* or *acquired but not learned*. The non-nativist, by contrast, denies the conjunction of (i) and (ii).

Notice that the non-nativist's rejection of unacquired but language-specialized cognitive mechanisms does not imply a rejection of unacquired *non-cognitive* mechanisms (e.g., perceptual ones) that constrain language acquisition. And of course the non-nativist view is compatible with general cognitive mechanisms acquiring language-specialized functions over (ontogenetic) time. Disputes about syntax acquisition between contemporary linguistic nativists and their opponents concern *what* constrains or biases language acquisition, not whether it is constrained or biased. Language acquisition is, for example, unquestionably constrained by quantitative resource bounds and sensory channel limits.

1 Contemporary Non-Nativism and Historical Empiricism

The classic empiricist slogan states that there is "nothing in the intellect which was not previously in the senses" (Aquinas, *Summa Theologica*, Ia). Nativism is often taken to be the negation of empiricism: the view that at least one thing is in the intellect that was *not* acquired from the senses. But this is too weak to be an interesting form of contemporary nativism. It would surely be a pyrrhic victory if linguistic nativism were true simply in virtue of one solitary unacquired or unlearned contentful linguistic principle, everything else being learned.[4] And it would make it a mystery why nativist linguists have attempted to establish the existence of so many such principles, and have emphasized their abundance.[5] For the purposes of this chapter, we take linguistic nativism to be the view stated in (1):

1   Most of the acquisition of natural languages by human beings depends on unacquired (or acquired but unlearned) linguistic knowledge or language-specialized cognitive mechanisms.

This psychological generalization quantifies over unacquired (or acquired but unlearned) knowledge and mechanisms specialized for language.[6] The research program of linguistic nativism aims to show, proposition by proposition and mechanism by mechanism, that very little knowledge of syntactic structure is acquired or learned from sensory stimuli. Thus the discovery of one (or even a few) language-specialized cognitive mechanisms does not resolve the partisan nativist/non-nativist dispute. Even after the discovery of one genuinely unacquired linguistic principle, the continued

Barbara C. Scholz and Geoffrey K. Pullum

development of both nativist and non-nativist research programs would and should continue.

Non-nativism with regard to language acquisition is the view stated in (2):

2 Very little of the acquisition of natural languages by human beings depends on unacquired (or acquired but unlearned) linguistic knowledge or language-specialized cognitive mechanisms.

This too is a psychological generalization about how particular languages are acquired, and it competes with (1). Advocates of (2) advance several distinct but related research programs in language acquisition that include stochastic, constructivist, and connectionist learning theories.

What exactly is at issue between linguistic nativists and non-nativists depends, in part, on identifying what being "innate" amounts to (which we turn to in section 2), and how the posited unacquired language-specialized mechanisms solve certain problems of language acquisition (which we address in section 3). But one thing is clear: contemporary non-nativism is not restricted to the vaguely delineated constellation of doctrines supposedly held by the likes of John Locke in the seventeenth century and B. F. Skinner in the twentieth. Non-nativists are not obliged to defend either Locke or Skinner as having proposed a productive research program on language acquisition (see Trout, 1998, on this point). Neither Lockean reductive empiricism nor Skinnerian behaviorism is entailed by the rejection of linguistic nativism. Unacquired sensory mechanisms (perhaps specialized for speech) and general computational mechanisms are, for the non-nativist, mechanisms of learning readiness. It is an error to assume that all linguistic non-nativism is a form of reductive empiricism.

Some nativists do commit this error. Fodor (1981) provides a particularly clear example. In the context of discussing both historical empiricist and contemporary non-nativist views of lexical concept acquisition, Fodor writes:

> [T]he Empiricist model says that there are two sorts of causal processes at play in concept acquisition: in the case of primitive concepts there are, one might say, brute-causal processes. The structure of the sensorium is such that certain inputs trigger the availability of certain concepts. Punkt. Whereas in the case of complex concepts, there are, as one might say, rational causal processes: the psychological mechanisms which mediate the availability of such concepts realize an inductive logic, and the experiences of the organism stand in a confirmation relation to the concepts whose availability they occasion. (Fodor, 1981, p. 273)

Fodor's "primitive concepts" correspond to the simple, unstructured ideas of British empiricism. Though activated or triggered by sensory experience, their acquisition is not explained by any psychological learning theory. Fodor alleges that all empiricist theories of concept acquisition are *reductive*: all learned complex concepts are reducible to triggered primitive concepts, and for the complex ones, "concept learning involves the inductive fixation of certain beliefs [complex concepts] and the mechanisms of concept learning are realizations of some species of inductive logic" (1981, p. 267).

Irrational Nativist Exuberance | 61 |

UNIVERSITY OF HERTFORDSHIRE LRC

Given this reductive characterization, Fodor struggles to specify the point of disagreement between nativists and both historical empiricists and contemporary non-nativists (1981, pp. 279–83). Do they disagree "over which concepts are primitive"? Do nativists deny "that the primitive concepts constitute an epistemologically interesting set"? Do contemporary empiricists accept that "the primitive concepts are the ones whose attainment I can't eventually account for by appeal to the mechanisms of concept learning"? Unsurprisingly, his effort to locate the precise point of difference fails. A dispute that is purportedly about the resources required for language acquisition is miscast as a dispute about the acquisition of unstructured concepts and the failure of reductive empiricism, all wrapped up in an empiricist theory of justification rather than a theory of concept acquisition.

Contemporary non-nativist psychology need not be either atomistic or reductive. Consider for example the non-reductive conjectures about the sense-based acquisition of natural-kind concepts developed by Boyd (1981, 1991) and Kornblith (1993), crucial to their understanding of scientific realism. Boyd finds in certain (unofficial) Lockean views the suggestion that natural kinds are primitive, complex, structured, homeostatic clusters of properties, and our sense-based concepts of them are complex homeostatic cluster concepts. What Boyd seems to reject is that primitive concepts are non-complex, and that non-complex concepts are epistemologically interesting. We will not extend these ideas to language acquisition here, but we note that Christiansen and Curtin (1999) appear to be applying them to word individuation.

Fodor, however, is certainly right about at least two things. First, any coherent research program in language acquisition must accept that some acquisition mechanisms are not acquired. All parties must concede this on pain of a vicious regress of acquired mechanisms for acquisition (see Block, 1981, p. 280). But Chomsky presses this point to a parodic extreme:

> To say that "language is not innate" is to say that there is no difference between my granddaughter, a rock, and a rabbit. In other words, if you take a rock, a rabbit, and my granddaughter and put them in a community where people are talking English, they'll all learn English. If people believe that, then they'll believe language is not innate. If they believe that there is a difference between my granddaughter, a rabbit, and a rock, then they believe that language is innate. (Chomsky, 2000, p. 50)

The very possibility of a non-nativist research program is trivialized by saddling it with the view (which no one holds) that humans have the same language acquisition mechanisms as rocks. If all the alternatives to nativism are malignly depicted as inherently dumb, then the triumph of nativism will be hollow.

The second thing Fodor is right about is that creatures who acquire *symbolic* representations or concepts by means of hypothesis formation and testing must antecedently have some concepts in which to frame hypotheses. But this is a claim about a specific kind of a prioristic learning theory and symbolic representationalism, not the distributed representations and stochastic learning theories investigated by contemporary non-nativist research programs.

It is also an error to understand non-nativism as claiming that what is learned or acquired by stochastic means can only be strictly proportional to the stimulus – as

Barbara C. Scholz and Geoffrey K. Pullum

if what is so acquired is never anything more than an exact copy of the statistical distributions in the stimulus. This error is frequently made by linguistic nativists. For example, Lidz et al. (2003) write that "It is hopeless to suppose that learning is responsive (solely) to input frequency, because the first word [that children acquire] in English vocabulary is not *the*." As Elman (2003) notes, it is an error to take stochastic learning theory to hypothesize that children learn statistics, i.e., they merely copy or memorize stimulus frequency patterns. On the contrary, stochastic learning theory holds that language learning is based on complex, higher-order properties of stochastic patterns in sensory experience, not a mere tabulation of frequency of patterns. To take children's (or adults') sense-based stochastic acquisition abilities to be limited to frequency detection and tabulation greatly underestimates their power. One leading question in statistical language acquisition research concerns the kinds of stochastic patterns infants can acquire (Saffran et al., 1996).

Nativists also sometimes mistakenly assume that the only kind of linguistic stimulus that could be relevant to language acquisition is the presence or absence of certain individual strings in the primary linguistic data. The assumption that rare or even absent strings would have to occur frequently for stochastically based learning to succeed oversimplifies (without investigation) the relevant distributional properties of the data (Lewis and Elman, 2001; Elman, 2003). Reali and Christiansen (forthcoming) provide further evidence that the relevant features of the stimulus for statistically based language acquisition models are the stochastic properties of the overall input, not just the presence or absence of individual strings therein. And see also Saffran et al. (1996), Aslin et al. (1998), Gomez (2002), and Saffran and Wilson (2003) for evidence that children are effective statistical learners.

Non-nativist researchers on language acquisition are free to either accept or reject historical empiricist doctrines, because contemporary linguistic non-nativism is not a form of reductive empiricism. It is merely a rejection of (1).

2 What Innateness Is

The hypothesis that some features of natural languages are acquired by triggering is characteristic of the "principles and parameters" theory.[7] Parameters are supposed to "reduce the difficulty of the learning problem" (Gibson and Wexler, 1994, p. 407). Parametrized universal principles are hypothesized to facilitate language acquisition by reducing what must be learned from sensory experience about the systematic parochial variations of natural languages.[8] A parameter does not specify a single property common to all natural languages. Rather, it specifies a fixed set of mutually exclusive linguistic properties, of which any given natural language can have exactly one.

Parameters are alleged to be unacquired. What is acquired is a particular setting of a parameter, by the process of being triggered by an environmental stimulus or range of stimuli. For example, "initial" might be one possible setting for a parameter governing position of lexical head (e.g., the verb in a verb phrase), and "final" the other setting, ruling out the possibility of any language in which lexical heads are positioned, say, as close to the middle of a phrase as possible. The debated issue in the philosophy of linguistics literature is whether the *products* of triggering processes (parameters set to particular values) count as being innate.

On one side of the debate, Samuels (2002), developing Fodor's view, claims that a cognitive structure (e.g., a parameter or a concept) is innate if and only if it is *psychologically primitive*. For Samuels a structure is psychologically primitive when it is "posited by some correct scientific psychological theory" but its acquisition has *no* explanation in that theory (Samuels, 2002, p. 246). A primitive process is "a 'brute causal' process that is not mediated by any psychological states," e.g., not mediated by information uptake or processing. Samuels takes triggering to be a paradigmatically primitive psychological process (p. 247), since he thinks any explanation of triggering will be biological, not psychological. He also seems to think that the products of triggering processes are themselves psychologically primitive.

On the other hand, Ariew (1996, 1999, 2003), following Waddington (1940), has argued that innateness is *environmental canalization*, which entails that "development is *insensitive* to particular environmental conditions." This is the idea that what is innate is developmentally rigid and hard to change. Any trait that is environmentally canalized is "buffered against environmental perturbation" (Ariew, 2003). Processes like triggering and their products are sensitive to, and depend on, particular environmental cues. Thus they are *not* innate in Ariew's sense. However, on his view, traits acquired by triggering are not learned either. Whatever is acquired by triggering is the result of a *sui generis* developmental process that is sensitive to environmental stimuli but is neither innate nor learned.

Samuels stipulates that whatever is innate is not learned. Ariew replaces that traditional dichotomy with a trichotomy: *innate* versus *triggered* versus *learned*. Our interest in this dispute is not in taking sides, but in pointing out that Samuels and Ariew are probably both right about triggering because both "innateness" and "triggering" are used polysemously in the linguistics literature.

The ambiguous use of "triggering" was noticed 30 years ago by Stich (1975). At least two undeveloped metaphors of acquisition by triggering are found in the literature. One is based on Plato's parable of the slave boy in the *Meno*. Stich writes:

> a trigger or a catalyst . . . sets off a process that results in the acquisition of the belief. But, as a catalyst it is not part of the end product of the chemical reaction, so the questioning process [of the slave boy by Socrates] does not supply the content of the belief . . . the content of the belief was contained in the boy. (Stich, 1975, p. 14)

The antecedently given range of possible parameter settings are "in the slave boy." The information in the activated parameter is *not* acquired by reasoning or inference from information in the environmental trigger. It is inherent in the boy's pre-existing parameter.

In what follows we use *instantaneous acquisition* for this kind of parameter setting by (Fodorian) triggering. In instantaneous acquisition no information in the environmental trigger informs or is taken up into the product of the triggering process: e.g., exposure to ambient temperatures of above 90°F might cause the head parameter to be set to strict verb-final clause structure.

Barbara C. Scholz and Geoffrey K. Pullum

Under the second triggering metaphor (Stich, 1975, p. 15), the parameter is not merely set off or activated. Rather, the *information* in the environmental trigger is relevant to the information content of the product of the triggering process (though the latter is not inferred from the former). As Gibson and Wexler (1994, p. 408) characterize it, triggers are "sentences in the child's experience that point directly to the correct settings of parameters"; indeed, for any setting of a parameter "there is a sentence that is grammatical under that setting but not under any other." Exposure to a trigger "allows the learner to determine that the appropriate parameter setting is the one that allows for the grammaticality of the sentence." Gibson and Wexler go on to develop this view (see their "Triggering Learning Algorithm," 1994, pp. 409–10): if a trigger fails to be grammatical as analyzed by the currently entertained grammar, the learning algorithm modifies a parameter setting to see if that will permit the trigger to be analyzed successfully (and changes it back again if not).

Henceforth we use the term *accelerated acquisition* for this kind of informationally triggered parameter setting.

By claiming that the learner determines the setting, Gibson and Wexler mean that the uptake of linguistic information in the trigger is necessary for the acquisition of a particular setting for a parameter. The familiar expression "poverty of the stimulus" picks up on impoverished information in the triggering stimulus by contrast with the richness of the information in the set parameter in both instantaneous and accelerated acquisition. But the two triggering processes are distinct. We speculate that an over-emphasis on arguments from the poverty of the stimulus has led many philosophers and linguists to overlook the differences between these two kinds of triggering.

However, Gibson and Wexler do distinguish sharply between their concept of triggering and Fodorian triggering (instantaneous acquisition) which is "supposed to mean something like an experience that has nothing theoretically to do with a parameter setting, but nevertheless determines the setting of a parameter" (Gibson and Wexler, 1994, p. 408, n. 2).

Instantaneous acquisition is a brute-causal psychological process, unmediated by intervening psychological states, exactly as Samuels says. Thus the product of instantaneous acquisition is innate for Samuels. For Gibson and Wexler, on the other hand, discrimination and uptake of the *information* in the stimulus mediates the setting of a parameter. Parameter setting by accelerated acquisition is neither psychologically primitive nor environmentally canalized, so its products are not innate in either Samuels' or Ariew's sense.

Doubtless Gibson and Wexler would reject both Samuels' and Ariew's concepts of innateness because they claim the product of their preferred triggering process is innate, although neither psychologically primitive nor canalized. But if it is, then there must be some other concept of innateness to vindicate their claim. Quite a few are on offer.

Sober (1998) has argued that all that is left of the pre-scientific concept of innateness is the idea that what is innate is *invariant* across environments. But it is immediately clear that invariance innateness won't do: triggering is supposed to explain the acquisition of linguistic structures that systematically vary across natural languages. Of course, parameters that have not yet been set are in a sense invariant. But they do not explain how infants acquire knowledge of parochial aspects of their languages.

Some scientists talk as if what is *universal* across all typical members of the species, or across all natural languages, is innate (see, e.g., Barkow et al., 1992); but, *ex hypothesi*, the products of triggering are not universal.

Stich (1975, p. 12) considers a Cartesian *dispositional* analysis of innate beliefs: a belief is innate for a person just in case "that person is disposed to acquire it under any circumstances sufficient for the acquisition of any belief." But this lends no support to any advocate of the idea that the products of triggering are innate. Knowledge of particular languages that is acquired by the triggering of a parameter requires special circumstances.

Gibson and Wexler should probably not consider reverting to the idea that what is innate is *known a priori*. First, if a priori acquisition is defined as "what is acquired independently of any specific experience," then the products of instantaneous and accelerated acquisition, which depend on the experience of specific sensory triggers, are not innate; and defining a priori knowledge as "what is known on the basis of reason alone" fails because the products of all triggering processes are, by definition, not acquired by means of inference or reason.

Bealer (1999) has more recently articulated a concept of the a priori through evidence that "is not imparted through experiences but rather through intuitions" (p. 245). According to Bealer, "For you to have an intuition that A is just for it to *seem* to you that A" (p. 247). Thus, we might say that

> a trait or structure, *A*, is innate for *S* just in case *S*'s evidence for *A* is *a priori*, i.e., it cognitively, consciously, and reliably seems to *S* that *A*.

But the triggering process is, *ex hypothesi*, not consciously accessible. And the idea that a trait is innate just in case it is due to our "biological endowment" fails, since even a behaviorist thinks association mechanisms are part of our biology.

At least three of the senses of "*X* is innate" in the linguistics literature that we have discussed here are empirically dissociated: (i) *X* is a psychological primitive, (ii) *X* is canalized, and (iii) *X* is universal across all natural languages. We have also seen that linguistic nativism hypothesizes at least three distinct specialized mechanisms of language acquisition that correspond to each of these kinds of innateness: instantaneous acquisition, accelerated acquisition, and unacquired universal principles. Our point is not that any one of these conceptions of innateness is somehow illegitimate, or that one is to be preferred to the others. So far as we can tell each of these kinds of innateness could plausibly play a role in the explanation of language acquisition. Rather, our worry is that treating empirically dissociated mechanisms with the single label "innate" only obscures the detailed and accurate understanding of language acquisition that is the goal of cognitive psychology.

We are certainly not the first to notice that the blanket labeling of distinct developmental trajectories as "innate" (or "learned") impedes scientific understanding. Bateson (1991; 2004, pp. 37–9) has identified seven ways in which "instinct" and "innate" are polysemous in the behavioral ecology literature, and notes that few traits are innate in all seven senses. Griffiths (2002) argues that "innateness" is undesirable as a theoretical term, since it confuses exactly what needs to be clarified. We join Bateson, Griffiths, and others in recommending that the term "innate" be abandoned in theorizing about language acquisition, because it impedes the study of language acquisition.

Barbara C. Scholz and Geoffrey K. Pullum

This recommendation is not anti-nativist. Marler (1999) posits highly specialized innate abilities, but nonetheless advocates abandoning the use of the terms "innate" and "learned":

> As all students of behavior are aware, arguments about where the emphasis should be placed in discussions of the *innate-learned* dichotomy are notoriously contentious, often becoming so strident that their scientific productivity is questionable . . . Thus one drawback to the *learned-innate* dichotomy is that it tends to polarize our thinking about how a particular behavior develops. Perhaps most importantly, it encourages us to underestimate genetic contributions to the development of *learned* behaviors. (Marler, 1999, p. 311)

Marler is not advocating some bland form of interactionism. Rather, he is suggesting that the innate-learned dichotomy encourages the "black-boxing" of significant genetic factors in a way that undermines our understanding of birdsong acquisition.

If this recommendation is followed, then partisan nativist/non-nativist disputes will be less likely to be polarized. And they might be more productive if they focused on a detailed examination of *all* the mechanisms that play a role in language acquisition.

3 Unacquired Linguistic Universals: What Are They Good For?

Linguistic nativists have repeatedly emphasized that they think that the human infant *must* be in possession of unacquired linguistic universals (which we will henceforth refer to as ULUs). The following remarks of Hauser, Chomsky, and Fitch are representative:

> No known "general learning mechanism" can acquire a natural language solely on the basis of positive or negative evidence, and the prospects for finding any such domain-independent device seem rather dim. The difficulty of this problem leads to the hypothesis that whatever system is responsible must be biased or constrained in certain ways. Such constraints have historically been termed "innate predispositions," with those underlying language referred to as "universal grammar." Although these particular terms have been forcibly rejected by many researchers, and the nature of the particular constraints on human (or animal) learning mechanisms is currently unresolved, the existence of some such constraints cannot be seriously doubted. (Hauser et al., 2002, p. 1577)

This recapitulates earlier claims frequently repeated and endorsed by philosophers sympathetic to linguistic nativism. Thus Lipton (1991) characterizes the linguistic nativist as holding that "children must be born with strong linguistic rules or principles that further restrict the class of languages they will learn [and are not] peculiar to a particular human language" (Lipton, 1998, p. 413), stressing the necessity of ULUs. And Laurence and Margolis (2001, p. 221) claim that "an empiricist learner . . . wouldn't have any innate domain-specific knowledge or biases to guide her learning and, in particular, wouldn't have any innate *language-specific* knowledge or biases."

But from the claim that language acquisition must be affected by some sorts of bias or constraint it does not follow that those biases or constraints must stem from either ULUs or parameters. A non-nativist can readily accept biases or constraints stemming from sensory mechanisms that are specific to language but non-cognitive, or cognitive-computational mechanisms that are not language-specialized.

What tempts the defenders of nativism to believe otherwise? The matter is complex. In brief, we see three factors conspiring to tempt nativists into thinking that only ULUs could guide language acquisition: (i) an inappropriately selective skepticism based on Humean underdetermination; (ii) a highly selective faith in lexical learning by hypothesis formation and testing; and (iii) a failure to appreciate the breadth of scope of the important mathematical results set out by E. Mark Gold (1967).

The idea of studying learning by investigating the limits of an abstract pattern-learning machine originates with Ray Solomonoff in work done at the end of the 1950s (Li and Vitányi, 1997, pp. 86–92 provides a very useful history with references). Independently, it would seem, Hilary Putnam (1963a, 1963b) provided a basic impossibility result about what a machine for inductive learning could in principle accomplish: there can never be a "perfect" learning machine, because for any proposed such machine we can define a regularity that it cannot induce. Putnam's proof strategy was later used by Gold (again, independently, it would appear) to prove a key result in the narrower domain of language learning by guessing grammars (Gold, 1967).

Gold's enormously influential paper stimulated the development of a whole subfield of mathematical work on learning based on recursive function theory (see Jain et al., 1999, for a comprehensive survey). Conceptualizing language learning as a process of guessing a generative grammar (or, in a separate series of results, guessing a parser), Gold advocated investigation of "the limiting behavior of the guesses as successively larger and larger bodies of information are considered" (Gold, 1967, p. 465). He obtained both pessimistic and optimistic results. On one hand, he showed that there was a sense in which for all interesting classes of generative grammars[9] the learning problem was unsolvable, because what has to be learned is deductively underdetermined by the positive evidence (evidence about what *is* in the language; successful learning from such evidence is called "identification in the limit from text"). On the other hand, he showed that if the evidence is an information sequence covering both *what is* and *what is not* in the language, the learning problem is solvable for a huge range of classes of languages.

The pessimistic results depend on a number of assumptions. We summarize those relevant to "identification in the limit from text" in (3).

3 (a) The input to the learning procedure consists of strings.
     (b) The strings presented are all from the target language (no evidence about what is not in the language is provided).
     (c) Success is defined as reaching, in the limit, a unique correct generative grammar for the target language after a finite number of inputs, and sticking with it in the face of all further data.
     (d) The learning procedure selects a generative grammar to be the current hypothesis, testing it against the current datum, abandoning it permanently if it is incompatible with that datum, and sticking with it otherwise.

Barbara C. Scholz and Geoffrey K. Pullum

Since human children do learn languages, and Gold has apparently proved that they can't, we face a paradox. The only plausible response is to reject one or more of the assumptions leading to it. That is, one or more of Gold's assumptions must not hold for child language learners (see Scholz, 2004, for further discussion of this point). Many contemporary linguistic nativists respond by rejecting one them, namely (3d), the assumption that language acquisition proceeds by hypothesis formation and testing. The positive alternative they propose is that ULUs do essentially all the work.

This move might seem to obviate any need for an algorithm that could acquire a natural language by hypothesis formation and testing: such an algorithm would be otiose. No significant linguistic generalizations are learned, because none need to be. But in fact Gold's paradox recurs for learning *any* parochial linguistic generalization that involves universal quantification over an unbounded domain, even a lexical generalization. The fact that natural languages are lexically open (see Johnson and Postal, 1980, ch. 14; Pullum and Scholz, 2001, 2003; Postal, 2004) is relevant. Many purely parochial lexical generalizations are highly productive, because it is always possible to add another word to the lexicon of a natural language. Take the English prefix *anti-*, or the suffix *-ish*. It appears that any noun will allow them: we can form words like *anti-borogove, anti-chatroom, anti-humvee, anti-Yushchenko* (though perhaps some of these have not yet been coined); similarly for *borogovish, chatroomish, humveeish, Yushchenko-ish*. Thus the Gold paradox returns: the learner must in effect identify a grammar for the lexicon, a grammar generating indefinitely many derived words; and that cannot be done from positive input alone. For what is the generalization for *anti-*, or for *-ish*? Permissible with all bases beginning with *b*, *ch*, *h*, or *y*? Or all nouns other than *arachnophobe*? Or all non-Latinate roots? Or all bases of two or more syllables? All these and indefinitely many other hypotheses entail the finite corpus of English words considered above. But lexical generalizations are just as under-determined by the evidence as hypotheses about syntactic structure are, so expanding the evidence won't determine a hypothesis. Yet neither ULUs nor parameters can help here: ex hypothesi these parochial lexical generalizations are just those that are acquired from evidence of use.[10]

Something more than ULUs and various sorts of parameters will be required for the full story about language acquisition. Unless anyone wants to propose the extremely implausible view that no one ever learns anything about any language, we will need a theory of how people learn what *is* learned. And developing such a theory is exactly the non-nativist research program.

If nativists respond to Gold by rejecting learning by hypothesis formation and testing, how do contemporary non-nativists respond? There are many current non-nativist programs, but none of Gold's assumptions are accepted by all of them as relevant to children's first language acquisition:

- Instead of an input of individual strings, the input is taken to be a corpus with rich stochastic information (Lewis and Elman, 2001);
- Instead of acquiring a grammar, the child is assumed to acquire "multiple, simultaneous, probabilistic constraints defined over different types of linguistic and nonlinguistic information" (Seidenberg and MacDonald, 1999, p. 569);

- Instead of only positive data, the child's experience has been investigated and shown to offer plenty of information about what is not in the language (Chouinard and Clark, 2004), and the underdetermination problem is addressed through Bayesian inference, which rules out many accidental generalizations that are supported by the corpus, using probability computations to determine whether certain absences from the corpus are systematic or accidental (Elman, 2005);
- Instead of success being defined as hitting upon a perfectly correct generative grammar, approximative definitions of success have been proposed (the whole field of "probably approximately correct" or "PAC" learning in computer science is based on this move);
- Instead of a hypothesis-testing procedure with whole grammars as hypotheses and only strings as relevant evidence, various monotonic and incremental procedures for approaching a workable grammar are proposed.

The leading challenge these research programs present for linguistic nativism is this: If some of the above proposed methods are utilized by children to learn lexical generalizations, why are ULUs and linguistic parameters required for the acquisition of natural language syntax, but not lexical structure?

4 Two Examples of Current Non-nativist Research

So far we have presented some of our reasons for doubting the triumphalist claims made by some linguistic nativists and for doubting that the linguistic nativist/non-nativist dispute is well formed enough to be adjudicated. In what follows, we present two striking research results that have made us optimistic that general cognitive computational mechanisms will explain much more of syntax acquisition than the linguistic nativist has so far acknowledged.

4.1 What auxiliary inversion shows

Lewis and Elman (2001) demonstrate that a Simple Recurrent Network (henceforth, SRN) correctly models the acquisition of what linguistic nativists thought required unacquired representations of hierarchical syntactic structure.[11] The case Lewis and Elman consider is the one that Crain (1991) calls the "parade case of an innate constraint." Nativist researchers take it to be one of the strongest arguments for linguistic nativism from the poverty of the stimulus. The reader is typically introduced to the acquisition problem via contrasting pairs of sentences (we cite examples from Laurence and Margolis, 2001, p. 222):

4 (a) Ecuador is in South America.
   (b) Is Ecuador in South America?
5 (a) The telephone is working again now the storm is over.
   (b) Is the telephone working again now the storm is over?

Barbara C. Scholz and Geoffrey K. Pullum

Given just these four types of sentences, the nativist's assumption is that the child (or is it the linguist?) would be tempted to hypothesize the following kind of syntactic generalization:

6 A closed interrogative sentence corresponding to a declarative sentence with *is* as its first verb may be formed by taking the first occurrence of *is* and putting it at the beginning of the sentence, before the subject.

(Set aside for now that (6) contains the linguistic concepts "sentence" and "subject.") The hypothesized (6) turns out to be one of the seductive accidental generalizations that is not supported by further data, as the following pair of sentences shows.

7 (a) That woman who is walking her dog is Tom's neighbor.
  (b) *Is that woman who walking her dog is Tom's neighbor?

The correct yes/no question formed from (7a) is (8), where the second *is* has been repositioned:

8 Is that woman who is walking her dog Tom's neighbor?

The right hypothesis could be framed in various ways, but a straightforward one would be this:[12]

9 All closed interrogative clauses formed from declarative clauses, are formed by placing the main clause auxiliary verb at the beginning of the sentence, before the subject.

If this is the child's generalization about the structure of English, then lexical concepts like "main clause" and "auxiliary verb" must, it is supposed, be antecedently known (Fodor, 1981), or the generalization cannot even be entertained. The concept "main clause" relates to hierarchical syntactic structure, not just the linear order of words (the presumed stimulus). So there is every reason for the nativist to suppose that children couldn't frame (9) from stimuli that consist merely of unstructured strings of words.

Certainly, children are reported not to make mistakes like (7b). Crain and Nakayama (1987) ran a study of thirty children (ages 3 to 5 years) who were told to "Ask Jabba if the man who is running is bald." Crain (1991) reports that the outcome was as predicted: children never produced incorrect sentences like (7b). From this Crain (1991) concludes, "The findings of this study then, lend support to one of the central claims of universal grammar, that state that the initial state of the language faculty contains structure-dependence as an inherent property."[13]

If replicable, the finding that 3- to 5-year-old children don't make mistakes like (7b) would be interesting to nativists and non-nativists alike. But it does not support the idea that children have a particular ULU or parameter. And the finding only supports the idea that children have some ULU or other if there is no better explanation.

Could children learn not to make mistakes like (7b) from linguistic stimuli? Chomsky has asserted (without citing evidence) that "A person might go through much or all of his life without ever having been exposed to relevant evidence" of this kind; he states (see Piattelli-Palmarini, 1980, pp. 114–15) that "you can go over a vast amount of data of experience without ever finding such a case" – i.e., a sentence with this structural property. Sampson (1989, 2002) and Pullum and Scholz (2002) question whether such strings are all that rare, providing evidence that relevantly similar strings are found in a variety of texts, including spoken English sources, some of them aimed at fairly young children.[14] But Lewis and Elman (2001) did something particularly interesting that took a different approach.

Lewis and Elman showed that "the stochastic information in the data that is uncontroversially available to children is sufficient to allow learning." SRNs will "generalize to predict" (2001) in a word-by-word fashion that English has interrogatives like (8), but not like (7b), from training sets that contained strings with the structure of (4) and (5), but not the supposedly rare (8). These training sets encoded "no grammatical information beyond what can be determined from statistical regularities." Thus, from finite training sets, their SRN does not generalize in hopelessly wrong ways. Nor is learning accomplished by ignoring rich stochastic information in the data.

More recently, Reali and Christiansen (forthcoming) have obtained similar results using a noisy corpus of language addressed to children. These results should be very surprising and intriguing to a linguistic nativist like Crain.

The moral Lewis and Elman draw is that "assumptions about the nature of the input, and the ability of the learner to utilize the information therein, clearly play a critical role in determining which properties of language to attribute to UG" (2001, p. 11). If the relevant stimulus is underestimated to exclude its relevant stochastic features and if the mechanisms of language acquisition are assumed not to exploit them, too much will be taken to be unacquired or triggered. The linguistic nativist seems to tacitly assume that the relevant stimuli for acquisition are simply strings observed in a context of use. But as Lewis and Elman put it: "the statistical structure of language provides for far more sophisticated inferences than those which can be made within a theory that considers only whether or not a particular form appears." The relevant input includes distributional information about the set of acquisition stimuli (for an SRN, what is in the training set).

Suddenly it begins to look as if what matters for language acquisition is what information is present in the overall stimulus and *how* the stimulus is impoverished, not just *whether* it is impoverished. Lewis and Elman's training sets included none of the supposedly crucial rare sentences like (8). It begins to seem that structure-dependence can be acquired from the stimuli, even if sentences like (8) are entirely absent in it, contrary to over 25 years of nativist claims.

Of course, there might be other linguistic universals that can't be learned. But these findings about SRNs raise a series of further questions for both types of research programs. One wants to know exactly which kinds of gaps in training sets SRNs do and do not fill in, and extend this line of work to children's language acquisition. If children fail to fill in as SRNs do, then that might be grist for the nativist's mill.

Indeed, the results of these computational experiments suggest that Jerry Fodor's (1981) claims about the necessity of unacquired linguistic concepts and the impossibility of

Barbara C. Scholz and Geoffrey K. Pullum

learning a language by hypothesis formation and testing only hold for symbolic representations and for the particular learning theory he considers. But they seem irrelevant to the acquisition of distributed representations by means of learning theories based on information-rich statistical regularities in the stimulus, which is a serious contender as a better explanation of the phenomena.[15]

4.2 What Simon says

The research program of Newport and Aslin (2000) has found that children might well acquire some morphological/syntactic categories and generalizations from inconsistent and error-ridden data by attending to the stochastic properties of the stimulus. They studied children whose linguistic input is "entirely from speakers who are themselves not fluent or native users of the language" (Newport and Aslin, 2000, p. 12). Their subjects were congenitally and profoundly deaf children acquiring American Sign Language (ASL) as a first language in families with only very imperfect proficiency in ASL. They describe these children's ASL input as "very reduced and inconsistent." We will focus on two of their case studies: one involving a child they call Simon and the other involving two children they call Stewart and Sarah.

Simon is widely celebrated in the popular literature on language acquisition; see Pinker (1994, pp. 38–9) for an often cited discussion. Simon's acquisition of ASL is taken to provide powerful support for linguistic nativism. The case study as reported in Newport and Aslin (2000), however, does not vindicate a nativist interpretation.

Simon is an only child, with deaf parents who were not exposed to ASL until their teens. None of Simon's teachers knew ASL, so his ASL input was all from his parents. Stewart and Sarah are different in that their parents are hearing, though similar to Simon in other relevant respects. Newport and Aslin report:

> Simon's parents sign are like other late learners: they use virtually all of the obligatory ASL morphemes, but only with middling levels of consistency. On relatively simple morphemes (the movement morphemes of ASL), they average 65–75 percent correct usage. In contrast, Simon uses these morphemes much more consistently (almost 90 percent correct, fully equal to children whose parents are native ASL signers. Thus, when input is quite inconsistent, Simon is nonetheless able to regularize the language and surpass input models. On more difficult morphemes (the hand shape classifiers of ASL), where his parents were extremely inconsistent (about 45 percent correct), Simon did not perform at native levels by age seven; but even there he did surpass his parents. (Newport and Aslin, 2000, p. 13)

Newport and Aslin state competing hypotheses that might explain this finding. The linguistic nativist hypothesis is "that children know, innately, that natural language morphology is deterministic, not probabilistic" (2000, p. 14) and regularize the inconsistent morphological stimuli of their parents' signing to conform with ULUs. But they consider one non-nativist alternative: that children have general cognitive mechanisms that "sharpen and regularize" inconsistent patterns in the stimuli.

Newport and Aslin elaborate the latter hypothesis in their discussion of Stewart and Sarah. They note that the correct (native) ASL pattern was used by the parents "with some moderate degree of consistency, while the errors are highly inconsistent"

(2000, p. 19). On the second hypothesis, Simon, Stewart, and Sarah, have acquired ASL from the consistent patterns in their parents overall inconsistent ASL use. This suggests that the overall stochastic information in the inconsistent stimulus is exploited in child language acquisition. That is, learning that is based on the rich stochastic information in the degraded, inconsistent, and messy ASL use of their parents is regularized by children's general stochastic learning mechanisms.[16]

These case studies do not, of course, refute the view stated in (1), that most of the acquisition of natural languages depends on unacquired or unlearned linguistic knowledge. But a clear moral is that without careful attention to the stochastic properties of the stimulus, the hypothesis that general cognitive mechanisms play a significant role in language acquisition is *not* ruled out. Perhaps because of the way Newport and Aslin's research has been publicized, the finding that Simon regularized over inconsistent input has been taken as clear support for linguistic nativism by means of a poverty of the stimulus argument. But this interpretation is premature. It looks as if the relative frequencies of patterns and inconsistencies in the overall stimulus is more important than the mere fact that it contains errors or is inconsistent.[17] Children have unacquired and unlearned mechanisms that regularize partial patterns that they detect – whether linguistic or not. That (if true) is certainly an inherent fact about children that assists in their language acquisition; but it does not imply possession of ULUs.

5 Conclusion

We have argued that, as of today, to maintain that linguistic nativism has triumphed over non-nativism demands tacitly accepting at least one of three rather unappealing views.

The first is to accept that linguistic nativism is the negation of reductive empiricism – that is, to depict all contemporary non-nativists as defenders of John Locke and B. F. Skinner – and declare victory. But that will necessitate ignoring the content of actual contemporary non-nativist theories.

The second is to take it on faith that one day an appropriate sense of "innate" will be discovered that makes it a coherent and contentful theoretical term with all the relevant specialized language acquisition mechanisms in its extension. But the meanings of "innate" that are in current use in linguistics are not all empirically equivalent, and the currently hypothesized mechanisms of language acquisition do not fall under a definite concept.

And the third strategy is to posit parameters, set by triggering (in some sense of "triggering"), for absolutely every parochial peculiarity of every natural language, even lexical generalizations. But if the set of posited parameters tracks the set of parochial features of natural languages, the theory is rendered vacuous as a theory of language acquisition: instead of an explanation of how language is acquired we get just a list of ways natural languages can differ.

None of these three strategies looks productive to us. But the defender of the claim that linguistic nativism has vanquished rival non-nativist views is in the unfortunate position of tacitly accepting at least one of them.

Barbara C. Scholz and Geoffrey K. Pullum

Acknowledgments

This work was supported in part by the Radcliffe Institute for Advanced Study at Harvard University, where the authors completed the final version of the chapter. We are grateful to Eve Clark, Shalom Lappin, Ivan Sag, and Stuart Shieber for useful discussions and correspondence; to Claire Creffield for highly intelligent copy-editing assistance; and to Jeff Elman, Mark Liberman, Diana Raffman, J. D. Trout, and Robert Stainton for their valuable comments on an earlier draft. No one mentioned here should be assumed to agree with the views we express, of course.

Notes

1   Before you charge us with being unfair, take a look at some quotes: "Chomsky's demonstration . . . is *the* existence proof for the possibility of a cognitive science" (Fodor, 1981, p. 258); "How can a system of ideas like this have succeeded in capturing the intellectual allegiance of so many educated people?" (Sampson, 1997, p. 159); "A glance at any textbook shows that . . . generative syntax has uncovered innumerable such examples" (Smith, 1999, p. 42); "Is the idea supposed to be that there is no (relevant) difference between my granddaughter, her pet kitten, a rock, a chimpanzee?" (Chomsky, quoted by Smith, 1999, pp. 169–70); "Her rhetorical stance . . . invites comparison with creationists' attacks on the hegemony of evolution" (Antony, 2001, p. 194, referring to Cowie, 1999). There is more wild-eyed stuff where this came from, and it is spouted by both sides.

2   Several commentators seem to have assumed this about Pullum and Scholz 2002, which is actually framed as an effort at stimulating nativists to present evidence that would actually count in favor of their view. Scholz and Pullum (2002) reply to several critics and tries to make the goals clearer.

3   Of course, it's premature to celebrate a non-nativist victory too. Geoffrey Sampson's announcement in a newspaper article that nativism has collapsed (Sampson, 1999) is an example of excess at the other extreme.

4   We note that Hauser, Chomsky, and Fitch, 2002, claim that the core language faculty comprises just "recursion" and nothing else, apparently accepting such a pyrrhic nativism; but they are answered on this point in great detail by Pinker and Jackendoff 2005.

5   "The linguistic literature is full of arguments of this type" (Lightfoot, 1998, p. 585); "A glance at any textbook shows that half a century of research in generative syntax has uncovered innumerable such examples" (Smith, 1999, p. 42).

6   Notice, we take "linguistic nativism" to denote a claim, not just a strategy. Some psycholinguists clearly differ. Fodor and Crowther (2002), for example, think linguistic nativism is a methodology that "assumes everything to be innate that could be innate." This would presumably contrast with a non-nativist methodology that assumes everything to be acquired that could be acquired. But these are not the forms of linguistic nativism and non-nativism we address.

7   The principles and parameters approach is basically abandoned in the controversial recent development known as the "minimalist program"; see Pinker and Jackendoff 2005 for a critique from a standpoint that is decidedly skeptical but nonetheless clearly nativist.

8   "Parochial" here means varying between natural languages, rather than being true of all of them.

9   "Interesting" is used here in a sense stemming from formal language theory, where finite or specially gerrymandered classes are not interesting, but broad and mathematically natural classes such as the regular languages or the context-free languages are interesting.

An excellent introduction to both the mathematics and the linguistic and psycholinguistic relevance can be found in Levelt 1974.

10   Janet Fodor (1989) wrestles with this issue, without arriving at a satisfying resolution. See Culicover (1999, p. 15) for remarks with which we agree: "Since human beings acquire both the general and the idiosyncratic, there must be a mechanism or mechanisms that can accommodate both . . . Even if we assume that the most general correspondences are instantiations of linguistic universals that permit only simple parametric variation, the question of how the rest of linguistic knowledge is acquired is left completely unexplored."

11   The SRN is a "three-layer feed-forward network – made up of the input, hidden, and output layers – augmented by a context layer." We should note that Prinz 2002 – a work which unfortunately we encountered only after this chapter was almost completed – describes Elman's work as showing "that a dumb pattern detector can pick up on structural relations" (p. 206). This seems overstated. Prinz seems unaware of the growing literature suggesting an alternative interpretation: that children are very capable and sophisticated learners of transition probabilities. Elman's computational models are particularly important in light of the discovery of children's stochastic learning capacities.

12   We're ignoring one complication, as other discussions generally do: if there is no main clause auxiliary verb, the auxiliary verb *do* is required.

13   There is actually a great deal to be made clear about just what the higher-order property of "structure-dependence" is. The statement in (9) is not universal: other languages do not form interrogative sentences in the same way as English. What could perhaps be universal is some metaprinciple about the form of suitable candidates for tentative consideration as principles of grammar. No one has ever really made this precise. We will ignore the matter here.

14   It is worth pointing out that there is a deep inconsistency in the nativist literature concerning the kind of stimulus that is relevant to showing that the stimulus for auxiliary inversion is impoverished. On the one hand, nativists often claim that only the characteristics of child-directed speech are relevant for child language acquisition, since children acquire language primarily from child-directed speech. On the other hand, it is often pointed out that in some cultures adults do not direct speech to children until they are verbally fluent, so ex hypothesi, in these cultures the relevant stimulus is not speech directed specifically toward children. The reason this is important is that how impoverished the stimulus is depends on what stimuli are counted as relevant. For an informed discussion see Clark 2003.

15   Fodor 1981 ignores stochastically based learning. Pessimistic results like those of Gold 1967 simply do not apply under the assumption that linguistic input is modeled as a stochastic process and not text (see Scholz, 2004). Elsewhere, Fodor claims that stochastic learning can do nothing but recapitulate the distributional properties of the input. Elman's SRN is a counterexample to that claim. However, this is not the place to reply to Fodor's criticisms of connectionism.

16   Prinz (2002, pp. 209–10) takes Singleton and Newport (2004) to show that "children can turn a moderate statistical regularity into a consistently applied rule." But Simon's regularization of morphological structure need not be seen as evidence for the acquisition of rules in the linguist's sense. Simon's accomplishment is to exhibit more statistical regularity than his input did. This does not of itself tell us that any rules were acquired (though they might have been).

There is more to be said about sign language, though we have insufficient space here. Findings about language acquisition from inconsistent stimuli have played an important role in research on cross-cohort syntactic change in Nicaraguan Sign Language where there is iterated regularization across successive stages in the development of the

Barbara C. Scholz and Geoffrey K. Pullum

language. Here part of what is being investigated is syntactic regularization across a range of different inconsistent stimuli. And this line of research promises to provide insights into creolization, another controversial topic relating to language acquisition (see Bickerton, 1984).

17 Notice, inconsistency and error were *not* features of the input to the learner considered by Lewis and Elman; they assumed that the consistent and correct data lacked instances of one particular kind of sentence.

References and further reading

Antony, L. M. (2001). Empty heads. *Mind and Language,* 16, 193–214.

Ariew, A. (1996). Innateness and canalization. *Philosophy of Science Supplement*, 63, 19–27.

— (1999). Innateness is canalization: A defense of a developmental account of innateness. In V. Hardcastle (ed.), *Biology Meets Psychology: Conjectures, Connections, Constraints.* Cambridge, MA: MIT Press.

— (2003). Innateness and triggering: Biologically grounded nativism. Manuscript, University of Rhode Island.

Aslin, R. N., Saffran, J. R., and Newport, E. L. (1998). Computation of conditional probability statistics by 8-month-old infants. *Psychological Science*, 9, 321–4.

Barkow, J., Cosmides, L., and Tooby, J. (1992). *The Adapted Mind.* Oxford: Oxford University Press.

Bateson, P. P. G. (ed.) (1991). *The Development and Integration of Behaviour.* Cambridge: Cambridge University Press.

— (2004). The origins of human differences. *Daedalus*, 133/4, 36–46.

Bealer, G. (1999). The a priori. In J. Greco and E. Sosa (eds.), *The Blackwell Guide to Epistemology.* Oxford: Blackwell.

Bickerton, D. (1984). The language bioprogram hypothesis. *Behavioral and Brain Sciences*, 7, 173–221.

Block, N. (1981). *Readings in the Philosophy of Psychology*, vol. 2. Cambridge, MA: Harvard University Press.

Boyd, R. N. (1981). Scientific realism and naturalistic epistemology. In P. Asquith and R. Giere (eds.), *PSA: Proceedings of the Biennial Meeting of the Philosophy of Science Association 1980*, vol. 2, 613–62. East Lansing, MI: Philosophy of Science Association.

— (1991). Realism, anti-foundationalism and the enthusiasm for natural kinds. *Philosophical Studies,* 61, 127–48.

Chomsky, N. (2000). *The Architecture of Language.* New Delhi: Oxford University Press.

Chouinard, M. and Clark, E. (2004). Adult reformulations of child errors as negative evidence. *Journal of Child Language*, 30, 637–69.

Christiansen, M. H. and Curtin, S. L. (1999). The power of statistical learning: No need for algebraic rules. *Proceedings of the 21st Annual Conference of the Cognitive Science Society.* Mahwah, NJ: Erlbaum.

Clark, E. (2003). *First Language Acquisition.* Cambridge: Cambridge University Press.

Cowie, F. (1999). *What's Within? Nativism Reconsidered.* New York: Oxford University Press.

Crain, S. (1991). Language acquisition in the absence of experience. *Behavioral and Brain Sciences*, 14, 597–650.

Crain, S. and Nakayama, M. (1987). Structure dependence in grammar formation. *Language*, 63, 522–43.

Culicover, P. W. (1999). *Syntactic Nuts: Hard Cases, Syntactic Theory, and Language Acquisition.* Oxford: Oxford University Press.

Elman, J. L. (2003). Generalization from sparse input. *Proceedings of the 38th Annual Meeting of the Chicago Linguistic Society.* Chicago: Chicago Linguistic Society.

— (2005). Connectionist models of cognitive development: Where next? *Trends in Cognitive Sciences,* 9, 111–17.

Fodor, J. A. (1981). The current status of the innateness controversy. In *Representations: Philosophical Essays on the Foundations of Cognitive Science.* Cambridge, MA: MIT Press.

Fodor, J. D. (1989). Learning the periphery. In R. J. Matthews and W. Demopoulos (eds.), *Learnability and Linguistic Theory.* Dordrecht: Kluwer.

Fodor, J. D. and Crowther, C. (2002). Understanding stimulus poverty arguments. *The Linguistic Review,* 19, 105–45.

Gibson, E. and Wexler, K. (1994). Triggers. *Linguistic Inquiry,* 25, 407–54.

Gold, E. M. (1967). Language identification in the limit. *Information and Control,* 10, 447–74.

Gomez, R. L. (2002). Variability and detection of invariant structure. *Psychological Science,* 13, 431–6.

Griffiths, P. E. (2002). What is innateness? *The Monist,* 85, 70–85.

Hauser, M. D., Chomsky, N., and Fitch, W. T. (2002). The faculty of language: What is it, who has it, and how did it evolve? *Science,* 298, 1569–79.

Jain, S., Osherson, D., Royer, J. S., and Sharma, A. (1999). *Systems That Learn* (2nd edn.). Cambridge, MA: MIT Press.

Johnson, D. E. and Postal, P. M. (1980). *Arc Pair Grammar.* Princeton, NJ: Princeton University Press.

Kornblith, H. (1993). *Inductive Inference and Its Natural Ground: An Essay in Naturalistic Epistemology.* Cambridge, MA: MIT Press.

Laurence, S. and Margolis, E. (2001). The poverty of the stimulus argument. *British Journal for the Philosophy of Science,* 52, 217–76.

Levelt, W. J. M. (1974). *Formal Grammars in Linguistics and Psycholinguistics* (3 vols). The Hague: Mouton.

Lewis, J. D. and Elman, J. L. (2001). Learnability and the statistical structure of language: Poverty of stimulus arguments revisited. *Proceedings of the 26th Annual Boston University Conference on Language Development.* Somerville, MA: Cascadilla Press.

Li, M. and Vitányi, P. (1997). *An Introduction to Kolmogorov Complexity and Its Applications* (2nd edn.). New York: Springer.

Lidz, J., Gleitman, H., and Gleitman, L. (2003). Understanding how input matters: Verb learning and the footprint of Universal Grammar. *Cognition,* 87, 151–78.

Lightfoot, D. (1998). Promises, promises: General learning algorithms. *Mind and Language,* 13, 582–7.

Lipton, P. (1991). *Inference to the Best Explanation.* New York: Routledge.

— (1998). Induction. In M. Curd and J. A. Cover (eds.), *Philosophy of Science: The Central Issues.* New York: Norton. (Reprint of a passage from Lipton, 1991.)

Marler, P. (1999). On innateness: Are sparrow songs "learned" or "innate"? In M. D. Hauser and M. Konishi (eds.), *The Design of Animal Communication.* Cambridge, MA: MIT Press.

Matthews, R. J. and Demopoulos, W. (eds.) (1989). *Learnability and Linguistic Theory.* Dordrecht: Kluwer.

Newport, E. L. and Aslin, R. N. (2000). Innately constrained learning: blending old and new approaches to language acquisition. In S. C. Howell, S. A. Fish, and T. Keith-Lucas (eds.), *Proceedings of the 24th Annual Boston University Conference on Language Development.* Somerville, MA: Cascadilla Press.

Barbara C. Scholz and Geoffrey K. Pullum

— and — (2003). Learning at a distance: I. Statistical learning of non-adjacent dependencies. *Cognitive Psychology*, 48, 127–62.

Piattelli-Palmarini, M. (1980). *Language and Learning: The Debate Between Jean Piaget and Noam Chomsky*. London: Routledge and Kegan Paul.

Pinker, S. (1994). *The Language Instinct: How the Mind Creates Language*. New York: William Morrow.

Pinker, S. and Jackendoff, R. S. (2005). The faculty of language: What's special about it? *Cognition*, 95, 201–36.

Postal, P. M. (2004). The openness of natural languages. In P. M. Postal, *Skeptical Linguistic Essays*. New York: Oxford University Press.

Prinz, J. (2002). *Furnishing the Mind: Concepts and Their Perceptual Basis*. Cambridge, MA: MIT Press.

Pullum, G. K. and Scholz, B. C. (2001). On the distinction between model-theoretic and generative-enumerative syntactic frameworks. In P. de Groote, G. Morrill, and C. Retoré (eds.), *Logical Aspects of Computational Linguistics: 4th International Conference*. Berlin: Springer Verlag.

— and — (2002). Empirical assessment of stimulus poverty arguments. *The Linguistic Review*, 19, 9–50.

— and — (2003). Linguistic models. In M. T. Banich and M. Mack (eds.), *Mind, Brain, and Language: Multidisciplinary Perspectives*. Mahwah, NJ: Erlbaum.

Putnam, H. (1963a). Degree of confirmation and inductive logic. In P. A. Schilpp (ed.), *The Philosophy of Rudolf Carnap*. La Salle, IL: Open Court. (Reprinted in Putnam, 1979.)

— (1963b). Probability and confirmation. *The Voice of America, Forum Lectures, Philosophy of Science Series*, 10. Washington DC: US Information Agency. (Reprinted in Putnam, 1979.)

— (1979). *Mathematics, Matter and Method: Philosophical Papers*, vol. 1 (2nd edn.). New York: Cambridge University Press.

Reali, F. and Christiansen, M. (forthcoming). Uncovering the richness of the stimulus: structure dependence and indirect statistical evidence. *Cognitive Science*.

Saffran, J. R., Aslin, R. N., and Newport, E. L. (1996). Statistical learning by 8-month-old infants. *Science*, 274, 1926–8.

Saffran, J. R. and Wilson, D. P. (2003). From syllables to syntax: Multi-level statistical learning by 12-month-old infants. *Infancy*, 4, 273–84.

Sampson, G. (1989). Language acquisition: Growth or learning? *Philosophical Papers*, 18, 203–40.

— (1997). *Educating Eve*. London: Cassell.

— (1999). Collapse of the language nativists. *The Independent* (April 9), 7.

— (2002). Exploring the richness of the stimulus. *The Linguistic Review*, 19, 73–104.

Samuels, R. (2002). Nativism in cognitive science. *Mind and Language*, 17, 233–65.

Scholz, B. C. (2004). Gold's theorems and the logical problem of language acquisition. *Journal of Child Language*, 31, 959–61.

Scholz, B. C. and Pullum, G. K. (2002). Searching for arguments to support linguistic nativism. *The Linguistic Review*, 19, 185–223.

Seidenberg, M. S. and MacDonald, M. C. (1999). A probabilistic constraints approach to language acquisition and processing. *Cognitive Science*, 23, 569–88.

Singleton, J. L. and Newport, E. L. (2004). When learners surpass their models: The acquisition of American Sign Language from inconsistent input. *Cognitive Psychology*, 49, 370–407.

Smith, N. (1999). *Chomsky: Ideas and Ideals*. Cambridge: Cambridge University Press.

Sober, E. (1998). Innate knowledge. In E. Craig (ed.), *Routledge Encyclopedia of Philosophy*, vol. 4. London: Routledge.

Stich, S. (1975). *Innate Ideas*. Berkeley, LA: University of California Press.

Trout, J. D. (1998). Nativism, statistical complexity, and speech. Presented at the 24th Annual Meeting of the Society for Philosophy and Psychology, Minneapolis, MN.

Waddington, C. H. (1940). *Organizers and Genes*. Cambridge: Cambridge University Press.

The Case for
Linguistic Nativism

Robert J. Matthews

Linguistic nativists hold that child-learners come to the language acquisition task equipped with certain domain-specific innate knowledge that enables them to succeed in this task in which they would otherwise fail. Many of these nativists further hold that this innate knowledge is in fact knowledge of certain grammatical principles true of all natural languages. These principles, the set of which they dub "universal grammar" (UG, for short), are said to constrain severely the class of possible natural languages, thereby making successful acquisition possible on the basis of the limited empirical evidence available to child-learners in the learning environment about the language to be learned.[1] In the years since the demise of behaviorism in the late 1950s and early 1960s, linguistic nativism has gradually become the received view within cognitive science on matters concerning the innate contribution of the learner to language acquisition,[2] though there continues to be significant empirical debate among nativists as to just what exactly is innate and how it is to be characterized. There also continues to be a number of linguists, philosophers, and psychologists who either reject linguistic nativism out of hand in favor of what might be described as a broadly empiricist conception of language acquisition or else argue that a compelling case has yet to be made for linguistic nativism.[3] These critics do not have anything that could be described as a reasonably well-developed alternative to the increasingly detailed models of child language acquisition presented by nativists and based on nativist principles. Rather they tend to focus critically on the arguments advanced in support of linguistic nativism, most notably on so-called poverty of the stimulus arguments (discussed below). These critics allege that for various reasons these arguments fail to establish the nativist conclusion that they are intended to establish; they argue that these arguments are formally invalid, or they fail to rise to a sufficient standard of proof, or they rest on certain dubious unstated assumptions, or they are crucially vague at critical points, or they depend on empirical premises that are either false or at least not empirical proven. So at the very least, according to these critics, the case for linguistic nativism has yet to be made, and empiricism in these matters is still a live option.

The arguments for linguistic nativism are certainly not apodictic, but, then, virtually no arguments for any claim of any importance in empirical science ever are. Nevertheless these arguments are considerably stronger than anti-nativist critics admit. The case for linguistic nativism is compelling – enough so that researchers are certainly justified in attempting to work out the details of a nativist account of language acquisition. Of course, many such details remain to be worked out, and currently accepted hypotheses about the learning environment, learning mechanisms, and what is acquired will undoubtedly suffer the fate of most other empirical scientific hypotheses, turning out to be at best only rough approximations of the truth. But the attempt to work out a nativist account is not the fool's errand that some empiricists have attempted to make it out to be. And if bets were being taken on how the debate between nativists and anti-nativists will turn out, the smart money would be on the nativists.

In the present paper we examine the case for linguistic nativism, focusing first on the so-called "poverty of the stimulus" arguments on which linguistic nativists commonly rely. We consider the reasons that anti-nativists find these arguments unconvincing, concluding that while anti-nativists typically hold these arguments to an unreasonably high standard of proof, they are right to complain that these arguments, as they are actually presented, are often lacking in crucial empirical detail. Without such detail, these arguments are best construed, we argue, as a kind of "demonstration" argument for linguistic nativism. We conclude our examination of the case for linguistic nativism by considering a kind of argument provided by formal learning theory that is arguably more empirically robust and thus less vulnerable to anti-nativist criticisms. We begin our discussion by providing some historical background for the current debate between nativists and anti-nativists.

Some Historical Background

The current debate between linguistic nativists and their critics is hardly new. In many ways it is a rerun, if not simply a continuation, of a debate that begin in the seventeenth century, one that finds even earlier echoes in Plato's *Meno*, where Socrates undertakes to establish that an untutored slave boy has unlearned knowledge of certain necessary truths of geometry.[4] Like Plato, seventeenth-century rationalists such as Descartes and Leibniz were impressed by the fact that we seem to know a great deal that cannot possibly have been acquired only through the senses. But whereas Socrates attributed such knowledge to a dim remembrance of things learned in a previous existence, seventeenth-century rationalists attributed such unlearned knowledge to innate endowment. Learners, they argued, come to the learning task with certain innate domain-specific knowledge that enables them to learn what they do. Thus, for example, we have, rationalists argued, knowledge of God as a necessary being with all perfections, despite our never having had sensory experience of any such being; similarly, we have knowledge of an isosceles triangle as one that has two sides of (absolutely) equal length, despite our never having had sensory experience

Robert J. Matthews

of such a triangle, in both cases because we are innately endowed with that knowledge. Seventeenth- and eighteenth-century empiricists such as Locke, Berkeley, and Hume, for their part, argued that such knowledge could be, and in fact was, acquired on the basis of sensory experience alone, using the domain-general inductive learning mechanisms hypothesized by empiricists.

The issue separating rationalists and empiricists has never been, as some believe, that empiricists failed to credit the mind with any innate structure.[5] Empiricists clearly assumed that the hypothesized perceptual apparatus and domain-general inductive learning mechanisms were innate. But unlike rationalists, empiricists assumed that this innate structure imposed no substantive restrictions on the knowledge that could be acquired. Empiricists identified knowledge with complex ideas constructed out of sensory experience, and there were, as they saw it, no restrictions on the sorts of complex ideas that the hypothesized innate inductive mechanisms could cobble out of the deliveries of innate sensory mechanisms. Rationalist accounts, by contrast, denied that knowledge acquisition involved inductive generalization over the deliveries of the senses. They regarded knowledge acquisition as a non-inferential, brute causal process that mapped a course of sensory experience into a body of knowledge. On the rationalist account, sensory experience played a quite different role in knowledge acquisition than empiricists imagined: specific sensory experiences served to occasion specific innate knowledge that was latently present in the mind. This innate knowledge effectively constrained what one could possibly learn and thus know, for one could come to know only what was innately (and latently) present in the mind.

For all the polemics and spilling of ink that characterized the debate between seventeenth- and eighteenth-century rationalists and empiricists, the debate was ultimately inconclusive, both because the issues in dispute were not framed with sufficient precision, and because the relevant empirical evidence was not in hand. Neither party had anything like a concrete proposal for how we come to know what we know; indeed, neither party had a precise, empirically well-supported specification of what it is that is learned and hence known. As well, neither party had anything more than the glimmer of an idea of what aspects of sensory experience were relevant to the acquisition of specific sorts of knowledge. Thus, neither party was in a position to decide the crucial question of whether sensory experience in combination with inductive learning strategies was even in principle sufficient to account for the knowledge that we in fact have. But all this began to change with the advent of modern generative linguistics in the late 1950s and early 1960s. First, linguists developed a reasonably precise characterization of one particular domain of human knowledge, viz., what it is one knows when one knows a natural language. Subsequently, developmental psycholinguists working largely within the generative linguistics tradition began to develop increasingly precise characterization of the primary linguistic data available to the child-learner. Learning theorists were finally in a position to begin to address fruitfully the crucial question of whether, as empiricists claimed, domain-general learning strategies were sufficient to account for the ability of child-learners to acquire any natural language on the basis of their access of data, or whether, as rationalists (now calling themselves nativists) claimed, successful language acquisition required that child-learners come to the acquisition task equipped with certain innate domain-specific knowledge about the language they would learn, knowledge that would effectively constrain the class of languages that they could learn (on the basis of available primary linguistic data). Much of the discussion and debate, especially within linguistics, focused on so-called poverty of the stimulus arguments, which linguistic nativists such as Chomsky argued provided compelling empirical support for their position.

Poverty of the Stimulus Arguments

Linguistic nativists rely heavily on poverty of the stimulus arguments (PoS arguments, for short) to make their case that acquisition of a natural language requires that the child-learner come to the learning task with certain innate domain-specific knowledge of language. PoS arguments take a variety of forms, but the basic idea is that you don't get rich output from impoverished input without a significant, specific contribution from the learner that makes up for the impoverished nature of the input. As applied to language acquisition, the basic idea is that if you consider both the rich complexity of the languages that learners acquire and the relatively impoverished data on the basis of which they acquire their languages, one must conclude that learners succeed in this acquisition task only because they come to the task already knowing a lot about the languages that they will eventually acquire. Here is Chomsky's well-known formulation of the argument:

> It is clear that the language each person acquires is a rich and complex construction hopelessly underdetermined by the fragmentary evidence available.... Nevertheless, individuals in a speech community have developed essentially the same language. This fact can be explained only on the assumption that these individuals employ highly restrictive principles that guide the construction of grammar. Furthermore, humans are, obviously, not designed to learn one human language rather than another.... Powerful constraints must be operative restricting the variety of languages.[6] (Chomsky, 1975, pp. 10–11)

The conclusion of the argument, it should be noticed, is *not* that knowledge of these grammatical principles is innate; rather it is that in order to come to know what they do on the basis of such impoverished data, learners must come to the learning task with certain domain-specific knowledge (specifically, of grammatical principles) – knowledge that will enable them to acquire any natural language on the basis of the relevant, impoverished data for that language. The PoS argument itself is *non*committal as to whether this knowledge that the successful learner must bring to the learning task is innate, or whether, as some (e.g., Piaget) believe, it is acquired earlier, perhaps on the basis of nonlinguistic sensory experience.

The argument for linguistic nativism therefore involves more than the direct inference from the poverty of linguistic data to the innateness of linguistic knowledge. Rather the argument involves two steps: (i) a PoS argument from the poverty of linguistic data to the conclusion that the learner must come to the learning task with certain domain-specific knowledge about what is to be learned, and (ii) a second argument, not necessarily a PoS argument, to the effect that this antecedent domain-specific knowledge could not itself be learned and must therefore be innate. And if, as Chomskyans claim, this innate knowledge takes the form of a universal grammar

(UG), i.e., a set of grammatical principles true of all possible natural languages, then there will have to be a third argument to the effect that (iii) this innate, domain-specific knowledge is properly characterized in terms of such universal principles.

Nativists, including Chomsky himself, have tended to focus almost exclusively on the first step in this argument for linguistic nativism, which establishes only that the learner must come to the learning task with certain domain-specific knowledge. They do this, not because they think that this is all there is to the argument for linguistic nativism, but rather because they think, correctly it seems, that recognizing the need for this domain-specific knowledge is the crucial step in the argument for linguistic nativism that empiricists have traditionally and stubbornly resisted. As long as empiricists remain convinced that language acquisition can be accounted for in terms of domain-general learning mechanisms, they will find any sort of nativism unmotivated. But if they can be brought to recognize the need for domain-specific knowledge, they will be forced, nativists assume, to face the question that will eventually drive them to nativism, namely, how could such knowledge possibly be acquired.[7]

Chomsky's own conclusion that the domain-specific knowledge that learners bring to the learning task is innate, i.e., that it is determined endogenously and not on the basis of sense experience, rests on the following argument from theoretical parsimony:

1 There are at present no substantive proposals as to how such domain-specific knowledge might be acquired.
2 In the absence of any such proposal, it is reasonable on grounds of theoretical parsimony to conclude that this knowledge, which is apparently species-specific, is, like other species-specific traits, innate; i.e., it is endogenously determined, since to conclude otherwise would be to presume that the development of cognitive structures is to be treated differently than the development of physical structures elsewhere in the body.
3 Hence, it is reasonable in the absence of such proposals to conclude that this domain-specific knowledge is innate.

Chomsky presents just this argument from theoretical parsimony in his reply to Piaget, who famously held that the required constraints were "constructions of sensorimotor intelligence":

> I see no basis for Piaget's conclusion. There are, to my knowledge, no substantive proposals involving "constructions of sensorimotor intelligence" that offer any hope of accounting for the phenomena of language that demand explanation. Nor is there any plausibility to the suggestion, so far as I can see. . . . The expectation that constructions of sensorimotor intelligence determine the character of a mental organ such as language seems to me hardly more plausible than a proposal that the fundamental properties of the eye or the visual cortex or the heart develop on this basis. Furthermore, when we turn to specific properties of this mental organ, we find little justification for any such belief, so far as I can see. (Chomsky, 1980b, pp. 36–7)

Other nativists have offered a different sort of argument for the claim that the domain-specific knowledge is innate.[8] This argument, which might be dubbed the "impossibility-of-acquisition argument," runs as follows: If domain-specific knowledge of the constraints on possible natural languages is acquired, then it must be acquired on the basis of either linguistic data or nonlinguistic data. It cannot be acquired on the basis of linguistic data, since even if sufficient linguistic data were available, the learner would be able to induce the relevant constraints from this data only if he or she, acting as a "little linguist," already understood the language or languages that exhibit the constraints, which by assumption the learner does not. But the learner is not going to be able to induce the constraints in question from nonlinguistic data either, for the simple reason that these data do not exhibit these domain-specific constraints. Hence, the learner is not able to acquire knowledge of the constraints in question, and such knowledge must be innate. While this impossibility-of-acquisition argument might be described as a kind of PoS argument, inasmuch as the argument trades on the absence of relevant evidence, Chomsky's argument from theoretical parsimony clearly is not. But the crucial point remains: there is more to the argument for linguistic nativism than simply a PoS argument from impoverished linguistic data.

The Anti-Nativist Response to PoS Arguments

Over the years nativists have focused on a small number of poster examples of PoS arguments to make their case for linguistic nativism. The best known of these examples is, no doubt, Chomsky's PoS argument regarding polar (yes/no) interrogative constructions in support of the claim that child-learners come to the acquisition task knowing that grammatical rules and principles are *structure dependent* (in the sense of being defined over specific syntactic structures rather than over non-structural features such as ordinal position in the sentence).[9] Chomsky argues that in learning to form polar interrogatives, child-learners hear sentences such as (1) and (2):

1   The man is wearing a jacket.

2   Is the man   wearing a jacket?

On the basis of such pairs, child-learners come to know that (2) is formed by "moving" the auxiliary "is" to the front of the sentence. But then when faced with the task of forming the polar interrogative corresponding to (3), they unerringly produce sentences such as (4), but never (5), despite the fact that they have, Chomsky claims, never heard sentences such as (4):

3   The man that is standing on the corner is wearing a jacket.

4   Is the man that is standing on the corner   wearing a jacket?

5   *Is the man that   standing on the corner is wearing a jacket?

Robert J. Matthews

Child-learners seemingly know that it is the main clause auxiliary that is to be moved, despite the fact that based solely upon the linguistic data available to them, viz., sentences such as (1) and (2), (5) is equally plausible. Chomsky concludes that the child-learner comes to the learning task knowing that grammatical rules and principles are structure dependent, so that in constructing the rule for polar interrogatives, the child-learner never entertains the possibility that the relevant rule is something like "move the first auxiliary to the front of the phrase," despite the fact that such a rule is consistent with the empirical data available to the child; instead, the child-learner presumes, correctly, that the rule is something like "move the main clause auxiliary to the front of the phrase," since this rule is consistent both with the available data and the knowledge that grammatical rules and principles are structure dependent.

Other well-known examples of PoS arguments endeavor to show: (i) that child-learners of English must come to the acquisition task knowing the structure of complex noun phrases, based upon their understanding that an anaphoric pronoun such as the English "one" can have as its referent a complex noun phrase, despite the fact that linguistic data available to the learner may include only sentences in which the anaphoric "one" takes a noun as its referent (see Hornstein and Lightfoot, 1981); and (ii) that child-learners of English come to the acquisition task knowing the possible parametric variation exhibited by natural languages (as regards binding relations, word order, null subjects, and so on) as well as the default values of each of the parameters that define a language (see, e.g., Wexler, 1991; Gibson and Wexler, 1994).

Anti-nativist critics have challenged these PoS-based arguments for linguistic nativism on a number of different (but quite predictable) grounds. Some, like Piaget, have been prepared to concede the conclusion of the PoS argument to the effect that success in these learning tasks requires that the learner come to the task with certain domain-specific knowledge of language, but they deny that this antecedent knowledge need be innate. The relevant knowledge, they argue, could have been acquired elsewhere, on the basis of nonlinguistic experience. Others concede that the PoS arguments establish that the child-learner must come to the learning task with certain innate domain-specific biases, but they deny that these biases need take the form of innate *knowledge*. Rather child-learners are said to come to the learning task furnished with certain innate learning *mechanisms*, rather than knowledge, that in some manner impose certain domain-specific learning biases.[10] Most anti-nativist critics, however, are not prepared simply to concede the conclusions of PoS arguments; they recognize the difficulty of blunting the nativist implications of these arguments once conceded. They challenge the PoS arguments themselves, arguing on one ground or another that the arguments fail to establish what they claim to establish, namely, that the child-learner comes to the learning task with certain domain-specific knowledge or biases that make language learning possible. For most anti-nativist critics, there is in fact *no* poverty of the stimulus, either because (i) the linguistic data upon which the learner acquires language is not as impoverished as nativists claim, or because (ii) the language acquired is not as complex as nativists claim, or both. Or if there is a poverty of the stimulus, it is one that (iii) a learner could remedy in ways other than by a domain-specific contribution on the part of the learner. Most critics adopt the first of these three positions, arguing that contrary to what nativists claim, the relevant evidence that would allow acquisition of the relevant knowledge is, as a matter of empirical fact, available to the learner in the learning environment, so that at the very least nativists have not made a case for a poverty of the stimulus. Thus, for example, Cowie (1999) and Pullum and Scholz (2002) argue against the assumption, widely held by developmental psycholinguistics, that child-learners acquire language on the basis of positive evidence only, i.e., on the basis of data drawn from the language to be acquired; they argue that at the very least there is what they call "indirect" negative evidence.[11] With respect to Chomsky's PoS argument from polar interrogatives, they argue that contrary to what Chomsky claims, learners do in fact have access in the learning environment to sentences such as (4), and they present as evidence for this claim the fact that such sentences appear with some frequency in the *Wall Street Journal*. They don't actually establish the frequency with which such sentences appear in the linguistic corpus to which child-learners are exposed, much less that child-learners actually register and make use of such sentences as are available in the learning corpus.[12] It is enough to discredit the argument, they assume, simply to show that the child-learner *might* have access to the relevant data. Anti-nativists also argue against PoS arguments by challenging nativist characterizations of what is learned, arguing that PoS arguments presume defective, or at least contentious, grammatical characterizations of what's learned, so that one can have no grounds for confidence in any nativist conclusions based on them.

The aim in virtually every case is to discredit PoS arguments by challenging the nativist's characterization of input data or output knowledge. Anti-nativists rarely claim to have proven the nativist's characterizations to be false, which of course would be a decisive refutation of their arguments; rather they claim, more modestly, to have shown that nativists have failed to shoulder the burden of proof to the anti-nativist's satisfaction. For all the nativist has shown, these anti-nativists argue, the characterizations of input data and output knowledge, and hence the conclusion of the PoS arguments, *might* be false, and this bare possibility, they argue, leaves open the possibility both that nativism is false and (consequently) that some form of empiricism is true.

Anti-nativists critics often write as if they imagine that PoS-based arguments are intended to convert the committed anti-nativist. This is simply not the case. It would be a fool's errand to undertake to convert anyone who holds PoS arguments to the unreasonable standard of having conclusions that are not possibly false, for no empirical argument can meet that standard. But even if PoS arguments are evaluated under some more reasonable standard of acceptability, anti-nativists will probably remain unconvinced, and for basically two reasons. First, as presented these arguments typically do not provide adequate empirical evidence in support of the crucial premises about what is acquired and the linguistic evidence on the basis of which it is acquired, thus permitting anti-nativists to question the truth of the premises. Second, in themselves these arguments provide no reason to suppose that their conclusions are empirically robust, in the sense of continuing to hold under "perturbtions," i.e., different reformulations, of the premises that reflect the our uncertainty about the relevant empirical facts. Put another way, given our uncertainty about the relevant empirical facts, anti-nativists question whether we can have any confidence in an argument based on any particular specification of these admittedly uncertain facts.

This lack of detailed accompanying empirical support for the premises, coupled with the lack of demonstrated empirical robustness of the conclusions, makes it difficult

Robert J. Matthews

to regard these arguments, at least as they have been presented, as anything more than demonstration arguments, i.e., arguments that are intended to demonstrate the sort of reasoning that leads linguistic nativists to their view. Given the obvious theoretical and empirical complexity of the acquisition problem, specifically, the difficulty of specifying (i) what precisely is acquired in acquiring a language, (ii) the data on the basis of which whatever is acquired is acquired, and (iii) the cognitive processes, including any innate biases, that effect the acquisition – such arguments alone *cannot* make a compelling case for linguistic nativism. Indeed, they cannot make a compelling case even for the crucial claim that learners come to the learning task with certain domain-specific knowledge that makes successful acquisition possible. Nothing less than the following two theoretical developments would turn the trick: (i) a theoretically well-developed, empirically well-supported nativist account, i.e., one that makes essential use of nativist assumptions, of how child-learners acquire the languages that they do on the basis of their access to linguistic data, and (ii) the concomitant failure of empiricist efforts to develop a similarly theoretically well-developed, empirically well-supported account which does *not* make essential use of nativist assumptions.[13]

Although there has been considerable progress over the last 25 years in the development of nativist computational accounts of natural language acquisition, at present neither nativists nor empiricists have accounts that are sufficiently well developed theoretically and well supported empirically to bring final closure to the dispute over linguistic nativism. There has been a great deal of empirical work within generative linguistics to specify in precise terms what it is that a child-learner acquires when he or she acquires a natural language, and these specifications have become increasingly sensitive over the years to the obvious requirement that whatever is acquired must be the sort of thing that *provably* can be acquired on the basis of the child-learner's given access to data in the learning environment. There has also been considerable empirical work within developmental linguistics to specify precisely what data is available to learners regarding the specific linguistic constructions that they master. There has, at the same time, been a growing body of research in "formal learning theory" (discussed below) that attempts to integrate these specifications of what is learned and the data on the basis of which it is learned into a computationally explicit account of the cognitive processes that map the latter into the former.[14] It is not possible to survey this work here, but suffice it to say that nativist assumptions underpin it at every turn (see Wexler, 1991). PoS-based considerations, for example, guide the development of the computational account of acquisition processes, suggesting to researchers the sorts of biases that have to be built into these processes if they are to succeed in their task. During this same period in which nativist assumptions have so dominated psycholinguistic research, *nothing* has emerged that could plausibly be described as even the beginnings of a non-nativist account of language acquisition. In the absence of such an account, anti-nativists have been reduced to playing the role of a loyal opposition (some would say fighting a rearguard action), criticizing nativist PoS arguments, objecting to specific nativist proposals, pointing out research results that might possibly favour a non-nativist account, and so on. Thus, for example, one finds many anti-nativist criticisms of the well-known poster examples of PoS arguments, criticisms that, as I said above, typically focus on establishing that these demonstration arguments are not decisive disproofs of the possibility of an anti-nativist account (e.g., Cowie, 1999; Pullum and Scholz, 2002). One finds arguments to the effect that certain connectionist architectures, e.g., simple recurrent networks, hold promise as a way of explaining how learners might exhibit the learning biases that they do, though without the intervention of domain-specific antecedent knowledge (e.g., Elman et al., 1996, but see Sharkey et al., 2000). One similarly finds arguments to the effect that learners are able to compensate for the apparent poverty of the stimulus by employing certain stochastic procedures (again, Cowie, 1999; Pullum and Scholz, 2002). But as suggestive as these criticisms and results may be, they don't really add up to anything that suggests that empiricist accounts are a live option at this point. All this of course could change, but at this point in time there is simply no evidence of an impending empiricist renaissance. Perhaps the most that anti-nativists might reasonably hope for is that as the nativist research program is elaborated and modified in response to the usual theoretical and empirical pressures that drive research programs we might eventually reach a point where the resulting account of language acquisition becomes unrecognizable as either nativist or empiricist, as least as we presently understand these terms. In such event, the question of which view turned out to be correct will be moot, and anti-nativists might take some solace in the fact that nativism, as currently conceived, turned out not to be correct.[15]

The Formal Learning-Theoretic Case for Linguistic Nativism

For some four decades now, Chomksyan linguists, most notably Chomsky himself, have been the principal advocates for linguistic nativism, making the case for that view in terms of PoS arguments of the sort described above. During this same time period, there has emerged from the intersection of formal language theory and recursive function theory, and largely independently of empirical generative linguistics, a field of mathematical inquiry known as "formal learning theory" (FLT). Over the last 25 years, acquisition theorists have increasingly availed themselves of the analytically powerful, mathematically precise framework that FLT provides for conceptualizing the acquisition of natural language. Serious acquisition theories are now routinely formulated in FLT terms, and proposed acquisition theories are expected to satisfy the following FLT-based adequacy condition:

> the learning procedure attributed to child-learners by the acquisition theory should *provably* be able to acquire the hypothesized class of natural languages on the basis of the data that the theory hypothesizes child-learners utilize in acquiring the languages that they do.

Many acquisition theorists who have adopted the FLT framework find in the results of their FLT-based acquisition research, *empirically robust* support for linguistic nativism that is independent of that provided by PoS arguments of the sort described above. It is not possible to spell out in any detail here the support that FLT provides for linguistic nativism, but we can provide some sense of its tenor.

Robert J. Matthews

Formal learning theory, as the name suggests, studies the learnability of different classes of formal objects (languages, grammars, theories, etc.) under different formal models of learning.[16] The specification of such a model, which specifies in formally precise terms (i) *a learning environment* (i.e., the data which the learner uses to learn whatever is learned), (ii) *a learning function*, and (iii) *a criterion for successful learning*, determines (iv) *a class of formal objects* (e.g., a class of languages), namely, the class that can be acquired to the level of the specified success criterion by a learner implementing the specified learning function in the specified learning environment.[17]

Much of the early work in FLT concerned itself with extensions and generalizations of the so-called Gold paradigm, initiated by Gold's 1967 seminal paper "Language identification in the limit." In this paper Gold examined the learnability of different classes of formal languages on the basis of two different data formats, under a success criterion of strict identification in the limit. Gold proved a number of important learnability results, most famously an unsolvability theorem for text presentation whose interpretation and import for linguistic nativism has been the subject of continuing debate within cognitive science.[18] Subsequent work in FLT has examined learning models that differ widely in their specification of all three parameters of the model (viz., learning environment, learning function, and success criterion). Formal learning-theoretic results typically compare models that differ only in their specification of one of the three parameters, showing that a class of languages learnable on one specification of the parameter in question is not learnable on a different specification of that same parameter. Many of the results are unsurprising: there are learnable classes of languages that cannot be learned by computable learning functions, that cannot be learned on noisy text (i.e., text that includes sentences drawn from the complement of the language to be acquired), that cannot be learned on incomplete text, and so on. But there are also some very surprising results, some of which refute very basic theoretical assumptions within psychology. (For example, there is a widely held assumption that a "conservative" learning-on-errors strategy, of abandoning a hypothesis only when it fails to explain the data, is not restrictive as regards what can be learned. FLT shows this to be false.)[19]

There is no direct or immediate application of these various learnability results to the current debate regarding linguistic nativism; in themselves these results do not make a case for linguistic nativism. But they do serve to map out the conceptual space within which any plausible theory of natural language acquisition must be articulated, and they do provide researchers familiar with these results with a pretty good sense, "intuitions" as mathematicians might put it, as to the learnability of particular classes of languages under different specifications of the three parameters that define a learning model. And it is here, arguably, that the FLT case for linguistic nativism begins to emerge.

From studying the learnability consequences of varying the three parameters that define a particular formal learning model, FLT theorists develop a rather clear understanding of how changes to the different parameters interact with one another to affect the learnability of broad classes of formal languages. As they study the learnability properties of what linguists take to be the class of possible natural languages, these theorists also develop a pretty clear sense of the sort of restrictions that must be imposed on that class (in the form of restrictions on the hypotheses that a learner implementing a certain learning strategy can entertain and conjecture) if it is to be learnable (to the level of the empirically relevant success criterion) on the basis of the kind of data that developmental psycholinguists hypothesize that child-learners employ in the course of language acquisition. As a result of this research, virtually all FLT theorists have concluded that, as Chomsky argued on the basis of PoS considerations, these restrictions have to be pretty severe in order to assure learnability: successful child-learners must come to the learning task with significant domain-specific knowledge of the languages that they will acquire, where this knowledge is realized in the form of constraints on the sort of hypotheses they will entertain and conjecture in the course of the learning task.

The FLT case for linguistic nativism just outlined is not, as Cowie (1999) and other anti-nativist critics have supposed, simply a kind of PoS argument. Obviously, the FLT case for linguistic nativism concludes, as do the PoS arguments, that learners are successful in acquiring the natural languages that they do on the basis of the sort of data children acquire languages only because they come to the learning task with certain domain-specific knowledge. But these FLT-based arguments do not turn, as PoS arguments do, on specific, detailed assumptions either about the principles that characterize the grammatical competence that learners acquire or about the linguistic data on the basis of which they acquire this competence. For this reason, FLT-based arguments for linguistic nativism are not vulnerable, in the way PoS arguments are, to the usual sorts of criticisms raised by anti-nativists. Nor do these arguments rely on detailed assumptions about the learning mechanisms employed by learners. Rather FLT-based arguments rely only on *very general* assumptions about the nature of the acquired competence, learning data, and learning mechanisms.

FLT-based arguments are also not vulnerable, as PoS arguments seemingly are, to the anti-nativist objection that the knowledge of specific grammatical principles that PoS arguments propose to explain *might* be the consequence of the acquisition, *in the learning environment*, of other linguistic knowledge, on the basis of other linguistic data. Consider once again Chomsky's PoS argument, based on polar interrogatives, for the claim that child-learners come to the learning task knowing that linguistic rules are structure dependent. Nothing in that argument precludes the possibility that the child-learners acquire this knowledge, perhaps as an interaction effect, in the course of acquiring other linguistic knowledge. FLT-based arguments avoid this vulnerability because they concern themselves with the antecedent knowledge required to acquire *entire* languages (or grammars) rather than simply specific grammatical components thereof.

The FLT case for linguistic nativism becomes only stronger as one starts to incorporate within the learning model empirically more plausible and detailed specifications of (i) the class of possible natural languages, (ii) the learning environment in which child-learners acquire the languages that they do, and (iii) the cognitive capacities that learners exercise in the course of language acquisition (learning strategies, memory limitations, etc.). FLT theorists find themselves forced even more strongly to the conclusion that Chomsky is right in thinking that there must be fairly severe constraints on the class of possible natural languages, and that to succeed in the acquisition task learners must come to the task knowing these constraints.

Robert J. Matthews

Importantly, FLT also provides a mathematically precise framework within which one can address the question of just *how empirically robust* one's nativist conclusions are in the face of uncertainty regarding the empirically correct specification of (i) the learning environment, (ii) the learning function, (iii) the success criterion, and (iv) the class of possible natural languages. One can vary (i), (iii), and (iv), both separately and in combination with one another and to a degree that reflects one's empirical uncertainty about empirically correct specification of each. One then determines for each of these variations the learning function provably required in order to acquire the specified class of possible natural language to the specified success criterion in the specified learning environment. To the extent that under all such variations the required learning function entails that learners come to the learning task with domain-specific knowledge about the languages they will acquire, then to that extent one's nativist conclusions are empirically robust. Thus far there has been no systematic undertaking of this sort, but it would be fair to say, based on the formal learnability results to date for proposed formal acquisition theories, the case for linguistic nativism looks to be empirically quite robust. Put more simply, the conclusion that linguistic nativism is true appears to be pretty stable over a wide range of different but empirically plausible assumptions about both the parameters that define the learning model and the class of possible natural languages.

Conclusion

In conclusion, five points deserve emphasis. (i) The case for linguistic nativism finds independent support from both PoS arguments and FLT-based arguments. (ii) These arguments are not apodictic; like any argument based on empirical premises, they are only as good as their premises. But (iii) the preponderance of available evidence suggests that these arguments are generally sound and empirically robust, and hence (iv) child-learners do come to the learning task with antecedent domain-specific knowledge, and the most plausible explanation of how learners come by this knowledge is that it is innate. But (v) any final verdict on linguistic nativism must await the development of a theoretically well-developed, empirically well-supported account of natural language acquisition, one that satisfies the minimal adequacy condition imposed by FLT, namely, that the hypothesized learning procedures provably be able to acquire the class of natural languages, to the empirically appropriate success criterion, on the basis of the sort of evidence that child-learners in fact employ in the course of language acquisition.

Notes

1 Classical statements of linguistic nativism are to be founded throughout the writings of Noam Chomsky, especially in Chomsky, 1966, 1975, 1980a, 1980b, 1988.
2 For a popular exposition of this received view, see Pinker, 1994.
3 E.g., Elman et al., 1996; Cowie, 1999; Sampson, 1999; Pullum and Scholz, 2002; and Scholz and Pullum, 2002.

4 See Chomsky, 1966 for his perspective on the seventeenth-century debate. See also Cowie 1999, pp. 3–66.

5 See Katz, 1967, pp. 240–68.

6 In an earlier formulation, Chomsky put the argument this way:

> It seems plain that language acquisition is based on the child's discovery of what from a formal point of view is a deep and abstract theory – a generative grammar of his language – many of the concepts and principles of which are only remotely related to experience by long and intricate chains of quasi-inferential steps. A consideration of . . . the degenerate quality and narrowly limited extent of the available data . . . leave[s] little hope that much of the structure of the language can be learned by an organism initially uninformed as to its general character. (Chomsky, 1965, p. 58)

7 Failure to appreciate that PoS arguments are intended to establish only that successful learners must come to the learning task with certain domain-specific knowledge has led empiricist critics such as Cowie (1999) to complain that these arguments establish less than they are supposed to establish, namely that learners come to the learning task with certain innate knowledge of language. It has led nativist supporters such as Nowak et al. (2002) to conclude that by "innate" linguistic nativists really mean "before data," i.e., knowledge that learners bring with them to the learning task.

8 See, e.g., Matthews, 2001.

9 See, e.g., Chomsky, 1975, pp. 30–3; 1980a, pp. 114–15; 1980b, pp. 41–7, 1986, pp. 7–13; also Lightfoot, 1991, pp. 3–4 and Pinker, 1994, pp. 233–4. For a nuanced discussion of PoS arguments, see Wexler, 1991.

10 Whether there is a substantive issue here depends crucially on how, computationally speaking, such knowledge is realized. Most critics who have pressed this issue presume without argument a representationalist theory of propositional attitudes (cf. Fodor, 1987) according to which having an attitude toward some proposition (e.g., knowing that P) is a matter of having a mental representation with the propositional content P that plays the appropriate functional/causal role in cognition. This presumption is especially evident in the arguments of Elman et al. (1996) against the position that they term "representational nativism."

11 For a defense of the standard assumption, see Marcus, 1993.

12 For discussion, see Matthews, 2001 and Crain and Pietrowski, 2002.

13 But even this might not be enough to bring the committed anti-nativist on board. If the history of science is any indication, many anti-nativists would remain unconverted. For as historians of science are fond of pointing out, scientific progress generally comes not through conversion of an entrenched scientific community to a new view, but through attrition: defenders of discredited theories simply die off, leaving the field to younger proponents of the replacing view.

14 Wexler and Culicover, 1980, and Berwick, 1985 are early examples of such work. More recent examples include Gibson and Wexler, 1994; Bertolo, 1995; Niyogi and Berwick, 1996; Sakas and Fodor, 2001; and Yang, 2002.

15 I am reminded here of the remark, cited by Hilary Putnam, of a famous Nobel laureate in chemistry who wryly noted that contrary to what historians of science always teach, the existence of phlogiston was never disproved, by Joseph Priestley or anyone else, that, on the contrary, phlogiston turned out to be valence electrons!

16 A class of languages is counted as learnable just in case every language in the class is learnable, to the specified success criterion, on the basis of the specified kind of data for that language.

17 For a general introduction, see Feldman, 1972; Valiant, 1984; Kelly, 1996; and Jain et al., 1999. For applications to the problem of natural language acquisition, see, e.g., Wexler and Culicover, 1980; Berwick, 1985; Matthews and Demopoulos, 1989; and Bertolo, 2001.
18 For a careful discussion of Gold's unsolvability result and its implications for the current nativist/empiricist debate, See Johnson (2004). See also Matthews, 1984; Demopoulos, 1989; and Nowak et al., 2002.
19 See Jain et al., 1999 and Osherson et al., 1984.

References

Bertolo, S. (1995). Maturation and learnability in parametric systems, *Language Acquisition*, 4, 277–318.
— (ed.) (2001). *Language Acquisition and Learnability*. Cambridge: Cambridge University Press.
Berwick, R. (1985). *The Acquisition of Syntactic Knowledge*. Cambridge, MA: MIT Press.
Chomsky, N. (1965). *Aspects of the Theory of Syntax*. Cambridge, MA: MIT Press.
— (1966). *Cartesian Linguistics*. New York: Harper & Row.
— (1975). *Reflections on Language*. New York: Pantheon.
— (1980a). *Rules and Representations*. New York: Columbia University Press.
— (1980b). On cognitive structures and their development: a reply to Piaget. In M. Piattelli-Palmarini (ed.), *Language and Learning: The Debate between Jean Piaget and Noam Chomsky*. Cambridge, MA: Harvard University Press.
— (1986). *Knowledge of Language*. Westport, CT: Praeger.
— (1988). Generative grammar: Its basis, development and prospects. *Studies in English Linguistics and Literature*, special issue. Kyoto: Kyoto University of Foreign Studies. (Reprinted as On the nature, acquisition, and use of language, in W. Lycan (ed.), *Mind and Cognition*. Oxford: Blackwell, 1990.)
Cowie, Fiona (1999). *What's Within: Nativism Reconsidered*. Oxford: Oxford University Press.
Crain, S. and Pietrowski, P. (2002). Why language acquisition is a snap. *The Linguistic Review*, 19, 163–83.
Demopoulos, W. (1989). On applying learnability theory to the rationalism-empiricism controversy. In R. Matthews and W. Demopoulos (eds.), *Learnability and Linguistic Theory*. Dordrecht: Kluwer.
Elman, J., Bates, E., Johnson, M., Karmiloff-Smith, A., Parisi, D., and Plunkett, K. (1996). *Rethinking Innateness*. Cambridge, MA: MIT Press.
Feldman, J. (1972). Some decidability results on grammatical inference and complexity. *Information and Control*, 20, 244–62.
Fodor, J. (1987). *Psychosemantics*. Cambridge, MA: MIT Press.
Gibson, E. and Wexler, K. (1994). Triggers. *Linguistic Inquiry*, 25, 407–54.
Gold, E. M. (1967). Language identification in the limit. *Information and Control*, 10, 447–74.
Hornstein, N. and Lightfoot, D. (1981). Introduction. In *Explanation in Linguistics: The Logical Problem of Language Acquisition*. London: Longman.
Jain, S., Osherson, D., Royer, J. S., and Sharma, A. K. (1999). *Systems That Learn* (2nd edn.). Cambridge, MA: MIT Press.
Johnson, K. (2004). Gold's theorem and cognitive science. *Philosophy of Science*, 71, 571–92.
Katz, J. (1967). *Philosophy of Language*. New York: Harper & Row.
Kelly, K. (1996). *The Logic of Reliable Inquiry*. Oxford: Oxford University Press.
Lightfoot, D. (1991). *How to Set Parameters*. Cambridge, MA: MIT Press.
Marcus, G. (1993). Negative evidence in language acquisition. *Cognition*, 46, 53–85.

Matthews, R. (1984). The plausibility of rationalism. *Journal of Philosophy*, 81, 492–515. (Reprinted in Matthews and Demopoulos (eds.) (1989). *Learnability and Linguistic Theory*. Dordrecht: Kluwer.)

— (2001). Cowie's anti-nativism. *Mind and Language*, 16, 215–30.

Matthews, R. and Demopoulos, W. (eds.) (1989). *Learnability and Linguistic Theory*. Dordrecht: Kluwer.

Niyogi, P. and Berwick, R. (1996). A language learning model for finite parameter spaces. *Cognition*, 17, 1–28.

Nowak, M., Komarova, N., and Niyogi, P. (2002). Computational and evolutionary aspects of language. *Nature*, 417, 611–17.

Osherson, D., Stob, M., and Weinstein, S. (1984). Learning theory and natural language. *Cognition*, 17, 1–28.

Pinker, S. (1994). *The Language Instinct: How the Mind Creates Language*. New York: William Morrow.

Pullum, G. and Scholz, B. (2002). Empirical assessment of stimulus of poverty arguments. *The Linguistic Review*, 19, 8–50.

Sakas, W. and Fodor, J. (2001). The structural triggers learner. In S. Bertolo (ed.) *Language Acquisition and Learnability*. Cambridge: Cambridge University Press.

Sampson, G. (1999). *Educating Eve*. London: Cassell.

Sharkey, N., Sharkey, A., and Jackson, S. (2000). Are SRNs sufficient for modelling language acquisition? In P. Broeder and J. Murre, *Models of Language Acquisition*. Oxford: Oxford University Press.

Scholz, B. and Pullum, G. (2002). Searching for arguments to support linguistic nativism. *The Linguistic Review*, 19, 185–223.

Valiant, L. G. (1984). A theory of the learnable. *Communications of the ACM*, 27, 1134–42.

Wexler, K. (1991). On the argument from the poverty of the stimulus. In A. Kasher (ed.), *The Chomskyan Turn*. Oxford: Blackwell.

Wexler, K. and Culicover, P. (1980). *Formal Principles of Language Acquisition*. Cambridge, MA: MIT Press.

Yang, C. (2002). *Knowledge and Learning in Natural Language*. Oxford: Oxford University Press.

On the Innateness
of Language

James McGilvray

Introduction

Barbara Scholz and Geoffrey Pullum in this volume (chapter 4, IRRATIONAL NATIVIST EXUBERANCE) review some of the current discussion on innateness of language. They express frustration at the nativist's lack of sympathy with what they call "sense based" approaches to language learning. Specifically, they suggest looking at the studies of language learning found in two works, Newport and Aslin, 2000, and Lewis and Elman, 2001. Both claim a role for statistical analysis in language acquisition. That seems to be what Scholz and Pullum have in mind by "sense based" approaches.

I want to emphasize the kinds of considerations that lead some of those who work on natural languages and their acquisition to adopt what I call, following Chomsky, a "rationalist" research program.[1] Scholz and Pullum's suggestions help in this, for – I suggest – Newport and Aslin's work can be understood as a contribution to a rationalist project, while Lewis and Elman's has a very different, empiricist aim. Distinguishing the two reveals what is at stake.

The question of the innateness of language should, I think, be seen as a matter of choosing the most fruitful research program for the science of language. This is an empirical question, decided by which program yields the best theory,[2] or naturalistic understanding of language. It is clear what Chomsky's rationalist choice was and is (Chomsky, 2000, 2005): treat linguistics as naturalistic scientific inquiry, using the same methodology as that of physics and biology, and think of language as a natural object, a kind of organ that grows under normal conditions to a state that the biophysical nature of that organ permits. That invites thinking of the innateness of language as a matter of internal biophysical machinery that sets an internally determined course of language growth or development for the child's mind. Biophysical machinery selects incoming signals according to its inbuilt criteria of relevance, "looking" for patterns and elements. It also sets an agenda for a normal course of development to an individual's linguistic perception, comprehension, and production of linguistic sounds and meanings over an unbounded range. The machinery allows for various courses of development; these are captured by parameters. A developed language organ is a child's I-language (to use Chomsky's terminology); a child who has one has a language and "cognizes" it. In general, internal machinery selects data, offers options, regulates coordination and growth, and thus determines a space of biophysically possible I-languages.

Newport and Aslin (2000) present a research program consistent with this view of linguistic innateness. They do not claim that the mind is nothing but a statistical analyzing device; they hold that it must have "hardware" that in some specific ways performs a kind of statistical analysis. Nor–crucially – do they hold that language develops in the child under *external* guidance and control. Their primary interest is in how the *human child's mind actually does* process signals when at a stage or stages of language development. That is fine with the internalist nativist. If it turns out that the mind performs statistical analysis on input in fixing on syllabic structure, word boundaries, and parametric options (Yang, 2002, 2004), so be it – so long as the aim is to find out how the child's mind actually does accomplish this *and everything else needed to acquire a language* in the relevant time period. Newport and Aslin do suggest that their research might undermine a nonstatistical story of development sometimes told about a deaf child called Simon. But acknowledging machinery that performs statistical analysis is consistent with internalist nativism.

Lewis and Elman (2001) have different commitments. On matters of methodology, target of research, and the kind of "object" a language is, and on the nature of a child's mind, they hold that the linguist interested in an account of acquisition should not only allow a role for statistical analysis, but should assume that there is little or no role for internal signal selection and agenda-setting – so that language develops almost entirely by statistical sampling procedures and language learning proceeds under external guidance and control. A language is not a natural object that grows naturally inside the head; they think of it as a social entity learned by the young by statistically discerning patterns in, and coming to duplicate, the linguistic usage that a child encounters.[3] As models of minds, they offer simple recurrent networks (SRNs) that are trained. And judging by Lewis and Elman (2001), demonstrating that these assumptions are correct might consist in getting an SRN – given massive amounts of data chosen by the experimenter – to predict word type and order in a way that models the "predictions" of a rule such as AUX-fronting for question formation (for example, in English, moving the main-clause auxiliary *is* of *The horse that Mary is fond of is in the stable* to the front, forming the question *Is the horse Mary is fond of in the stable?*). Their project is firmly within the empiricist camp. Languages are external, manufactured objects – E-languages, in Chomsky's terminology. SRNs have minimal internal agenda-setting powers (perhaps statistical algorithms in a "context layer" that can be tweaked by the experimenter to get the "right" outputs); they are fed input chosen by the experimenter, not selected by the device; they have "learned" when they yield the "right" predictions. Their focus is on languages as sets of behaviors; they want to get a device to simulate those behaviors (make the right "predictions"); their technique is focused on, and aims to simulate, the behaviors exhibited in a single speech population, not all people,

James McGilvray

anywhere. Perhaps friends of SRNs can get SRNs to manage this, to some degree. But no matter how close they might come to convincing people that a device "speaks English" (Chinese, etc), their effort has no demonstrable relevance to the issue of how a child actually does acquire a language.

What's Wrong with Connectionist Empiricism?

What's wrong? For one thing, thinking of a language as a set of behaviors; I'll come back to that. For another, reliance on external channeling and control. In Lewis and Elman, 2001, the authors get "Englishy" AUX-fronting predictions for questions out of SRNs subjected to staged sets of training sessions with corpora.[4] They show that SRNs can be made to produce fairly reliable next-element-in-a-string predictions after massive training – several "epochs" of repetition (with stored assessments of their "progress" in a "context layer") through three stages of training. One can complain about the amount of repetition needed, the lack of parallelism to child learning, and the like; but those are not points I focus on here. And I'll grant that the SRNs and the conditions under which training sessions proceed do not somehow provide information about structure (relative clauses, phrasal structure) that is not extracted from the stimulus sets. The issue is this: would an SRN, given not just the sets of strings Lewis and Elman use in their procedure, but *everything* a child encounters in his or her experience, be able to decide *at the appropriate stage of development* which strings are *relevant* to developing natural language "output" that models a principle of structure dependence amounting to requiring main clause fronting of AUX for questions? In Lewis and Elman, 2001, task-devoted SRNs are kept on track through three stages of training by providing them with specific sets of data, those needed to produce – given sufficient repetition – what the experimenters take to be the right predictions at the various stages. An SRN given a large channeled data set eventually "solves" (to an extent) that problem.[5] But children's data are not channeled. They don't have to be; their minds have machinery that selects, organizes, and grows into a form that the machinery allows.

Children acquire several principles – phonological, morphological, structural, semantic – in short order, not all of them quite as transparent and "on the surface" as the one(s) that underlie AUX-fronting. Children in multilingual environments acquire two or more sets of principles with little, if any, change in rate. They do so, apparently, with little or no training or direction; their parents, other children, and other speakers in their environments do not stream data to them and keep them "on track." To a reasonable degree, the orders in which they acquire principles for specific languages reflect the statistical distribution of evidence in their environments (Yang, 2004); but that is not evidence that they acquire languages in the way that Lewis and Elman would have us believe. Nativist internalist reasoning here is more plausible: children's minds (not children as agents) must "know" ahead of time what the "choice space" is for not just a single, but any natural language. The child's mind needs to know what principles must be acquired, what kinds of choices must be made, and what kind(s) of data are relevant to acquiring a principle and – where relevant – making a choice. The child's mind cannot rely on other speakers channeling and coordinating what the child receives. The child's mind must have a biophysical system that "contains" the principles and options for any natural language. The child's mind must have an *internal* data-selection and option-setting device.

Given sufficient time and devoted effort, a connectionist empiricist story might possibly be told about SRNs with external guidance exploiting whatever statistical distributions are to be found in an extremely large set of signals of an English-appearing sort, so as to eventually produce sets of behaviors that some judge or another (who decides who is to judge?) says shows that it has learned English. To the rationalist, that would be about as interesting as being told that someone has decided that such-and-such a program yields a machine that thinks. The rationalist sees the production of behaviors that "pass" as thinking as a matter of *decision* about *usage* of *think*. So too of *learned English*: unless it is demonstrated that children's developing minds *are* SRNs and that they *do* learn in the way the connectionist empiricist story says they do, it is of no interest to the natural science of language and of how language develops. It might interest software engineers who want to produce "talking" robots. But that is quite a different enterprise.

To someone trying to find out how children's minds actually acquire a language, facts such as that they seem to employ statistical sampling in "looking for" local minima in *linguistic* sounds and in tracking the extent of available data in setting parametric options (Saffran et al., 1996; Yang, 2004) *are* interesting. The first indicates that the mind *has* a device that seeks local minima in *language*-like signals. It is interesting because only *children*'s minds automatically recognize the patterns and their relevance. Note that detection must be at least *bimodal* (auditory and spatial for speech and sign), and must be somehow exploited by a growth control system that brings the detected patterns to bear in the earliest forms of linguistic production – among others, babbling (Petitto et al., 2000; Petitto, 2005). How is a statistical sampling system – likely located in the superior temporal gyrus – made to perform this task, keeping in mind that among organisms, only human minds seem to "look" for the patterns and "know" how to put them to use? There must be some kind of selection and control mechanism that is "prepared" for information of this sort, "seeks" it and in this sense selects it, and quickly sets to putting it to use, in either speech or sign, or both (Petitto, 2005).

Consider next that a child's mind sets parameters in a sequence that tracks the extent of available data; that process too shows the mind "anticipating" what is relevant. Children developing English sometimes produce constructions that English does not allow. Their errors extinguish gradually, not with a sharp cutoff; that indicates that something like the statistical distribution of data available in a child's experience not only plays a role in "choosing," but in setting the order in which parameters are set. Crucially, though, the process is not random; children's minds are constrained to producing constructions available only in *other* natural languages. A child developing English might at one stage of development (2 years and 7 months, according to one study – Crain and Thornton, 1998) say *What do you think what pigs eat* – fine in some dialects of German, but not in English. Or a child might produce pro-drop or topic-drop constructions – fine under specific conditions in some languages (Italian, Chinese), but ruled out of English (cf. Wang, 2004, p. 254). The choice space seems to be closed. The only plausible way to make sense of that

James McGilvray

is to assume that their minds entertain only certain options – in Chomskyan terminology, parameters – even though they exploit statistical sampling to "choose" among them.

Further, the child who speaks by three and a half or so already has an integrated, coordinated knowledge of language that s/he brings to bear in speaking and comprehending others. S/he also has acquired a considerable vocabulary. And s/he has shown evidence of comprehension during growth that exceeds production capacity. An example of integration is found in a response to Scholz and Pullum's paper "Empirical assessments of stimulus poverty arguments" (2002). Pietroski and Crain (2002; see also 2005) show that a child of this age understands what negative polarity items, downward-entailing environments, and default readings of *or* sentences are (one or the other or both: not exclusive *or*). With these and a Gricean principle of economy, the child has also – automatically – an understanding of when *or* constructions are to be read exclusively (*You may have a piece of cake or a piece of pie*) or inclusively (*If Jane has invited witches or warlocks, you must leave*). The complex of knowledge needed for understanding is explained only by assuming that the information relevant to it and the principles governing it come as an interlocking – although unexpected – package of syntactic-semantic information. Interestingly, the child's mind must develop this package in the face of statistically dominant evidence that the reading of an *or* sentence is an exclusive one.

Given this and other such facts, plus a limited choice space, plus a need for some kind of selection mechanism, surely the learning child needs a selection and control mechanism. Let us say it is Universal Grammar (UG) – written into the human genome – *plus* other systems and constraints involved in development. I'll call the total selection and agenda-setting system "UG+"; UG+ selects data it considers relevant and determines the course of development for acquiring a language – and not just for a single language, but for all the possible languages that humans can produce. For without UG+, the selecting, staging, and coordination in language acquisition across the human species cannot be explained. Communities of speakers just won't do, and children are not in labs, subjected to streamed data. Biology and general physical and information-gathering principles (cf. Cherniak, forthcoming) must serve. So we should speak not of learning but of language growth.

Another problem with connectionist stories is found in a lack of parallelism. No doubt statistical sampling plays some role in vision acquisition too, but Lewis and Elman's effort to rely on statistics all the way up would not even be considered by someone hoping to explain how the child's mind normally develops the capacity to see and visually discriminate. With vision, the scientist simply assumes that the agenda is set biophysically, guided by control mechanisms, some of which are genetically encoded. The Pax-6 gene, for example, has been held to be involved in and to guide visual development in multiple species (Callaerts et al., 1997) – and to be itself controlled by a Notch gene (Onuma et al., 2002). And it is extremely likely that general physical constraints play a role too – those that play a role in skeletal and overall structural development (cf. Thompson, 1917), neuron axon connection lengths (Cherniak et al., 2004), etc. No doubt certain inputs – physical, informational, etc. – are required at certain stages of growth to enable growth at all. But the selection and control mechanisms say which inputs are relevant, when. In effect, they serve as internal, not external, principles of growth regulation and data relevance. The nativist says that we can tell a similar tale about language. With language, of course, several courses of development are allowed – French, Swahili, Miskito, etc. So the internal system must allow for options – described, in current work, by parameters. These aside, and ignoring "Saussurean arbitrariness" with lexical items (not something a naturalistic theory can deal with), grammar itself (largely Merge[6]) may well be uniform and extremely simple (Hauser et al., 2002; Chomsky, 2005).

And finally, there is a problem with connectionist hardware and "wiring" commitments. At this stage it is premature at best to adopt research programs that assume that human brains are sufficiently like SRNs wired up in the way connectionist empiricists insist so that we can take seriously their use in proving or even suggesting that brains learn language in the way Lewis and Elman suggest. It is not an accident that rationalist approaches to the science of language leave decisions about what hardware/instantiation computes language aside until a future date – perhaps the distant future. It is unwise to be confident at this stage about what the brain is, not to mention how the brain is "wired up" to understand and produce language. Basically, we really don't know very much – as indicated by the remarks about the (typically) single-track system vision, where genetic control (Pax-6, Notch . . .) and who knows what physical developmental constraints seem to play roles, but no one knows exactly which, or how, or when. Yes, we know something about brains and wiring them up – although almost nothing about language in this regard. But we know a considerable amount about language and how it develops.

These last points – perhaps especially the one about parallels to visual system growth – give me an opportunity to emphasize that the advent of the principles and parameters approach to grammar in the early 1980s and recent developments in what Chomskyans call "minimalism" have eliminated with respect to "core grammar" the prima facie implausibility of linguistic nativism. The implausibility arose from early Chomskyan proposals – for example, those found in Chomsky, 1965. In them, innate endowment for grammar was assumed to consist in a "format" for a possible grammar and, to make acquisition possible in real time, it had to be assumed that the child's mind was genetically endowed with a "rich and articulate" (Chomsky, 2005) set of language-specific principles and elements that make up the format. Parameters changed that. By the time of Hauser et al., 2002 and Chomsky, 2005, perhaps all that must be language-specific and *genetically* specified for grammar is Merge – the one clear case of a computational capacity that humans have that no other organism does. Chomsky (2005) calls this the "first factor" in language growth. Parameters might be written into our genes; but they might also be written into another factor in language growth – what Chomsky (2005) calls the "third factor" that includes general principles of data analysis and (perhaps most important) "principles of structural architecture and developmental constraints" that canalize, set up organic form and development, provide for aspects of efficient computation, etc. So if "language specific" means "written into our genes" (first factor) and core grammar is language specific and unique to us (Hauser et al., 2002), perhaps only Merge is written into our genes. On the other hand, the *entire* process of language development – that yields core grammar, concepts and sounds – is biophysically "guided"; I-languages are products of a process of growth. There must be input (the "second

James McGilvray

factor"), of course. But what, when, and how input contributes is determined by an internal biophysical system (first and third factors = UG+).[7]

But is UG+ a single system: is it *an* internal biophysical selection and agenda-setting device? The set of biophysically possible human visual systems is fixed. The set of biophysically possible human languages is too. If you think a person's vision is the product of *a* biophysical system of growth, you should think a person's I-language is the product of *a* single system too.

Representation, Knowledge of Language, and What it is to be Innate

In the rest of this chapter I review the basic case for a nativist internalist research program for language. First, I define terms, suggesting what are – I think – plausible conceptions of innateness and knowledge of language. Then – by going back to the observational roots that led to the rationalist (nativist internalist) research program for language – I explain why an internalist and nativist strategy is the best option. Those observational roots are found in what Chomsky calls the "creative aspect of language use" and the "poverty of the stimulus" observations. The first are largely ignored and, where not, they and their implications are usually misunderstood. The second, and their implications, are usually just misunderstood.

To speak to innateness and knowledge of language, let us start with Scholz and Pullum's distinction (chapter 4) between "contentful" and "architectural" linguistic representations. Only the contentful representations, they suggest, represent linguistic knowledge. Assuming that an architectural representation might be something like, say, Chomsky's Merge (internal and external), the internalist rationalist holds that it *is* a form of linguistic knowledge, "information" concerning how structure is built, resulting in how an expression is interpreted. Recursivity and cyclicity are linguistic knowledge, as is the fact that the concept WATER– contentful, perhaps, for Scholz and Pullum – contains information that says where water comes from. Linguistic knowledge includes any information that is relevant to a linguistic derivation/computation and the information it provides other systems at "interfaces." Most of this knowledge can be taken to be innate.

One source of distrust of the idea that the mind has innate linguistic knowledge or information is the intuition that ideas and knowledge are *about* or *of* something or another in the sense of standing in some determinate, scientifically describable way to some thing, property, class of things, even semantic value, whatever that might be – all of them outside the representation.[8] These supposed targets of a linguistic representation often receive the label "contents," and linguistic representations are said to "have content" to the extent that they are related to these entities or properties outside the representation itself. If they have content in this sense, they are "of" or "about" or "denote" or "refer to" some thing or property. Jerry Fodor (1981, 1998) is attracted to this way of speaking; the internalist rationalist nativist rejects it. Saddling a theory of linguistic representations with a need to deal with relations to world or something else in the head leads to no progress and no theory at all (Pietroski, 2002; Hornstein 2005). Abandoning it, one can still have a notion of innate content: it is provided by the information/knowledge contained in the syntax of a linguistic representation, and its being innate is a matter of it being "anticipated" in the mind's biophysical machinery.

The internalist nativist does not deny – no one sane is likely to – that sometimes *people* use (say) a sentence to refer to something in the outside world, or perhaps a fictional or notional world, or fragment of world, etc. I might use the sentences

Dubya is in Washington.
Hamlet is in Denmark.

to do that, even by stressing *is* to declare that I *know* that Dubya is in Washington and Hamlet in Denmark. But this is a matter of my using a sentence/words to do this, not a matter of something in my head that is fixed by some naturalistically described relationship of "ofness" (denotation, reference . . .) to Dubya, Washington, and perhaps "in-ness" and "what I know." It is a matter of a person, using a linguistic tool with the information that it contains, to refer. There is no science of human action – and likely never will be. If representation–world (or representation–something-else) relations depend on human action, we will likely never have a theory of external-to-representation contents. But because linguistic representations contain information made available at language system "interfaces," they *do* have "content" internally and intrinsically.

Representation need not be a matter of being "of" something else. Saying that the mind has a noun phrase (NP) representation is saying that a part of the mind is in an NP kind of state. That state – and any other specifically linguistic state – is described by a theory of that part of the mind, the language faculty. Representations are, then, described intensionally ("under" a theory), not intentionally (as being of things or properties). Representations in this sense aren't of anything else, although people can use them to speak of things, using the information they contain.

Nevertheless, in another sense of "representation of," the part/element/event of the mind that is a noun phrase representation can be said to "have a *representation of a noun phrase* (of such-and-such a sort)." Goodman exploited this in his discussion of art (1967), and before that in his early (1952) suggestions concerning how to deal with linguistic meanings if one wants to be a nominalist. In his discussion of art, he argued that it is fine to think of a picture as a picture of Pegasus, even given a commitment to nominalism and an extensional conception of people referring. We read *picture of Pegasus* as *Pegasus-picture*, so that *of* here is a matter of classifying the picture, not remarking a relationship between it and a non-existent thing. The result is what he called an account of "representation-as" – a way of classifying the picture. Similar moves, he held, are possible with language. The meaning of *left the store* is not an event somewhere in the world. Speaking of the meaning of *left the store* (what this phrase is "of"), is speaking of a syntactic object that has whatever character it does.[9]

One of the very few positive things one can say about Goodman's conception of linguistic syntax is that he realized that syntax deals with features "inside" a "word." We can do much better. A theory of language like Chomsky's aims to say what is "inside" those "words" that appear at internal linguistic interfaces. Specifically, "words" offer, in phonetic and semantic features, information that "instructs" other systems inside the head. Syntactic theory says what this information is, and describes the means by which an internal organ can yield (compute) this information in the form of potentially infinite sets of sentences. In current terminology, linguistic meanings (semantic information) are SEMs; linguistic sounds are PHONs. All the information in SEMs and PHONs is intrinsic to these linguistic representations – it is "inside" a PHON or SEM. So the syntactic theory of language provides a syntactic theory of meaning in Goodman's sense – a syntactic classification of what a sentence provides at SEM. This internalist syntactic program is ambitious: it aims to characterize all possible sounds, meanings, and structures – and how they are integrated – in all the heads of all speakers of natural languages, those who were and now are, and those who might be. It does that by saying what languages are, and how they grow.

If one is careful, this notion of representation that is non-re-presenting can also be extended to the idea that computations are *represented in* some biophysical state(s)/event(s) in the mind. That is, they are embodied in whatever we discover to be the "machinery" that carries out a derivation/computation. The linguist constructing a naturalistic theory of language describes the various states and possible configurations of this machinery – presumably biophysical machinery – with a (computational) theory of linguistic syntax. This seems to be what Chomsky has in mind when he speaks of a theory of natural languages as biology (plus – as Chomsky, 2005, emphasizes – various background physical and information-processing factors that constrain and guide language growth) at an abstract level of description.

This points to how to view natural-language "ideas," information, etc, as innate. They are contained in a system that grows and develops according to its own agenda. The innateness of I-languages – the information concerning merging elements, recursion, structures, sounds, and meanings – is the innateness of linguistic syntax and the factors that serve as selectors and guide its growth. It is the innateness of a biophysical system – on which, see above. The overall theory of linguistic growth – UG+ – "says" what a biophysically possible human language is. What a particular person has in his or her head at a specific stage of development – his or her I-language – is likely to be unique to him or her: lexical items, parametric settings, etc, yield any number of different I-languages. Yet the theory of growth says what any one of them can be.

An informal way to make sense of this notion of innateness is found in Ralph Cudworth's work (1688). Descartes's notion of innateness as something like a congenital disease is too passive, as is the terminology of dispositions. Cudworth, a seventeenthth-century Cambridge Platonist, did better. He said that the human mind has an "innate cognoscitive power" that, when "occasioned" by sense, manufactures the required idea or concept, perhaps thereafter placing it in a memory store. He suggested thinking of this power as *anticipating* (he spoke of "prolepsis") what is needed for that occasion. This is a useful metaphor for UG+ and its development into a specific relatively steady state, an I-language: the growing child's language faculty anticipates its possible future states in that the powers of the faculty consist in selecting relevant data, allowing various options, and determining the potential developed states. A UG+-type theory describes the powers involved in acquiring and producing linguistic sounds, meanings, and their complexes – expressions. UG+ "says" what counts. I-languages – indefinite numbers of them – are anticipated in the machinery; they are innate.

What about innate linguistic *knowledge*? Having a language is having a massive amount of information (in a non-intentional sense) that can be brought together in indefinitely large, structured sets of meaning and sound specifications. Perhaps others would agree to that. But the internalist nativist goes on to say that all this knowledge is – as an I-language is – contained in the growth system UG+ that itself must be innate in order for it to yield what it does in the way it does in the time that it does. If I were an ancient Mesopotamian, I would not have "grown" the concept REFRIGERATOR. But I could have quickly, had I need for it. That's because I'm endowed with an innate cognoscitive power that anticipated it, and others I might need.

The Internalist Nativist Program: Coping with Linguistic Creativity

Poverty of the stimulus (PoS) facts typically take center stage in discussions of why one should adopt an internalist, nativist research strategy. But other, too often neglected factors need mention – specifically, what Chomsky calls the "creative aspect of language use" (CALU) observations. They suggest that if you want an objective science of language, look inside to what our languages offer *for* use, rather than trying to construct a theory *of* use. And they advise against what Morris et al. (2000, p. 7) call a "usage-based acquisition system."

The CALU observations concern how people routinely use language. The observations can be made by anyone of anyone, including oneself when one inspects the perhaps 98 percent or more of language use that stays in the head. The basic facts were in the background of Chomsky's review of Skinner's *Verbal Behavior* in 1959, but were not addressed systematically until *Cartesian Linguistics* (1966/2002). As that title suggests, Descartes recognized the facts when he considered extending his (he incorrectly believed) adequate contact mechanical explanation of animal and machine behaviors to the linguistic behavior of human beings. His attempt failed, and he described the factors that, taken together, make it impossible. One is that the use of language is stimulus-free and apparently (both internally and externally) uncaused. Another is that it seems to be unbounded in possible forms and contents – it offers unlimited scope for innovation, providing what would later be identified as a discrete infinity of possible cognitive perspectives. The third is that although uncaused and innovative, it typically remains appropriate to whatever circumstances – fictional or real – are relevant to a specific discourse. All this is true of everyone's language use: general intelligence, education, and social status play no role.

Nor does age. Linguistic creativity is found even in children of a very young age. At play and in fantasy, children invent, speculate, and engage in wonder – using novel sentence constructions to do so. The only way to make sense of this early display of linguistic creativity, Chomsky and other rationalists discussed in (Chomsky, 1966/2002) point out, is to assume that children have available to them, virtually at birth, inside their heads, a rich, cohesive, endless resource of "ideas" or – we could say – linguistically expressed cognitive perspectives. The source of these could be some mysterious, innate faculty of the mind, perhaps beyond the reach of scientific inquiry. Or it is language itself, and language is innate. It *must* be one of these – and surely the latter – otherwise children could not display linguistic creativity and factors that depend on it at such an early age. If they had to "learn" language in the way Morris et al. (2000) suggest, they would have to spend a lot of time in regimented training sessions. Creativity – were it to arise at all – would come very late indeed.

There is also advice in favor of linguistic internalism, and a modular form of it at that. The cognitive perspectives the child uses are not tied to input, either external or internal. They must be freely provided by a modular system that operates without external control. And the study of them, if it is to be accomplished at all, must be offered in terms of the internal system that provides them. If objectivity is characteristic of scientific inquiry, scientific study of language had better try to offer an account of how it can readily arise in the mind of *any* child, how it reaches a relatively steady state – an I-language – and how it "computes" sentences. There is little alternative but to adopt a research strategy that constructs a biophysical UG+-type theory that deals with all human languages.

Poverty and its Implications

The poverty of the stimulus (PoS) observations cover the full range of linguistic phenomena – sound, meaning, and structure. They are readily made, for there are plenty: virtually every acquisition of a single word by a child provides an example.[10] The observations note that children appear to acquire language quickly and display virtual adult competence by age 3 or 4.[11] They do this without regard to which language(s) they acquire – or to the child's general intelligence, educational or social status, etc. Across the human population, and without regard to whether they are acquiring sign or spoken natural languages, they do so in what appears to be an order that begins with spoken or sign babbling (a phenomenon unique to human beings) at age 6 to 9 months and quickly progresses through stages thereafter. In early stages, understanding – even of relatively complex constructions – outpaces production. Children manage this with little or no training ("negative evidence" in one use of this term, where there is little indication that members of the "community" – parents, other children, etc – try to correct a child's performance) and on the basis of input or experience that is impoverished (given what is acquired) and often fragmentary and corrupt. Recognition of "mother" tongue sounds as opposed to others appears early. Further, another and more interesting case of "negative evidence": children do not make some mistakes that one would think that they might, especially if they – or some system inside them – were thought to be constructing hypotheses, testing, and rejecting or accepting them. And finally, setting a frame around the matter, language is unique to human beings. No ape, no matter how trained, has understood the abstract sense of *fruit*, worked out or understood morphological variants (*fruity, fruitful* . . .), or had an inkling of recursion and linguistic structure.

Appreciating the force of these observations requires holding them up against the rich and structured information that a speaker with a language has available and can put to use. Consider words – sound–meaning pairs. Linguistic sounds have qualities and features that it takes special training and theoretical terminology to characterize and understand, and yet infants manage to distinguish "Englishy" sounds from Japanese (and others) quickly. Concepts/meanings have structure and detail revealed in the ways people use and understand language, although they have never been instructed in any of it. One of the more interesting cases in this respect is the concept WATER – a philosopher's favorite, often appearing in identity sentences with H_2O. My point has nothing to do with the fact that our concept WATER – the one(s) we express in our natural languages – has no single scientific counterpart,[12] although that is true and belies the (misguided) hope of finding *the* meaning (content) of water in some supposed "natural" object H_2O. It is that WATER, the concept we have, is a complex with structure and richness we have only begun to appreciate (for discussion, see Moravcsik, 1975; Chomsky, 1995, 2000). WATER is sensitive to matters of agency: put a tea bag in water, and it becomes tea. It is sensitive to source: if from a lake, a river, or even a tap, it's water. Tap water is water, even though it has been filtered through tea. Heavily polluted, if in a river, it's water: the St Lawrence is filled with it (a quirky feature of RIVER – why isn't the river the water, rather than being filled with water?), supposedly – although the water there includes an unhealthy proportion of other substances too. And so on. WATER is a single example; there are thousands more.

I mentioned early in this chapter that PoS observations are almost always misunderstood; now I can explain what I mean. They are *not* an argument; they present a problem for the theorist. PoS observations do not stand to theories that try to explain them as arguments and assumptions stand to conclusions. They commend to theorists an internalist, nativist research strategy, rather than an empiricist account like the connectionist story that Scholz and Pullum would like to tell. It is almost a commonplace that Chomsky offers a poverty of the stimulus "argument for the innateness of language." But when he speaks of PoS observations as constituting an argument – as in his discursive *Rules and Representations* (1980) – he speaks informally. Like Descartes in "Comments on a certain broadsheet" (to which Chomsky, 1980, referred when speaking of an "argument from the poverty of the stimulus"), he is saying that an internalist, nativist program looks more fruitful than an empiricist effort. "Language is innate" is not something that the scientist offers as an hypothesis, much less tests.[13] The only scientific hypothesis at issue is the (naturalistic, scientific) theory that – prompted by what the CALU and PoS observations suggest – one constructs to describe and explain and make sense of these observed facts, plus any number of other facts having to do with grammaticality, the character of use, other languages, truth indications, language impairment . . . – an expanding and changing set as the theory develops.

The would-be scientist of language or any other domain tries what Peirce called "abduction" or hypothesis-formation. Abduction is not argument. People now are fond of speaking of an inference to the best explanation, but "inference" fares little better than "argument": the mystery is relocated to "inference." If scientists had reliable inferential principles to follow when they constructed hypotheses, they would have discovery procedures. If they did, we would either be done by now, or have found that our principles are useless. Instead, we proceed incrementally, making jumps here and there. The process of constructing and refining a theory goes on – usually for centuries – with many contributing. And we feel justified in taking that course of research if it looks like there is improvement.

There is, however, an empirical issue. For language, it is whether, having adopted the internalist nativist strategy characteristic of rationalist (internalist nativist) views of language and its study, one gets successful scientific theories. On this, surely the record of the last fifty years or so indicates that the answer is yes. The internalist and nativist science of language that results does not, of course, explain language use. But the CALU observations indicate that it would be unwise to try.

Summary

In sum, rationalist nativism is a nativism of "machinery" – biophysical machinery of language growth and syntactic machinery of I-languages. Rationalists attempt to construct a natural science of that machinery. They want to get to know how *children* acquire languages and what *I-languages* are. The rationalist (nativist, internalist) research program seems to be on the right track; it speaks to the facts and aims to meet the standards of natural science. And it has made progress. While there are many outstanding issues – coming to understand exactly what is language-specific, for example, and developing an account of just how languages grow – we have reached the point that we can now begin to address the question of why language is the way it is ("principled explanation," Chomsky, 2005).

There are no obvious challenges to the rationalist program. Newport and Aslin (2000) contributes to it. Lewis and Elman's (2001) empiricist (anti-nativist, externalist) program seems to be devoted to trying to show that there is a different way to produce language-like behavior. Perhaps there is. But what they propose is not relevant to the science of human language.

Acknowledgments

I am very grateful to Rob Stainton for comments on an early draft and to Sam Epstein, Paul Pietroski, and Steve McKay for comments on others.

Notes

1   A rationalist program is an empirical program that maintains that acquisition of rich cognitive capacities such as language depends on innate resources. Rationalists are typically also – with a few exceptions, such as Fodor – internalists. Rationalist programs contrast with anti-nativist and externalist empiricist programs. For discussion, see Chomsky, 1966/2002; McGilvray, 1999; Hornstein, 2005.
2   Best by the standards of successful scientific projects: these are descriptively and explanatorily adequate to their domains, simple, formal, allow for accommodation to other sciences, and make progress in all these respects.

3   The commitments of connectionist views of language, data (usage), mind, learning, and the role of the experimenter are not obvious in Lewis and Elman, 2001. They are in Morris et al., 2000): children "learn grammatical relations over time, and in the process accommodate to whatever language-specific behaviors . . . [their] target language exhibits." Further: "From beginning to end this is a usage-based acquisition system. It starts with rote-acquisition of verb-argument structures, and by finding commonalities, it slowly builds levels of abstraction. Through this bottom-up process, it accommodates to the target language." Taking apart all the commitments in these passages is a project for a much longer paper.

4   Children never "front" the first *is* in the sentence *The dog that is shedding is under the table* to form a question. They never say *Is the dog that shedding is under the table*; they always say *Is the dog that is shedding under the table*. Chomsky often uses examples like this to emphasize that children's minds must implicitly know the principle(s) that govern the relevant phenomena.

5   A related point: SRNs are designed by experimenters to "solve" virtually any pattern-acquisition "problem"; they are made to be plastic, an enduring trait of empiricist doctrine. Because of this, they can acquire non-natural language patternings as easily – or not – as natural. Children acquire natural languages easily; they do not acquire non-natural languages easily. Machinery in their minds "anticipates" natural languages, not other kinds of system. It excludes other possibilities. For example, children's minds assign *The billionaire called the representative from Alberta* readings on which the call or the representative is from Alberta, but excludes a reading on which the billionaire is from Alberta (Pietroski, 2002).

6   Intuitively, Merge is a structure-building operation. It has two forms, External Merge and Internal Merge. One can think of the former as an operation that takes two lexical items and concatenates them, puts them together, or joins them; essentially, one starts with {x} and {y} and gets {x, y}. The second puts one item of the set "at the edge"; it replaces what Chomsky used to call "Move." External Merge yields sentential argument structure; Internal yields various discourse effects.

7   In case concepts and sounds look to you to be fertile areas for empiricist (externalist) acquisition stories, see the next two sections and Chomsky, 1966/2002, 2000 and McGilvray, 1998, 1999, 2005. That said, a lot needs to be done with concepts before anyone can plausibly say that as natural scientists they know what they are.

8   The externalist nativist must deal with two problems – establishing connections to external contents and dealing with the fact that reference/denotation is a form of human free action, not a naturalistic "locking" (Fodor, 1998). Moving contents inside the head but outside the linguistic representation avoids the agent control problem. But if the nativist continued to hold that contents were located somewhere else in the head (in Fodor's language of thought, perhaps), s/he would still have to deal with the problem of establishing connections. Chomskyan nativists locate their "contents" in linguistic representations themselves, avoiding both problems.

9   That said, this object and the "information" it contains constrain its possible uses and what would count as its correct uses. Meaning guides ("instructs") use, in this sense.

10   In their (2002) discussion of PoS "arguments for innateness," Scholz and Pullum seem to accept without qualm (2002, p. 31) that the informational "content" of many words such as *house* is easily learned at an early age. They should be worried by that: word-acquisition offers any number of examples of easy and apparently automatic acquisition of rich forms of packaged "information" – phonological and semantic. On that, see Chomsky, 2000 and McGilvray, 1998, 1999, 2005. For a good description of lexical acquisition timing, although little on sounds and meanings themselves, see Gleitman and Fisher, 2005.

James McGilvray

11 That is, core competence: they have fully developed I-languages, but haven't contended with all the irregular constructions and their root vocabularies are smaller than most adults'.
12 There are various states of H_2O as the scientist conceives it. See, for example, Ruan et al., 2004; Wernet et al., 2004; and Zubavicus and Grunze, 2004.
13 In Chomsky, 1980, to which Scholz and Pullum refer for what they take to be Chomsky's canonical view of the "argument from the poverty of the stimulus," the term "argument from the poverty of the stimulus" is introduced by reference to Descartes and his view that you can't find colors, things with the structure of our ideas, triangles, etc. "in the world" in the form you find them in our heads, so they must be contributed by what we have in our heads. The rest of the discussion proceeds in a similarly informal fashion.

References and further reading

Baker, M. (2001). *The Atoms of Language.* New York: Basic Books.

Callaerts, P., Halder, G., and Gehring, W. J. (1997). Pax-6 in development and evolution. *Annual Review of Neuroscience*, 20, 483–532.

Cherniak, C. (forthcoming). Innateness and brain-wiring optimization: non-genomic nativism. In A. Zilhao (ed.), *Cognition, Evolution, and Rationality.* Oxford: Blackwell.

Cherniak, C., Mokhtarzada, Z., Rodriguez-Esteban, R., and Changizi, K. (2004). Global optimization of cerebral cortex layout. *Proceedings of the National Academy of the Sciences*, 101/4, 1081–6.

Chomsky, N. (1959). Review of B. F. Skinner, *Verbal Behavior. Language*, 35/1, 26–57. (Reprinted with added preface in L. A. Jakobovits and M. S. Miron (eds.), *Readings in the Psychology of Language.* Englewood Cliffs, NJ: Prentice-Hall, 1967.)

— (1965). *Aspects of the Theory of Syntax.* Cambridge, MA: MIT Press.

— (1966/2002). *Cartesian Linguisitics.* (2nd edn. edited with a new introduction by J. McGilvray). Newcastle, NZ: Cybereditions.

— (1980). *Rules and Representations.* New York: Columbia University Press.

— (1995). Language and nature. *Mind*, 104, 1–61.

— (2000). *Reflections on Language.* Cambridge: Cambridge University Press.

— (2005). Three factors in language design. *Linguistic Inquiry*, 36/1, 1–22.

Crain, S. and Thornton, R. (1998). *Investigations in Universal Grammar. A Guide to Experiments on the Acquisition of Syntax and Semantics.* Cambridge, MA: MIT Press.

Cudworth, R. (1688). *A Treatise Concerning Eternal and Immutable Morality.* (Reprinted as *Ralph Cudworth: A Treatise Concerning Eternal and Immutable Morality*, ed. S. Hutton, Cambridge: Cambridge University Press, 1995.)

Fodor, J. (1981). The current status of the innateness controversy. In *Representations.* Cambridge, MA: MIT Press.

— (1998). *Concepts.* Cambridge, MA: MIT Press.

Gleitman, L. and Fisher, C. (2005). Universal aspects of word learning. In J. McGilvray (ed.), *The Cambridge Companion to Chomsky.* Cambridge: Cambridge University Press.

Goodman, N. (1952). On likeness of meaning. In L. Linsky (ed.), *Semantics and the Philosophy of Langauge.* Urbana, IL: University of Illinois Press.

— (1967). *Languages of Art.* Cambridge, MA: Harvard University Press.

Hauser, M., Chomsky, N., and Fitch, W. T. (2002). The faculty of language: What is it, who has it, and how did it evolve? *Science*, 298, 1569–79.

Hornstein, N. (2005). Empiricism and rationalism as research strategies. In J. McGilvray (ed.), *The Cambridge Companion to Chomsky.* Cambridge: Cambridge University Press.

Lewis, J. D. and Elman, J. (2001). Learnability and the statistical structure of language: Poverty of stimulus arguments revisited. *Proceedings of the 26th Annual Boston University Conference on Language Development*, 359–70. (Electronic version at http://crl.ucsd.edu/~elman/Papers/morris.pdf.)

McGilvray, J. (1998). Meanings are syntactically individuated and found in the head. *Mind and Language*, 13, 225–80.

—— (1999). *Chomsky: Language, Mind, and Politics*. Cambridge: Polity.

—— (2005). Meaning and creativity. In J. McGilvray (ed.), *The Cambridge Companion to Chomsky*. Cambridge: Cambridge University Press.

Moravcsik, J. (1975). *Aitia* as generative factor in Aristotle's philosophy of language. *Dialogue*, 14, 622–36.

Morris, W., Cottrell, G., and Elman, G. (2000). A connectionist simulation of the empirical acquisition of grammatical relations. In S. Wermter and R. Sun (eds.), *Hybrid Neural Systems Integration*. Heidelberg: Springer-Verlag. (Pagination is from the electronic version at http://crl.ucsd.edu/~elman/Papers/morris.)

Newport, E. and Aslin, R. (2000). Innately constrained learning: blending old and new approaches to language acquisition. In S. Howell, S. Fish, and T. Keith-Lucas (eds), *Proceedings of the Annual Boston University Conference on Language Development*, 24, 1–21.

Onuma, Y., Takahashi, S., Asashima, M., Kurata, S., and Gehring, W. J. (2002). Conservation of Pax 6 function and upstream activation by *Notch* signaling in eye development of frogs and flies. *Proceedings of the National Academy of Sciences*, 99/4, 2020–5.

Petitto, L. (2005). How the brain begets language. In J. McGilvray (ed.), *The Cambridge Companion to Chomsky*. Cambridge: Cambridge University Press.

Petitto, L., Zatorre, R., Gauna, K., Nikelski, E. J., Dostie, D., and Evans, A. C. (2000). Speech-like cerebral activity in profoundly deaf people while processing signed languages: implications for the neural basis of all human language. *Proceedings of the National Academy of the Sciences*, 97/25, 13961–6.

Pietroski, P. (2002). Meaning before truth. In G. Preyer and G. Peter (eds.), *Contextualism in Philosophy*. Oxford: Oxford University Press.

Pietroski, P. and Crain, S. (2002). Why language acquisition is a snap. *Linguistic Review*, 19, 63–83.

—— and —— (2005). Innate ideas. In J. McGilvray (ed.), *The Cambridge Companion to Chomsky*. Cambridge: Cambridge University Press.

Ruan, C-Y., Lobastov, V. A., Vigliotti, F., Chen, S., and Zewail, A. H. (2004). Ultrafast electron crystallography of interfacial water. *Science*, 304, 80–4.

Saffran, J. R., Aslin, R. N., and Newport, E. L. (1996). Statistical learning by 8-month-old infants. *Science*, 274, 1926–8.

Scholz, B. and Pullum, G. (2002). Empirical assessment of stimulus poverty arguments. *Linguistic Review*, 19, 9–50.

Thompson, W. D'Arcy (1917). *On Growth and Form*. Cambridge: Cambridge University Press.

Wernet, Ph., Nordlund, D., Bergmann, U., et al. (2004). The structure of the first coordination shell in liquid water. *Science*, 304, 995–9.

Yang, C. D. (2002). *Knowledge and Learning in Natural Language*. New York: Oxford University Press.

—— (2004). Universal Grammar, statistics, or both? *Trends in Cognitive Sciences*, 8/10, 1–6.

Zubavicus, Y. and Grunze, M. (2004). New insights into the structure of water with ultrafast probes. *Science*, 304, 974–6.

HAS COGNITIVE SCIENCE SHOWN THAT HUMAN BEINGS ARE COGNITIVELY BOUNDED, OR IRRATIONAL?

Bounded and Rational

Gerd Gigerenzer

At first glance, *Homo sapiens* is an unlikely contestant for taking over the world. "Man the wise" would not likely win an Olympic medal against animals in wrestling, weight lifting, jumping, swimming, or running. The fossil record suggests that *Homo sapiens* is perhaps 400,000 years old, and is currently the only existing species of the genus *Homo*. Unlike our ancestor, *Homo erectus*, we are not named after our bipedal stance, nor are we named after our abilities to laugh, weep, and joke. Our family name refers to our wisdom and rationality. Yet what is the nature of that wisdom? Are we natural philosophers equipped with logic in search of truth? Or are we intuitive economists who maximize our expected utilities? Or perhaps moral utilitarians, optimizing happiness for everyone?

Why should we care about this question? There is little choice, I believe. The nature of *sapiens* is a no-escape issue. As with moral values, it can be ignored yet will nonetheless be acted upon. When psychologists maintain that people are unreasonably overconfident and fall prey to the base rate fallacy or to a litany of other reasoning errors, each of their claims is based on an assumption about the nature of *sapiens* – as are entire theories of mind. For instance, virtually everything that Jean Piaget examined, the development of perception, memory, and thinking, is depicted as a change in logical structure (Gruber and Voneche, 1977). Piaget's ideal image of *sapiens* was logic. It is not mine.

Disputes about the nature of human rationality are as old as the concept of rationality itself, which emerged during the Enlightenment (Daston, 1988). These controversies are about norms, that is, the evaluation of moral, social, and intellectual judgment (e.g., Cohen, 1981; Lopes, 1991). The most recent debate involves four sets of scholars, who think that one can understand the nature of *sapiens* by (i) constructing *as-if theories of unbounded rationality*, (ii) constructing *as-if theories of optimization under constraints*, (iii) demonstrating *irrational cognitive illusions*, or (iv) studying *ecological rationality*. Being engaged in this controversy, I am far from dispassionate, and have placed my bets on ecological rationality. Yet I promise that I will try to be as impartial as I can.

Four Visions of Human Rationality

The heavenly ideal of perfect knowledge, impossible on earth, provides the gold standard for many ideals of rationality. From antiquity to the Enlightenment, knowledge – as opposed to opinion – was thought to require certainty. Such certainty was promised by Christianity, but began to be eroded by the events surrounding the reformation and counter-reformation. The French astronomer and physicist Pierre-Simon Laplace (1749–1827), who made seminal contributions to probability theory and was one of the most influential scientists ever, created a fictional being known as Laplace's super-intelligence or demon. The demon, a secularized version of God, knows everything about the past and present, and can deduce the future with certitude. This ideal underlies the first three of the four positions on rationality, even though they seem to be directly opposed to one another. The first two picture human behavior as an approximation to the demon, while the third blames humans for failing to reach this ideal.

I will use the term *omniscience* to refer to this ideal of perfect knowledge (of past and present, not of the future). The mental ability to deduce the future from perfect knowledge requires *unlimited computational power*. To be able to deduce the future with certainty implies that the structure of the world is *deterministic*. Omniscience, unbounded computational abilities, and determinism are ideals that have shaped many theories of rationality. Laplace's demon is fascinating precisely because he is so unlike us. Yet as the Bible tells us, God created humans in his own image. In my opinion, social science took this model too seriously and, in many a theory, recreated us in close proximity of that image.

Unbounded rationality

The demon's nearest relative is a being with "unbounded rationality" or "full rationality." For an unboundedly rational person, the world is no longer fully predictable, that is, the experienced world is not deterministic. Unlike the demon, unboundedly rational beings make errors. Yet it is assumed that they can find the *optimal* (best) strategy – that is, the one that maximizes some criterion (such as correct predictions, monetary gains, or happiness) and minimizes error. The seventeenth-century French mathematicians Blaise Pascal and Pierre Fermat have been credited with this more modest view of rationality, defined as the maximization of the expected value, later changed to the maximization of expected utility by Daniel Bernoulli (Hacking, 1975; Gigerenzer et al., 1989). In unbounded rationality, *optimization* (such as maximization) replaces determinism, whereas the assumptions of omniscience and unlimited computational power are maintained. I will use the term "optimization" in the following way:

> *Optimization* refers to a *strategy* for solving a problem, not to an *outcome*. An optimal strategy is the *best* for a given class of problems (but not necessarily

Gerd Gigerenzer

a perfect one, for it can lead to errors). To refer to a strategy as optimal, one must be able to prove that there is no better strategy (although there can be equally good ones).

Because of their lack of psychological realism, theories that assume unbounded rationality are often called *as-if* theories. They do not aim at describing the actual cognitive processes, but are only concerned with predicting behavior. In this program of research, the question is: If people were omniscient and had all the necessary time and computational power to optimize, how would they behave? The preference for unbounded rationality is widespread. This is illustrated by some consequentionalist theories of moral action, which assume that people consider (or should consider) the consequences of all possible actions for all other people before choosing the action with the best consequences for the largest number of people (Williams, 1988). It is illustrated by theories of cognitive consistency, which assume that our minds check each new belief for consistency with all previous beliefs encountered and perfectly memorized; theories of optimal foraging, which assume that animals have perfect knowledge of the distribution of food and of competitors; and economic theories that assume that actors or firms know all relevant options, consequences, benefits, costs, and probabilities.

Optimization under constraints

Unbounded rationality ignores the constraints imposed on human beings. A *constraint* refers to a limited mental or environmental resource. Limited memory span is a constraint of the mind, and information cost is a constraint on the environment. The term *optimization under constraints* refers to a class of theories that assume that one or several constraints exist.

Lack of omniscience – together with its consequence, the need to search for information – is the key issue in optimization under constraints, whereas the absence of search is a defining feature of theories of unbounded rationality. Models of search specify a searching direction (where to look for information) and a stopping rule (when to stop search). The prototype is Wald's (1950) sequential decision theory. In Stigler's (1961) classical example, a customer wants to buy a used car. He continues to visit used car dealers until the expected costs of further search exceed its expected benefits. Here, search takes place in the environment. Similarly, in Anderson's (1990) rational theory of memory, search for an item in memory continues until the expected costs of further search exceed the expected benefits. Here, search occurs inside the mind. In each case, omniscience is dropped but optimization is retained: the stopping point is the optimal cost-benefit trade-off.

Optimization and realism can inhibit one another, with a paradoxical consequence. Each new realistic constraint makes optimization calculations more difficult, and eventually impossible. The ideal of optimization, in turn, can undermine the attempt to make a theory more realistic by demanding new unrealistic assumptions – such as the knowledge concerning cost and benefits necessary for estimating the optimal stopping point. As a consequence, models of optimization under constraints tend to be more complex than models of unbounded rationality, depicting people in the image of econometricians (Sargent, 1993). This unresolved paradox is one reason why constraints are often ignored and theories of unbounded rationality preferred. Since economists and biologists (wrongly) tend to equate optimization under constraints with *bounded rationality*, bounded rationality is often dismissed as an unpromisingly complicated enterprise and ultimately nothing but full rationality in disguise (Arrow, 2004). Theories of optimization under constraints tend to be presented as as-if theories, with the goal of predicting behavior but not the mental process – just as models of unbounded rationality do.

Heuristics and biases: cognitive illusions

Unbounded rationality and optimization under constraints conceive of humans as essentially rational. This is sometimes justified by the regulating forces of the market, by natural selection, or by legal institutions that eliminate irrational behavior. The "heuristics and biases" or "cognitive illusions" program (Kahneman et al., 1982; Gilovich et al., 2002) opposes theories assuming that humans are basically rational. It has two stated goals. The main goal is to understand the cognitive processes that produce both valid and invalid judgments. Its second goal (or method to achieve the first one) is to demonstrate errors of judgment, that is, systematic deviations from rationality also known as cognitive illusions (Kahneman and Tversky, 1996, p. 582). The cognitive processes underlying these errors are called heuristics, and the major three proposed are representativeness, availability, and anchoring and adjustment. The program has produced a long list of biases (see Krueger and Funder, 2004). It has shaped many fields, such as social psychology and behavioral decision making, and helped to create new fields such as behavioral economics and behavioral law and economics.

Although the heuristics-and-biases program disagrees with rational theories on whether or not people follow some norm of rationality, it does not question the norms themselves. Rather, it retains the norms and interprets deviations from these norms as cognitive illusions: "The presence of an error of judgment is demonstrated by comparing people's responses either with an established fact … or with an accepted rule of arithmetic, logic, or statistics" (Kahneman and Tversky, 1982, p. 493). For instance, when Wason and Johnson-Laird (1972) criticized Piaget's logical theory of thinking as descriptively incorrect, they nevertheless retained the same logical standards as normatively correct for the behavior studied. When Tversky and Kahneman (1983) reported that people's reasoning violated the laws of logic ("conjunction rule"), they nevertheless retained logic as the norm for rational judgment.

The heuristics-and-biases program correctly argues that people's judgments do in fact systematically deviate from the content-blind laws of logic or optimization. But it has hesitated to take two necessary further steps: to rethink the norms, and to provide testable theories of heuristics. The laws of logic and probability are neither necessary nor sufficient for rational behavior in the real world (see below), and mere verbal labels for heuristics can be used post hoc to "explain" almost everything.

The term "bounded rationality" has been used both by proponents of optimization under constraints, emphasizing rationality, and by the heuristics-and-biases program, emphasizing irrationality. Even more confusing is the fact that the term was coined by Herbert A. Simon, who was not referring to optimization or irrationality, but to

Gerd Gigerenzer

an ecological view of rationality (see next section), which was revolutionary in thinking about norms, not just behavior (Simon, 1956; Selten, 2001; Gigerenzer, 2004b).

The science of heuristics: ecological rationality

The starting point for the science of heuristics is the relation between mind and environment, rather than between mind and logic (Gigerenzer et al., 1999; Gigerenzer and Selten, 2001). Humans have evolved in natural environments, both social and physical. To survive, reproduce, and evolve, the task is to adapt to these environments, or else to change them. Piaget called these two fundamental processes assimilation and accommodation, but he continued to focus on logic. The structure of natural environments, however, is ecological rather than logical. In Simon's (1990) words: "Human rational behavior is shaped by a scissors whose two blades are the structure of task environments and the computational capabilities of the actor" (p. 7). Just as one cannot understand how scissors cut by looking only at one blade, one will not understand human behavior by studying cognition or the environment alone.

The two key concepts are *adaptive toolbox* and *ecological rationality*. The analysis of the adaptive toolbox is descriptive, whereas that of ecological rationality is normative. The adaptive toolbox contains the *building blocks* for *fast and frugal heuristics*. A heuristic is fast if it can solve a problem in little time, and frugal if it can solve it with little information. Unlike as-if optimization models, heuristics can find good solutions independent of whether an optimal solution exists. As a consequence, one does not need to "edit" a real world problem in order to make it accessible to the optimization calculus (e.g., by limiting the number of competitors and choice alternatives, by providing quantitative probabilities and utilities, or by ignoring constraints). Heuristics work in real-world environments of natural complexity, where an optimal strategy is typically unknown.

The study of ecological rationality answers the question: In what environments will a given heuristic work? Where will it fail? Note that this normative question can only be answered if there is a process model of the heuristic in the first place, and the results are gained by proof or simulation. As mentioned beforehand, the ecological rationality of a verbal label such as representativeness cannot be determined. At most one can say that representativeness is sometimes good and sometimes bad – without being able to explicate the "sometimes."

Let me illustrate the difference between the adaptive toolbox program and the previous visions of rationality with the example of problem solving in baseball and cricket.

How does an outfielder catch a flyball? In Richard Dawkins' words: "When a man throws a ball high in the air and catches it again, he behaves as if he had solved a set of differential equations in predicting the trajectory of the ball" (1989, p. 96). Note that Dawkins invokes a form of omniscience. The trajectory of a ball is determined by a number of causal factors, including the ball's initial velocity, angle, and distance from the player; the air resistance; the speed and direction of the wind at each point of the trajectory, and spin. An unboundedly rational player would measure all causally relevant factors for computing the ball's trajectory in no time, would know the optimal formula to compute the trajectory, and run to the point where the ball lands. A player who optimizes under constraints would not be able to measure all factors given the time constraint of a few seconds, but would know the optimal formula to compute the trajectory given these constraints. These are as-if theories. Real humans perform poorly in estimating the location where the ball will strike the ground (Saxberg, 1987; Babler and Dannemiller, 1993). Note also that as-if theories have limited practical use for instructing novice players or building a robot player. The heuristics-and-biases program might respond with an experiment demonstrating that experienced players make systematic errors in estimating the point where the ball lands, such as underestimating the distance to the player. Tentatively, these errors might be attributed to player's overconfidence bias or optimism bias (underestimating the distance creates a false certainty that one can actually catch a ball). The demonstration of a discrepancy between judgment and norm, however, does not lead to an explanation of how players actually catch a ball. One reason for this is that the critique is merely descriptive, that is, what players can do, and does not extend to the norm, that is, what players should do. The norm is the same – to compute the trajectory correctly, requiring knowledge of the causal factors.

Yet it is time to rethink the norms, such as the ideal of omniscience. The normative challenge is that real humans do not need a full representation and unlimited computational power. In my view, humans have an adaptive toolbox at their disposal, which may contain heuristics that can catch balls in a fast and frugal way. Thus, the research question is: Is there a fast and frugal heuristic that can solve the problem? Experiments have shown that experienced players in fact use several heuristics (e.g., McLeod and Dienes, 1996). One of these is the *gaze heuristic*, which works only when the ball is already high up in the air:

> *Gaze heuristic*: Fixate your gaze on the ball, start running, and adjust your speed so that the angle of gaze remains constant.

The angle of gaze is between the eye and the ball, relative to the ground. The gaze heuristic ignores all causally relevant factors when estimating the ball's trajectory. It attends to only one variable: the angle of gaze. This heuristic belongs to the class of *one-reason decision making heuristics*. A player relying on this heuristic cannot predict where the ball will land, but the heuristic will lead him to that spot. In other words, computing the trajectory is not necessary; it is not an appropriate norm. The use of heuristics crosses species borders. People rely on the gaze heuristic and related heuristics in sailing and flying to avoid collisions with other boats or planes; and bats, birds, and flies use the same heuristics for predation and pursuit (Shaffer et al., 2004).

To repeat, the gaze heuristic consists of three building blocks: fixate your gaze on the ball, start running, and adjust running speed. These building blocks can be part of other heuristics, too.

> *Definition*: A fast and frugal heuristic is a (conscious or unconscious) strategy that searches for minimal information and consists of building blocks that exploit evolved abilities and environmental structures.

Heuristics can be highly effective because they are anchored in the evolved brain and in the external environment. Let me explain.

Embodiment: heuristics exploit evolved abilities. For instance, the first building block "fixate your gaze on the ball" exploits the evolved ability of *object tracking*, in this

Gerd Gigerenzer

case, to track a moving object against a noisy background. It is easy for humans to do this; 3-month-old babies can already hold their gaze on moving targets (Rosander and Hofsten, 2002). Tracking objects, however, is difficult for a robot; a computer program that can track objects as well as a human mind can does not yet exist. Thus, the gaze heuristic is simple for humans but not for today's generation of robots. The standard definition of optimization as computing the maximum or minimum of a function, however, ignores the "hardware" of the human brain. In contrast, a heuristic exploits hard-wired or learned cognitive and motor processes, and these abilities make it simple. This is the first reason why fast and frugal heuristics can, in the real world, be superior to some optimization strategy.

Situatedness: heuristics exploit structures of environments. The rationality of heuristics is not logical, but ecological. The study of the ecological rationality of a heuristic answers the normative question concerning the environments in which a heuristic will succeed and in which it will fail. It specifies the class of problems a given heuristic can solve (Martignon and Hoffrage, 1999; Goldstein et al., 2001). Ecological rationality implies that a heuristic is not good or bad, rational or irrational per se, but only relative to an environment. It can exploit certain structures of environments or change them. For instance, the gaze heuristic transforms the complex trajectory of the ball in the environment into a straight line.

Note that as-if optimization theories – because they ignore the human mind – are formulated more or less independently of the hardware of the brain. Any computer can compute the maximum of a function. Heuristics, in contrast, exploit the specific hardware and are dependent on it. Social heuristics, for instance, exploit the evolved or learned abilities of humans for cooperation, reciprocal altruism, and identification (Laland, 2001). The principles of embodiment and situatedness are also central for "New AI" (Brooks, 2002). For an introduction to the study of fast and frugal heuristics, see Payne et al., 1993; Gigerenzer et al., 1999; and Gigerenzer and Selten 2001.

The Problem With Content-Blind Norms

In the heuristics-and-biases program, a norm is typically a law (axiom, rule) of logic or probability rather than a full optimization model. A law of logic or probability is used as a *content-blind norm* for a problem if the "rational" solution is determined independently of its content. For instance, the truth table of the material implication *if P then Q* is defined independently of the content of the Ps and Qs. The definition is in terms of a specific syntax. By content, I mean the semantics (what are the Ps and Qs?) and the pragmatics (what is the goal?). The heuristics-and-biases program of studying whether people's judgments deviate from content-blind norms proceeds in four steps:

1 *Syntax first*: Start with a law of logic or probability.
2 *Add semantics and pragmatics*: Replace the logical terms (e.g., material implication, mathematical probability) by English terms (e.g., if . . . then; probable), add content, and define a problem to be solved.
3 *Content-blind norm*: Use the syntax to define the "rational" answer to the problem. Ignore semantics and pragmatics.

4 *Cognitive illusion*: If people's judgments deviate from the "rational" answer, call the discrepancy a cognitive illusion. Attribute it to some deficit in the human mind (not to your norms).

Content-blind norms derive from an internalist conception of rationality. Examples are the use of the material implication as a norm for reasoning about any content (Wason and Johnson-Laird, 1972), the set-inclusion or "conjunction rule" (Tversky and Kahneman, 1983), and Bayes's rule (Kahneman and Frederick, 2002; see also Matheson, chapter 8, BOUNDED RATIONALITY AND THE ENLIGHTENMENT PICTURE OF COGNITIVE VIRTUE). Proponents of content-blind norms do not use this term, but instead speak of "universal principles of logic, arithmetic, and probability calculus" that tell us what we should think (Piatelli-Palmarini, 1994, p. 158). Consider the material implication.

In 1966, the British psychologist Peter Wason invented the *selection task*, also known as the *four-card problem*, to study reasoning about conditional statements. This was to become the most frequently studied task in the psychology of reasoning. Wason's starting point was the material implication $P \rightarrow Q$, as defined by the truth table in elementary logic. In the second step, the Ps and Qs are substituted by some content, such as "numbers" (odd/even) and "letters" (consonants/vowels). The material implication "$\rightarrow$" is replaced by the English terms "if . . . then," and a rule is introduced: "If there is an even number on one side of the card, there is a consonant on the other." Four cards are placed on the table, showing an even number, an odd number, a consonant, and a vowel on the surface side. People are asked which cards need to be turned around in order to see whether the rule has been violated. In the third step, the "correct" answer is defined by the truth table: to turn around the P and the not-Q card, and nothing else, because the material conditional is false if and only if $P \cap \neg Q$. However, in a series of experiments, most people picked other combinations of cards, which was evaluated as a reasoning error, due to some cognitive illusion. In subsequent experiments, it was found that the cards picked depended on the content of the Ps and Qs, and this was labeled the "content effect." Taken together, these results were interpreted as a demonstration of human irrationality and a refutation of Piaget's theory of operational thinking. Ironically, as mentioned before, Wason and Johnson-Laird (1972) and their followers held up truth-table logic as normative even after they criticized it as descriptively false.

Are content-blind norms reasonable norms? Should one's reasoning always follow truth-table logic, the conjunction rule, Bayes's rule, the law of large numbers, or some other syntactic law, irrespective of the content of the problem? The answer is no, and for several reasons. A most elementary point is that English terms such as "if . . . then" are not identical to logical terms such as the material conditional "$\rightarrow$" (Fillenbaum, 1977). This confusion is sufficient to reject logic as a content-blind norm. More interesting, adaptive behavior has other goals than logical truth or consistency, such as dealing intelligently with other people. For instance, according to Trivers' (1971, 2002) theory of reciprocal altruism, each human possesses altruistic and cheating tendencies. Therefore, one goal in a social contract is to search for information revealing whether one has been cheated by the other party (Cosmides, 1989). Note that the perspective is essential: you want to find out whether you were cheated by the other party, not whether you cheated the other. Logic, in contrast, is without

Gerd Gigerenzer

perspective. Consider a four-cards task whose content is a social contract between an employer and an employee (Gigerenzer and Hug, 1992):

If a previous employee gets a pension from the firm, then that person must have worked for the firm for at least ten years.

The four cards read: got a pension, worked ten years for the firm, did not get a pension, worked eight years for the firm. One group of participants was cued into the role of the employer, and asked to check those cards (representing files of previous employees) that could reveal whether the rule was violated. The far majority picked "got a pension" and "worked for eight years." Note that this choice is consistent with both the laws of the truth table and the goal of cheater detection. Proponents of content-blind norms (mis-)interpreted this and similar results as indicating that social contracts somehow facilitated logical reasoning. But when we cued the participants into the role of an employee, the far majority picked "did not get a pension" and "worked for ten years." (In contrast, in the employer's group, no participant had checked this information.) Now the result was inconsistent with the truth table, but, from the employee's perspective, again consistent with the goal of not being cheated. Search for information was Machiavellian: to avoid being cheated oneself, not avoiding cheating others.

The perspective experiment clearly demonstrates that logical thinking is not central to human reasoning about these problems, as well as that truth-table logic is an inappropriate norm (Cosmides and Tooby, 1992; Gigerenzer, 2000). Yet several decades and hundreds of thousands of dollars of grant money have been wasted trying to show that human thinking violates the laws of logic. We have learned next to nothing about the nature of thinking or other cognitive processes. The same holds for research on other content-blind norms (Gigerenzer, 1996, 2001). Inappropriate norms tend to suggest wrong questions, and the answers to these generate more confusion than insight into the nature of human judgment (Gigerenzer, 2000). My point is not new. Wilhelm Wundt (1912/1973), known as the father of experimental psychology, concluded that logical norms have little to do with thought processes, and that attempts to apply them to learn about psychological processes have been absolutely fruitless. But at least some psychologists have learned. For instance, Lance Rips, who had argued that deductive logic might play a central rule in cognitive architecture (Rips, 1994), declared that he would not defend this "imperialist" theory anymore (Rips, 2002).

The Ecological Rationality of Heuristics

Is there an alternative to optimization and content-blind norms? The alternatives are external forms of rationality, where reasonableness is measured by the actual success in solving problems. Success has several aspects, depending on the problem. These include predictive accuracy of a strategy, how much information it needs to search, and how fast it leads to a decision – in some situations, to act now is better than to wait until the best action is found. Ecological rationality can be expressed in comparative terms: a given heuristic performs better in environment A than in B. For instance, imitation of others' successful behavior (as opposed to individual learning) works in environments that change slowly, but not in environments under rapid change (Boyd and Richerson, 2001). Ecological rationality can also be analyzed in quantitative terms: a heuristic will make 80 percent correct predictions in environment E, and requires only 30 percent of the information.

The ecological rationality of a heuristic is conditional on an environment. Content-blind norms, in contrast, are defined without consideration of any environment. Ecological rationality is comparative or quantitative; it is not necessarily about the best strategy. This provides it with an advantage: ecological rationality can be determined in all situations where optimization is out of reach, and one does not need to edit the problem so that optimization can be applied. In what follows, I describe the ecological rationality of three classes of heuristics. For a more extensive analysis, see Gigerenzer et al., 1999; Goldstein et al., 2001; and Smith, 2003.

Recognition heuristic

Daniel Goldstein and I asked American and German students the following question (Goldstein and Gigerenzer, 2002):

> Which city has more inhabitants: San Diego or San Antonio?

Sixty-two percent of Americans answered correctly: San Diego. The Germans knew little of San Diego, and many had never heard of San Antonio. What percentage of the more ignorant Germans found the right answer? One hundred percent. How can people who know less make more correct inferences? The answer is that the Germans used the *recognition heuristic*:

> If you recognize one city, but not the other, infer that it has the larger population.

The Americans could not use this heuristic. They knew too much. The Americans had heard of both cities, and had to rely on their recall knowledge. Exploiting the wisdom in partial ignorance, the recognition heuristic is an example of ignorance-based decision making. It guides behavior in a large variety of situations: rats choose food they recognize on the breath of a fellow rat and tend to avoid novel food; children tend to approach people they recognize and avoid those they don't; teenagers tend to buy CDs of bands whose name they have heard of; adults tend to buy products whose brand name they recognize; participants in large conferences tend to watch out for faces they recognize; university departments sometimes hire professors by name recognition; and institutions, colleges, and companies compete for a place in the public's recognition memory through advertisement.

Like all heuristics, the recognition heuristic works better in certain environments than in others. The question of when it works is the question of its ecological rationality:

> The recognition heuristic is ecologically rational in environments where the recognition validity α is larger than chance: $\alpha > 0.5$.

The validity α is defined as the proportion of cases where a recognized object has a higher criterion value (such as population) than the unrecognized object, for a given set of objects. This provides a quantitative measure for ecological rationality.

Gerd Gigerenzer

For instance, α is typically around 0.8 for inferring population (Goldstein and Gigerenzer, 2002), 0.7 for inferring who will win a Grand Slam tennis match (Serwe and Frings, 2004), and 0.6 for inferring disease prevalence (Pachur and Hertwig, 2004).

Take The Best

As a second illustration of ecological rationality, consider a heuristic from the family of one-reason decision-making. The task is to infer which of two objects has a higher value on a criterion, based on binary cues. The heuristic is called Take The Best, because it relies on only one cue to make this inference, the cue with the highest validity on which the objects differ. The rest of the cues are ignored. Take The Best has three building blocks, a search rule, stopping rule, and decision rule:

1   *Search rule*: Search through cues in order of their validity. Look up the cue values of the cue with the highest validity first.
2   *Stopping rule*: If one object has a positive cue value and the other does not (or is unknown), then stop search and proceed to Step 3. Otherwise exclude this cue and return to Step 1. If no more cues are found, guess.
3   *Decision rule*: Predict that the object with the positive cue value has the higher value on the criterion.

The validity of a cue i is defined as $v_i = R_i/P_i$, where R_i = number of correct predictions by cue i, and P_i = number of pairs where the values of cue i differ between objects.

When is relying on only one cue rational? Consider an environment with M binary cues ordered according to their weights W_j (such as beta weights), with $1 \leq j \leq M$. A set of cue weights is noncompensatory if for every weight:

$$W_j > \sum_{k>j} W_k$$

I refer to this environmental structure as *noncompensatory information*. An example is the set of weights 1, $^1/_2$, $^1/_4$, $^1/_8$, and so on. The sum of the cue weights to the right of a cue can never be larger than this cue's weight – the sum cannot compensate for a cue with a higher weight. Here, Take The Best makes the same inferences as any linear strategy (with the same order of weights). Thus, we get the following result (Martignon and Hoffrage, 1999):

> In an environment with non-compensatory information, no linear strategy can outperform the faster and more frugal Take The Best heuristic.

A second environmental structure that Take The Best can exploit is scarce information:

$$M < \log_2 N,$$

where M and N are the number of cues and objects, respectively (Martignon and Hoffrage, 2002). An example of scarce information is a sample with 30 objects measured on 5 cues or predictors ($\log_2 30 < 5$). Related environmental structures are discussed in Hogarth and Karelaia, 2005. Consistent with these results, Take The Best and other one-reason decision making heuristics have been proven to be, on average, more accurate than multiple regression in making various economic, demographic, environmental, and health forecasts, as well as in the prediction of heart attacks (Green and Mehr, 1997; Czerlinski et al., 1999). Todorov (2003) showed that Take The Best predicted the outcomes of basketball games during the 1996/97 NBA season as accurately as Bayes's rule did, but with less information. Chater et al. (2003) demonstrated that Take The Best matched highly complex computational methods such as a three-layer feedforward connectionist network, Quinlan's (1993) decision three algorithm, and two exemplar-based models, Nearest Neighbor and Nosofsky's (1990) Generalized Context Model. When the environment had scarce information, specifically when the training set included less than 40 percent of all objects, Take The Best was more accurate than any of these computationally expensive strategies. The effectiveness of one-reason decision making has been demonstrated, among others, in the diagnosis of heart attacks (Green and Mehr, 1997) and in the simple heuristic for prescribing antibiotics to children (Fischer et al., 2002).

Follow the majority

Social heuristics exploit the capacity of humans for social learning and imitation (imitation need not result in learning), which is unmatched among the animal species. For instance, just like the recognition heuristic, the following social heuristic allows an individual to act with only a surface analysis of the situation:

> *Do-what-the-majority-do heuristic*: If you see the majority of your peers display a behavior, engage in the same behavior.

This simple social heuristic seems to cause a broad range of adaptive behaviors (Laland, 2001). It saves an organism from having to extract information anew from the environment, and hence starting from scratch. It facilitates the spread of cultural behavior, from religious ceremonies to rules of conduct to riots against minorities. Imitating the majority – as opposed to imitating one skilled individual – is characteristic of adaptive behaviors related to social issues, such as moral and political actions (Gigerenzer, 2004a). Studies have reported behavior copying in animals and humans. Dugatkin (1992) argued that female guppies choose between males by copying the mate preferences of other females. In modern human societies, teenagers admire a movie star because everyone else in their peer group adulates that person. Advertisement exploits this heuristic by portraying a product surrounded by many admirers (not just one). People may display disgust for members of a minority because they notice that most of their peers do the same. A man may start thinking of marriage at a time when most other men in his social group do, say, around age 30. Copying the behavior of one's peers is a most frugal heuristic, for it almost guarantees the peer group's approbation, is sometimes even a condition for peer acceptance, and one does not need to consider the pros and cons of one's behavior.

Do-what-the-majority-do tends to be ecologically rational in situations where:

1 the observer and the demonstrators of the behavior are exposed to similar environments, such as social systems;
2 the environment is stable or changing slowly rather than quickly;
3 the environment is noisy and consequences are not immediate, that is, it is hard or time-consuming to figure out whether a choice is good or bad, such as which political or moral system is preferable (Boyd and Richerson, 1985; Goldstein et al., 2001).

In environments where these conditions do not hold, copying the behavior of the majority can lead to disaster. For instance, copying the production and distribution systems of traditional firms can be detrimental when an economy changes from local to globalized.

Cognitive Luck

In this volume, Matheson discusses the study of ecological (bounded) rationality as a way to overcome the epistemic internalism of the Enlightenment tradition. But he raises a worry:

> If cognitive virtue is located outside the mind in the way that the Post-Enlightenment Picture suggests, then it turns out to be something bestowed on us by features of the world not under our control: it involves an intolerable degree of something analogous to what theoretical ethicists call "moral luck"... [cf. Williams, 1981; Nagel, 1993] – "cognitive luck," we might say. (Matheson, chapter 8, p. 143)

This worry is based on the assumption that internal ways to improve cognition are under our control, whereas the external ones are not.

This assumption, however, is often incorrect, and reveals a limit of an internalist view of cognitive virtue. I conjecture that changing environments can in fact be easier than changing minds. Consider the serious problem of innumerate physicians, as illustrated by screening for colorectal cancer. A man tests positive on the FOB (fecal occult blood) test and asks the physician what the probability is that he actually has cancer. What do physicians tell that worried man? We (Hoffrage and Gigerenzer, 1998) gave exper-ienced physicians the best estimates of base rate (0.3 percent), sensitivity (50 percent), and false positive rate (3 percent), and asked them to estimate the probability of colorectal cancer given a positive test. Their estimates ranged between 1 percent and 99 percent. If patients knew about this variability, they would be rightly scared.

This result illustrates a larger problem: When physicians try to draw a conclusion from probabilities, their minds typically cloud over (Gigerenzer, 2002). What can be done to correct this? An internalist might recommend training physicians to use Bayes's rule in order to compute the posterior probability. In theory, this training should work wonders, but in reality, it does not. One week after students successfully passed such a course, for instance, their performance was already down by 50 percent, and it continued to fade away week by week (Sedlmeier and Gigerenzer, 2001). Moreover, the chance of convincing physicians to take a statistics course in the first place is almost nil; most have no time or little motivation, while others believe they are incurably innumerate. Are we stuck for eternity with innumerate physicians? No. In the ecological view, thinking does not happen simply in the mind, but in interaction between the mind and its environment. This adds a second, and more efficient, way to improve the situation: to edit the environment. The relevant part of the environment is the representation of the information, because the representation does part of the Bayesian computation. Natural (non-normalized) frequencies are such an efficient representation; they mimic the way information has been encountered before the advent of writing and statistics, throughout most of human evolution. For instance: 30 out of every 10,000 people have colorectal cancer, 15 of these will have a positive test; of the remaining people without colorectal cancer, 300 will still have a positive test. When we presented the numerical information in natural frequencies as opposed to conditional probabilities, then the huge variability in physicians' judgments disappeared. They all gave reasonable estimates, with the majority hitting exactly on the Bayesian posterior of about 5 percent, or 1 in 20.

Similarly, by changing the environment, we can make many so-called cognitive illusions largely disappear (Gigerenzer, 2000), enable fifth and sixth graders to solve Bayesian problems before they even heard of probabilities (Zhu and Gigerenzer, forthcoming), and help judges and law students understand DNA evidence (Hoffrage et al., 2000). Thus, an ecological view actually extends the possibilities to improve judgment, whereas an internal view limits the chances. To summarize, the term "cognitive luck" only makes sense from an internalist view, where luck in fact refers to the theory's ignorance concerning the environment, including the social environment. From an ecological view, environmental structures, not luck, directly influence cognition and can be designed to improve it. Cognitive virtue is, in my view, a relation between a mind and its environment, very much like the notion of ecological rationality (see also Bishop, 2000).

What Is the Rationality of Homo Sapiens?

What makes us so smart? I have discussed four answers. The first is that we are smart because we behave as if we were omniscient and had unlimited computational power to find the optimal strategy for each problem. This is the beautiful fiction of unbounded rationality. The second is a modification of the first that diminishes omniscience by introducing the need for searching for information and the resulting costs, but insists on the ideal of optimization. These two programs define the theories in much of economics, biology, philosophy, and the social sciences. Both have an antipsychological bias: they try to define rational behavior without psychology, promoting as-if theories. The assumption is that one can predict behavior while ignoring what we know about the human mind, an assumption that is not always true. In the image of Laplace's demon, *Homo economicus* has defined *Homo sapiens*: we are basically rational beings, and the nature of our rationality can be understood through the fictions of omniscience and optimization. The heuristics-and-biases program has attacked that position, but only on the descriptive level, using content-blind norms as the yardstick to diagnose human irrationality. The result has been that we are mostly or sometimes – the quantifiers keep changing – irrational, committing systematic errors of reasoning.

There is now a literature that tries to determine which of these positions is correct. Are we rational or irrational? Or perhaps 80 percent rational and 20 percent irrational? Some blessed peacemakers propose that the truth is in the middle and we are a little of both, so there is no real disagreement. For instance, the debate between Kahneman and Tversky and myself (e.g., Gigerenzer, 1996; Kahneman and Tversky, 1996) has been sometimes misunderstood as concerning the question of *how much* rationality or irrationality people have. In this view, rationality is like a glass of water, and Kahneman and Tversky see the glass as half empty, whereas I see it as half full. For instance, Samuels et al. conclude their call for "ending the rationality war" with the assertion that the two parties "do not have any deep disagreement over the extent of human rationality" (2004, p. 264). However, the issue is not quantity, but quality: *what* exactly rationality and irrationality are in the first place. We can easily agree how often experiment participants have violated the truth-table logic or some other logical law in an experimental task, and how often not. But proponents of the heuristics-and-biases program count the first as human irrationality, and the second as rationality. I do not. I believe that we need a better understanding of human rationality than relative to content-blind norms. These were of little relevance for *Homo sapiens*, who had to adapt to a social and physical world, not to systems with content-free syntax, such as the laws of logic.

The concept of ecological rationality is my answer to the question of the nature of *Homo sapiens*. It defines the rationality of heuristics independently of optimization and content-blind norms, by the degree to which they are adapted to environments. The study of ecological rationality facilitates understanding a variety of counter-intuitive phenomena, including when one reason is better than many, when less is more, and when partial ignorance pays. *Homo sapiens* has been characterized as a tool-user. There is some deeper wisdom in that phrase. The tools that make us smart are not bones and stones, but the heuristics in the adaptive toolbox.

References

Anderson, J. R. (1990). *The Adaptive Character of Thought*. Hillsdale, NJ: Erlbaum.

Arrow, K. J. (2004). Is bounded rationality unboundedly rational? Some ruminations. In M. Augier and J. G. March (eds.), *Models of a Man: Essays in Memory of Herbert A. Simon*. Cambridge, MA: MIT Press.

Babler, T. G. and Dannemiller, J. L. (1993). Role of image acceleration in judging landing location of free-falling projectiles. *Journal of Experimental Psychology: Human Perception and Performance*, 19, 15–31.

Bishop, M. A. (2000). In praise of epistemic irresponsibility: How lazy and ignorant can you be? *Synthese*, 122, 179–208.

Boyd, R. and Richerson, P. J. (1985). *Culture and the Evolutionary Process*. Chicago: University of Chicago Press.

— and — (2001). Norms and bounded rationality. In G. Gigerenzer and R. Selten (eds.), *Bounded Rationality: The Adaptive Toolbox*. Cambridge, MA: MIT Press.

Brooks, R. (2002). *Robot: The Future of Flesh and Machines*. London: Penguin Books.

Chater, N., Oaksford, M., Nakisa, R., and Redington, M. (2003). Fast, frugal, and rational: How rational norms explain behavior. *Organizational Behavior and Human Decision Processes*, 90, 63–86.

Cohen, L. J. (1981). Can human irrationality be experimentally demonstrated? *Behavioral and Brain Sciences*, 4, 317–70.

Cosmides, L. (1989). The logic of social exchange: Has natural selection shaped how humans reason? Studies with the Wason selection task. *Cognition*, 31, 187–276.

Cosmides, L. and Tooby, J. (1992). Cognitive adaptions for social exchange. In J. H. Barkow, L. Cosmides, and J. Tooby (eds.), *The Adapted Mind: Evolutionary Psychology and the Generation of Culture*. New York: Oxford University Press.

Czerlinski, J., Gigerenzer, G., and Goldstein, D. G. (1999). How good are simple heuristics? In G. Gigerenzer, P. M. Todd, and the ABC Research Group, *Simple Heuristics that Make Us Smart*. New York: Oxford University Press.

Daston, L. (1988). *Classical Probability in the Enlightenment*. Princeton, NJ: Princeton University Press.

Dawkins, R. (1989). *The Selfish Gene* (2nd edn.). Oxford: Oxford University Press.

Dugatkin, L. A. (1992). Sexual selection and imitation: Females copy the mate choice of others. *The American Naturalist*, 139, 1384–9.

Fillenbaum, S. (1977). Mind your p's and q's: the role of content and context in some uses of and, or, and if. *Psychology of Learning and Motivation*, 11, 41–100.

Fischer, J. E., Steiner, F., Zucol, F., et al. (2002). Use of simple heuristics to target macrolide prescription in children with community-acquired pneumonia. *Archives of Pediatrics and Adolescent Medicine*, 156, 1005–8.

Gigerenzer, G. (1996). On narrow norms and vague heuristics: A reply to Kahneman and Tversky (1996). *Psychological Review*, 103, 592–6.

— (2000). *Adaptive Thinking: Rationality in the Real World*. New York: Oxford University Press.

— (2001). Content-blind norms, no norms, or good norms? A reply to Vranas. *Cognition*, 81, 93–103.

— (2002). *Calculated Risks: How to Know When Numbers Deceive You*. New York: Simon and Schuster. (Published in UK as *Reckoning with Risk: Learning to Live with Uncertainty*. London: Penguin Books.)

— (2004a). Fast and frugal heuristics: The tools of bounded rationality. In D. Koehler and N. Harvey (eds.), *Handbook of Judgment and Decision Making*. Oxford: Blackwell.

— (2004b). Striking a blow for sanity in theories of rationality. In R. B. Augier and J. G. March (eds.), *Models of a Man: Essays in Honor of Herbert A. Simon*. Cambridge, MA: MIT Press.

Gigerenzer, G. and Hug, K. (1992). Domain-specific reasoning: Social contracts, cheating, and perspective change. *Cognition*, 43, 127–71.

Gigerenzer, G. and Selten, R. (eds.) (2001). *Bounded Rationality: The Adaptive Toolbox*. Cambridge, MA: MIT Press.

Gigerenzer, G., Swijtink, Z., Porter, T., Daston, L., Beatty, J., and Krüger, L. (1989). *The Empire of Chance: How Probability Changed Science and Everyday Life*. Cambridge: Cambridge University Press.

Gigerenzer, G., Todd, P. M., and the ABC Research Group (1999). *Simple Heuristics that Make Us Smart.* New York: Oxford University Press.

Gilovich, T., Vallone, R., and Tversky, A. (1985). The hot hand in basketball: On the misconception of random sequences. *Cognitive Psychology*, 17, 295–314.

Goldstein, D. G. and Gigerenzer, G. (2002). Models of ecological rationality: The recognition heuristic. *Psychological Review*, 109, 75–90.

Goldstein, D. G., Gigerenzer, G., Hogarth, R. M., et al. (2001). Group report: Why and when do simple heuristics work? In G. Gigerenzer and R. Selten (eds.), *Bounded Rationality: The Adaptive Toolbox.* Cambridge, MA: MIT Press.

Green, L. and Mehr, D. R. (1997). What alters physicians' decisions to admit to the coronary care unit? *Journal of Family Practice*, 45, 219–26.

Gruber, H. E. and Vonèche, J. J. (1977). *The Essential Piaget.* New York: Basic Books.

Hacking, I. (1975). *The Emergence of Probability.* Cambridge: Cambridge University Press.

Hoffrage, U. and Gigerenzer, G. (1998). Using natural frequencies to improve diagnostic inferences. *Academic Medicine*, 73, 538–40.

Hoffrage, U., Lindsay, S., Hertwig, R., and Gigerenzer, G. (2000). Communicating statistical information. *Science*, 290, 2261–2.

Hogarth, R. M. and Karelaia, N. (2005). Ignoring information in binary choice with continuous variables: When is less "more"? *Journal of Mathematical Psychology*, 49, 115–25.

Kahneman, D. and Frederick, S. (2002). Representativeness revisited: Attribute substitution in intuitive judgment. In T. Gilovich, D. Griffin, and D. Kahneman (eds.), *Heuristics and Biases: The Psychology of Intuitive Judgment.* New York: Cambridge University Press.

Kahneman, D. and Tversky, A. (1982). On the study of statistical intuitions. In D. Kahneman, P. Slovic, and A. Tversky (eds.), *Judgment Under Uncertainty: Heuristics and Biases.* Cambridge: Cambridge University Press.

— and — (1996). On the reality of cognitive illusions. A reply to Gigerenzer's critique. *Psychological Review*, 103, 582–91.

Kahneman, D., Slovic, P., and Tversky, A. (eds.) (1982). *Judgment Under Uncertainty: Heuristics and Biases.* Cambridge: Cambridge University Press.

Krueger, J. I. and Funder, D. C. (2004). Towards a balanced social psychology: Causes, consequences, and cures for the problem-seeking approach to social behavior and cognition. *Behavioral and Brain Sciences*, 27, 313–27.

Laland, K. (2001). Imitation, social learning, and preparedness as mechanisms of bounded rationality. In G. Gigerenzer and R. Selten (eds.), *Bounded Rationality: The Adaptive Toolbox.* Cambridge, MA: MIT Press.

Lopes, L. L. (1991). The rhetoric of irrationality. *Theory and Psychology*, 1, 65–82.

Martignon, L. and Hoffrage, U. (1999). Why does one-reason decision making work? A case study in ecological rationality. In G. Gigerenzer, P. M. Todd, and the ABC Research Group, *Simple Heuristics that Make Us Smart.* New York: Oxford University Press.

— (2002). Fast, frugal and fit: Lexicographic heuristics for paired comparison. *Theory and Decision*, 52, 29–71.

McLeod, P. and Dienes, Z. (1996). Do fielders know where to go to catch the ball or only how to get there? *Journal of Experimental Psychology: Human Perception and Performance*, 22, 531–43.

Nagel, T. (1993). Moral luck. In D. Statman (ed.), *Moral Luck.* Albany, NY: State University of New York Press.

Nosofsky, R. M. (1990). Relations between exemplar-similarity and likelihood models of classification. *Journal of Mathematical Psychology*, 34, 393–418.

Pachur, T. and Hertwig, R. (2004). *How Adaptive is the Use of the Recognition Heuristic?* Poster session presented at the Annual Meeting of the Society for Judgment and Decision Making, Minneapolis, MN.

Payne, J. W., Bettman, J. R., and Johnson, E. J. (1993). *The Adaptive Decision Maker.* Cambridge: Cambridge University Press.

Piattelli-Palmarini, M. (1994). *Inevitable Illusions: How Mistakes of Reason Rule our Minds.* New York: Wiley.

Quinlan, J. R. (1993). *C4.5: Programs for Machine Learning.* Los Altos, CA: Morgan Kaufmann.

Rips, L. J. (1994). *The Psychology of Proof: Deductive Reasoning in Human Thinking.* Cambridge, MA: MIT Press.

— (2002). Circular reasoning. *Cognitive Science,* 26, 767–95.

Rosander, K. and Hofsten, C. von (2002). Development of gaze tracking of small and large objects. *Experimental Brain Research,* 146, 257–64.

Samuels, R., Stich, S., and Bishop, M. (2004). Ending the rationality wars: How to make disputes about human rationality disappear. In R. Elio (ed.), *Common Sense, Reasoning and Rationality.* New York: Oxford University Press.

Sargent, T. J. (1993). *Bounded Rationality in Macroeconomics.* New York: Oxford University Press.

Saxberg, B. V. H. (1987). Projected free fall trajectories: I. Theory and simulation. *Biological Cybernetics,* 56, 159–75.

Sedlmeier, P. and Gigerenzer, G. (2001). Teaching Bayesian reasoning in less than two hours. *Journal of Experimental Psychology: General,* 130, 380–400.

Selten, R. (2001). What is bounded rationality? In G. Gigerenzer and R. Selten, *Bounded Rationality: The Adaptive Toolbox.* Cambridge, MA: MIT Press.

Serwe, S. and Frings, C. (2004). *Predicting Wimbledon*: Poster presented at the 4th Summer Institute for Bounded Rationality in Psychology and Economics, Berlin.

Shaffer, D. M., Krauchunas, S. M., Eddy, M., and McBeath, M. K. (2004). How dogs navigate to catch frisbees. *Psychological Science,* 15, 437–41.

Simon, H. A. (1956). Rational choice and the structure of environments. *Psychological Review,* 63, 129–38.

— (1990). Invariants of human behavior. *Annual Review of Psychology,* 41, 1–19.

Smith, V. L. (2003). Constructivist and ecological rationality in economics. *The American Economic Review,* 93, 465–508.

Stigler, G. J. (1961). The economics of information. *Journal of Political Economy,* 69, 213–25.

Todorov, A. (2003). Cognitive procedures for correcting proxy-response biases in surveys. *Applied Cognitive Psychology,* 17, 215–24.

Trivers, R. L. (1971). The evolution of reciprocal altruism. *Quarterly Review of Biology,* 46, 35–57.

— (2002). *Natural Selection and Social Theory: Selected Papers of Robert Trivers.* New York: Oxford University Press.

Tversky, A. and Kahneman, D. (1983). Extensional versus intuitive reasoning: The conjunction fallacy in probability judgment. *Psychological Review,* 90, 293–315.

Wald, A. (1950). *Statistical Decision Functions.* New York: Wiley.

Wason, P. C. (1966). Reasoning. In B. M. Foss (ed.), *New Horizons in Psychology.* London: Penguin Books.

Wason, P. C. and Johnson-Laird, P. N. (1972). *Psychology of Reasoning: Structure and Content.* Cambridge, MA: Harvard University Press.

Williams, B. (1981). *Moral Luck.* Cambridge: Cambridge University Press.

— (1988). Consequentialism and integrity. In S. Scheffler (ed.), *Consequentialism and its Critics*. New York: Oxford University Press. (Reprinted from B. Williams and J. J. C. Smart, *Utilitarianism: For and Against*. Cambridge: Cambridge University Press, 1973).

Wundt, W. (1912/1973). *An Introduction to Psychology* (R. Pintner, trans.). New York: Arno.

Zhu, L. and Gigerenzer, G. (forthcoming). Children can solve Bayesian problems: The role of representation in computation. *Cognition*.

Bounded Rationality and the Enlightenment Picture of Cognitive Virtue

David Matheson

Introduction

Broadly speaking, a virtue is a feature of something that enables it to perform well along a relevant dimension of evaluation. Sympathy and courage are moral virtues because, all else being equal, the sympathetic and courageous tend to act morally more often than the cold-hearted and cowardly. Ease of handling and fuel efficiency are automotive virtues because automobiles that possess them are better suited to serve the typical interests of drivers than those that do not. Clarity and relevance are virtues of communication because their absence impedes the flow of information.

A cognitive virtue pertains to the mental processes or mechanisms whereby we acquire our representations of (e.g., beliefs and judgments about) the world: it is a feature of these mechanisms that aids in the felicitous acquisition of representations. But what precisely is the dimension of cognitive evaluation picked out by "felicitous" here? Along one dimension, the immediate end of cognition is just the acquisition of numerous representations of the world, and the exercise of our representational mechanisms is evaluated simply in terms of how many representations they generate. Cognitive virtue as highlighted in this dimension is of a pretty weak sort, however, for its connection to representational *accuracy* is attenuated: here, representational mechanisms that consistently yield a large number of wildly false judgments about the world, for example, might count as no more vicious than ones that consistently yield a comparable number of true judgments.

Another dimension is concerned with how well our representational mechanisms do when it comes to the acquisition of prudentially (or practically) useful representations of the world. Here again, the weakness of the connection to accuracy makes for a rather weak form of cognitive virtue – no stronger, it would seem, than the sort at play in discussions about how well our representational mechanisms do when it comes to generating emotionally satisfying representations of the world. It may not seem very virtuous from the cognitive point of view, given the disheartening evidence afforded by the medical experts under whose care she falls, for a subject to believe that she will survive a recently diagnosed illness. But, for all that, it may be quite virtuous of her, along a prudential dimension of evaluation, to go ahead and form the belief. After all, the belief, against the evidence, may predictably result in a better quality of life for whatever time she has left.

A stronger dimension of cognitive evaluation, then, takes the immediate end of cognition to be the acquisition of *accurate* representations, and human representational mechanisms are now evaluated in terms of how well they generate representations of that sort. But this is still not a very strong evaluative dimension. For along this dimension a subject could be performing fully virtuously by the use of such representational mechanisms as wishful thinking and mere guesswork, provided only she happens to be lucky enough to have her representations so acquired turn out to be accurate.

Stronger yet is a dimension according to which the immediate end of cognition is the *stable* (alternatively, *non-accidental*) acquisition of accurate representations, and our representational mechanisms are evaluated in terms of how well they stably generate accurate representations. Wishful thinking and mere guesswork may with the right sort of luck generate accurate representations, but not stably: over the long haul, chances are that these representational mechanisms will yield as many (or more) inaccurate as accurate representations of the world.

This paper will be concerned with human cognitive virtue from the point of view of the last, strongest dimension of cognitive evaluation. There is a certain picture of cognitive virtue, so understood – call it the Enlightenment Picture – that portrays it as inhabiting the mind alone. In this picture, to borrow the words of Charles Taylor, the cognitively virtuous human agent is "ideally disengaged . . . rational to the extent that he has fully distinguished himself from the natural and social worlds, so that his identity is no longer to be defined in terms of what lies outside him in these worlds" (Taylor, 1995, p. 7). The alternative picture portrays cognitive virtue as inhabiting a broader domain: on the Post-Enlightenment Picture, cognitive virtue can be located only by looking simultaneously at mind and world.

The current psychological debate about the "boundedness" of human rationality – and more specifically about whether rational human judgment under uncertainty is "bounded" – has important implications for the respective plausibility of these competing pictures of cognitive virtue. On one side of the debate, we have those who read various recent results in experimental psychology as indicative of widespread irrationality in human judgment under uncertainty. On the other side, there are theorists like Gigerenzer who look at those experimental results and draw the conclusion that the judgments are generally rational but bounded in some important sense. One problem students of cognitive science are likely to encounter in their examination of the literature on this debate is that of finding a succinct formulation of what the relevant boundedness claim amounts to. In the next section, I will provide it, before going on to locate the debate against the background of the competing pictures of cognitive virtue. Given the nature of their boundedness claim, I will show, the boundedness theorists are committed to a rejection of the Enlightenment Picture. In my third section I will point to a reason for pause about the boundedness theorists' rejection: it seems to carry with it a worrisome consequence about the extent to which cognitive virtue is under the control of the subject who manifests it. Though I will offer some suggestions about how to mitigate the worrisome nature of this consequence, I would be most interested in hearing Gigerenzer's own.

Boundedness Theorists' Rejection of the Enlightenment Picture

The claim about the bounded nature of rational human judgment under uncertainty is best understood by contrasting it with an opposing claim of "unboundedness," as follows:

> *Unbounded Rationality Thesis:* the rationality of one's judgment under uncertainty consists of following rules for the formation of such judgment that are specifiable without reference to (i.e., unbounded by) one's environment.
> *Bounded Rationality Thesis:* the rationality of one's judgment under uncertainty consists of following rules for the formation of such judgment that are specifiable only by reference to (i.e., bounded by) one's environment.

There are three points to keep in mind about these two theses. First, they are theses about the rationality of *judgment* under uncertainty. The unbounded/bounded rationality distinction they carve out, therefore, applies to a narrower domain than certain other distinctions that go by the same name. Thus, for example, to talk about the boundedness, or by contrast unboundedness (or "fullness") of rational *decision* or *choice* under uncertainty is to point to a distinction that applies to more than merely the rationality of judgment, for there is more to the rationality of choice than simply the rationality of judgment: rational judgment is only one factor involved in rational choice – another, for example, being the desire, interest, or preference of the judging subject (cf. Simon, 1972; Gigerenzer and Selten, 2001; Selten, 2001). Even if it is quite rational for me to judge that investing in a certain company will maximize my financial returns, it may not, given my desire to maximize things other than my financial returns, be rational of me to choose to invest.

Second, the notion of *following rules* at play in each thesis need not require any explicitly conscious awareness of the rules, or awareness of satisfying their conditions, when followed. Undoubtedly, humans follow all kinds of rules in such cognitive activities as facial recognition and grammatical linguistic utterance; yet equally undoubtedly, they are typically quite unaware, at any conscious level, of the nature and content of those rules when followed.

Third, each thesis takes a contrasting stand on the nature of rationality itself as applied to judgment under uncertainty. According to the Bounded Rationality Thesis, the rationality of judgment under uncertainty is always a relative matter: to be cognitively rational in such judgement is always to be cognitively rational *relative to a given environment*. The Unbounded Rationality Thesis, by contrast, renders the rationality of the judgment an absolute, idealized matter: to be cognitively rational in one's judgment under uncertainty is never to be cognitively rational relative to a given environment, but simply cognitively rational in the judgment, full-stop.

With the competing theses of Unbounded and Bounded Rationality in hand, we are now in a position to begin to understand both what motivates theorists like Gigerenzer to adopt the Bounded Rationality Thesis, and why this commits them to a rejection of the Enlightenment Picture. From the early 1970s onward, a number of psychological experiments have been conducted that seem to show that ordinary adult humans do not arrive at their judgments under uncertainty (hereafter, uncertainty judgments) in accord with a class of rules that fit the description given in the Unbounded Rationality Thesis, viz., the entrenched rules of the probability calculus (cf. Kahneman and Tversky, 1972; Tversky and Kahneman, 1973a, 1973b, 1974, 1982a, 1982b, 1982c, 1983; Nisbett and Ross, 1980). Thus, for example, in the well-known experiment reported by Tversky and Kahneman, test subjects were presented with the following "Cab Problem":

> A cab was involved in a hit-and-run accident at night. Two cab companies, the Green and the Blue, operate in the city. You are given the following data:
> (a) 85 percent of the cabs in the city are Green and 15 percent are Blue.
> (b) A witness identified the cab as Blue. The court tested the reliability of the witness under the same circumstances that existed on the night of the accident and concluded that the witness correctly identified each one of the two colors 80 percent of the time and failed 20 percent of the time.
> What is the probability that the cab involved in the accident was Blue rather than Green? (Tversky and Kahneman, 1982b, pp. 156–7)

As compared to the result delivered by the probability calculus, test subjects performed very poorly when confronted with this problem. The probability calculus delivers the result that the probability that the cab involved in the accident was Blue is 0.41; test subjects' answers ranged wildly away from that answer, and their median was 0.80. This experimental result, in the eyes of many, including Tversky and Kahneman themselves, served as further evidence for the conclusion that ordinary adult humans do not follow the entrenched rules of the probability calculus in arriving at their uncertainty judgments, such as the sort of probability judgment asked for in the Cab Problem.

The reasoning behind this conclusion is as straightforward as it is compelling. The first step is just that test subjects are wrong much more often than not with respect to their uncertainty judgments in probabilistic reasoning tasks like the Cab Problem. The second step involves some sort of inference to the best available explanation: the best available explanation of why test subjects are wrong much more often than not with respect to their judgments is that they do not follow the entrenched rules of the probability calculus in arriving at those judgments. Hence, test subjects do not follow the entrenched rules of the probability calculus in arriving at their judgments in such probabilistic reasoning tasks. But now, the reasoning continues, on the plausible assumption that not only are the subjects representative of ordinary adult humans but also their uncertainty judgments in such probabilistic reasoning tasks are relevantly representative of their uncertainty judgments in general, we get the further conclusion that ordinary adult humans (hereafter, humans) do not follow the entrenched rules of the probability calculus in arriving at their uncertainty judgments.

So much seems relatively uncontroversial. The more controversial bit comes upon consideration of whether the foregoing conclusion carries any particularly disturbing implications with respect to the rationality of human uncertainty judgment.

If we add a premise to the effect that human uncertainty judgment is rational just in case it follows the entrenched rules of the probability calculus, we seem straightaway to land ourselves with a very disturbing, skeptical conclusion about the rationality of human uncertainty judgment, viz., that such judgment is typically *not* rational.

Notice, however, that the added premise – that human uncertainty judgment is rational just in case it follows the entrenched rules of the probability calculus – is an instance of the Unbounded Rationality Thesis. This is because the entrenched rules of the probability calculus are specifiable independently of any reference to the environment of the judging subject. To see why, consider one central entrenched rule of the probability calculus, built upon Bayes's Theorem. We may formulate the theorem as follows:

$$\text{Prob}(H|E) = \frac{\text{Prob}(E|H) \times \text{Prob}(H)}{[\text{Prob}(E|H) \times \text{Prob}(H)] + [\text{Prob}(E|{\sim}H) \times \text{Prob}({\sim}H)]}$$

That is, the conditional probability of a hypothesis H on evidence E is the product of (i) the conditional probability of E on H and (ii) the unconditional probability of H, divided by the sum of (i) (a) the product of the conditional probability of E on H and (b) the unconditional probability of H and (ii) (a) the product of the conditional probability of E on not-H and (b) the unconditional probability of not-H.

There are two difficulties with thinking of this equation as itself an entrenched rule for rational uncertainty judgment, i.e., as a rule that ought to be followed if the cognitive aim is not just making uncertainty judgments, but *rationally* making them. First, the equation does not have the form of a rule of rational uncertainty judgment at all. Second, it doesn't capture the entrenched nature of Bayes's Theorem as a rule of rational uncertainty judgment, for, as entrenched, the rules of the probability calculus restrict (typically implicitly) the format of the judgments involved in arriving at the judgment being evaluated to the standard format(s) of the probability calculus, e.g., single-event probability format. (A single-event format judgment about the conditional probability of H on E might be rendered as the judgment that the conditional probability of H on E is 0.8 or 80 percent; in frequency format, it might be rendered as the judgment that the conditional probability of H on E is 8/10, or 80/100.) So, to formulate Bayes's Theorem as a rule of the relevant sort, it would have to be rendered along the following lines:

A subject S rationally judges that $\text{Prob}(H|E) = n$ only if
(a) S judges in standard probability format(s) that $\text{Prob}(E|H) = o$
(b) S judges in standard probability format(s) that $\text{Prob}(H) = p$
(c) S judges in standard probability format(s) that $\text{Prob}(E|{\sim}H) = q$
(d) S judges in standard probability format(s) that $\text{Prob}({\sim}H) = r$
(e) S judges in standard probability format(s) that $op/op + qr = n$

And, clearly, this is a rule of Unbounded Rationality: nothing in its specification involves any reference to the subject S's environment.

If we accept the Unbounded Rationality Thesis in the form of such rules, then, we are committed to the skeptical conclusion that human uncertainty judgment is for the most part not rational. For, as the experimental evidence shows, humans simply do not typically follow the entrenched rules of the probability calculus such as the one based on Bayes's Theorem in forming their uncertainty judgments. The lesson to be learned from the Cab Problem experiment, for instance, is that humans fail to satisfy (a)–(e) of that rule in forming their conditional probability judgments. Since rational uncertainty judgment is supposed to require following the entrenched rules of the probability calculus, humans do not normally form rational uncertainty judgments.

To summarize the discussion thus far: results based on such experiments as the Cab Problem pull strongly in favor of (1):

1 Human uncertainty judgment does not follow the entrenched rules of the probability calculus.

If we add to this the premise captured by (2),

2 Human uncertainty judgment is rational just in case it follows the entrenched rules of the probability calculus,

we get the skeptical conclusion given in (3):

3 Therefore, human uncertainty judgment is not rational.

To block such an unpalatable conclusion – unpalatable at least partly in virtue of the difficulty of reconciling it with (i) the fact that humans seem to survive in and navigate the world pretty well, all things considered, and (ii) the plausible assumption that their uncertainty judgments play a crucial role in this survival and navigation (as W. V. O. Quine once remarked, "[c]reatures inveterately wrong in their inductions have a pathetic but praiseworthy tendency to die before reproducing their kind," Quine, 1969, p. 126) – theorists like Gigerenzer have in effect taken a long hard look at the likes of premise (2) and the Unbounded Rationality Thesis of which, as we saw, it is an instance. If we abandon that thesis in the form of (2) and replace it with an instance of the Bounded Rationality Thesis, the unpalatable conclusion (3) can be blocked: one can reasonably grant the experimentally supported (1) and yet remain uncommitted to the general irrationality of human uncertainty judgment.

The Bounded Rationality Thesis counsels replacement of absolute (unrelativized to environment) rules of rational uncertainty judgment with relativized ones. What form might these relativized rules take, specifically, and how exactly would their adoption block the skeptical conclusion (3)? It is worth noting that at one level, the rules might turn out to bear considerable similarity to their absolute counterparts. Thus, for example, it would be consistent with acceptance of the Bounded Rationality Thesis to endorse the following rule:

Relative to an information-representation environment I, a subject S rationally judges that $\text{Prob}(H|E) = n$ only if

(a) S judges, in the representation format F of I, that $\text{Prob}(E|H) = o$
(b) S judges, in the representation format F of I, that $\text{Prob}(H) = p$
(c) S judges, in the representation format F of I, that $\text{Prob}(E|\sim H) = q$
(d) S judges, in the representation format F of I, that $\text{Prob}(\sim H) = r$
(e) S judges, in the representation format F of I, that $op/op + qr = n$.

The consistency stems from the fact that this rule amounts to a rule for rational uncertainty judgment specifiable only by reference to the subject S's environment. The *information-representation environment* I is the external context in which S is presented with the relevant probabilistic information available to her. The *representation format* F of that environment is the way – guise – in which I typically encodes that information. There may well be a significant difference between the representation format of our (ordinary adult humans') *natural* probabilistic information-representation environments and the representation format(s) at play in the *artificial* information-representation environments of the Tversky and Kahneman experimental settings. In the natural environments, for example, probabilistic information may typically be represented in a natural frequency format; in the artificial environments, the information may typically represented in another format – e.g., that of the entrenched rules of the probability calculus. Thus, writes Gigerenzer:

> Consider numerical information as an example of external representation [i.e., of the representation format of a subject's environment]. Numbers can be represented in Roman, Arabic, and binary systems, among others. These representations can be mapped one to one onto each other and in this sense are mathematically equivalent. But the form of representation can make a difference for an algorithm that does, say, multiplication. The algorithms of our pocket calculators are tuned to Arabic numbers as input data and would fail badly if we entered binary numbers. Similarly, the arithmetic algorithms acquired by humans are designed for particular representations . . . Contemplate for a moment long division in Roman numerals. (Gigerenzer, 2000, p. 94)

> The experimenters who have amassed the apparently damning body of evidence that humans fail to meet the norms of Bayesian inference have usually given their research participants information in the standard probability format . . . Results from these [experiments] . . . have generally been taken as evidence that the human mind does not reason with Bayesian algorithms. Yet this conclusion is not warranted . . . One would be unable to detect a Bayesian algorithm within a system by feeding it information in a representation that does not match the representation with which the algorithm works [i.e., in a format different from that typical of the system's natural information-representation environment].
>   In the last few decades, the standard probability format has become a common way to communicate information ranging from medical and statistical textbooks to psychology experiments. But we should keep in mind that it is only one of many mathematically equivalent ways of representing information; it is, moreover, a recently invented notation. [T]he standard probability format [was not] used in Bayes's . . . original essay. [W]ith natural frequencies one does not need a pocket calculator to estimate the Bayesian posterior. (Gigerenzer, 2000, p. 98)

Similarly, as Cosmides and Tooby put it:

> [N]o computational mechanism can be expected to correctly produce an answer it was not designed to produce. For example, choosing food and choosing a spouse both involve "preferences." One can even ask questions about these choices in the same linguistic format: "How much do you like your salad/boyfriend?" But a mechanism that is well-designed for choosing nutritious food will not be able to choose the best spouse. Similarly, even though addition and finding a logarithm both involve numbers, a mechanism that is well-designed for adding will not be able to find a logarithm.

David Matheson

Suppose that people do have reliably developed mechanisms that allow them to apply a calculus of probability, but that these mechanisms are "frequentist": they are designed to accept probabilistic information when it is in the form of a frequency, and to produce a frequency as their output. Let us then suppose that experimental psychologists present subjects with problems that ask for the "probability" of a single event, rather than a frequency, as output, and that they present the information necessary to solve the problem in a format that is not obviously a frequency. Subjects' answers to such problems would not appear to have been generated by a calculus of probability, even though they have been designed to do just that. (Cosmides and Tooby, 1996, p. 18)

If we adopt the Bounded Rationality Thesis and as a result replace absolute rules like those of the entrenched probability calculus with relativized ones like the one just articulated above, how does the skeptical conclusion (3) get blocked? In place of premise (2), we would substitute a claim to the effect that human uncertainty judgment is rational *relative to an information-representation environment I* just in case it follows *relativized-to-I* (in the sense of the Bounded Rationality Thesis) rules of the probability calculus. But now the experimentally well-supported (1), even when combined with the new premise about relativized rationality will not yield the skeptical conclusion (3), at least not in any unqualified way. The most that will follow from the combination of (1) and the new premise is that human uncertainty judgment is not rational *relative to the artificial information-representation environment of the experimental settings*. At least, that's all that will follow given this instance of the Bounded Rationality Thesis: human uncertainty judgment is rational *relative to the artificial information-representation environment of the experimental settings* just in case it follows the entrenched rules of the probability calculus. But then again, the irrationality of judgment *relative to the artificial settings* is perfectly consistent with its rationality *relative to the natural information-representation environment*.

Moreover, the claim that human uncertainty judgment is rational in this way – relative to its natural information-representation environment – would follow from yet another instance of the Bounded Rationality Thesis perfectly consistent with the previous one – viz., that human uncertainty judgment is rational *relative to its natural information-representation environment* just in case it follows rules of the probability calculus specifiable only by reference to that natural information-representation environment – together with the assumption that humans do in fact generally follow rules of the probability calculus specifiable only by reference to the natural information-representation environment. And, interestingly enough, recent experimental results seem to confirm that this assumption is correct. (See, e.g., Gigerenzer and Hoffrage, 1995, 1998; Cosmides and Tooby, 1996; Gigerenzer, 2000; Cf. Gigerenzer, 1996; Kahneman and Tversky, 1996.)

Thus, in effect, boundedness theorists like Gigerenzer would have us replace the reasoning given above in (1)–(3) with the reasoning captured below by (4)–(6) – where, notice, the uncontroversial (1) is still accepted: it's identical with (5).

4   Relative to the artificial information-representation environment of the experimental settings, human uncertainty judgment is rational just in case it follows the entrenched rules of the probability calculus.

5   Human uncertainty judgment does not follow the entrenched rules of probability calculus.
6   Therefore, relative to the artificial information-representation environment of the experimental settings, human uncertainty judgment is not rational.

And they would have us keep in mind that the conclusion (6) is not to be confused with the earlier, skeptical conclusion (3), because it is perfectly consistent with the manifestly non-skeptical conclusion (9), as supported by (7) and (8):

7   Relative to its natural information-representation environment, human uncertainty judgment is rational just in case it follows rules of the probability calculus specifiable only by reference to the natural information-representation environment.
8   Human uncertainty judgment follows rules of the probability calculus specifiable only by reference to its natural information-representation environment.
9   Therefore, relative to its natural information-representation environment, human uncertainty judgment is rational.

By adopting the Bounded Rationality Thesis in the form of (4) and (7), as opposed to its Unbounded counterpart in the form of (2), Gigerenzer and other boundedness theorists thereby block the troubling skeptical conclusion that human uncertainty judgment is generally irrational, period, as (3) would have it. But notice that they also thereby maintain that what distinguishes rational from irrational uncertainty judgment – following rules for uncertainty judgment that are specifiable only by reference to the judging subject's external environment – is at least partly outside of the mind. And, since it is eminently plausible to treat this as precisely what serves to distinguish stably accurate probabilistic representational mechanisms from merely accurate probabilistic representational mechanisms, it follows (given the general notion of cognitive virtue articulated in my introduction) that one very important form of cognitive virtue – cognitive virtue with respect to our probabilistic representational mechanisms – is not wholly within the mind. By pushing us in the direction of the Bounded Rationality Thesis, therefore, theorists like Gigerenzer push us away from the Enlightenment Picture. For, according to that picture, cognitive virtue – in whatever form – is supposed to be located entirely within the mind.

A Worry about Cognitive Luck

In the previous section we saw how certain results in experimental psychology might lead one to the skeptical conclusion that human uncertainty judgment is generally not rational, and how the derivation of that conclusion leads to acceptance of the unboundedness of rational uncertainty judgment – the Unbounded Rationality Thesis. We also saw how the desire to avoid that skeptical conclusion has in effect led Gigerenzer and other boundedness theorists to reject the Unbounded Rationality Thesis in favor of its Bounded counterpart, which in turn commits them to a rejection of the Enlightenment Picture of cognitive virtue. I want to close by pointing to a worry that arises upon such a rejection. I will offer two suggestions as to how we might downplay the worry, leaving it to the reader to evaluate their plausibility. Also, I would be interested to hear any alternative suggestions that Gigerenzer might have.

David Matheson

The worry has been raised in one form or another by Kaplan (1985) and Cruz and Pollock (1999), and can be stated roughly as follows. If cognitive virtue is located outside the mind in the way that the Post-Enlightenment Picture suggests, then it turns out to be something bestowed on us by features of the world not under our control: it involves an intolerable degree of something analogous to what theoretical ethicists call "moral luck" (cf. Statman, 1993) – "cognitive luck," we might say. In that case, there is little we can do to improve our cognitive abilities, for – so the worry continues – such improvement requires manipulation of what it is within our power to change, and these external, cognitively fortuitous features are outside that domain. But consider: one important goal of the enterprise of cognitive science is precisely the improvement of our cognitive abilities. After all, surely *one* central reason why cognitive scientists are so concerned with understanding the nature of our representational mechanisms is that this understanding promises ultimately to lead to an increased ability to detect and correct faulty – unstable – deployments of those mechanisms (cf. Goldman, 1978, 1986). Hence, if the Post-Enlightenment Picture turns out to be accurate, one important goal of cognitive science goes by the wayside.

One response to the worry consists of pointing out that, even on the assumption that the relevant features outside the mind are not under our control, there is nothing in the Post-Enlightenment Picture that suggests that these are all of what makes for cognitive virtue. That the rationality of human uncertainty judgment involves following rules for such judgment that are specifiable only by reference to one's environment does not mean that it involves following rules specifiable exclusively by reference to one's environment; that cognitive virtue cannot be located entirely within the mind does not imply that it is located entirely outside the mind. So, perhaps there is a great deal we can do to improve our cognitive abilities, by manipulating those features of the mind that, together with those outside it, make for cognitive virtue.

Another response to the worry under consideration might be this: we ought not to accept the assumption that those features outside the mind that partly make for cognitive virtue are beyond our control. Consider, for example, one such representative feature: having the input to one's visual-belief-acquisition mechanisms – visual experience – caused under appropriate lighting and distance conditions. This is clearly a feature of the world outside the mind. But it is perhaps equally clearly a feature over which we can exercise control: we just have to take pains to ensure that our bodily location is apt when we deploy these visual-belief-acquisition mechanisms. Or consider another representative feature: having the informational input to our uncertainty-judgment-acquisition mechanisms structured in (say) a natural frequency format. Again, this is a feature outside the mind that is to some extent under our control. It is precisely by the manipulation of such features that the experimental results reported in Cosmides and Tooby 1996, *inter alia*, are generated.

Acknowledgments

I would like to express my thanks to Robert Stainton, Joseph Shieber, and Patrick Rysiew for their helpful feedback during my preparation of this chapter.

References

Cosmides, L. and Tooby, J. (1996). Are humans good intuitive statisticians after all? *Cognition*, 58, 1–73.

Cruz, J. and Pollock, J. (1999). *Contemporary Theories of Knowledge* (2nd edn.). Totowa, NJ: Rowman & Littlefield.

Gigerenzer, G. (1996). On narrow norms and vague heuristics: A reply to Kahneman and Tversky. *Psychological Review*, 103, 592–6.

— (2000). *Adaptive Thinking: Rationality in the Real World*. Oxford: Oxford University Press.

Gigerenzer, G. and Hoffrage, U. (1995). How to improve Bayesian reasoning without instruction: frequency formats. *Psychological Review*, 102, 684–704.

— and — (1998). AIDS counselling for low-risk clients. *AIDS Care*, 10, 197–211.

Gigerenzer, G. and Selten, R. (2001). Rethinking rationality. In G. Gigerenzer and R. Selten (eds.), *Bounded Rationality: The Adaptive Toolbox*. Cambridge, MA: MIT Press.

Goldman, A. (1978). Epistemics: The regulative theory of cognition. *Journal of Philosophy*, 75, 509–23.

— (1986). *Epistemology and Cognition*. Cambridge, MA: Harvard University Press.

Kahneman, D. and Tversky, A. (1972). Subjective probability: A judgment of representativeness. *Cognitive Psychology*, 3, 430–54.

— and — (1996). On the reality of cognitive illusions. *Psychological Review*, 103, 582–91.

Kaplan, M. (1985). It's not what you know that counts. *Journal of Philosophy*, 82, 350–63.

Nisbett, R. and Ross, L. (1980). *Human Inference: Strategies and Shortcomings of Social Judgment*. Englewood Cliffs, NJ: Prentice Hall.

Quine, W. V. O. (1969). Natural kinds. In *Ontological Relativity and Other Essays*. New York: Columbia University Press.

Selten, R. (2001). What Is bounded rationality? In G. Gigerenzer and R. Selten (eds.), *Bounded Rationality: The Adaptive Toolbox*. Cambridge, MA: MIT Press.

Simon, H. A. (1972). Theories of bounded rationality. In C. B. Radner and R. Radner (eds.), *Decision and Organization*. Amsterdam: North Holland Publishing.

Statman, D. (ed.) (1993). *Moral Luck*. Albany: State University of New York Press.

Taylor, C. (1995). Overcoming epistemology. In C. Taylor, *Philosophical Arguments*. Cambridge, MA: Harvard University Press.

Tversky, A. and Kahneman, D. (1973a). Availability: A heuristic for judging frequency and probability. *Cognitive Psychology*, 5, 207–32.

— and — (1973b). On the psychology of prediction. *Psychological Review*, 80, 237–51.

— and — (1974). Judgment under uncertainty: heuristics and biases. *Science*, 185, 1124–31.

— and — (1982a). Causal schemas in judgments under uncertainty. In D. Kahneman, P. Slovic, and A. Tversky (eds.), *Judgment under Uncertainty: Heuristics and Biases*. Cambridge: Cambridge University Press.

— and — (1982b). Evidential impact of base rates. In D. Kahneman, P. Slovic, and A. Tversky (eds.), *Judgment under Uncertainty: Heuristics and Biases*. Cambridge: Cambridge University Press.

— and — (1982c). Judgments of and by representativeness. In D. Kahneman, P. Slovic, and A. Tversky (eds.), *Judgment under Uncertainty: Heuristics and Biases*. Cambridge: Cambridge University Press.

— and — (1983). Extensional versus intuitive reasoning: The conjunction fallacy in probability judgment. *Psychological Review*, 90, 293–315.

David Matheson

ARE RULES AND REPRESENTATIONS NECESSARY TO EXPLAIN SYSTEMATICITY?

Cognition Needs Syntax but not Rules

Terence Horgan and John Tienson

Human cognition is rich, varied, and complex. In this chapter we argue that because of the richness of human cognition (and human mental life generally), there must be a syntax of cognitive states, but because of this very richness, cognitive processes cannot be describable by exceptionless rules.

The argument for syntax, in section 1, has to do with being able to get around in any number of possible environments in a complex world. Since nature did not know where in the world humans would find themselves – nor within pretty broad limits what the world would be like – nature had to provide them with a means of "representing" a great deal of information about any of indefinitely many locations. We see no way that this could be done except by way of syntax – that is, by a systematic way of producing new, appropriate representations *as needed*. We discuss what being systematic must amount to, and what, in consequence, syntax should mean. We hold that syntax does *not* require a part/whole relationship.

The argument for the claim that human cognitive processes cannot be described by exceptionless rules, in section 2, appeals to the fact that there is no limit to the factors one might consider in coming to a belief or deciding what to do, and to the fact that there is no limit in principle to the *number* of factors one might consider in coming to a belief or deciding what to do.

We argue not on the basis of models in cognitive science, but instead from reflections on thought and behavior. We do not take our argument to have obvious short-term implications for cognitive science practice; we are not seeking to tell cognitive scientists what specific sorts of modeling projects they should be pursuing in the immediate future. We do think that our arguments have longer-term implications for cognitive science, however, because if we are right about human cognition then adequate models would ultimately need to somehow provide for cognitive processes that (i) are too complex and subtle to conform to programmable, exceptionless rules for manipulating mental representations, (ii) employ syntactically structured representations, and (iii) operate on these representations in a highly structure-sensitive – and thereby highly content-appropriate – ways. We also think the views put forward in this chapter do have some significant links to certain leading ideas behind some extant models in cognitive science, especially models (connectionist, classical-computational, and hybrid) that incorporate syntactic structure and structure-sensitive processing, and/or operate via multiple soft-constraint satisfaction.

1 Syntax: The Tracking Argument

In order to survive in a complex, changing, and uncertain world, an organism must be able to keep track of enduring individuals and of their changing properties and relations. The number of potential predications of properties and relations to individuals that must be available to an organism, for it to be capable of surviving in a complex and uncertain world, is enormous – orders of magnitude too high for each to be pre-wired into the system as a simple representation without compositional structure. The needed compositional structure is syntactic structure. We call this the "tracking argument," because it involves the capacity to keep track of items in the environment. This argument will be illustrated and elaborated in what follows.

1.1 Beliefs about one's locale and the tracking capacities that subserve them

When philosophers talk about beliefs, they tend to consider examples such as your belief that George W. Bush is President of the United States. We want to focus on a different, more mundane, kind of belief. At this moment you have beliefs about the locations of literally hundreds, perhaps thousands, of small to medium-size objects in your vicinity, seen and unseen. You also have beliefs about the perceptual and nonperceptual properties of many of these objects. You have beliefs about the functions or uses of many of them, beliefs about what many of them are made of, beliefs about dispositional properties of many of them, and beliefs about the ages, parts, contents, etc. of some.

Take a moment to consider the many things in your present location about which you have such beliefs. I am in an academic office. I have beliefs, to begin with, about many of the hundreds of books in the office. Of course, I am not now aware of most of these beliefs, but any one of them could come to mind if something prompted it. I believe, for example, that Russell's *The Problems of Philosophy* is on such and such shelf, because I remember it being there. I believe that Wittgenstein's *Tractatus* is in the same vicinity, not because I specifically remember it being there, but because that is where the books in the history of analytic philosophy are. I might also wonder whether a certain book is in the office, or regret that another book is at home. Thus, I have thoughts representative of many different attitudes about books in the office. I also have beliefs about the color and size of many of these books, which beliefs are put to work in looking for books on the shelves. (I also have opinions about the contents of some of these books, but we need only concern ourselves with beliefs

Terence Horgan and John Tienson

about them as physical objects.) And, of course, I have beliefs about many other kinds of things in the office: furniture, decorations, supplies, files, etc.

Whenever you take up a new location, even for a short while, you acquire many new beliefs of this kind. Think, for example, of a campsite or hotel room, or a restaurant. On being seated in a restaurant, you quickly form numerous beliefs about the locations of typical restaurant items in this restaurant, about particular patrons, etc. You also, of course, have knowledge of the locations and properties of things in other familiar locations. Think, for example, of how much you know about items in your own kitchen. (And of course, you can quickly acquire a good deal of that same kind of information about a kitchen where you are visiting.)

So you have had an enormous number of beliefs about items in your vicinity. Such beliefs are obviously necessary to get around in the world and to make use of what the world provides. Most of the beliefs that any natural cognizer has in the course of its career are of this kind – beliefs about objects that it does or may have to deal with.

But reflect further. Nature did not know where on Earth you were going. You could have gone to different places; then you would have had different beliefs about your locale. Nature had to provide you with the capacity to take in – have beliefs about – the configuration of objects any place on Earth. But also, nature did not know exactly what Earth was going to be like. You have the capacity to take in many possible Earth-like locales that have never actually existed. You have, indeed, the capacity to take in many more possible locales that are not particularly Earth-like – witness e.g., *Star Trek*. The beliefs about your immediate environment that you are capable of having – and about potential immediate environments that you are capable of inhabiting – far outstrip the beliefs that you will ever actually have.

Of course, what we have been saying is true of every human being. And, to a significant extent, it must be true of most any cognitive system that is capable of getting around and surviving in the world. Any successful natural cognitive system must be capable of representing the situation in its locale for an indefinite number of possible locales – and representing the situation means representing a very large number of things and their numerous properties and relations.

The beliefs a cognizer forms about items in its environment must have content-appropriate causal roles – otherwise they would be of no help in survival. Thus, cognitive systems must be set up in such a way that each *potential* belief, should it occur, will have an appropriate causal role.[1]

1.2 What is syntax?

One might, perhaps, provide *ad hoc* for states with semantically appropriate causal roles in a simple system by wiring in all the potentially necessary states and causal relations, but that would hardly be possible for the complex cognitive systems we actually find in nature. The only way a cognitive system could have the vast supply of potential representations about the locations and properties of nearby objects that it needs is by having the capacity to *produce* the representations that are "needed" when they are needed. The system must generate beliefs from more basic content. Thus, the following must be at least approximately true: (i) For each individual *i* and property *P* that the system has a way of representing, a way of representing "that *i* has *P*" is automatically determined for that system. And the representation that "*i* has *P*" must automatically have its content-appropriate causal role. Thus, (ii) whenever the system discovers a new individual, potential states predicating old properties to the new individual must automatically be determined, and when the system discovers a new property, states predicating that property to old individuals must be determined. And, again, those new states must have their content-appropriate causal roles. (i) and (ii) are possible on such a vast scale only if representations that predicate different properties of the same individual are systematically related, and representations that predicate the same property of different individuals are systematically related. Then representations can be "constructed" when needed on the basis of those systematic relations. In no other way could there be the vast supply of potential representations that natural cognizers need in order to track their surroundings.

Any representational system with such relations has a syntax, and any such system is a language of thought. Syntax is simply the *systematic* and *productive* encoding of semantic relationships, understood as follows:

Systematic. When different representational states predicate the same property or relation to individuals, the fact that the same property or relation is predicated must be encoded within the structure of representations. And when different representational states predicate different properties or relations to the same individual, the fact that it is the same individual must be encoded in the structure of representations.

Productive. When a representation of a new property or relation is acquired, the representations that predicate that property of each individual must be automatically determined. When a representation for a new individual is acquired, the complex representations that predicate properties of that individual must be automatically determined.

In order for a system of syntactically structured representations to be a language of *thought,* one more thing is necessary. The representations must have semantically appropriate causal roles within a cognitive system. The causal roles of representations depend in part upon the semantic relationships of their constituents, which are encoded in syntactic structure. Thus, the fact that a representation has a particular syntactic structure must be capable of playing a causal role within the system – a causal role appropriate to the representational content that is syntactically encoded in the representation. Syntax in a language of thought must be, as we will say, *effective.*

When philosophers think of language, they tend to think of the languages of logic. In a theory formulated in the first-order predicate calculus the fact that two sentences of the theory predicate the same property of different individuals is encoded in the structure of representations by the presence of the same predicate at corresponding places in the two sentences. So a first order theory is systematic. And first order theories are productive. When a new predicate representing a new property is added to the theory, new sentences predicating that property of each individual represented in the theory are automatically determined. In logic, and in the syntax of classical cognitive science, systematicity and productivity are achieved by encoding identity of reference and identity of predication by shared *parts* of strings; syntax is realized as a part/whole relation. We will call such part/whole based syntax *classical syntax* (following Fodor and McLaughlin, 1990).

Terence Horgan and John Tienson

It is extremely important to understand the following point. It is by no means *necessary* that syntax – systematicity and productivity – be based on part/whole relationships. What is necessary for productivity and systematicity is this: there must be systematic formal relations between complex representations and their constituents which are used by the system in constructing complex representations. Nonclassical constituency is common in natural language. Irregular plural nouns and irregular verbs in English are examples of nonclassical syntax. It would be a mistake to think that these irregulars were syntactically simple (although perhaps semantically complex). Irregular verbs interact with auxiliaries – paradigmatically a matter of syntax – in just the way regular verbs do. "He may drank the water" is syntactically and not just (or even) semantically bad, and it is bad in just the same way as "He may poured the water." Nonclassical, non-part/whole, constituency is the norm in highly inflected languages such as Greek, Latin, and Sanskrit (and, of course, in many non-Indo-European languages). For instance, the one-word Latin sentence "Cogito" is syntactically complex, being translatable as "I now think"; it is a first-person, singular, present-tense, construction. If syntax meant classical syntax (in Fodor and McLaughlin's sense), then the classical natural languages would not have syntax.

Furthermore, it is easy to make up languages with nonclassical constituents. Imagine, for example, a language in which there is one class of pure wave forms that can be used as proper names and other classes of wave forms that can be used as general terms, relational terms, adverbs, connectives, and so on. When a general term is predicated of an individual, the general-term wave form and the individual name wave form are produced simultaneously. Sentences are analogous to *chords,* not to tunes. Slight conventional modifications of the basic pure wave forms indicate that a word is a direct object, an indirect object, etc. Sound waves, like all waves, superimpose; so in the chord none of the individual waves that went to make it up is tokened.[2] If there are creatures with such a system of communication, it would hardly be reasonable to deny that they have a language, or to say that their language lacks syntax. Likewise, if a system of mental representations encodes predication in a similar manner, it would be inappropriate to deny that this system has syntax or that it is a *language* of thought. Our suspicion is that the language of thought is more like this than it is like the first-order predicate calculus or LISP. Syntax is the effective, systematic, and productive encoding of representational content, however it is accomplished.

1.3 Complex skills

We first presented the tracking argument, in section 1.1, in terms of the representations that are necessary for dealing for the various environments that humans and other cognitive agents find themselves in. The argument was that in order to survive in a complex and changing world, an organism must possess a representational system that can generate far more predications of properties to and relations to individuals than would be possible via simple representations without compositional structure. It is important to this argument that physical skills have an essential, rich, and pervasive *cognitive* component that involves the capacity to represent features of the skill domain on a vast scale – so vast, again, that it requires a systematic way of constructing representations as they happen to be needed (i.e., syntax). We will take basketball as an example to illustrate the cognitive component of physical skills, but what we say about basketball can be applied, *mutatis mutandis*, to an indefinitely wide range of mundane physical activities, including hunting, gathering, housekeeping, and getting about in crowded shopping areas. One could not do any of these things without employing novel representations on a vast scale; hence, one could not do so without employing syntactically structured representations.

Hundreds of times in the course of a basketball game a player is faced with a decision that must be made very rapidly, to shoot or pass, for example, and if to pass, to which teammate. The player has to take in a complex, rapidly changing situation, and doing this no doubt takes a specialized, practiced kind of perceptual processing. What we want to call attention to here, however, is that there is a large amount of propositional, hence syntactically structured, information the player must apply to the scene to appropriately "take in" the situation.

First, there are the basic properties that structure the game, so obvious that one may overlook them. Who is in the game? Of those in the game, who is a teammate and who is an opponent? This information is *not* literally contained in a perceptual or image-like representation of the situation. There are also more global properties of the game, such as the score, the time left on the time clock, the time left in the game, the coach's game plan and/or latest instructions, and what defense the opposition is playing.

Second, there are specific properties of individual players: height, jumping ability, speed, shooting ability, and so forth. Third, there are more transient properties: who is guarding whom, what position each player is playing, who is having a good game and who isn't, who is shooting well, who is in foul trouble, etc.

All this language-like information must be related in the right way to the possibly more imagistic representation of the evolving scene. You must know *which* player you see is Jones who is on your team, in foul trouble, not a good shooter, etc. To play basketball one must predicate many nonperceptual properties to those one sees and to others one knows to be in the vicinity.

Thus, much of the information that goes into a basketball player's on-court decisions is language-like, coming in repeatable chunks. There are repeatable properties and relations that are attributed to different enduring individuals of different types – games, teams, persons, balls, etc. For a system of the size and complexity of a basketball cognizer there is no alternative to encoding identity of reference and of predication in the structure of representations themselves, so that representations can be constructed as needed on the basis of this structure. That is, what is needed is syntax.[3]

One response we have heard to this is that skilled basketball play does not involve representations at all. What the skilled player has acquired, so this response goes, is a system that issues in behavior, not representations. This is an expression of a common view about physical skills: that they are fancy, acquired systems of dispositions to respond to stimuli. One might suppose, then, that what one acquires in basketball practice is a system mapping perceptual input to responses, in effect extrapolating from experienced situations to new situations, so that variations in responses are correlated with variations in situations, in perceptual input. But to suppose this would

Terence Horgan and John Tienson

be to seriously misunderstand and underestimate what goes on in the exercise of physical skills.

Some players are better at recognizing situations than others. Thus, players with similar physical abilities do not always respond in physically or behaviorally similar ways to similar situations, because their cognitive abilities and responses are different. One way players improve is in their ability to recognize situations.

But there is a deeper flaw in the idea that physical skills are dispositions to respond. There is no such thing as *the* response a player would make to a specific court situation. A player can do many different things in a given situation, depending upon his current aims. A player's physical skills plus his understanding of the present court configuration are not sufficient to determine his action. Short-term strategic considerations figure importantly in determining a player's actions. The game plan for this game, the strategy currently in effect, the play called by the point guard, the time on the shot clock, the score, the time left in the game – all of these can influence what a player does. Indeed, they may all do so independently at once. None of these is a part of the court configuration, or perceived scene, or physical stimulus. Thus, there are many different responses a player might make to a given court configuration, depending upon various other considerations. The player's representation of the court configuration plus his understanding of the strategy in effect determine how he will exercise his physical skills. This would be impossible if he didn't *have* a representation of the court configuration – which, we repeat, must include attribution of various kinds of nonperceptual properties (teammate, center, etc.).

The phenomenon of shaving points (i.e., deliberately scoring fewer points than one can, or deliberately allowing one's opponent additional scoring opportunities) is interesting here. This is something a person can do for the first time, without practicing *or learning anything new.* Shaving points and throwing games are illegal and immoral in organized sports (though they happen). It is, therefore, worth noticing that shaving points is a common and useful occurrence in social sports. Think of individual sports like tennis and golf. You do not play the same way against a player you can beat easily as you do against one who is your equal or better, but you do not give points away either. And at very modest skill levels one can play in a way that will keep the score respectable without having to keep one's mind on it. One does this differently against different players, and often one can do it without conscious thought – even the first time one faces a particular player. Suppose you were determined to beat your opponent as badly as possible by playing as well as possible. You would play differently than you would against the same opponent if you wanted to keep the score respectably close. And that means you would respond to particular stimuli in a different manner. But you would be using the same knowledge and skills to do it.

A player can play and practice basketball with many different purposes, and with each different purpose, the player's responses to certain physical stimuli will be different than they would have been given other purposes. The same system of skills and abilities would be put to use to produce any of these different responses. Thus, basketball skills (including cognitive skills) do not alone determine responses on the court. So the basketball player cannot properly be thought of as having a system that merely produces responses to stimuli. Part of what the player has is a system that generates representations that can be put to use in determining responses, either typical or atypical, depending on other factors.

Furthermore, each of these different potential responses would be *appropriate* to the current situation. They would be recognizably basketball responses, if not optimal basketball responses. It would be impossible to be capable of so many different appropriate responses to a given situation without actually representing a great deal of the situation and without being capable of representing whatever might go into helping determine one of those responses. In general, physical skills can be exercised in a variety of ways, including novel ways, depending on present goals and purposes. This would be impossible if physical skills were simply learned systems of responses to stimuli. Basketball, and all physical skills, requires the capacity to bring a large amount of non-perceptual propositional, hence syntactically structured, information to bear on the present task.

1.4 A remark about the argument

We want to distinguish the tracking argument, rehearsed in this section, from an important argument in linguistics, known as the productivity argument. It goes as follows. Every speaker knows many ways of taking a given sentence and making a longer sentence. Hence, there is no longest sentence of a natural language; that is, every natural language contains infinitely many sentences. But speakers are finite. The only way a finite speaker could have such an infinite capacity is by having a capacity to construct sentences from a finite vocabulary by a finite set of processes – i.e., by having a system of rules that generates sentences from finite vocabulary (i.e., syntax).

The tracking argument differs from productivity arguments – and from similar arguments concerning infinite linguistic capacity. These arguments appeal to recursive processes and logically complex representations. The tracking argument, however, appeals only to states of the sort that would most naturally be represented in the predicate calculus as (monadic or n-adic) *atomic* sentences, without quantifiers or connectives – that is, to representations that predicate a property of an individual or a relation to two or three individuals. Thus, the vastness of potential representations we are talking about in the tracking argument depends not upon recursive features of thought, but only upon the vastness of potential simple representations.[4] The tracking argument therefore is not committed to recursiveness in the representational systems of cognitive agents to which the argument applies – which means that denying recursiveness would not be a basis for repudiating the argument.

2 No Exceptionless Rules

In section 1 we argued that cognition requires syntax, understood as any systematic and productive way of generating representations with appropriate causal roles. The most familiar, and perhaps most natural, setting for syntactically structured representations is so-called "classical" cognitive science – which construes cognition on the model of the digital computer, as the manipulation of representations in accordance

Terence Horgan and John Tienson

with exceptionless rules of the sort that could constitute a computer program. In this way of conceiving cognition, the rules are understood as applying to the representations themselves on the basis of their syntactic structures. Let us call these rules "programmable, representation-level rules" (PRL rules).

We maintain that human cognition is too rich and varied to be described by PRL rules. Hence, we hold that the classical, rules and representations, paradigm in cognitive science is ultimately not a correct model of human cognition. In this section we briefly present two closely related kinds of considerations that lead us to reject PRL rules. First, there is no limit to the exceptions that can be found to useful generalizations about human thought and behavior. Second, there is no limit to the *number* of considerations that one might bring to bear in belief formation or decision making. Since any PRL rules that might be proposed to characterize, explain, or predict some kind of human behavior would essentially impose a limit on relevant factors and on possible exceptions, such rules would go contrary to the limitless scope, in actual human cognition, of potential exceptions and potentially relevant considerations.

2.1 Basketball, again

These features of cognition are apparent in the basketball example. Players play differently in the same circumstances depending on their present aims and purposes, broadly speaking. As we said above, one's immediate purposes are influenced by factors such as game plan, score, time, and so forth. How one responds to a situation can also change when one goes to a new team, when the team gets a new coach, when one is injured, etc. We will mention two descriptions of factors that can influence how one plays in certain circumstances. Each of these descriptions in fact covers indefinitely many possible influencing factors of that type. First, one can attempt to play the role of a player on an upcoming opponent's team for the sake of team practice. Clearly, there are indefinitely many possible opponents one could attempt to imitate. Second, one's play may be influenced by one's knowledge of the health conditions of players in the game. Making such adjustments is fairly natural for human beings. But there is no way that a system based on PRL rules could do it with the open-ended range that humans seem to have; rather, the PRL rules would have to pre-specify – and thereby limit – what counts as a suitable way to mimic a player on another team, or what informational factors about opposing players can influence how one plays against them.

2.2 Ceteris paribus

Imagine being at someone's house at a gathering to discuss some particular topic, a philosophical issue, say, or the policy or actions of an organization. And imagine that you are very thirsty and know that refreshments have been provided in the kitchen. There is a widely accepted generalization concerning human action that is certainly at least approximately true:

1 If a person S wants something W, and believes that she can get W by doing A, then (other things equal) she will do A.

In the case at hand, if you want something to drink, and believe you can get something to drink in the kitchen, you will go to the kitchen. Neither (1) nor its typical instances are exceptionless, however – which is signaled by the parenthetical "other things equal." You might not go to the kitchen because you do not want to offend the person speaking; or you might not want to miss this particular bit of the conversation; or you might be new to the group and not know what expected etiquette is about such things; or there might be someone in the kitchen who you do not want to talk to. One could go on and on. And so far we have only mentioned factors that are more or less internal to the situation. You would also not go to the kitchen if, say, the house caught on fire.

Generalizations such as (1) are frequently called *ceteris paribus* (all else equal) generalizations. Some have suggested that they should be named "*impedimentus absentus* generalizations." Given your thirst, you will go to the kitchen *in the absence of impediments*. (The impediments can, of course, include your other beliefs and desires.) One thing that is important to see is that (1) is a generalization of a different logical form from the familiar universal generalizations of categorical logic and the predicate calculus. It is not like "All dogs have four legs," which is falsified by a single three-legged dog. It is like "Dogs have four legs." This is not falsified by dogs with more or less than four legs, provided the exceptions have explanations.[5]

Thus, (1) or something very like it is true; exceptions are permitted by the "other things equal" clause. The point we are emphasizing is that there is no end to the list of acceptable exceptions to typical instances of (1) such as the one about you going to the kitchen. One could, indeed, go on and on listing possible exceptions. Furthermore, the example we have used is just one of an indefinitely large number that we could have used. PRL rules are not the kinds of generalizations that apply to this aspect of human cognition. PRL rules cannot allow endless possible exceptions.

Finally, it bears emphasis that instances of (1) can be used to explain and predict human behavior. Very often it is possible to know that *ceteris* is *paribus*.[6]

2.3 Multiple simultaneous soft constraints

Think of ordering dinner in a restaurant. What you order is influenced by what kind of food you like, by how hungry you are, by the mood you are in, and perhaps by price. But what you order can be influenced by many other factors: what others in your party are ordering, what you had for lunch, what you expect to have later in the week, whether you have been to this restaurant before and what you thought of it, whether you think you might return to this restaurant. Again, we could go on and on.

There is no limit to the factors that could influence what you order. Each factor is a "constraint," pushing for some decisions and against others. But (typically) each of the constraints is "soft" – any one of them might be violated in the face of the others. The phenomenon of multiple, simultaneous, soft constraints seems to be ubiquitous in cognition. It is typical of "central processes": deciding, problem solving, and belief fixation.[7] (The classic detective story is a paradigm case in the realm of belief fixation, with multiple suspects and multiple defeasible clues.) In such cases one is often conscious of the factors one is considering – though often one is not

Terence Horgan and John Tienson

aware of how they conspired to lead to the final decision. If there are too many factors to keep in mind and the matter is important enough, one may recycle the factors mentally or write them down. (Imagine deciding what job to take supposing you are fortunate enough to have a choice, or what car to buy, for example.) But in other kinds of cases, such as social situations, physical emergencies, and playing basketball, multiple simultaneous soft-constraint satisfaction appears to occur quite rapidly (and often unconsciously).

In many instances, multiple simultaneous soft-constraint satisfaction permits indefinitely many factors to be influential at once – and generates outcomes that are appropriate to the specific mix of indefinitely many factors, however numerous and varied and heterogeneous they might be. Exceptionless rules cannot take account of indefinitely many heterogeneous factors and the indefinitely many ways they can combine to render some specific outcome most appropriate, because such rules would have to pre-specify – and thereby limit – all the potentially relevant factors and all the ways they might jointly render a particular outcome the overall most appropriate one.

3 Concluding Remarks

We have argued that complex cognition must utilize representations with syntactic structure because that is the only way for there to be the vast supply of representations that cognition requires. But we have also argued that many of the processes these representations undergo are too rich and flexible to be describable by exceptionless rules.

The heart of classical modeling is programs, hence exceptionless rules. Many connectionist models, on the other hand – and more generally, many dynamical-systems models – do not employ syntax. We have no quarrel with, and in fact applaud, (i) models that handle information-processing tasks via the classical rules and representations mode, and (ii) connectionist and dynamical systems models that handle information-processing tasks without resorting to syntax. Much can be learned from such models that is relevant to understanding human-like cognition. But if the arguments of this chapter are right, then neither kind of model can be expected to scale up well from handling simplified "toy problems" to handling the kinds of complex real-life cognitive tasks that are routinely encountered by human beings. Scaling up will require forms of multiple soft-constraint satisfaction that somehow incorporate effective syntax (as do many extant classical models), while also eschewing the pre-supposition of PRL rules (as do many extant connectionist and dynamical systems models, in which rules operate only locally and sub-representationally whereas representations are highly distributed).[8]

Notes

1 For any given belief, causal role is a complicated matter. If I believe there is a coffee cup just out of my sight on the table to my left, this may influence my behavior in many different ways. If I want some coffee, I may reach out, pick up the cup, and sip from it. (Note that

I may well not have to look at the cup.) If I want to take my time answering a question, I may pick up the cup, bring it to my lips, pause, and put it down again. If I want to create a distraction, I might "inadvertently" knock over the cup. And so forth.

2 Connectionist tensor product representations are relevantly similar to the chord language. Cf. Horgan and Tienson, 1992; 1996, pp. 74–81.

3 Do drawings or computer-generated images have syntax, in the sense here described? It depends on whether, and how, such items are used as representations by a given representational system. For instance, a system might use the height of stick-figure representations of basketball players to represent players' heights, might use the colors of the stick figures to represent players' team membership, etc. In such a case there is a systematic, productive, way of constructing representations – which counts as syntax.

4 Thus, we believe, the argument applies not only to human cognition but also to non-human animals, for whom it is difficult to find evidence for more than a minimum of recursive structure in representations. Birds and mammals have languages of thought.

5 It is probably not a good idea to call such generalizations *impedimentus absentus* generalizations, since one important class of such generalizations is simple moral principles: lying is wrong, stealing is wrong, etc, which have exceptions that are not *impediments*.

6 For more on this theme, see Horgan and Tienson, 1990; 1996, ch. 7.

7 Jerry Fodor (1983, 2001) has compared belief fixation to theory confirmation in science. Theory confirmation is "holistic"; the factors that might be relevant to the confirmation (or disconfirmation) of a particular theory may come from any part of science. (This, he suggests, is why confirmation theory is so underdeveloped compared to deductive logic. Deductive validity is a strictly local matter, determined by nothing but the premises and conclusion of the argument.) Likewise, anything one believes might turn out, under some circumstances, to be relevant to anything else you should believe – the potential relevance of anything to anything. And there are no general principles for determining in advance what might be relevant.

8 For a book-length articulation of one way of filling in some details of this sketch of a conception of human cognition, see Horgan and Tienson, 1996.

References

Fodor, J. (1983). *The Modularity of Mind: An Essay on Faculty Psychology*. Cambridge, MA: MIT Press.

— (2001). *The Mind Doesn't Work That Way: The Scope and Limits of Computational Psychology*. Cambridge, MA: MIT Press.

Fodor, J. and McLaughlin, B. (1990). Connectionism and the problem of systematicity: Why Smolensky's solution doesn't work. *Cognition*, 35, 183–204. (Reprinted in T. Horgan and J. Tienson (eds.), *Connectionism and the Philosophy of Mind*, 1991. Dordrecht: Kluwer.)

Horgan, T. and Tienson, J. (1990). Soft Laws. *Midwest Studies in Philosophy*, 15, 256–79.

— and — (1992). Structured representations in connectionist systems? In S. Davis (ed.), *Connectionism: Theory and Practice*. New York: Oxford University Press.

— and — (1996). *Connectionism and the Philosophy of Psychology*. Cambridge, MA: MIT Press.

CHAPTER
T E N

Phenomena and Mechanisms: Putting the Symbolic, Connectionist, and Dynamical Systems Debate in Broader Perspective

Adele Abrahamsen and William Bechtel

Cognitive science is, more than anything else, a pursuit of cognitive mechanisms. To make headway towards a mechanistic account of any particular cognitive phenomenon, a researcher must choose among the many architectures available to guide and constrain the account. It is thus fitting that this volume on contemporary debates in cognitive science includes two issues of architecture, each articulated in the 1980s but still unresolved:

- Just how modular is the mind? (Part 1) – a debate initially pitting encapsulated mechanisms (Fodorian modules that feed their ultimate outputs to a nonmodular central cognition) against highly interactive ones (e.g., connectionist networks that continuously feed streams of output to one another).
- Does the mind process language-like representations according to formal rules? (Part 4) – a debate initially pitting symbolic architectures (such as Chomsky's generative grammar or Fodor's language of thought) against less language-like architectures (such as connectionist or dynamical ones).

Our project here is to consider the second issue within the broader context of where cognitive science has been and where it is headed. The notion that cognition in general – not just language processing – involves rules operating on language-like representations actually predates cognitive science. In traditional philosophy of mind, mental life is construed as involving propositional attitudes – that is, such attitudes towards propositions as believing, fearing, and desiring that they be true – and logical inferences from them. On this view, if a person desires that a proposition be true and believes that if she performs a certain action it will become true, she will make the inference and (absent any overriding consideration) perform the action.

This is a prime exemplar of a symbolic architecture, and it has been claimed that all such architectures exhibit *systematicity* and other crucial properties. What gets debated is whether architectures with certain other design features (e.g., weighted connections between units) can, in their own ways, exhibit these properties. Or more fundamentally: What counts as systematicity, or as a rule, or as a representation? Are any of these essential? Horgan and Tienson offer their own definition of systematicity and also of syntax, arguing that syntax in their sense is required for cognition, but not necessarily part/whole constituent structures or exceptionless rules. They leave to others the task of discovering what architecture might meet their criteria at the scale needed to seriously model human capabilities.

Our own goal is to open up the debate about rules and representations by situating it within a framework taken from contemporary philosophy of science rather than philosophy of mind. First, we emphasize the benefits of clearly distinguishing phenomena from the mechanisms proposed to account for them. One might, for example, take a symbolic approach to describing certain linguistic and cognitive phenomena but a connectionist approach to specifying the mechanism that explains them. Thus, the mechanisms may perform symbolic activities but by means of parts that are not symbolic and operations that are not rules. Second, we point out that the mechanisms proposed to account for phenomena in cognitive science often do not fit the pure types debated by philosophers, but rather synthesize them in ways that give the field much of its energy and creativity. Third, we bring to the table a different range of phenomena highly relevant to psychologists and many other cognitive scientists that have received little attention from philosophers of mind or even of cognitive science – those that are best characterized in equations that relate variables. Fourth, we offer an inclusive discussion of the impact of dynamical systems theory on cognitive science. It offers ways to characterize phenomena (in terms of one or a few equations), explain them mechanistically (using certain kinds of lower-level models involving lattices or interactive connectionist networks), and obtain new understandings of development.

Phenomena and Two Ways of Explaining Them

Characterizing phenomena and explaining them are key tasks of any science. The nature of the characterization depends on the domain but, at least initially, tends to stay close to what can be observed or directly inferred. In the domain of language, many phenomena can be efficiently characterized in terms of rules and representations. For example, the phenomenon of past-tense formation can be expressed roughly as follows: for regular verbs, $V \rightarrow V + ed$ (the verb stem is represented categorically as V and linked to its past-tense form by a general rule); for irregular verbs, $eat \rightarrow ate$, $fly \rightarrow flew$, $give \rightarrow gave$, and so forth (specific pairs of representations are linked individually). In physics, many classic phenomena are characterized

Adele Abrahamsen and William Bechtel

in *empirical laws* that express idealized regularities in the relations between variables over a set of observations. According to the Boyle-Charles law, for example, the pressure, volume, and temperature of a gas are in the relation $pV = kT$. In psychology, there is a similar focus on relations between variables, but these relations are less likely to be quantified and designated as *laws*. Instead, psychologists probe for evidence that one variable causes an effect on another variable. Cummins (2000) noted that psychologists tend to call such relations *effects*, offering as an example the Garcia effect: animals tend to avoid distinctive foods which they ate prior to experiencing nausea, even if the actual cause of the nausea was something other than the food (Garcia et al., 1968).

In the traditional deductive-nomological (D-N) model (Hempel, 1965), characterizations of phenomena are regarded as explanatory. For example, determining that an individual case of nausea is "due to" the Garcia effect explains that case. On a more contemporary view, such as that of Cummins, identifying the relevant phenomenon is just a preliminary step towards explanation. The actual explanation typically involves one of two approaches:

- Re-characterizing the phenomenon in terms of such abstractions as *theoretical laws* or underlying principles. This approach to explanation originated in logical positivism and its hypothetico-deductive method (Hempel, 1965; Suppe, 1974) and produced an influential position holding that less basic theories can be reduced to more basic, fundamental ones (Nagel, 1961). On this view, a given science aims towards a parsimonious, interconnected system of laws (axioms) from which other laws or predictions can be deduced. Nagel's prime example is the derivation of the phenomena of thermodynamics (as expressed, for example, in the Boyle-Charles law) from the more fundamental theory of statistical mechanics (in which theoretical laws incorporate such abstract constructs as *mean kinetic energy*). Though the full apparatus lost its elegance and general acceptance due to a succession of criticisms and modifications, the impulse to find fundamental explanatory laws or principles survives. Scientists still propose laws, and philosophers of science still ask how they cohere across different sciences. (For a contemporary approach emphasizing unification, see Kitcher, 1999.)
- Uncovering and describing the *mechanism* responsible for the phenomenon, as emphasized in the mechanistic approach to explanation advocated since the 1980s by an emerging school of philosophers of science focusing on biology rather than physics. Examples include biologists' detailed accounts of such diverse phenomena as metabolism, blood circulation, and protein synthesis.

The phenomena of cognitive science are so varied that every kind of characterization is encountered: symbolic rules and representations, descriptive equations comparable to the empirical laws of classical physics, statements that certain variables are in a cause-effect relation, and perhaps more. Individual cognitive scientists tend to have a preferred mode of characterization and also a preferred mode of explaining the phenomena they have characterized. Those who propose theoretical laws or principles typically work in different circles than the somewhat larger number who propose mechanisms. We will discuss both, but begin by introducing mechanistic explanation. Historically, the conception of mechanism was drawn from inanimate machines, but it was extended by Descartes to apply to all physical phenomena, including those of organic life. It was further developed by biologists in the nineteenth and twentieth centuries who, in opposition to vitalists, viewed the pursuit of mechanism as the route to developing biology as a science. Explanatory accounts in modern biology predominantly involve mechanisms (rather than theoretical laws), and many parts of cognitive science have the same character. Here is a brief definition of mechanism that was inspired by its use in biology but is equally relevant to proposals about mental architecture:

> A mechanism is a structure performing a function in virtue of its component parts, component operations, and their organization. The orchestrated functioning of the mechanism is responsible for one or more phenomena. (Bechtel and Abrahamsen, 2005; for related accounts, see Bechtel and Richardson, 1993; Glennan, 1996, 2002; Machamer et al., 2000)

In an illustration from biology, the overall phenomenon of carbohydrate metabolism can be characterized as the harvesting of energy in the process of breaking down carbohydrates to carbon dioxide and water. This is explained by decomposing the responsible mechanism into various enzymes (parts) that catalyze intracellular biochemical reactions (operations) in molecular substrates (another kind of parts). For example, the enzyme succinate dehydrogenase oxidizes succinate to fumarate. But it is not sufficient to identify each reaction and the molecules involved; organization is equally important. For example, succinate $\to$ fumarate is followed by other reactions that include (omitting some intermediates, side reactions, and the ongoing provision of acetyl CoA at the step producing citrate): fumarate $\to$ malate $\to$ oxaloacetate $\to$ citrate $\to$ isocitrate $\to$ α-ketoglutarate $\to$ succinate. The complete set of reactions is known as the Krebs cycle (or citric acid cycle) – a submechanism of metabolism that is a well-known exemplar of cyclic organization. The account can be completed by describing the spaciotemporal orchestration of the organized components in real time, that is, their dynamics. (Note to low-carb diet fans: fats and proteins have their own routes into the Krebs cycle. Any diet relies on the metabolic system's ability to dynamically adjust to the ever-changing mix of incoming food molecules.)

For philosophers of science, it was increased attention to biology that provided the impetus towards an emphasis on explanation in terms of mechanisms rather than laws. This turn towards mechanism has brought new perspectives on fundamental issues in philosophy of science (Bechtel and Abrahamsen, 2005), but no new solutions to a problem known as *underdetermination*. Especially at the leading edge of any science, explanations tend to be underdetermined by available data. In the biochemistry of the 1930s, for example, there were a variety of partially correct proposals before Hans Krebs nailed the essentials of the mechanism named for him. Underdetermination is particularly pervasive in our era for cognitive science. Dramatically different mechanistic explanations are routinely championed for a given cognitive phenomenon, and consensus is elusive. In the next section we discuss past-tense

Adele Abrahamsen and William Bechtel

formation to illustrate the conflict between the symbolic and connectionist architectural frameworks for mechanistic explanation in cognitive science. More importantly, we then make the case that these architectures are not polar opposites for which one winner must emerge. After conceptually reframing the symbolic-connectionist debate in this way, we finish by pointing to two research programs that achieve a more integrative approach: optimality theory in linguistics and statistical learning of rules in psycholinguistics.

Getting Beyond the Symbolic–Connectionist Debate

The symbolic–connectionist debate over mechanisms of past-tense formation

If you are fluent in English, on a typical day you produce the correct past-tense form for hundreds of regular and irregular verbs without giving it a moment's thought. How? This capability may seem trivial, but proponents of two different mechanistic approaches have been using it as a battleground for more than 20 years. One approach – symbol processing – keeps the mechanistic explanation very close to the characterization of the phenomenon by positing two different mechanisms. Basically, the language production system performs one of two different operations, depending on the type of verb involved:

- Apply the rule $V \rightarrow V + ed$ if the verb is regular (e.g., *need* → *needed*), or
- Get the appropriate past-tense form from the mental lexicon if the verb is irregular (e.g., the lexical entry for the stem *give* specifies its past-tense form as *gave*).

There are further details, such as distinguishing among three allomorphs of the past-tense affix *ed*, but the key point is that the mechanisms are at the same scale as the phenomenon. Operations like rule application and lexical look-up are assumed to directly modify symbolic representations.

The other approach is to explain past-tense formation by means of a single mechanism situated at a finer-grained level that is sometimes called *subsymbolic*. The best-known subsymbolic models of cognition and language are feedforward connectionist networks. Architecturally, these originated in networks of *formal neurons* that were proposed in the 1940s and, in the guise of Frank Rosenblatt's (1962) *perceptrons*, shown to be capable of learning. Overall phenomena of pattern recognition were seen to emerge from the statistics of activity across numerous identical fine-grained units that influenced each other across weighted connections. Today these are sometimes called *artificial neural networks* (ANNs). The standard story is that network and symbolic architectures competed during the 1960s, ignored each other during the 1970s (the symbolic having won dominance), and began a new round of competition in the 1980s. We suggest, though, that the symbolic and network approaches were both at their best when contributing to new blended accounts. Notably, in the 1980s they came together in connectionism when a few cognitive scientists pursued the idea that a simple ANN architecture could (i) provide an alternative explanation for well-known

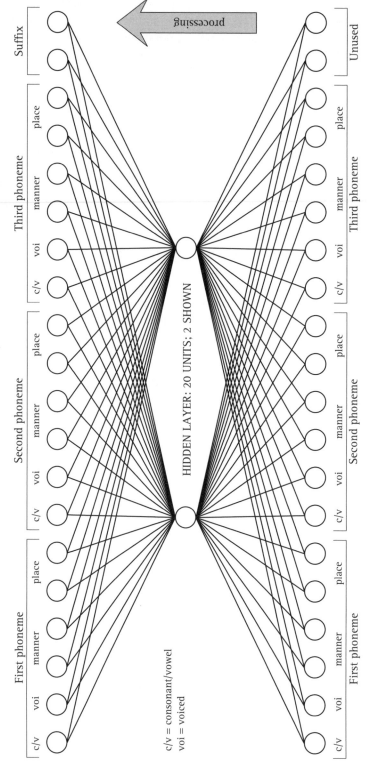

Figure 10.1 Plunkett and Marchman's (1991) feedforward network for past-tense formation. Each artificial verb stem gets a subsymbolic encoding on the input units, based on the phonological features of each of its phonemes. Propagation of activation across weighted connections (shown for two of the 20 hidden layer units) transforms the input pattern into a past-tense form on the output units.

human symbolic capabilities such as past-tense formation while also (ii) explaining additional phenomena of graceful degradation, constraint satisfaction, and learning that had been neglected (Rumelhart and McClelland, 1986b) Connectionist networks generally are construed as having representations across units, but no rules. The very idea that these representations are *sub*symbolic signals the ongoing relevance of the symbolic approach. Connectionists, unlike many other ANN designers, are grappling with the problem of how humans' internal networks function in a sea of external symbols – words, numbers, emoticons, and so forth. In fact, at least one of the pioneers of connectionism had pursued a different blend in the 1970s that leaned more towards the symbolic side – semantic networks – but became critical of their brittleness (see Norman and Rumelhart, 1975).

The first connectionist model of past-tense formation (Rumelhart and McClelland, 1986a) performed impressively, though not perfectly, and received such intense scrutiny that its limitations have long been known. It explored some intriguing ideas about representation (e.g., coarse-coding on context-dependent units), but for some years has been superseded by a sleeker model using a familiar network design. As illustrated in figure 10.1, Plunkett and Marchman's (1991, 1993) feedforward network represents verb stems subsymbolically as activation patterns across the binary units of its *input layer*. It propagates activation across weighted connections first from the input to *hidden layer* and then from the hidden to *output layer*. Each unit in one layer is connected to each unit in the next layer, as illustrated for two of the hidden units, and every such connection has its own weight as a result of repeated adaptive adjustments during learning (via back-propagation). An *activation function*, which typically is nonlinear, determines how the various weighted activations coming into a unit will be combined to determine its own activation. In this way, the network transforms the input representation twice – once for each pair of layers – to arrive at a subsymbolic representation of the past-tense form on the output layer. Although all three layers offer subsymbolic representations, it is the encoding scheme on the input layer that most readily illustrates this concept. The verb stems, which would be treated as morphemes by a rule appending *ed* in a symbolic account, are replaced here with a lower-level encoding in terms of the distinctive features of each constituent phoneme in three-phoneme stems. For example, the representation of *dez* (for convenience, they used artificial stems) would begin with an encoding of *d* as 011100 (0 = consonant, 1 = voiced, 11 = manner: stop, 10 = place: alveolar). With *e* encoded on the next six units and *z* on the last six units, *dez* is represented as a binary pattern across 18 subsymbols rather than symbolically as a single morpheme. Moreover, as the pattern gets transformed on the hidden and output layers, it is no longer binary but rather a vector of 20 real numbers, making the mapping of stem to past tense a statistical tendency. Connectionist networks are mechanisms – they have organized parts and operations – but the homogeneity, fine grain, and statistical functioning of their components make them quite distinct from traditional symbolic mechanisms. (See Bechtel and Abrahamsen, 2002, for an introduction to connectionist networks in chapters 2 and 3 and discussion of past-tense networks and their challenge to rules in chapter 5.)

The trained network in figure 10.1 can stand on its own as a mechanistic model accounting for past-tense formation by adult speakers. However, it is the network's

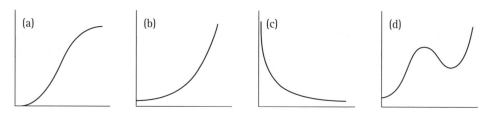

Figure 10.2 Some nonlinear curves: (a) sigmoidal (e.g., skill as a function of practice); (b) positively accelerated exponential (e.g., early vocabulary size as a function of time); (c) negatively accelerated exponential (e.g., number of items learned on a list as a function of list repetitions); (d) U-shaped acquisition (e.g., irregular past tense as a function of age).

behavior during training that has captured the greatest attention, due to claims that it provides a mechanistic explanation of an intriguing developmental phenomenon, U-shaped acquisition. It has long been known that in acquiring the regular past tense, children overgeneralize it to some of their irregular verbs – even some that had previously been correct (Ervin, 1964; Brown, 1973). For example, a child might correctly produce *went* and *sat* at age 2, switch to *goed* and *sitted* at age 3, and gradually return to *went* and *sat* at ages 4–5. Graphing the percentage of opportunities on which the correct form was used against age, a U-shaped acquisition function is obtained. This contrasts with typical learning curves, which tend to be sigmoidal or exponential. The phenomenon of interest is that acquisition of irregulars cannot be described by any of the usual functions but rather is U-shaped, as illustrated in figure 10.2. Advocates of the symbolic approach have interpreted this as favoring the two-mechanism account (applying a rule for regulars and looking up the verb in a mental lexicon for irregulars); specifically, they attribute the decline in performance on irregulars to the replacement of lexical look-up (which gives the correct form) with overgeneralization of the rule (yielding the regular past tense that is inappropriate for these verbs). The alternative proposal, initially advanced by Rumelhart and McClelland (1986a), acknowledged competition but relocated it within a single mechanism – their connectionist network in which the same units and connection weights were responsible for representing and forming the past tense of all verbs. Especially when an irregular verb was presented to the network, activation patterns appropriate to different past-tense forms would compete for dominance. Like children, their network showed a U-shaped acquisition curve for irregular verbs across its training epochs. Pinker and Prince (1988) and others objected to discontinuities in the input and to shortcomings in the performance of Rumelhart and McClelland's network relative to that of human children (based not only on linguistic analyses but also on detailed data gathered by Kuczaj, 1977, and later by Pinker, Marcus and others). Subsequent modeling efforts (Plunkett and Marchman, 1991, 1993) addressed some of the criticisms, but the critics responded with their own fairly specific, though unimplemented, model. A readable, fairly current exchange of views is available in a series of papers in *Trends in Cognitive Sciences* (McClelland and Patterson, 2002a, 2002b; Pinker and Ullman, 2002a, 2002b).

When competing groups of researchers are working within architectural frameworks as distinct as the symbolic and connectionist alternatives, data alone rarely generate

Adele Abrahamsen and William Bechtel

consensus. Advocates tend to adjust specific aspects of their account to accommodate new findings rather than abandon their architecture. In the long term, an architectural framework may fade away because necessary accommodations make it increasingly inelegant, or it may be absorbed into a more powerful framework when new phenomena are identified that it cannot handle, or some other fate may await it. In the shorter term, though, a notable byproduct of the competition is that the phenomenon of interest becomes much more precisely characterized as each group makes increasingly detailed predictions and obtains data to test them. This raises the bar not only for the competing explanations but also for any future ones. On occasion, either the additional data or a consequent revised understanding of the mechanism lead to a substantial reconstrual of the original phenomenon (Bechtel and Richardson, 1993, refer to this as "reconstituting the phenomenon"). More relevant to the case of past-tense acquisition is that the explanations themselves or the relation between them may get reconstrued in a way that reframes the debate. The next section pursues this possibility.

Reframing the debate

Symbolic and connectionist approaches are treated in exchanges like this as competitors, but there are at least two ways of reframing the discussion that make it less contentious and perhaps more satisfactory. One way, as we have noted previously, is to consider the implications of the fact that connectionist networks

> repeatedly find themselves in the same grooves. That is, they behave in ways that can be closely approximated by symbolic models, and for many purposes it is the symbolic models that are most convenient to use.... The real challenge for connectionists will not be to defeat symbolic theorists, but rather to come to terms with the ongoing relevance of the symbolic level of analysis. That is, the ultimate new alliance may be as simple, and as difficult, as forming a new relationship with the long-time opponent. (Bechtel and Abrahamsen, 2002, p. 16)

That is, the two competing approaches to past-tense formation might be given complementary roles. One way of construing this is to appreciate linguistic rules as well suited to characterizing the *phenomenon* of past-tense formation but to prefer feedforward networks as a plausible *mechanism* for producing the phenomenon. Alternatively, both architectures might be viewed as suitable for mechanistic accounts, but at different levels – one course-grained and symbolic, the other fine-grained and statistical. Whatever the exact roles, providing a place for more than one approach can move inquiry towards how they complement each other rather than seeking a winner. In particular, both approaches need not directly satisfy every evaluative criterion. For example, considerations of systematicity proceed most simply (though not necessarily exclusively) with respect to symbolic accounts, and graceful degradation is one of the advantages offered by a fine-grained statistical account.

Looking beyond the Chomskian-connectionist axis of the past-tense debate, an alternative linguistic theory exists that has been very amenable to – even inspired by – the idea that symbolic and subsymbolic approaches each have a role to play in an integrated account. *Optimality theory* emerged from the collaboration between two cognitive scientists who were opponents in the 1980s: connectionist Paul Smolensky and linguist Alan Prince. In a 1993 technical report (published as Prince and Smolensky, 2004), they showed that the constraint-satisfaction capabilities of networks could also be realized, though in a somewhat different way, at the linguistic level. Specifically, they succeeded in describing various phonological phenomena using a single universal set of soft rule-like constraints to select the optimal output among a large number of candidate outputs. A given language has its own rigid rank ordering of these constraints, which is used to settle conflicts between them. For example (see Tesar et al., 1999, for the full five-constraint version): the constraint NoCODA is violated by any syllable ending in a consonant (the coda), and the constraint NoINSV is violated if a vowel is inserted in the process of forming syllables (the output) from a phoneme string (the input). The input string /apot/ would be syllabified as *.a.pot.* in a language that ranks NoINSV higher (e.g., English), but in a vowel-final form like *.a.po.to.* in a language that ranks NoCODA higher (e.g., Japanese).

Optimality theory (OT) offers such an elegant explanation of diverse phenomena that a substantial number of phonologists have adopted it over classic rule-based theories. (Uptake in syntax has been slower.) For reasons difficult to explain without presenting OT in more detail, it is implausible as an explicit mechanistic account. Those with the ambition of integrating OT with an underlying mechanistic account have tended to assume a connectionist architecture. Prince and Smolensky (1997) posed, but did not solve, the most tantalizing question invited by such a marriage: Why would the computational power and flexibility offered by a statistical mechanism like a network be funneled into solutions (languages) that all exhibit the rigid rank-ordering phenomenon that makes OT a compelling theory?

A similar dilemma has been raised by a team of cognitive scientists whose integrative inclinations have operated on different commitments (their linguistic roots are Chomskian, and they regard learning as induction rather than adjustments to weights in a network). They have offered provocative evidence that the language acquisition mechanism is highly sensitive to distributional statistics in the available language input (Saffran et al., 1996), but seek to reconcile this with their view that the product of learning is akin to the rules and representations of linguistic theory. That is, a statistical learning mechanism is credited with somehow producing a nonstatistical mental grammar. This brings them into disagreement with symbolic theorists on one side, who deny that the learning mechanism operates statistically (see Marcus, 2001) and with connectionists on the other side, who deny that the product of learning is nonstatistical. In support of their nuanced position, Newport and Aslin (2000) cited the finding that children acquiring a signed language like American Sign Language from non-native signers get past the inconsistent input to achieve a more native-like morphological system. On their interpretation "the strongest consistencies are sharpened and systematized: statistics are turned into 'rules'" (p. 13). They and their collaborators have also contributed a growing body of ingenious studies of artificial language learning by infants, adults, and primates, from which they argue that the statistical learning mechanism has selectivities in its computations that bias it towards the phenomena of natural language (see Newport and Aslin, 2000, 2004).

Attempts like these to integrate connectionist or other statistical approaches with symbolic ones offer promising alternatives to polarization. We mentioned, though,

Adele Abrahamsen and William Bechtel

that there is a second way of reframing the discussion. Looking at the rise of connectionism in the early 1980s, it is seen to involve the confluence of a number of research streams. Among these are mathematical models, information processing models, artificial neural networks, and symbolic approaches to the representation of knowledge – especially semantic networks but extending even to the presumed foe, generative grammar. Some of these themselves originated in interactions between previously distinct approaches; for example, ANNs were a joint product of neural and computational perspectives in the 1940s, and semantic network models arose when an early artificial intelligence researcher (Quillian, 1968) put symbols at the nodes of networks rather than in rules. Some of the research streams leading to connectionism also had pairwise interactions, as when mathematical modeling was used to describe operations within components of information processing models. Finally, some of these research streams contributed not only to connectionism but also, when combined with other influences, to quite different alternatives. Most important here is that dynamical systems theory (DST) took shape in a quirky corner of mathematical modeling focused on nonlinear physical state changes. It found a place in cognitive science when combined with other influences, such as an emphasis on embodiment, and some of the bends in DST's path even intersected with connectionism when it was realized that such concepts as attractor states shed light on interactive networks. Another example (not discussed in this chapter) is that information processing models, neuroimaging, and other research streams in the cognitive and neural sciences came together in the 1990s, making cognitive neuroscience a fast moving field both on its own and within cognitive science. As well, the idea that cognition is distributed not only within a single mind, but also on a social scale, gave rise to socially distributed cognition as a distinct approach in cognitive science (see Bechtel et al., 1998, Part 3). Thus, an exclusive focus on polar points of contention would give a very distorted picture of cognitive science. This interdisciplinary research cluster in fact is remarkable for its protean nature across both short and long time-frames.

If one is seeking maximal contrast to symbolic rules and representations, it is to be found not in the pastiche of connectionism but rather within the tighter confines of one of its tributaries, mathematical modeling. Yet, except for DST, this approach has been mostly neglected in philosophical treatments of psychology and of the cognitive sciences more generally. In the next section we consider how mainstream mathematical psychology exemplifies the quantitative approach to characterizing and explaining phenomena in cognitive science. This provides conceptual context for then discussing DST and its merger with other commitments in the dynamical approach to perception, action, and cognition.

Mathematical Psychology and its Contributions to Cognitive Science

Mathematical psychology

In its simplest form, mathematical psychology offers the means of characterizing phenomena involving quantitative relations between variables. This is a very different class of phenomena than those characterized in terms of symbolic relations between representations, and accordingly, mathematical psychology has a distinctive look and feel. Although the term *mathematical psychology* only gained currency about the same time as the cognitive revolution,[1] its antecedents extend as far back as the nineteenth century.

The first area to be pioneered in what is now called mathematical psychology was psychophysics. A well-known example is Ernst Weber's (1834) investigation of the relation between physical dimensions such as an object's weight and psychological ones such as its perceived heaviness. He found that he could make the same generalization across a variety of dimensions: "we perceive not the difference between the things, but the ratio of this difference to the magnitude of the thing compared" (p. 172). Later this was expressed as Weber's law ($\Delta I/I = k$), where I is the intensity of a stimulus, ΔI is the *just noticeable difference* (the minimum increment over I that is detectable), and the value of k was constant except at extreme values for a given domain (e.g., approximately 0.15 for loudness). Gustav Fechner (1860) added an assumption of cumulativity to Weber's law to obtain a logarithmic function: $\Psi = c \log (I/I_0)$. That is, the intensity of a sensation is proportional to the logarithm of the intensity of the stimulus (relative to threshold intensity). The constant c depends on k and the logarithmic base. This would seem definitive, but even in this most physically grounded area of psychology conflicts sometimes emerge. Notably, Stevens (1957) proposed a power law that made stronger, and in some cases more accurate, predictions than Fechner's law. Although often regarded as theoretical due to its elegance and breadth of application, Stevens' law (like its predecessors and like the Boyle–Charles law in physics) is essentially an empirical law. Particular percepts can be explained by appeal to the law, but the law itself has not been explained – there has been no appeal to more fundamental laws and no plausible proposals regarding a mechanism. (Weber, 1834, p. 175), in applying his finding to perception of line length, noted that it ruled out a mechanism by which "the mind ... counts the nerve endings touched in the retina." However, he had no suggestions as to what kind of mechanism would make ΔI relative to I rather than constant.)

The next arena in which psychologists expressed empirical laws in equations was learning theory. Notably, a logarithmic retention curve was found to accurately relate the number of items retained from a list to the time elapsed since the list was studied (Ebbinghaus, 1885). As the field developed, a number of other empirical phenomena were identified, and ambitions to account for them culminated in the mathematico-deductive theory of Clark Hull (1943). Explicitly inspired by logical positivism, Hull crafted a formal theory in which empirical relationships between such observables as number of reinforcements and response latency were taken to be derived from theoretical laws (axioms) that included operationally defined *intervening variables*. For example, reinforcements affected habit strength, which was multiplied by drive to get excitatory potential, which affected response latency. Eventually Hull's theory came to be regarded as bloated and insufficiently explanatory. It was replaced by a *mathematical psychology* in which equations were expected to achieve explanatory power through parsimony:

> In principle, such a theory entails an economical representation of a particular set of data in mathematical terms, where "economical" means that the number of free parameters

of the theory is substantially smaller that the number of degrees of freedom (e.g., independent variables) in the data. (Falmagne, 2002, p. 9405)

The Markov models of William Estes (1950) and R. R. Bush and F. Mosteller (1951) satisfied this criterion and energized the field by elegantly accounting for a variety of empirical data and relationships. Their new mathematical psychology surpassed Hull in successfully arriving at equations that were more akin to the explanatory theoretical laws of physics than to its descriptive empirical laws.

On their own, equations are not mechanistic models. One equation might characterize a psychological phenomenon, and another might re-characterize it so as to provide a highly satisfactory theoretical explanation. Equations do not offer the right kind of format, however, for constructing a mechanistic explanation – they specify neither the component parts and operations of a mechanism nor how these are organized so as to produce the behavior. This suited the mathematical psychologists of the 1950s who, like other scientifically oriented psychologists, avoided any proposals that hinted at mentalism. When the computer metaphor made notions of internal information processing respectable, though, they began to ask what sorts of cognitive mechanisms might be responsible for phenomena that could be characterized, but not fully explained, using equations alone.

Mathematical psychology combined with symbolic mechanistic models

The development of *information processing models* in the 1960s and 1970s signaled that certain experimental and mathematical psychologists had become committed to mechanistic explanation. They did this by positing various representations that were processed (e.g., compared, moved, transformed) by operations similar to those in computer programs. Often the models were further influenced by symbolic disciplines such as linguistics and logic, making "rules and representations" a familiar phrase. (Models for visual imagery, though, usually specified analog representations and operations rather than discrete ones.) Another option was the introduction of equations with variables specifying quantitative properties of a part (e.g., the familiarity or concreteness rating of a word being encoded in memory) or of an operation (e.g., the rate of encoding). Thus, information processing models integrating computational, symbolic, and quantitative perspectives became widespread (and still are).

In one well-known exemplar, Saul Sternberg (1966) devised a task in which a set of items, typically a list of digits, must be held in short-term memory and retrieved for comparison to a probe item. Sternberg explicitly brought together the symbolic and computational perspectives in his very first sentence: "How is symbolic information retrieved from recent memory?" That is, each item on the list was regarded as an external symbol that needed to be represented as a mental symbol, and then subjected to discrete computational operations like retrieval. He found that $RT = 392.7 + 37.9\ s$, where s is set size and RT is the mean reaction time (in msec.) to respond whether or not a single probe item was in the set of items on the just-presented list. He interpreted this as sufficient basis for rejecting a common "implicit assumption that a short time after several items have been memorized, they can be immediately and simultaneously available for expression in recall or in other responses, rather than having to be retrieved first" (p. 652). Instead, it appeared that each item was retrieved and compared to the probe in succession (a process that has been called *serial search, serial retrieval, serial comparison,* or simply *scanning*). Moreover, because the reaction time functions were almost identical for trials in which there was and was not a match, Sternberg contended that this process was not only serial but also exhaustive. If, to the contrary, the process terminated once a match was found, positive trials should have had a shallower slope and averaged just half the total reaction time of negative trials for a given set size.

Sternberg's deceptively simple paper illustrates several key points.

- The linear equation initially played the same straightforward role as Fechner's logarithmic equation: it precisely characterized a phenomenon.
- Sternberg aspired to explain the phenomenon that he characterized, and departed from the mathematical psychology of the 1950s by proposing a mechanism, rather than a more fundamental equation, that could produce the phenomenon of a linear relation between set size and RT.
- In the proposed mechanism – one of the earliest information processing models – the most important parts were a short-term memory store and mental symbols representing the probe and list items, the most important operation was retrieval, and the system was organized such that retrieval was both serial and exhaustive.
- The mechanism combined computational and symbolic approaches, in that its operations were performed on discrete mental symbols.
- In addition to the computational and symbolic approaches, the mechanistic explanation incorporated the quantitative approach of mathematical psychology as well. That is, Sternberg used his linear equation not only to characterize the phenomenon, but also as a source of detail regarding an operation. Specifically, he interpreted the slope (37.9 msec.) as the time consumed by each iteration of the retrieval operation.
- The underdetermination of explanation is hard to avoid. For example, although Sternberg regarded his data as pointing to a mechanism with serial processing, competing mechanisms based on parallel processing have been proposed that can account for the same data. The slope of the linear function is interpreted quite differently in these accounts.

Information processing models of cognitive mechanisms like Sternberg's took shape in the 1960s, became more complex and dominant in the 1970s, and still play a major role today. They also were a major antecedent to connectionism and have competed with this offspring since the 1980s. Mathematical psychologists generally ally themselves with either information processing or connectionist models. As mentioned above, however, a different mathematical modeling approach from outside psychology – dynamical systems theory – caught the attention of certain psychologists focusing on perception or motor control in the 1980s and then of cognitive scientists in the 1990s. We consider it next.

Adele Abrahamsen and William Bechtel

Dynamical Systems Theory and its Contributions to Cognitive Science

Dynamical systems theory

Researchers like linear equations; they are simple, well behaved, and amenable to statistical analysis. Numerous phenomena of interest to cognitive scientists can be characterized using such equations, even when time is one of the variables. For example, mean IQ scores increased linearly across the years of the twentieth century (a little-known and surprising fact called the *Flynn effect*; Flynn, 1987; Neisser, 1997). Another example, in which time is a dependent rather than independent variable, is Sternberg's finding that reaction time in his memory scanning task increased linearly with set size. When relationships are not linear, sometimes they can be made linear by transforming the data. For example, population growth is exponential. For purposes of analysis (unfortunately not in reality) the relationship of population size to time can be made linear by performing a logarithmic transformation. Exponential functions are common in mathematical psychology, both in characterizing phenomena and in theoretical laws proposed to explain phenomena, and in these uses present no undue difficulties.

Nature, though, is much less attached to simple linear and nonlinear functions than are the researchers trying to make sense of nature. It presents us with numerous phenomena in which the changes of state are nonlinear in complex ways. Working outside the scientific mainstream in the twentieth century, the pioneers of dynamical systems theory (DST) developed mathematical, graphical, and conceptual tools for characterizing such phenomena and learning from them. Though DST is best known for such exotic concepts as chaotic trajectories, Lorenz attractors, and fractals, some of its essentials can be conveyed in a relatively straightforward example (adapted from Abraham and Shaw, 1992, pp. 82–5). In the 1920s, Lotka and Volterra considered how the number of prey (x) and predators (y) in an idealized two-species ecosystem would change over time. They saw that cyclic population swings, in which neither predators nor prey can retain a permanent advantage, are obtained from a system of just two nonlinear differential equations (if appropriate values are provided for its four parameters A–D):

$$dx/dt = (A - By)x$$
$$dy/dt = (Cx - D)y$$

The notation dx/dt refers to the rate of change in the number of prey x over time t and dy/dt to the rate of change in the number of predators y over time t. Figure 10.3a shows just three of the cyclic trajectories that can be obtained from these equations by specifying different initial values of x and y. They differ in the size of the population swings, but share the fate that whichever trajectory is embarked upon will be repeated *ad infinitum*. If the initial values are at the central equilibrium point, also shown, there are no population swings – it is as though births continuously replace deaths in each group. A more interesting situation arises if the equations are modified by adding "ecological friction" (similar to the physical friction that brings

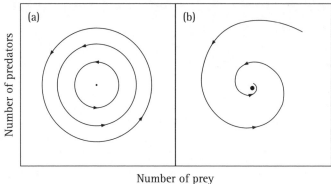

Figure 10.3 Two kinds of trajectories through state space for a predator and prey population: (a) cyclic trajectory (equilibrium point is not an attractor) and (b) spiraling trajectory (equilibrium point is a point attractor).

a pendulum asymptotically to rest by damping its oscillations). Now the swings decrease over time as the system spirals towards, but never quite reaches, its point of equilibrium. In this modified system the point of equilibrium is an *attractor state* (specifically, a *point attractor* in *state space*, or equivalently, a *limit point* in *phase space*) – one of the simplest concepts in DST and very influential in some parts of cognitive science. Figure 10.3b shows a point attractor and one of the trajectories spiraling towards it. The type of graphic display used in figure 10.3, called a *phase portrait*, is one of DST's useful innovations. Time is indicated by the continuous sequence of states in each sample trajectory. This leaves all dimensions available for showing the state space, at a cost of not displaying the rate (or changes in rate) at which the trajectory is traversed. If graphic display of the rate is desired, a more traditional plot with time on the abscissa can be used.

In the 1980s DST captured the attention of a few psychologists who recognized its advantages for characterizing phenomena of perception, motor behavior and development. By the 1990s DST was having a broader impact in cognitive science. As in the case of mathematical psychology before it, the use of DST progressed through phases:

- First, primarily exploring how dynamic phenomena, especially of motor behavior and development, could be characterized using the mathematical, graphical, and conceptual tools of DST;
- Increasingly with experience, also extracting or applying theoretical principles, for example, metastability (see below) or the well-known "sensitivity to initial conditions" with regards to those dynamic systems that behave chaotically;
- Finally, combining the theoretical principles and the tools for characterizing phenomena with other commitments so as to achieve a dynamical framework specifically tailored to cognitive science.

In recognition of the additional commitments involved in tailoring dynamical accounts to cognitive science, reference is most often made to the *dynamical approach* to cognition rather than *DST* as such. And given that individuals disagree about some of

Adele Abrahamsen and William Bechtel

those commitments, it is best understood as a family of approaches. One of the major disagreements involves mechanistic explanation. On one view, the dynamical approach is valuable for its way of characterizing phenomena and its theoretical explanations, and that style of explanation is preferable to mechanistic explanation. Thus, the dynamical approach should be adopted in preference to symbolic, connectionist, or any other mechanistic accounts (see, for example, papers in Port and van Gelder, 1995). Opposing this are dynamical approaches that combine aspects of DST with mechanistic modeling of cognition (e.g., Elman's use of dynamical concepts such as attractors to better understand interactive connectionist models, or van Leeuwen's use of dynamical tools in constructing small-grained coupled map lattice models). Another axis of difference is the timescale involved. In addition to models targeting the fleeting dynamics of motor, perceptual, or cognitive acts, there are highly influential models of change across developmental time. In each of the next three sections we offer a glimpse of one of these dynamical approaches to cognition.

A dynamical approach with no mechanisms

Dynamicists in cognitive science who refrain from mechanistic explanation tend to advocate holism. Making the assumption that all aspects of a system are changing simultaneously, they "focus on how a system changes from one total state to another. . . . The distinctive character of some cognitive process as it unfolds over time is a matter of how the total states the system passes through are spatially located with respect to one another and the dynamical landscape of the system" (van Gelder and Port, 1995, pp. 14–15). Timothy van Gelder contrasts this holism with several characteristics he attributes to the symbolic approach – homuncularity, representation, computation, and sequential and cyclic operation – and maintains that "a device with any one of them will standardly possess others" (van Gelder, 1995, p. 351). *Homuncularity* refers to Dennett's (1978) conception of cognitive explanation as a decomposition of cognitive processes into little agents, each responsible for one operation in the overall activity of the cognitive system. This approach is often referred to as *homuncular functionalism* (Lycan, 1979) and involves a kind of decomposition that is characteristic of mechanistic explanations. In arguing instead for a dynamical alternative, van Gelder cites James Watt's governor for the steam engine (figure 10.4) and maintains that it is best understood in terms of the dynamical equations Maxwell developed for describing its activity. But Bechtel (1997) argued that the smooth overall functioning of Watt's governor offers insufficient grounds for the extreme holism espoused by van Gelder and some other dynamicists. As with any mechanism, component parts and operations can be identified: the flywheel rotates, the spindle arms become extended, the valve closes. The parts are spatially organized in ways that help organize the operations. It makes sense, for example, to ask why Watt attached the spindle arms to the spindle coming out of the flywheel and to answer that question in terms of the resulting relationship between two of the operations: as the flywheel rotates, the angle arms become extended. These relationships can be quantified by defining variables corresponding to properties of the operations and measuring their values under a variety of circumstances; Maxwell's equations economically express the outcome of such a procedure. They permit, for example,

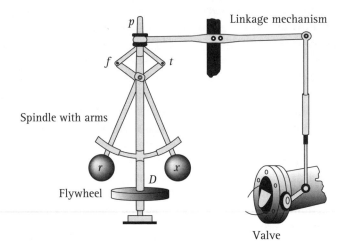

Figure 10.4 Watt's centrifugal governor for a steam engine. Drawing from Farley (1827).

prediction of the angle of the spindle arms given any particular speed at which the flywheel rotates. This is very useful, but does not imply holism.

In addition to their holism, these dynamicists also have a preference for parsimony that is similar to that of classic mathematical psychologists (those who had not yet adopted a mechanistic information processing framework within which to apply their mathematical techniques). A simple dynamical account typically targets phenomena involving a small number of quantitative variables and parameters. One of the earliest examples relevant to cognitive science is Scott Kelso's account of the complex dynamics evoked in a deceptively simple task used to study motor control. Participants were asked to repeatedly move their index fingers either in phase (both move up together, then down together) or antiphase (one moves up while the other moves down) in time with a metronome (Kelso, 1995). As the metronome speed increases, people can no longer maintain the antiphase movement and involuntarily switch to in-phase movement. In DST terms, the two moving fingers are *coupled oscillators*. Slow speeds (low frequencies) permit a stable coupling either in-phase or antiphase: the state space has two attractors. At high speeds only in-phase coupling is possible: the state space has only one attractor. Kelso offered a relatively simple equation that provides for characterization of the attractor landscape (*V*) as parameter values change:

$$V = -\,\varphi\delta\omega - a\cos\varphi - b\cos 2\varphi$$

Here φ is the degree of asynchrony between the two fingers (*relative phase*), $\delta\omega$ reflects the difference between the metronome's frequency and the spontaneous oscillation frequency of the fingers, and a and b indirectly reflect the actual oscillation frequency of the fingers. When the ratio b/a is small, oscillation is fast and only the in-phase attractor exists. When it is large, there are two attractors: people can produce in-phase or antiphase movement as instructed or voluntarily traverse a trajectory between them.

Adele Abrahamsen and William Bechtel

Things get interesting when the ratio a/b is intermediate between values that clearly provide either one or two attractors. The attractors disappear but each "leaves behind a remnant or a phantom of itself" (Kelso, 1995, p. 109). The system's trajectory now exhibits *intermittency*, approaching but then swinging away from the phantom attractors. Putting it more concretely, the two index fingers fluctuate chaotically between in-phase and antiphase movement. Although such intermittency may not seem particularly important, if we shift to a different domain we can recognize it as a significant characteristic of cognition. Most people have had the experience, when looking long enough at an ambiguous figure such as the Necker cube, of an irregular series of shifts between the two interpretations. The temporal pattern of these spontaneous shifts is *chaotic* – a technical concept in DST that refers to trajectories in state space in which no point is revisited (such trajectories appear random but in fact are deterministic). Kelso remarked on the similarity between the finger-movement and Necker cube tasks, not only in the switching-time data he displayed but also in the quantitative and graphical analyses of the systems. Given the wide range of applicability of these analyses, their elegance, and their depth, they clearly go beyond characterizing phenomena to explaining them via re-characterization. Nonetheless, they provide only one of the two types of explanation we have discussed. In the next section we introduce an alternative dynamical approach that offers intriguing new ideas about mechanistic explanation.

A dynamical approach with subsymbolic mechanisms

Kelso chose to focus on switching time phenomena and center his explanation on a single dynamical equation with variables capturing aspects of the system as a whole. Here we look at a mechanistic explanation for the same phenomenon. Cees van Leeuwen and his collaborators (van Leeuwen et al., 1997) developed a model that is both dynamical and mechanistic by using a dynamical equation to govern (not only to describe) the operations of the fine-grained component parts of a mechanism. It is similar to a connectionist model insofar as its component parts are numerous homogeneous units, some with pairwise connections, that become activated in response to an input. However, in this case the units are more sparsely connected and are designed as oscillators that can synchronize or desynchronize their oscillations. Particular patterns of synchronization across the units are treated as constituting different interpretations of the input.

More specifically, van Leeuwen et al. employed a *coupled map lattice* (CML) of the sort first explored by Kaneko (1990). A *lattice* is a sparsely connected network in which only neighboring units are connected (*coupled*); the basic idea is illustrated by a large construction from Tinkertoys or a fishnet. A *map* is a type of function in which values are iteratively determined in discrete time. Kaneko employed the logistic equation

$$x_{t+1} = A \, x_t (1 - x_t)$$

to govern the activation (x) of units at a future time $t + 1$ on the basis of their current activation. Depending on the value of the parameter A, such units will oscillate between a small number of values or behave chaotically. For nearby units to influence each other, there must be connections between them. Although van Leeuwen's proposed mechanistic model used 50 × 50 arrays of units, with each unit coupled to four neighbors, his analysis of a CML with just two units suffices for illustration. In his account, the net input to unit x is determined from the activation of x and the other unit y:

$$netinput_x = Ca_y + (1 - C)a_x$$

The logistic function is then applied to the resulting net input to determine the activation of unit x:

$$a_{x,t+1} = A\ netinput_{x,t}(1 - netinput_{x,t})$$

The behavior of the resulting network is determined by the two parameters, A and C. For a range of values of A relative to C, the two units will come to change their activation values in synchrony. Outside this range, however, the system exhibits the same kind of intermittency as did Kelso's higher-level system. For some values, the two units approach synchrony, only to spontaneously depart from synchrony and wander through state space until they again approach synchrony. With larger networks, one constellation of nearby units may approach synchrony only to break free; then another constellation of units may approach synchrony. These temporary approaches to synchrony were interpreted by van Leeuwen et al. as realizing a particular interpretation of an ambiguous figure. Thus, there are echoes of Kelso not only in the achievement of intermittency but also in its interpretation. Nonetheless, van Leeuwen et al's full-scale CML is clearly mechanistic: it explains a higher-level phenomenon as emerging from the dynamics of numerous, finer-grained parts and operations at a lower level. This contrasts with the more typical dynamical approach, exemplified by Kelso, of describing a phenomenon at its own level using just a few variables in a global equation.

Dynamical approaches to development

The earliest dynamical approaches to development were more in the vein of Kelso than of van Leeuwen. Notably, Esther Thelen (1985) initially drew attention to dynamics by showing how global equations could account elegantly for phenomena of infant motor development. She saw bipedal locomotion, for example, as residing "in the dynamics of two coupled pendulums" (limbs). Collaboration with colleagues at Indiana University, especially Linda Smith and Michael Gasser, yielded a more ambitious, potent package of theoretical elaborations and extended the empirical work to cognitive and linguistic development. Their fresh ideas are best conveyed in quotations (taken from Smith and Gasser, 2005): "Babies begin with a body richly endowed with multiple sensory and action systems." Those systems are coupled to a heterogeneous physical world and also, via "smart social partners," to social and linguistic worlds. The developing intelligence of babies is embodied. That is, it resides "not just inside themselves but . . . distributed across their interactions and experiences in the physical world" – interactions that are exploratory, multimodal, incremental, simultaneous, and continuous. The physical world is "full of rich regularities that organize perception [and] action" and offer opportunities for offloading aspects of

Adele Abrahamsen and William Bechtel

cognition that might otherwise require internal inferences or predicate bindings. Experience with this world "serves to bootstrap higher mental functions," but once in the system, language in particular provides computational power that "profoundly changes the learner."

These ideas did not take shape in an armchair, but rather emerged as the Indiana team extended their range to a variety of developmental domains and moved towards a more mechanistic style of dynamical modeling. Though some of the mechanisms they have proposed are connectionist networks, most innovative is their dynamic field model of the A-not-B error in Piaget's classic object concept task (Thelen et al., 2001). They explored many variations of this task, but essentially a researcher places two cups in front of a baby (7 to 12 months old) and repeatedly hides an enticing object under the cup on the left. Each time it is hidden, the baby retrieves it. Then, making a great show of it, the researcher hides the object under the cup on the right. The baby watches what is happening on the *right* like a hawk, but then picks up the cup on the *left* and hence fails to get the desired object. What went wrong? Piaget's interpretation involves an intermediate stage in development of the concept of object. In the dynamic field model, equations specify activation functions that are continuous across the left-right spatial field, coupled, and dynamically changing at multiple timescales. Essentially, the influence of the memory field (which has a peak on the left) can override that of the perception field (which has a peak on the right during the critical trial) as they dynamically mesh in the motor planning field. If an above-threshold peak on the left dominates that field, the baby will reach to the left. Nothing in these exquisite equations could be interpreted as a representation of an object. Although this account does not rule out positing that such a representation also exists, this strikes Thelen and her colleagues as superfluous and non-parsimonious.

Dynamical approaches to development have also been adopted by cognitive scientists whose initial domains of interest were language and cognition rather than motor development and whose modeling preferences have ranged from the competition model to connectionist networks. For a lucid review bristling with examples and recent innovations see MacWhinney, 2005. For a longer exploration that is thought provoking but accessible even to novices, see Elman et al. (1996) *Rethinking Innateness*, The product of an unusual collaboration involving six leading developmental theorists, this wide-ranging book includes a number of illustrations of different roles played by equations.

We have already seen, in the differing accounts of the U-shaped function relating age and past-tense formation for irregular verbs, that dissimilar mechanistic proposals can compete as explanations for a single nonlinear developmental phenomenon. Sometimes these disputes are rooted in choices researchers make at the outset about the equations used to characterize the phenomenon. *Rethinking Innateness* offers a very readable guide to the kinds of equations used and their implications. It also covers both kinds of explanation for nonlinear phenomena: mechanistic models (in the form of connectionist networks) and global theoretical equations. One example discussed by Elman et al. involves the shape of early vocabulary acquisition: slow growth to about 50 words and then a "vocabulary burst" initiating a period of rapid growth that can add several hundred words in a few months. The most obvious way to characterize this phenomenon mathematically is to posit two separate linear equations with different slopes, one for the first 50 words and the other beyond 50 words. Among the explanations invited by this characterization are a sudden insight that things have names (Baldwin, 1989) and a change in categorization (Gopnik and Meltzoff, 1987). These explanations seem far less apt when the same vocabulary data are characterized using a single nonlinear equation. Elman et al. offered the following exponential function for data from 10–24 months of age (p. 182):

$$y = y_0\, e^{b(t-t_0)}$$

where the number of words known at t_0 (10 months) is y_0 and at any other t is y. When displayed graphically, y is seen to increase slowly, then bend upwards, then increase rapidly. Thus, this function can fit the acquisition data about as well as the two straight lines – so well that a choice cannot be made based on fit. What is appealing about the single nonlinear function is that there is an underlying simplicity. The amount y will increase in the next unit of time is proportional to the current value of y:

$$dy/dt = by$$

where dy/dt is a notation indicating that we are concerned with the number of additional words to be added per unit of time, b is the percentage increase across that time (which does not change), and y is the current number of words (which increases with t). This equation arguably is explanatory, in that it re-characterizes the first equation so as to explicate that a constant *percentage* increase is responsible for its exponential *absolute* increase.

Elman et al. emphasize that a single mechanism can produce slow initial vocabulary growth as well as a later vocabulary burst. This does not mean nothing else can be involved; they themselves go on to consider a more complicated version of their initial account. The point is that the burst, as such, does not require any special explanation such as a naming insight; "the behavior of the system can have different characteristics at different times although the same mechanisms are always operating" (p. 185). In another part of their book (pp. 124–9), Elman et al. describe an auto-associative connectionist network that, though limited to simplified representations, suggests a mechanistic explanation. It replicates not only the quantitative phenomenon of a vocabulary burst (exponential growth), but also such phenomena as a tendency to underextension prior to the burst and overextension thereafter.

Abrupt transitions are not uncommon in development, and connectionist networks excel at producing this kind of nonlinear dynamic. Another example discussed by Elman et al. targets the transitions observed by Robert Siegler (1981) when children try to solve balance-scale problems. They appear to progress through stages in which different rules are used (roughly: weight, then distance, then whichever of these is more appropriate). McClelland and Jenkins (1991) created a connectionist network that offered a simplified simulation of the abrupt transitions between these three stages. While intrigued by this capability, Elman et al. commented that "simulating one black box with another does us little good. What we really want is to understand exactly what the underlying mechanism is in the network which gives rise to such behavior" (p. 230).

Adele Abrahamsen and William Bechtel

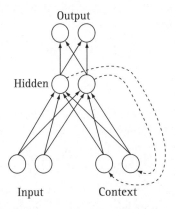

Output

Hidden

Input   Context

Figure 10.5 Simple recurrent network as proposed by Jeffrey Elman (1990). For clarity, fewer units are shown than would be typical. The solid arrows represent feedforward connections used to connect each unit in one layer with each unit in the next layer. The dotted arrows indicate the recurrent (backwards) connections that connect the hidden units to specialized input units called *context units*.

To address this question they explored a type of connectionist network that exhibits time dynamics in its behavior. Unlike feedforward networks, such as those used in the past tense, vocabulary, and balance-scale simulations, *recurrent networks* include recurrent (backwards) connections between certain sets of units (figure 10.5). Rather than a single forward pass of activation changes, each unit in a recurrent network repeatedly has its activation recalculated as the network (typically) settles gradually into a stable response to the input – an attractor state. Elman et al. began by training a recurrent network to perform a simple demonstration task: determining parity for a long string of 1s and 0s (that is, deciding whether the number of 1s is odd or even). They succeeded in simulating the phenomenon of abrupt transitions; in fact, after 17,999 training cycles the network could not do the task and after just one more training trial it could. To understand why, they simplified further by examining a single unit with a nonlinear activation function commonly employed in connectionist modeling. This unit starts with an initial activation and on successive time-steps receives input from a constant input (called a *bias*) and a recurrent connection from itself. With a weight on the recurrent connection of 1.0 and a bias of −0.5, the unit after several iterations settles to an activation of 0.5 and remains there. With a weight of 10.0 and a bias of −5.0, however, the unit will settle to an activation of 0.0 when its initial activation is below 0.5, to an activation of 1.0 when its initial activation is above 0.5, and to 0.5 when its initial activation is 0.5. These two kinds of behavior reflect a network unable to retain information versus one able to retain information. Further exploration of values of weight and bias enabled the researchers to map the response of such a unit. They found a region in which a very small change in the weight created a large change in behavior, and noted that DST could provide exactly the right tools for pursuing and understanding this kind of nonlinearity.

Phenomena and Mechanisms

Conclusions

Our strategy through this paper has been to show that the range of phenomena for which mechanistic models are sought is extremely varied and to illustrate briefly some of the kinds of models of mechanisms that have been advanced to account for different phenomena. The focus in the philosophical literature on systematicity and other general properties of cognitive architectures presents a distorted view of the actual debates in the psychological literature over the types of mechanisms required to account for cognitive behavior. Even in the domain of language, where systematicity is best exemplified, many additional phenomena claim the attention of cognitive scientists. We discussed two that are quantitative in nature: the U-shaped acquisition of irregular past-tense forms and the exponential acquisition of early vocabulary. Beyond language we have alluded to work targeting the rich domains of perceptual and motor behavior, memory, and problem solving. Phenomena in all of these domains are part of the explanandum of mechanistic explanation in cognitive science. Such explanatory attempts, which like the phenomena themselves often are quantitative, go back as far as Weber's psychophysics and currently are moving forward in dynamical approaches to perception, cognition, and development.

We have also emphasized that cognitive science, despite its many disputes, has progressed by continually combining and recombining a variety of influences. The use of equations both in characterizing and explaining phenomena are among these. When combined with other influences and commitments, the outcomes discussed here have ranged from information processing models with quantified operations to connectionist networks to both global and mechanistic dynamical accounts. Each of these approaches has provided a different answer to the question of whether the mind processes language-like representations according to formal rules, and we have argued that the overall answer need not be limited to just one of these. Cognitive science takes multiple shapes at a given time, and is protean across time.

> I am large, I contain multitudes.
> (Walt Whitman, *Leaves of Grass*)

Note

1 According to Estes (2002), the publication of the three-volume *Handbook of Mathematical Psychology* (Luce et al., 1963–5) galvanized development of professional organizations for mathematical psychologists. The *Journal of Mathematical Psychology* began publishing in 1964. The Society for Mathematical Psychology began holding meetings in 1968, although official establishment of the society and legal incorporation only occurred in 1977.

References

Abraham, R. H. and Shaw, C. D. (1992). *Dynamics: The Geometry of Behavior.* Redwood City, CA: Addison-Wesley.

Adele Abrahamsen and William Bechtel

Baldwin, D. A. (1989). Establishing word–object relations: a first step. *Child Development*, 60, 381–98.

Bechtel, W. (1997). Dynamics and decomposition: are they compatible? *Proceedings of the Australasian Cognitive Science Society*.

Bechtel, W. and Abrahamsen, A. (2002). *Connectionism and the Mind: Parallel Processing, Dynamics, and Evolution in Networks* (2nd edn.). Oxford: Blackwell.

— and — (2005). Explanation: A mechanist alternative. *Studies in History and Philosophy of Biological and Biomedical Sciences*, 36, 421–41.

Bechtel, W. and Richardson, R. C. (1993). *Discovering Complexity: Decomposition and Localization as Scientific Research Strategies*. Princeton, NJ: Princeton University Press.

Bechtel, W., Abrahamsen, A., and Graham, G. (1998). The life of cognitive science. In W. Bechtel and G. Graham (eds.), *A Companion to Cognitive Science*. Oxford: Blackwell.

Brown, R. (1973). *A First Language: The Early Stages*. Cambridge, MA: Harvard University Press.

Bush, R. R. and Mosteller, F. (1951). A mathematical model for simple learning. *Psychological Review*, 58, 313–23.

Cummins, R. (2000). "How does it work?" versus "what are the laws?": Two conceptions of psychological explanation. In F. Keil and R. Wilson (eds.), *Explanation and Cognition*. Cambridge, MA: MIT Press.

Dennett, D. C. (1978). *Brainstorms*. Cambridge, MA: MIT Press.

Ebbinghaus, H. (1885). *Über das Gedächtnis: Untersuchungen zur Experimentellen Psychologie*. Leipzig: Duncker & Humblot.

Elman, J. L. (1990). Finding structure in time. *Cognitive Science*, 14, 179–211.

Elman, J. L., Bates, E. A., Johnson, M. H., Karmiloff-Smith, A., Parisi, D., and Plunkett, K. (1996). *Rethinking Innateness: A Connectionist Perspective on Development*. Cambridge, MA: MIT Press.

Ervin, S. (1964). Imitation and structural change in children's language. In E. Lenneberg (ed.), *New Directions in the Study of Language*. Cambridge, MA: MIT Press.

Estes, W. K. (1950). Towards a statistical theory of learning. *Psychological Review*, 57, 94–107.

— (2002). Mathematical psychology, history of. In *International Encyclopedia of the Social and Behavioral Sciences*. New York: Elsevier.

Falmagne, J.-C. (2002). Mathematical psychology. In *International Encyclopedia of the Social and Behavioral Sciences*. New York: Elsevier.

Farley, J. (1827). *A Treatise on the Steam Engine: Historical, Practical, and Descriptive*. London: Longman, Rees, Orme, Brown, and Green.

Fechner, G. T. (1860). *Elemente der Psychophysik*. Leipzig: Breitkopf und Härtel.

Flynn, J. R. (1987). Massive IQ gains in 14 nations: What IQ tests really measure. *Psychological Bulletin*, 101, 171–91.

Garcia, J., McGowan, B. K., Ervin, F. R., and Koelling, R. A. (1968). Cues: Their relative effectiveness as a function of the reinforcer. *Science*, 160, 794–5.

Glennan, S. (1996). Mechanisms and the nature of causation. *Erkenntnis*, 44, 50–71.

— (2002). Rethinking mechanistic explanation. *Philosophy of Science*, 69, S342–53.

Gopnik, A. and Meltzoff, A. N. (1987). The development of categorization in the second year and its relation to other cognitive linguistic developments. *Child Development*, 58, 1523–31.

Hempel, C. G. (1965). Aspects of scientific explanation. In C. G. Hempel (ed.), *Aspects of Scientific Explanation and Other Essays in the Philosophy of Science*. New York: Macmillan.

Hull, C. L. (1943). *Principles of Behavior*. New York: Appleton-Century-Crofts.

Kaneko, K. (1990). Clustering, coding, switching, hierarchical ordering, and control in a network of chaotic elements. *Physica D*, 41, 137–42.

Kelso, J. A. S. (1995). *Dynamic Patterns: The Self Organization of Brain and Behavior*. Cambridge, MA: MIT Press.

Kitcher, P. (1999). Unification as a regulative ideal. *Perspectives on Science*, 7, 337–48.

Kuczaj, S. A. (1977). The acquisition of regular and irregular past tense forms. *Journal of Verbal Learning and Verbal Behavior*, 16, 589–600.

Luce, R. D., Bush, R. R. B., and Galanter, E. (eds.) (1963–5). *Handbook of Mathematical Psychology*. New York: Wiley.

Lycan, W. G. (1979). Form, function, and feel. *Journal of Philosophy*, 78, 24–49.

Machamer, P., Darden, L., and Craver, C. (2000). Thinking about mechanisms. *Philosophy of Science*, 67, 1–25.

MacWhinney, B. (2005). The emergence of linguistic form in time. *Connection Science*, 17, 191–211.

Marcus, G. F. (2001). *The Algebraic Mind: Integrating Connectionism and Cognitive Science*. Cambridge, MA: MIT Press.

McClelland, J. L. and Jenkins, E. (1991). Nature, nurture and connectionism: implications for connectionist models of development. In K. van Lehn (ed.), *Architectures for Intelligence: The Twenty-second (1988) Carnegie Symposium on Cognition*, 41–73. Hillsdale: Erlbaum.

McClelland, J. L. and Patterson, K. (2002a). 'Words or Rules' cannot exploit the regularity in exceptions. *Trends in Cognitive Sciences*, 6, 464–5.

— and — (2002b). Rules or connections in past-tense inflections: What does the evidence rule out? *Trends in Cognitive Sciences*, 6, 465–72.

Nagel, E. (1961). *The Structure of Science*. New York: Harcourt, Brace.

Neisser, U. (1997). Rising scores on intelligence tests. *American Scientist*, 85, 440–7.

Newport, E. L. and Aslin, R. N. (2000). Innately constrained learning: Blending old and new approaches to language acquisition. In S. C. Howell, S. A. Fish, and T. Keith-Lucas (eds.), *Proceedings of the 24th Annual Boston University Conference on Language Development*, 1–21. Somerville, MA: Cascadilla Press.

— and — (2004). Learning at a distance: I. Statistical learning of non-adjacent dependencies. *Cognitive Psychology*, 48, 127–62.

Norman, D. A. and Rumelhart, D. E. (1975). *Explorations in Cognition*. San Francisco: Freeman.

Pinker, S. and Prince, A. (1988). On language and connectionism: Analysis of a parallel distributed processing model of language acquisition. *Cognition*, 28, 73–193.

Pinker, S. and Ullman, M. T. (2002a). The past and future of the past tense. *Trends in Cognitive Sciences*, 6, 456–63.

— and — (2002b). Combination and structure, not gradedness, is the issue. *Trends in Cognitive Sciences*, 6, 472–4.

Plunkett, K. and Marchman, V. (1991). U-shaped learning and frequency effects in a multilayered perceptron. *Cognition*, 38, 43–102.

— and — (1993). From rote learning to system building: Acquiring verb morphology in children and connectionist nets. *Cognition*, 48, 21–69.

Port, R. and van Gelder, T. (1995). *It's About Time*. Cambridge, MA: MIT Press.

Prince, A. and Smolensky, P. (1997). Optimality: From neural networks to universal grammar. *Science*, 275, 1604–10.

— and — (2004). *Optimality Theory: Constraint Interaction in Generative Grammar*. Oxford: Blackwell.

Quillian, M. R. (1968). Semantic memory. In M. Minsky (ed.), *Semantic Information Processing*. Cambridge, MA: MIT Press.

Rosenblatt, F. (1962). *Principles of Neurodynamics: Perceptrons and the Theory of Brain Mechanisms*. Washington: Spartan Books.

Rumelhart, D. E. and McClelland, J. L. (1986a). On learning the past tenses of English verbs. In J. L. McClelland and D. E. Rumelhart (eds.), *Parallel Distributed Processing: Explorations*

Adele Abrahamsen and William Bechtel

in the Microstructure of Cognition, vol. 2: Psychological and Biological Models. Cambridge, MA: MIT Press.

— and — (eds.) (1986b). *Parallel Distributed Processing: Explorations in the Microstructure of Cognition*, vol. 1: *Foundations*. Cambridge, MA: MIT Press.

Saffran, J. R., Aslin, R. N., and Newport, E. L. (1996). Statistical learning by 8-month-old infants. *Science*, 274, 1926–8.

Siegler, R. (1981). Developmental sequences within and between concepts. *Monographs of the Society for Research in Child Development*, 46/2.

Smith, L. B. and Gasser, M. (2005). The development of embodied cognition: six lessons from babies. *Artificial Life*, 11, 13–30.

Sternberg, S. (1966). High-speed scanning in human memory. *Science*, 153, 652–4.

Stevens, S. S. (1957). On the psychophysical law. *Psychological Review*, 64, 153–81.

Suppe, F. (1974). The search for philosophical understanding of scientific theories. In F. Suppe (ed.), *The Structure of Scientific Theories*. Urbana, IL: University of Illinois Press.

Tesar, B., Grimshaw, J., and Prince, A. (1999). Linguistic and cognitive explanation in optimality theory. In E. Lepore and Z. W. Pylyshyn (eds.), *What is Cognitive Science?*. Oxford: Blackwell.

Thelen, E. (1985). Developmental origins of motor coordination: leg movements in human infants. *Developmental Psychobiology*, 18, 1–22.

Thelen, E., Schöner, G., Scheier, C., and Smith, L. B. (2001). The dynamics of embodiment: A field theory of infant perseverative reaching. *Behavioral and Brain Sciences*, 24, 1–34.

Van Gelder, T. (1995). What might cognition be, if not computation. *The Journal of Philosophy*, 92, 345–81.

Van Gelder, T. and Port, R. (1995). It's about time: An overview of the dynamical approach to cognition. In R. Port and T. van Gelder (eds.), *It's About Time*. Cambridge, MA: MIT Press.

Van Leeuwen, C., Steyvers, M., and Nooter, M. (1997). Stability and intermittency in large-scale coupled oscillator models for perceptual segmentation. *Journal of Mathematical Psychology*, 41, 319–44.

Weber, E. H. (1834). *De pulsu, resorpitione, auditu et tactu: annotationes anatomicae et physiologicae*. Leipzig: Koehlor.

CAN CONSCIOUSNESS AND QUALIA BE REDUCED?

CHAPTER ELEVEN

Consciousness and Qualia Can be Reduced

William G. Lycan

Whether consciousness and qualia can be reduced depends on what is meant by "consciousness," "qualia," and "reduced." "Consciousness" has been used to mean nearly anything, and the variety of intellectual structures that have been called "theories of consciousness" is astonishing. (Brian Smith once said of computation that it "is a *site*, not a subject-matter"; "consciousness" is a flea market or jumble sale, not even a site.) And even the deliberately technical term "qualia" has a surprising number of importantly distinct senses in the literature.

Explananda

I shall address just three notions of consciousness, the three that seem to occupy most theorists in contemporary philosophy of mind:

1 Conscious awareness, and "conscious states" in the sense of mental states whose subjects are directly aware of being in them.[1]
2 "Phenomenal consciousness," as Block (1995) calls it, viz., being in a sensory state that has a distinctive qualitative or phenomenal character.
3 The matter of "what it is like" for the subject to experience a particular phenomenal property – which many writers (including Block) fail to distinguish from (2). It too is sometimes called "phenomenal consciousness."

The main uses of the term "qualia" (singular, "quale") parallel (2) and (3). A quale in the sense of C. I. Lewis (1929) is the sort of qualitative or phenomenal property mentioned in (2): the color of an after-image, or of a more ordinary patch in one's visual field; the pitch or volume or timbre of a subjectively heard sound; the smell of an odor; a particular taste; the texture encountered by touch in feeling some object in the dark.

Some writers, in my view inaccurately, have used the phrase "what it is like" (hereafter "w.i.l."), brought to the fore by Farrell (1950) and Nagel (1974) to mean just a quale in the sense just mentioned. But the more common use is as in (3) above: what it is like for the subject to experience a particular phenomenal property or quale, a higher-order property of the quale itself. Just as unfortunately, "qualia" and "quale" themselves have been used in the higher-order sense of (3). I shall here reserve "quale" for (2) and "w.i.l." for (3).

It is important to see that those two uses differ. First, just to make the obvious point, if w.i.l. is a higher-order property of a quale, it cannot be the quale itself. Second, as Carruthers (2000) points out, a quale presents itself as part of the world, not as part of one's mind. It is the apparent color of an apparently physical object (or, if you are a Russellian, the color of a sense-datum that you have happened to encounter as an object of consciousness); as Carruthers says, a quale is what *the world* is or seems like. But w.i.l. to experience that color is what your first-order perceptual state is like, quintessentially mental and experienced as such.

Third, a quale can be described in one's public natural language, while what it is like to experience the quale seems to be ineffable. If you are experiencing a reddish after-image and I ask you, "What color does it look to you?", you will reply, "It looks red." But if I persevere and ask you w.i.l. to experience that "red" look, you can only go comparative: "It looks the same color as that," pointing to some nearby object. If I press further and insist on an intrinsic characterization, you will probably go blank. In one way, you can describe the phenomenal color, as "red," but when asked w.i.l. to experience that red, you cannot describe that directly. So there is a difference between "w.i.l" in the bare sense of the quale, the phenomenal color that can be described using ordinary color words, and w.i.l. to experience that phenomenal color, which cannot easily be described in public natural language at all.

And fourth, a bit more tendentiously, Armstrong (1968), Nelkin (1989), Rosenthal (1991), and Lycan (1996) have argued that qualia can fail to be conscious in the earlier sense (1) of awareness. That is, a quale can occur without its being noticed by its subject. But in such a case, it would not be like anything for the subject to experience that quale. So even when one is aware of a quale, the "w.i.l." requires awareness and so is something distinct from the quale itself.

Reduction

Reduction is sometimes understood as a relation between theories, typically as a derivational relation between sets of sentences or propositions. But in our title question it is applied to consciousness and qualia themselves, so its sense is ontological. It may apply to individual entities, to properties, to events, processes, or states of affairs.

Let us further distinguish type reduction from token reduction. Token reduction is the weaker notion: A's are token-reducible to B's iff every A is entirely constituted by some arrangement of B's. Thus, chess pieces are token-reducible to the micro-entities of physics, because every individual chess piece is entirely constituted by

William G. Lycan

such entities. But chess pieces are not type-reducible to physics, because there is no correlation between rooks (or for that matter between chess pieces as such) and any particular type of configuration of subatomic particles described in the language of physics. A's are type-reducible to B's iff every standard type of A is constituted by a specific type of configuration described in B language. Thus, lightning is type-reducible to high-voltage electrical discharge in the sky, table salt to the compound NaCl, and so on.

The identity of *properties* as conceived here is a matter of type-reduction of their instances. The property of being salt reduces to the property of being NaCl, since quantities of salt are type-reducible to quantities of NaCl; the property of being cash is that of having been made legal or quasi-legal tender in a given population; etc. (But type-reduction of instances as defined above does not entail property identity, since it may involve only constitution rather than strict identity.)

Consciousness(es) and qualia are even less likely to be type-reduced to physics than are chess pieces, but I will suggest that they are token-reducible, and that they can be type-reduced to functional and information-theoretic properties located at various higher levels of a creature's physical organization.

Conscious Awareness and Conscious States

Again, a "conscious state" in the present sense is a mental state whose subject is directly aware of being in it. Not all mental states have that awareness property. Sometimes I am in a mental state without being aware of that state, though I could have been aware of it had I paid introspective attention. Some of my psychological states, such as language-processing or texture-gradient-computing states, are structurally inaccessible to introspection. Can we type-identify the awareness property with anything less problematic?

There are several theories of conscious awareness and conscious states: Dennett's (1978) Volume Control theory; and two rival "higher-order representation" (HOR) accounts. The two HOR accounts are the Lockean "inner sense" or "higher-order perception" (HOP) theory offered by Armstrong (1968, 1981) and Lycan (1987, 1996), and the "higher-order thought" (HOT) theory defended by Rosenthal (1993; see also Gennaro, 1995, and Carruthers, 2000).[2] According to HOR theories, which currently prevail, a subject's awareness of her/his own mental state consists in a representing of that state itself. HOP has it that the representing is done quasi-perceptually, by a set of functionally specified internal attention mechanisms of some kind that scan or monitor "first-order" mental/brain states. HOT theorists say that merely having a thought about the first-order state will suffice, provided that the thought was directly caused by the state itself or at least not be the result of "ordinary inference" in Rosenthal's phrase.

Any version of HOR easily explains the differences between conscious and non-conscious first-order states; a state is, or is not, or could not be a conscious state accordingly as it itself is, or is not, or psychofunctionally could not be the object of a higher-order quasi-perception or thought. Further motivation for a HOR theory of awareness is obvious enough as well: in general, to be aware of any thing or state of affairs is to represent that item in some way, and to be unaware or unconscious of it is to fail to represent it. And when we deliberately introspect and thereby become aware of a first-order mental state that we had not realized we were in, the awareness is quasi-perceptual or at least takes the form of some mental state itself directed upon the first-order state; it feels as though we are "looking at" a particular sector of our phenomenal field.

Two very bad but still prevalent objections to HOR theories need to be disposed of at once. First, it is pointed out (correctly) that such theories do not in any way explain the qualitative or phenomenal character of experience; a mere higher-order representation could hardly bring a quale or phenomenal property into being. How, then, can they claim to be theories of *consciousness*? But to my knowledge no HOR theorist has ever claimed to have explained anything about qualia; HOR views aim to explain only the distinction between mental states one is aware of being in and mental states one is not aware of being in. Some other theory must be given of qualia and phenomenal character.

Second, some philosophers have yelled regress. If the second-order representation is to confer consciousness on the first-order state, it must itself be a conscious state; so there must be a third-order representation of it, and so on forever. But HOR theorists reject the opening premise. The second-order representation need not itself be a conscious state. (It will be one only if there happens to be a higher-order representation of it in turn.) The higher-order representation need not "confer" consciousness on the first-order state in the strong sense of itself first having the property of consciousness and then passing on that property.

But some further criticisms of HOR views are more serious.

Fallibility and false positives. An internal monitor or the like is a *device* or mechanism that scans first-order states, and a higher-order thought about a first-order state is produced causally by that state. Shoemaker (1994b) complains therefore that on a HOR view, my awareness of a first-order state is entirely contingent. There could be unfelt pains, and other sensations of which I might be systematically unaware, and this could happen regularly, not just occasionally or under strange conditions. And the fallibility problem gets worse: Neander (1998) points out in detail that there is also a danger of false positives. Might not an internal scanner, or whatever mechanism produces a higher-order thought, be defective in that it fires mistakenly, introspecting a visual sensation or a pain that never occurred? A subject whose device was seriously out of whack might seem to herself or himself to suffer a ghastly, excruciating pain, while actually having no pain at all. It is not obvious that that consequence of HOR theories even makes sense.[3]

Ubiquity. Rey (1983) objects that if all it takes to make a first-order state a conscious state is that the state be the object of a higher-order representation, then consciousness is everywhere. Any laptop computer, for example, has monitoring devices that keep track of its "psychological" states. To the obvious rejoinder that no existing laptop has genuinely psychological states in the first place, Rey replies that, once we had done whatever needs to be done in order to fashion a being that did have nonconscious first-order intentional and sensory states, the addition of an internal monitor or two would be a trifling afterthought, not the sort of thing that could turn a simply nonconscious being into a conscious being.

William G. Lycan

This objection demands a careful response. White (1987) and Lycan (1996) have tried to rebut it.

Computational/cognitive overload. Carruthers (2000) points out that, given the richness of a person's conscious experience at a time, the alleged higher-order representing agencies would be kept very busy. The higher-order representations would have to keep pace with every nuance of the total experience. The complexity of the experience would have to be matched in every detail by a higher-order perception or thought. It is hard to imagine that a human being would have so great a capacity for complex higher-order representation, much less that a small child or a nonhuman animal would have it. Carruthers concludes that if any HOR theory is true, then to say the least, few if any creatures besides human adults have conscious experiences.

Some HOR theorists can live with that apparent consequence. Lycan (1999a) maintains, *contra* Carruthers' premise, that in the present sense of "conscious," very few of our mental states are conscious states.

Qualia and Phenomenal Character

Qualia in sense (2) above pose a problem for materialist theories of the mind. For where, ontologically speaking, are they located? Suppose I am having a reddish after-image, and suppose for the sake of argument that there is no red physical object in my visible environment either. Nor is there relevant redness in my brain (blood is dark red, but the after-image's redness is not that one). So there is no relevantly red physical thing inside my head, and there is none outside it. But there is a red thing that I am experiencing. You do the math: it must after all be a nonphysical, immaterial thing, like a Russellian sense-datum. But that is incompatible with materialism.

There is one theory of qualia in sense (2) that avoids that outcome: a representational theory (Anscombe, 1965, and Hintikka, 1969; followed by Kraut, 1982; Lewis, 1983; Lycan, 1987, 1996; Harman, 1990; Shoemaker, 1994a; Tye, 1994, 1995; and Dretske, 1995). The theory has it that qualia are intentional contents, represented properties of represented objects. If I am seeing a real banana under normal conditions, the banana looks yellow to me, and there is a corresponding banana-shaped yellow patch in my visual field. I am visually representing the actual yellowness of the banana, and the yellowness of the patch is just that of the banana itself.[4] But now suppose that I am hallucinating a similar banana, and there is an exactly similar banana-shaped yellow patch in my visual field just as there was in the veridical case. Then too I am representing the yellowness of an external, physical banana. The only difference is that in this second case the banana is not real; it and its yellowness are intentional inexistents. The yellowness is still that of a physical object, the hallucinated banana, even though the banana is not real.

After-images are subject to the same treatment, and that is how the representational theorist gets around the foregoing dilemma. When I experience the red after-image, I am visually-representing a red blob. The blob is located at such-and-such a spot in the room (just this side of the source of green light that caused the after-image). As before, there is no real red physical object in the room, my visual experience is unveridical. After-images are, after all, optical illusions. The quale, the redness of the blob, is, like the blob itself, an intentional inexistent. And that is how the dilemma is resolved: There is a red thing that I am experiencing, but it is not an actual thing. (I like to say: in defending sense-data, Russell mistook a nonactual physical thing for an actual nonphysical thing.) The "there is" in "There is a red thing that ..." is the same existentially noncommittal "there is" that occurs in "There is an allegedly Christian god that is not immaterial, but lives on a real planet somewhere in the universe" and in "There is a growth effect that a few loony economists believe in but that doesn't exist and never will."

The main argument in favor of the representational theory has in effect already been given: that otherwise our dilemma succeeds in refuting materialism, and commits us to actual Russellian sense-data. Of course that is only grist to the mill of someone who points to qualia in sense (2) by way of arguing against materialism, but representationalism is a reductive strategy, and shows that such a refutation does not succeed as it stands, and so contributes to an affirmative answer to the question "Can consciousness and qualia be reduced?"

A second argument is Harman's (1990) transparency argument: We normally "see right through" perceptual states to external objects and do not even notice that we are in perceptual states; the properties we are aware of in perception are attributed to the objects perceived.

> Look at a tree and try to turn your attention to intrinsic features of your visual experience. I predict you will find that the only features there to turn your attention to will be features of the presented tree, including relational features of the tree "from here". (Harman, 1990, p. 39)

Tye (1995) extends this argument to bodily sensations such as pain. It can be extended further to the hallucinatory case. Again I am looking at a real, bright yellow banana in normal conditions. Suppose also that I simultaneously hallucinate a second, identical banana to the left of the real one. The relevant two regions of my visual field are phenomenally just the same; the banana and color appearances are just the same in structure. The yellowness inhering in the second-banana appearance is exactly the same property as that inhering in the first. But if we agree that the yellowness perceived in the real banana is just the actual color of the banana itself, then the yellowness perceived in the hallucinated banana is just the yellowness of the hallucinated banana itself. And that accounts for the yellow quale involved in the second banana appearance.

I believe the transparency argument shows that visual experience represents external objects and their apparent properties. But that is something we really knew anyway. What the argument does not show, but only claims, is that experience has no other qualitative properties that pose problems for materialism. The obvious candidate for such a property is a w.i.l. property – sense (3) – but there are other candidates as well (Block, 1996); see below.

A variation on the transparency argument begins with our need to explain the distinction between veridical and unveridical visual experiences. My veridical experience of the banana is as of a yellow banana, and has yellowness as one of its

William G. Lycan

intentional objects. My simultaneous unveridical experience of the second banana has similar intentional contents, but what that experience reports is false. Each of the qualia, the yellownesses, has been entirely accounted for; what matter of qualitative or phenomenal character remains to be explained? (But, as before, there is the higher-order w.i.l. property.)

The representational theory faces a number of objections.

Cheapness. The mere representation of yellowness does not suffice for phenomenal yellow, for something's actually looking yellow to a subject. Representation of yellow is cheap: I can shout the word "yellow" aloud, or telegraph it in Morse code, or write the German word "gelb" in purple paint on a large poster.

This ignores the provision that the representation must be specifically a visual one, produced by either a normal human visual system or by something functionally parallel to one. Admittedly, the representational theory of qualia cannot appeal only to representation, but must invoke some further factor. Dretske (1995) cites only the fact that visual representation is sensory and what he calls "systemic." Tye (1995) requires that the representation be nonconceptual and "poised," and he also argues that visual representations of color would differ from other sorts of representations in being accompanied by further representational differences. Lycan (1996) appeals to functional considerations, principally those that make the representation visual in the first place. A mixed view of the latter sort is what Block (1996) calls "quasi-representationism."

Color realism. The representational theory seems to require color realism. In our discussion so far, "yellow" has meant the objective, public property that inheres in bananas and some other physical objects. One could not, without circularity, explicate phenomenal yellowness in terms of represented real-world yellowness and then turn around and construe real physical yellowness as a disposition to produce sensations of phenomenal yellowness. But color realism is a widely despised minority view. What sort of real-world property is an "objective," physical color? There is no easily specifiable physical property (such as a wavelength measured in Ångstrom units, as touted 50 years ago) that all yellow objects have in common.

There is a variety of realist answers, though none of them is unproblematic. Dretske (1995), Tye (1995), Lycan (1996), Lewis (1997), and Watkins (2002) each gesture toward one. But I am not sure that the representational theory does absolutely require color realism, even though such realism helps by avoiding even the appearance of circularity. So far as I can see, one might hold an error theory of physical color, but still maintain that physical color concepts are explanatorily and/or conceptually prior to phenomenal ones.

Psychosemantics. Representationalists agree that the relevant representations of color and other sensible properties are in some sense "nonconceptual," at least in that the qualitative representations need not be translatable into the subject's natural language. But some psychosemantics (in Fodor's, 1987, sense) would be needed to explain what it is in virtue of which a brain item represents a particular shade of yellow in particular. Dretske (1995) offers one, as does Tye (1995); both accounts are teleologized versions of "indicator" semantics.

I believe a large problem looms here. While such semantics may be fairly plausible for perceptual representations, a *fully general* teleologized indicator psychosemantics would never do. (Does some brain state have the function of indicating ashtrays? angels? Ariel? Anabaptists? Arcturus? algebra? aleph-null?) More generally, though I cannot argue this here, I judge that psychosemantics is in very bad shape. Though naturalist and reductionist by temperament, I am not optimistic about the onto-logical reduction of intentionality to matter. Now, like HOR theories of conscious awareness, the representational theory reduces qualia, not to matter itself, but to inten-tionality. If intentionality cannot be reduced, then we will not have reduced either conscious awareness or qualia to the material.

Still, it is a prevalent opinion that although intentionality is a problem for the materialist, consciousness and qualia are a much greater difficulty. So it is worth arguing that consciousness and qualia can be reduced to representation, even if in the end representation remains unreduced.

Counterexamples. Allegedly there are cases in which either two experiences share their intentional content and differ in their qualia or they differ entirely in their inten-tional content but share qualia. Peacocke (1983) gave three examples of the former kind, Block (1990) one of the latter. (Block, 1995 and 1996, also offers some of the former kind; for discussion, see Lycan, 1996.)

In Peacocke's first example, you experience two (actual) trees, at different distances from you but as being of the same physical height and breadth; "[y]et there is also some sense in which the nearest tree occupies more of your visual field than the more distant tree" (Peacocke, 1983, p. 12). Peacocke maintains that that sense is qualitative, and the qualitative difference is unmatched by any representational dif-ference. The second and third examples concern, respectively, binocular vision and the reversible-cube illusion.

In each case, Tye (1995) and Lycan (1996) have rejoined that there are after all identifiable representational differences constituting the qualitative differences. Tye (2003) continues this project *vis-à-vis* further alleged counterexamples, to good effect.

Block appeals to an "Inverted Earth," a planet exactly like Earth except that its real physical colors are (somehow) inverted with respect to ours. The Twin Earthlings' speech sounds just like English, but their intentional contents in regard to color are inverted relative to ours: When they say "red," they mean green (if it is green Twin objects that correspond to red Earthly objects under the inversion in question), and green things *look* green to them even though they call those things "red." Now, an Earthling victim is chosen by the usual mad scientists, knocked out, fitted with color inverting lenses, transported to Inverted Earth, and repainted to match that planet's human skin and hair coloring. Block contends that after some length of time, short or very long, the victim's word meanings and propositional-attitude contents and all other intentional contents would shift to match the Twin Earthlings' contents, but, intuitively, the victim's qualia would remain the same. Thus, qualia are not inten-tional contents.

The obvious representationalist reply is to insist that if the intentional contents would change, so too would the qualitative contents. Block's nearly explicit argu-ment to the contrary is that qualia are "narrow" in that they supervene on head con-tents (on this view, two molecularly indistinguishable people could not experience different qualia), while the intentional contents shift under environmental pressure precisely because they are wide. If qualia are indeed narrow, and all the intentional

William G. Lycan

contents are wide and would shift, then Block's argument succeeds. (Stalnaker, 1996, gives a version of Block's argument that does not depend on the assumption that qualia are narrow; Lycan, 1996, rebuts it.)

Three rejoinders are available. The first is to insist that not all the intentional contents would shift. Word meanings would shift, but it does not follow that visual contents ever would. Lycan (1996) argues that we have no reason to think that visual contents would shift. The second rejoinder is to hold that although all the ordinary intentional contents would shift, there is a special class of narrow though still representational contents underlying the wide contents; qualia can be identified with the special narrow contents. That view has been upheld by Shoemaker (1994a), Tye (1994), and especially Rey (1998). Rey argues vigorously that qualia are narrow, and then offers a narrow representational theory. (But it turns out that Rey's theory is not a theory of qualia in sense (2); see below.)

The third rejoinder is to deny that qualitative content is narrow and to argue that it is wide, i.e., that two molecularly indistinguishable people could indeed experience different qualia. This last is the position that Dretske (1996) has labeled "phenomenal externalism." It is maintained by Dretske, Tye (1995), and Lycan (1996, 2001). A number of people – even Tye himself (1998) – have since called the original contrary assumption that qualia are narrow a "deep/powerful/compelling intuition," but it proves to be highly disputable.

If the representational theory is correct, then qualia are determined by whatever determines a perceptual state's intentional content. In particular, the color properties represented are taken to be physical properties instanced in the subject's environment. What determines a psychological state's intentional content is given by a psychosemantics. But every even faintly plausible psychosemantics makes intentional contents wide. Of course, the representational theory is just what is in question; but this argument does not beg that question; it merely points out that the anti-representationalist is not entitled to the bare assumption that qualia are narrow. And notice that that assumption is a positive modal claim, a claim of necessitation; we representationalists have no a priori reason to accept it.

Although until recently the assumption that qualia are narrow had been tacit and entirely undefended, opponents of representationalism have since begun defending it with vigor. Here are two of their arguments, with sample replies.

Introspection. An Earthling suddenly fitted with inverting lenses and transported to Inverted Earth would notice nothing introspectively, despite a change in representational content; so the qualia must remain unchanged and so are narrow.

Reply: The same goes for propositional attitudes, i.e., the transported Earthling would notice nothing introspectively. Yet the attitude contents are still wide. Wideness does not predict introspective change under transportation. (Which perhaps is odd.)

Modes of presentation (Rey, 1998). There is no such thing as representation without a mode of presentation. If a quale is a represented property, then it is represented under some mode of presentation, and modes of presentation may be narrow even when the representational content itself is wide. Indeed, many philosophers of mind take modes of presentation to be internal causal or functional roles played by the representations in question. Surely they are strong candidates for qualitative content. So are they not narrow qualia?

Reply: Remember, qualia in sense (2) are properties like phenomenal yellowness and redness, which according to the representational theory are representata. The mode or guise *under which* yellowness and redness are represented in vision is something else again. (It can plausibly be argued that such modes and guises are qualitative or phenomenal properties of some sort, perhaps higher-order properties. See the next section.)

There are at least ten more such arguments, and few will be convinced by all of the externalist replies to them. But no one should find it obvious that qualia are narrow.

The representationalist reduction of qualia is subject to a more general sort of objection that has been raised against many forms of materialism: a *conceivability argument*. On those, see Gertler (chapter 12, CONSCIOUSNESS AND QUALIA CANNOT BE REDUCED).[5]

"What it is Like"

It is "w.i.l." in sense (3) that figures in anti-materialist arguments from subjects' "knowing what it is like," primarily Nagel's (1974) "Bat" argument and Jackson's (1982) "Knowledge" argument. Jackson's character Mary, a brilliant color scientist trapped in an entirely black-and-white laboratory, nonetheless becomes omniscient as regards the physics and chemistry of color, the neurophysiology of color vision, and every other public, objective fact conceivably relevant to human color experience. Yet when she is finally released from her captivity and emerges into the outside world, she sees colored objects for the first time, and learns something: she learns what it is like to see red and the other colors. Thus she seems to have learned a new fact, the fact of w.i.l. to see red. By hypothesis, that fact is not a public, objective one, but is an intrinsically perspectival fact. This is what would refute materialism, since materialism has it that every fact about every human mind is ultimately a public, objective fact.

Upon her release, Mary has done two things: She has at last hosted a red quale in sense (2), and she has learned what it is like to experience a red quale. The fact she has learned has the ineffability characteristic of w.i.l. in sense (3); were Mary to try to pass on her new knowledge to a still color-deprived colleague, she would not be able to express it in English.

As there are representational theories of qualia in sense (2), there are representational theories of w.i.l. in sense (3). The most common answer to the arguments of Nagel and Jackson is what may be called the "perspectivalist" reply (Horgan, 1984; Churchland, 1985; Van Gulick, 1985; Tye, 1986, 1995; Lycan, 1987, 1996, 2003; Loar, 1990; Rey, 1991; Leeds, 1993). The perspectivalist notes that a knowledge difference does not entail a difference in fact known, for one can know a fact under one representation or mode of presentation but fail to know one and the same fact under a different mode of presentation. Someone might know that lightning is flashing but not know that electrical discharge was taking place in the sky, and vice versa; someone might know that person X is much gossiped about without knowing that she herself is much gossiped about, even if she herself is in fact person X. So, from Mary's knowledge difference following her release, Jackson is not entitled to infer the existence of a new, weird fact, but at most that of a new way of representing a fact that

William G. Lycan

Mary already knew in a different guise. She has not learned a new fact, but has only acquired a new, introspective or first-person way of representing one that she already knew under its neurophysiological aspect.

This response to Nagel and Jackson requires that the first-order qualitative state itself be represented (else how could it be newly known under Mary's new mode of presentation?). And that hypothesis in turn encourages a HOR theory of awareness and introspection. Since we have seen that HOR theories of awareness face significant objections, the perspectivalist must either buy into such a theory despite its drawbacks or find some other way of explicating the idea of an introspective or first-person perspective without appealing to higher-order representation. But I myself am a happy HOR partisan, and find the idea of an introspective perspective entirely congenial despite its unfortunate assonance.

Notes

1 Important: the phrase "conscious state" has been used in at least one entirely different sense, as by Dretske (1993). Failure to keep these senses straight has led to much confusion. The present use is as in "conscious memory" or "conscious decision."
2 For extensive general discussion of HOR views, see Gennaro, 2004. A more recent competitor is Van Gulick's (2001) "HOGS" (Higher-Order Global State) theory.
3 Lycan (1998) answers this objection, not very convincingly.
4 On this view, perhaps surprisingly, qualia turn out not to be properties *of* the experiences that present them: qualia are represented properties of represented objects, and so they are only intentionally present in experiences. The relevant properties of the experiences are just their representative properties, such as representing yellow.
5 Lycan (2004) rebuts one of the latest conceivability arguments.

References and further reading

Anscombe, G. E. M. (1965). The intentionality of sensation: a grammatical feature. In R. J. Butler (ed.), *Analytical Philosophy: Second Series*. Oxford: Blackwell.
Armstrong, D. M. (1968). *A Materialist Theory of the Mind*. London: Routledge & Kegan Paul.
— (1981). What is consciousness? In D. M. Armstrong, *The Nature of Mind*. Ithaca, NY: Cornell University Press.
Block, N. J. (1990). Inverted Earth. In J. E. Tomberlin (ed.), *Philosophical Perspectives*, vol. 4: *Action Theory and Philosophy of Mind*. Atascadero, CA: Ridgeview Publishing. (Reprinted in W. G. Lycan (ed.), *Mind and Cognition* (2nd edn.). Oxford: Blackwell.)
— (1995). On a confusion about a function of consciousness. *Behavioral and Brain Sciences*, 18, 227–47.
— (1996). Mental paint and mental latex. In E. Villanueva (ed.), *Philosophical Issues*, vol. 7: *Perception*. Atascadero, CA: Ridgeview Publishing.
Burge, T. (1988). Individualism and self-knowledge. *Journal of Philosophy*, 85, 649–53.
Carruthers, P. (2000). *Phenomenal Consciousness*. Cambridge: Cambridge University Press.
Churchland, P. M. (1985). Reduction, qualia, and the direct introspection of brain states. *Journal of Philosophy*, 82, 8–28.
Davies, M. and Humphreys, G. (eds.) (1993). *Consciousness*. Oxford: Blackwell.

Dennett, D. C. (1978). Why you can't make a computer that feels pain. In *Brainstorms*. Montgomery, VT: Bradford Books.

Dretske, F. (1993). Conscious experience. *Mind*, 102, 263–83.

— (1995). *Naturalizing the Mind*. Cambridge, MA: Bradford Books/MIT Press.

— (1996). Phenomenal externalism. In E. Villanueva (ed.), *Philosophical Issues*, vol. 7: *Perception*. Atascadero, CA: Ridgeview Publishing.

Farrell, B. A. (1950). Experience. *Mind*, 59, 170–98.

Fodor, J. A. (1987). *Psychosemantics*. Cambridge, MA: Bradford Books/MIT Press.

Gennaro, R. (1995). *Consciousness and Self-Consciousness*. Philadelphia: John Benjamins.

— (ed.) (2004). *Higher-Order Theories of Consciousness*. Philadelphia: John Benjamins.

Harman, G. (1990). The intrinsic quality of experience. In J. E. Tomberlin (ed.) *Philosophical Perspectives*, vol. 4: *Action Theory and Philosophy of Mind*. Atascadero, CA: Ridgeview Publishing. (Reprinted in W. G. Lycan (ed.), *Mind and Cognition* (2nd edn.). Oxford: Blackwell.)

Heil, J. (1988). Privileged access. *Mind*, 47, 238–51. (Reprinted in W. G. Lycan (ed.), *Mind and Cognition* (2nd edn.). Oxford: Blackwell.)

Hintikka, K. J. J. (1969). On the logic of perception. In N. S. Care and R. H. Grimm (eds.), *Perception and Personal Identity*. Cleveland, OH: Case Western Reserve University Press.

Horgan, T. (1984). Jackson on physical information and qualia. *Philosophical Quarterly*, 34, 147–52.

Jackson, F. (1982). Epiphenomenal qualia. *Philosophical Quarterly*, 32, 127–36. (Reprinted in W. G. Lycan (ed.), *Mind and Cognition* (2nd edn.). Oxford: Blackwell.)

Kim, J. (1995). Mental causation: What, me worry? In E. Villanueva (ed.), *Philosophical Issues*, vol 6: *Content*. Atascadero, CA: Ridgeview Publishing.

Kraut, R. (1982). Sensory states and sensory objects. *Noûs*, 16, 277–95.

Leeds, S. (1993). Qualia, awareness, Sellars. *Noûs*, 27, 303–30.

Lewis, C. I. (1929). *Mind and the World Order*. New York: C. Scribner's Sons.

Lewis, D. (1983). Individuation by acquaintance and by stipulation. *Philosophical Review*, 92, 3–32.

— (1997). Naming the colours. *Australasian Journal of Philosophy*, 75, 325–42.

Loar, B. (1990). Phenomenal states. In J. E. Tomberlin (ed.), *Philosophical Perspectives*, vol. 4: *Action Theory and Philosophy of Mind*. Atascadero, CA: Ridgeview Publishing.

Lycan, W. G. (1987). *Consciousness*. Cambridge, MA: Bradford Books/MIT Press.

— (1996). *Consciousness and Experience*. Cambridge, MA: Bradford Books/MIT Press.

— (1998). In defense of the representational theory of qualia. (Replies to Neander, Rey, and Tye.) In J. E. Tomberlin (ed.), *Philosophical Perspectives*, vol. 12: *Language, Mind, and Ontology*. Atascadero, CA: Ridgeview Publishing.

— (1999a). A response to Carruthers' "natural theories of consciousness." *Psyche*, 5. http://psyche.cs.monash.edu.au/v5/psyche-5-11-lycan.html.

— (ed.) (1999b). *Mind and Cognition* (2nd edn.). Oxford: Blackwell.

— (2001). The case for phenomenal externalism. In J. E. Tomberlin (ed.), *Philosophical Perspectives*, vol. 15: *Metaphysics*. Atascadero, CA: Ridgeview Publishing.

— (2003). Perspectivalism and the knowledge argument. In Q. Smith and A. Jokic (eds.), *Consciousness: New Philosophical Perspectives*. Oxford: Oxford University Press.

— (2004). Vs. a new a priorist argument for dualism. In E. Sosa and E. Villanueva (eds.), *Philosophical Issues*, vol. 13. Oxford: Blackwell.

Nagel, T. (1974). What is it like to be a bat? *Philosophical Review*, 82, 435–56.

Neander, K. (1998). The division of phenomenal labor: A problem for representational theories of consciousness. In J. E. Tomberlin (ed.), *Philosophical Perspectives*, vol. 12: *Language, Mind, and Ontology*. Atascadero, CA: Ridgeview Publishing.

Nelkin, N. (1989). Unconscious sensations. *Philosophical Psychology*, 2, 129–41.

Peacocke, C. (1983). *Sense and Content*. Oxford: Oxford University Press.

Rey, G. (1983). A reason for doubting the existence of consciousness. In R. Davidson, G. E. Schwartz, and D. Shapiro (eds.), *Consciousness and Self-Regulation*, vol. 3. New York: Plenum Press.

— (1991). Sensations in a language of thought. In E. Villanueva (ed.), *Philosophical Issues*, vol. 1: *Consciousness*. Atascadero, CA: Ridgeview Publishing.

— (1998). A narrow representationalist account of qualitative experience. In J. E. Tomberlin (ed.), *Philosophical Perspectives*, vol. 12: *Language, Mind, and Ontology*. Atascadero, CA: Ridgeview Publishing.

Rosenthal, D. (1991). The independence of consciousness and sensory quality. In E. Villanueva (ed.), *Philosophical Issues*, vol. 1: *Consciousness*. Atascadero, CA: Ridgeview Publishing.

— (1993). Thinking that one thinks. In M. Davies and G. Humphreys (eds.), *Consciousness*. Oxford: Blackwell.

Sellars, W. (1956). Empiricism and the philosophy of mind. In H. Feigl and M. Scriven (eds.), *Minnesota Studies in the Philosophy of Science*, vol. 1. Minneapolis: University of Minnesota Press.

Shoemaker, S. (1994a). Phenomenal character. *Noûs*, 28, 21–38.

— (1994b). Self-knowledge and "inner sense." Lecture II: the broad perceptual model. *Philosophy and Phenomenological Research*, 54, 271–90.

Stalnaker, R. (1996). On a defense of the hegemony of representation. In E. Villanueva (ed.), *Philosophical Issues*, vol. 7: *Perception*. Atascadero, CA: Ridgeview Publishing.

Tomberlin, J. E. (ed.) (1990). *Philosophical Perspectives*, vol. 4: *Action Theory and Philosophy of Mind*. Atascadero, CA: Ridgeview Publishing.

— (ed.) (1998). *Philosophical Perspectives*, vol. 12: *Language, Mind, and Ontology*. Atascadero, CA: Ridgeview Publishing.

Tye, M. (1986). The subjectivity of experience. *Mind*, 95, 1–17.

— (1992). Visual qualia and visual content. In T. Crane (ed.), *The Contents of Experience*. Cambridge: Cambridge University Press.

— (1994). Qualia, content, and the inverted spectrum. *Noûs*, 28, 159–83.

— (1995). *Ten Problems of Consciousness*. Cambridge, MA: Bradford Books/MIT Press.

— (1998). Inverted Earth, Swampman, and representationism. In J. E. Tomberlin (ed.), *Philosophical Perspectives*, vol. 12: *Language, Mind, and Ontology*. Atascadero, CA: Ridgeview Publishing.

— (2003). Blurry images, double vision, and other oddities: New problems for representationalism? In Q. Smith and A. Jokic (eds.), *Consciousness: New Philosophical Perspectives*. Oxford: Oxford University Press.

Van Gulick, R. (1985). Physicalism and the subjectivity of the mental. *Philosophical Topics*, 13, 51–70.

— (2001). Inward and upward: Reflection, introspection, and self-awareness. *Philosophical Topics*, 28, 275–305.

Villanueva, E. (ed.) (1991). *Philosophical Issues*, vol. 1: *Consciousness*. Atascadero, CA: Ridgeview Publishing.

— (ed.) (1996). *Philosophical Issues*, vol. 7: *Perception*. Atascadero, CA: Ridgeview Publishing.

Watkins, M. (2002). *Rediscovering Colors*. Philosophical Studies series. Dordrecht: Kluwer.

White, S. (1987). What is it like to be a homunculus? *Pacific Philosophical Quarterly*, 68, 148–74.

Consciousness and Qualia Cannot Be Reduced

Brie Gertler

Reductionism is currently the favored position in the philosophy of mind, and I surmise that it enjoys an even wider margin of popularity among cognitive scientists. Accordingly, my aspirations here are limited. I hope to show that reductionism faces serious difficulties, and that anti-reductionism may be more palatable than usually believed.

Preliminaries

I will focus on consciousness in Lycan's sense (2): qualia. (See chapter 11, CONSCIOUSNESS AND QUALIA CAN BE REDUCED.) Qualia are the first-order phenomenal properties of (some) mental states. They are also called "qualitative features," and are said to make up a state's "phenomenal character." I won't address the other two senses of "consciousness" that Lycan more briefly discusses; these are (1) "conscious awareness" and (3) the second-order property of qualia that he terms "what it's like." For I think that it is the first-order phenomenal features of mental states that generate the core of what Chalmers (1996) aptly calls "the hard problem of consciousness." In any case, it is first-order qualia that pose the *hardest* part of the philosophical problem.

I will argue that qualia cannot be reduced to physical, functional, and/or computational ("information-theoretic," in Lycan's phrase) properties of the organism. What exactly does it mean to say that qualia are thus irreducible? As Lycan says, the notion of reduction at issue here is an ontological one; it does not chiefly concern concepts or predicates, and there is no guarantee that truths about reduction are available to a priori reflection. While the precise requirements for reduction are a matter of controversy, one point is clear. Any plausible theory of reduction will gloss the relation between the reduced properties (or tokens) and the reducing properties (or tokens) as *necessary*. That is, in a genuine case of reduction the relationship between what is reduced and the reductive base cannot be mere correlation, or even lawlike correlation.

For an anti-reductionist can allow that physical properties *cause* irreducibly non-physical qualia, and that these causal connections are lawlike.[1] Compare: someone who believes in ghosts can claim that certain physical processes – those involved in a séance, say – causally suffice for the presence of ghosts. But clearly this does not commit her to physicalist reductionism about ghosts. I will not attempt to offer necessary and sufficient conditions for reduction. Instead, because I will be arguing against reduction, I will specify one necessary condition that, I think, cannot be met in the current case. This necessary condition involves *necessary supervenience*. It says that Q-properties are reducible to P-properties only if Q-properties necessarily supervene on P-properties. That is,

> Q-properties are reducible to P-properties only if, for all x and all y, x is exactly similar to y as regards P-properties $\Rightarrow$ x is exactly similar to y as regards Q-properties.

Put simply, reduction requires that any difference in reduced properties must be grounded in some difference in reducing properties. So if qualia are reducible to physical (functional, computational) properties, then two persons that are physically, functionally, and computationally alike must be alike in their qualia properties. The necessary supervenience of qualia on physical properties is sometimes expressed by saying "Once God fixed the physical facts, the qualia facts were also fixed." This way of expressing necessary supervenience illustrates why reduction requires necessary supervenience. For if qualia facts reduce to physical facts, fixing the former should require no work beyond fixing the latter.

While reduction requires necessary supervenience, necessary supervenience may not suffice for reduction. For instance, many have worried that the fact (if it is a fact[2]) that a variety of physical properties can realize qualia – the "multiple realizability" of qualia – may thwart attempts at reduction. And one may consistently accept necessary supervenience while rejecting reduction because of concerns about multiple realizability. The fact that necessary supervenience is a relatively weak notion, as compared with the more full-blooded notion of reduction, allows the strategy to sidestep the issues about multiple realizability that are, I suspect, behind Lycan's qualms about type-reduction to the physical. For my approach allows the argument to apply to type- and token-reduction equally, since both require necessary supervenience. Lycan's criterion for the token-reducibility of A's to B's is that "every A is entirely constituted by some arrangement of B's." Taking A's to be entities individuated by their Q-properties, and B's to be individuated by their P-properties, the relation of constitution demands that there is no difference in Q-properties without a corresponding difference in P-properties. (The requirement of necessary supervenience is even clearer in the case of type reduction, which, as Lycan notes, is a more stringent relation than token reduction.)

Why Conceivability Arguments are Indispensable

The requirement that reduced properties *necessarily* supervene on reducing properties opens the door to conceivability arguments against reductionism. Even if qualia never actually vary independently of the physical (functional, computational), physicalist reductionism fails so long as qualia *can* vary independently of the physical (functional, computational). Because evaluating a claim about what is (or is not) possible requires considering non-actual scenarios, conceivability arguments are indispensable in evaluating the prospects for reductionism. Or so I shall argue here.

The most straightforward conceivability arguments against reductionism use one of two claims. (i) We can conceive of a scenario in which particular qualia are present, but the physical, functional, and/or computational properties to which they allegedly reduce are absent. (ii) We can conceive of a scenario in which qualia are absent, but the allegedly reducing properties are present. The argument that uses (i) is what I'll call the "disembodiment argument": I can conceive of my qualia tokens occurring in the absence of a body; whatever I can conceive is possible; so my mind is not reducible to any body. (Descartes, 1641/1984).[3] The argument that uses (ii) is the "zombie argument": I can conceive of a creature that shares my physical, functional, and computational properties, but that lacks qualia altogether; so qualia are not reducible to those properties (Kirk, 1974; Chalmers, 1996). A third anti-reductionist argument, the "knowledge argument," is less straightforward but very influential (Jackson, 1982). Jackson asks us to imagine Mary, a neuroscientist of the future who knows all of the physical (functional, computational) facts about color vision, but who has spent her entire life in a black-and-white room, and has never perceived any other colors. He argues that Mary would not be in a position to determine which qualia are associated with any particular neurophysiological state. As its name suggests, this argument is more explicitly epistemic than the disembodiment and zombie arguments. But I will argue below that this difference is not as significant as it may at first appear, for the disembodiment and zombie arguments also have a crucial epistemic dimension.

Before assessing these particular arguments, I want to address one source of qualms about using conceivability arguments. The worry is that conceivability arguments tell us, at most, about *our concepts* of qualia (or whatever else they concern). But qualia themselves may not neatly fit our concepts. So it's illegitimate to use conceivability arguments to determine the nature of qualia, including whether qualia are ultimately reducible. I think that conceivability arguments are not only legitimate, but also indispensable for evaluating reductionism. First, as explained above, the relation between a reducing property and a reduced property is *necessary*. This means that we cannot evaluate a claim about reducibility simply by examining *actual* correlations between P-properties and Q-properties. For such correlations may be accidental or, more plausibly, they may be a result of natural law. So assessing reductionist claims requires considering whether non-actual scenarios are possible; and this is precisely the method of conceivability arguments. Now in a sense it's true that conceivability arguments are based in our concepts. But it is only by exercising our concepts that we are able to think about the world; and it is only by exercising our concept of qualia that we are able to think about qualia. Of course, our concepts may be seriously incomplete, and so we may not have clear intuitions about whether a described scenario is possible.[4] More to the point, conceivability arguments are plainly fallible. We may be using concepts that nothing satisfies; and inattention or sloppiness may lead us to mistakenly think that we are conceiving of a particular scenario when in fact we are conceiving of a slightly different scenario. But even if our methods are imperfect, they may nonetheless be indispensable. Conceivability is the only guide to necessity;

our concepts, and the intuitions about possibility that derive from them, provide our only grip on modal claims.[5]

Finally, it's worth mentioning that modal intuitions – intuitions about what is possible and impossible, which it is the aim of conceivability arguments to reveal – are as important to arguments for reductionism as they are to anti-reductionist claims. Again, reductionism entails that it's *impossible* for the reduced property to vary independently of the reducing property. Since a claim of impossibility cannot be established by considering the actual world alone (though of course it can be refuted in this way), the reductionist must consider whether certain non-actual scenarios are possible. And the only way to determine this is to use the method of conceivability.

Objections from Ignorance

It appears, then, that conceivability arguments are crucial as a means of evaluating reductionism. Above, I outlined three general anti-reductionist conceivability arguments: the disembodiment argument, the zombie argument, and the knowledge argument. The knowledge argument is explicitly epistemic. But the others have a deep epistemic dimension as well; as we will see, many of the objections to these three arguments target the particular epistemic assumptions on which each relies.

What are these epistemic assumptions? Descartes recognized that his argument would fail unless our conception of the mental was comprehensive enough to exhaust its essential features. (In his terms, this conception must be "complete and adequate.") For suppose that one has only a partial grasp of the mental; in that case, what one fails to grasp might be precisely the mental's underlying physical nature. And clearly, in that circumstance the conceivability of a disembodied mind does nothing to establish its possibility. Parallel considerations apply to the zombie case: an incomplete understanding of the physical (functional, computational) might lead one to overlook the phenomenal aspect of physical (functional, computational) states, and so allow one to conceive a scenario in which those states are present while the relevant qualia are absent. Finally, the epistemic assumption of the knowledge argument might appear to be the assumption that Mary's knowledge of the physical is complete: for it is only by this assumption that one can conclude, from the fact that Mary doesn't know the phenomenal character of a particular neurophysiological state, that that character is not a physical feature of the state. (In Jackson's terms, the *information* about qualia is not physical *information*.) But Jackson stipulates, rather than assumes, that Mary's physical knowledge is complete. The real epistemic assumption of the knowledge argument is that *our* grasp of the physical, while not as detailed as Mary's, is nonetheless comprehensive enough to afford us an adequate conception of Mary's situation. That is, our grasp of the physical must not be so impoverished that it fails as a model for Mary's exhaustive physical knowledge.

Not surprisingly, the epistemic prerequisites of these conceivability arguments provide fodder for many of their critics. To name just a few: Arnauld (1641/1984) claimed that Descartes' meditator had no reason to think that his grasp of mentality was complete and adequate; Stoljar (2002) argues that we don't understand the physical completely enough to conclude, from the apparent conceivability of zombies, that zombies are possible; and Lycan (this volume, chapter 11) contends that it is ignorance about the relation between phenomenal and physical modes of presentation that leads us to mistakenly conclude, from Mary's inability to determine the phenomenal properties of physical states, that qualia are irreducible to the physical. Since these objections target the epistemic dimension of anti-reductionist conceivability arguments by contending that ignorance blocks the inference from conceivability to possibility, I'll call them "objections from ignorance."

The key responses to objections from ignorance maintain that, even if our current understanding of qualia and/or physical (functional, computational) properties is limited, these limitations do not block the inference to the envisaged ontological conclusion. For instance, Descartes himself argued that there is much we do not know about the mental: in particular, introspection may not afford knowledge of its causal etiology.[6] But he did think that introspection yields a complete and adequate picture of the *essential* features of mentality. Others have argued that, even if we don't understand the physical in all its specificity, we do have a concept of the physical that, in its very nature, seems to exclude the phenomenal (Chalmers, 1996). And I have argued that the "same fact, different mode of presentation" objection to the knowledge argument at best re-describes the knowledge Mary gains, leaving an epistemic gap that is best explained ontologically (Gertler, 1999).

Before turning to specific objections to each of the three conceivability arguments, I want to make two general remarks about objections from ignorance. First, appeals to ignorance must be carefully restricted. In particular, objections from ignorance cannot claim that we have *no* clear notion of qualia, or of the physical, or of the relation between the two; otherwise, the claim that qualia are (or are not) reducible to the physical is empty. And so it is entirely legitimate to offer, in defense of these conceivability arguments, some gloss of our concept of qualia and/or the physical. In fact, it's hard to see how there could be any basis for evaluating a claim about reductionism, either in favor of it or against it, that doesn't use at least a tentative outline of these notions. This isn't to say that we need a thoroughly detailed description. But we do need some criterion, even if this is simply "physical properties are whatever properties will explain rocks, trees, and planets . . ."[7] Moreover, a blanket skepticism about the relations between qualia and physical properties would block reductionist and anti-reductionist arguments equally.

Second, there appears to be a tension between the objections from ignorance and the larger impetus for physicalist reduction. One advantage that physicalist reduction purportedly confers is epistemic: if qualia are physically reducible, then the scientific methods used in explaining physical phenomena will explain qualia as well. But now suppose that we are in fact ignorant about the physical, as some of the objections from ignorance maintain. In that case, the scientific methods used to explain physical phenomena are either limited or faulty; hence, the idea of applying these methods to qualia seems less promising.

I can see two ways for the reductionist to respond to this tension. I'll address each of these in turn.

First reductionist response. Reductionism holds out the hope that all of reality is ultimately explainable by the methods used by natural science. For despite the fact that we don't have the explanations in hand, such explanations are *in principle* possible

Brie Gertler

so long as reductionism is true. And surely the idea that a single set of methods could yield a coherent account of all of reality is epistemologically promising.

Reply. To assess this response, we must understand what is meant by "the methods used by natural science." If this phrase is interpreted narrowly, to refer to the *particular techniques* of current science, then the claim that such methods will explain all of reality loses plausibility. For the history of science has shown us that a thorough account of reality often demands the development of new investigative methods. Now suppose that we interpret this phrase more liberally, so that it encompasses specific innovations within the larger, relatively stable framework of what might be called the "scientific approach" to the world. In that case, the anti-reductionist will argue that a core tenet of the scientific approach is that one must follow the data where they lead, without prejudging the outcome of an experiment; and the conceivability arguments provide data that call for explanation. Of course, reductionists do offer alternative explanations of that data, and I will consider some of these below. My point is just that an appeal to the general epistemological benefits of scientific methodology in no way diminishes the force of the conceivability arguments.

The anti-reductionist will make a similar reply to a reductionist appeal to a general methodological principle, like Occam's razor. Occam's razor prohibits multiplying entities (and, by extension, properties) without need; but of course what is at issue here is precisely whether there *is* need. Finally, the reductionist may claim that physicalistic theories have more explanatory power, since they allow for a greater simplicity in laws, etc., and thereby yield more powerful explanations of observed phenomena. But anti-reductionists will maintain that, inasmuch as reductionist theories fail to explain qualia, they are less explanatorily powerful. Again, my point here is just that this sort of general methodological stance does not eliminate the need for specific responses to the conceivability arguments.

Second reductionist response. Even if reductionism isn't supported on general epistemic grounds, it carries ontological benefits. Specifically, it allows us to avoid "spooky" properties like irreducibly nonphysical qualia, and thus allows for a larger naturalistic picture of the world.

Reply. Whether naturalism supports physicalist reductionism depends, of course, on what is meant by "naturalism." Suppose that naturalism is understood methodologically, as the claim that empirical science represents the only legitimate method of understanding the universe. In that case, my reply to the previous response applies: either this is unduly restrictive, or a naturalist account of reality must accommodate the data revealed by the conceivability arguments. Alternatively, naturalism may be given an ontological gloss: in this sense, naturalistic properties are (reducible to) physical properties. But an appeal to naturalism in that sense is, of course, question-begging. Relatedly, irreducibly nonphysical qualia should not be dismissed on the grounds that they're "spooky" unless it can be shown that there are less spooky alternatives. As I will explain below, anti-reductionists claim that reductionism is committed to brute, unexplained, necessary correlations between qualia and physical properties – what Chalmers (1999) calls "strong necessities" – that are, they think, spookier than irreducible qualia. Much more can be said about these issues. But I hope that these brief remarks illustrate that objections from ignorance and appeals to naturalism do not easily defeat anti-reductionism.

Consciousness and Qualia Cannot Be Reduced

The Three Arguments: Objections and Replies

In this section, I will examine the three conceivability arguments more closely, and explain how the anti-reductionist will defend each argument from specific objections. This section will cover a fairly broad range of objections; it should be clear that, at times, my responses to an objection could be modified to defend another of the arguments against a similar objection.

The disembodiment argument

The disembodiment argument runs as follows. I can conceive of my qualia existing in the absence of anything physical; whatever is conceivable is possible; therefore, my qualia do not necessarily supervene on the physical, and reductionism is false. Now it may seem that the disembodiment argument doesn't, in fact, weigh against the necessary supervenience thesis. For that thesis says that if A and B are physically identical, then they share qualia, whereas the possibility of disembodied qualia is the possibility that my twin and I differ physically while sharing qualia. Exposing the incompatibility between the conceived scenario and reductionism requires a few steps. First, if my soul can be disembodied (I'll call this "the Cartesian scenario"), then surely there could be a disembodied soul *other than mine* that is qualitatively identical to my soul, i.e., that tokens precisely those qualia that I token. Therefore, there is a possible world that is physically just like ours (and that contains me as I am, that is, with both qualia and physical properties) except that it contains, in addition, one disembodied soul. But this possibility means that once God fixed the physical facts – that is, once she narrowed down the candidates for *actual world* to those which were physically the same – she still had another choice to make. Should she actualize the world that she did in fact actualize, in which there are, let us grant, no disembodied souls? Or should she actualize the world just like the actual world except that it contains, in addition, one disembodied soul? (These do not exhaust her choices, of course.) This choice is a choice between which qualia tokens to actualize. So when God made this choice, she was in the following situation: she'd fixed the physical facts, but she still had to fix the qualia facts, if only to exclude disembodied souls. Hence, the Cartesian scenario is incompatible with the necessary supervenience thesis.

Objections and replies

The basic objection to the disembodiment argument is an objection from ignorance. The disembodiment argument uses a conception of qualia that derives from our introspective grasp of qualia tokens. But, the objector contends, this introspective grasp does not afford a complete understanding of qualia. In particular, the apparent conceivability of a disembodied soul shows only that the introspective mode of presentation of qualia is not a physical mode of presentation. Unless we can show that the introspective mode of presentation *exhausts* the essential features of qualia, we have no grounds for concluding that the object of introspection (the qualia) are not essentially physical. I expect that this may be the sort of objection Lycan would make.

For he says that when we introspect qualia, we are presented with *properties of* qualia: where qualia are first-order properties, introspection reveals higher-order properties, "what it's like" to have qualia. And the higher-order properties grasped through introspection need not yield a complete grasp of the first-order qualia.

As I see it, introspection can yield direct knowledge of first-order qualia properties. (This is not to say that introspection always *does* yield direct knowledge; only that, in optimal cases, it *can*.) For I believe that, through introspection, one does not encounter only second-order properties of qualia that are distinct from the first-order qualia; rather, one can directly encounter the qualia themselves. I have defended an account of introspecting qualia along these lines (Gertler, 2001a; see also Chalmers, 2003). But the basic idea that introspection gives us unmediated access to qualia doesn't depend on the details of that account; it is familiar from several sources.

> Pain ... is not picked out by one of its accidental properties; rather it is picked out by the property of being pain itself, by its immediate phenomenological quality. (Kripke, 1980, pp. 152–3)

> [T]here is no appearance/reality distinction in the case of sensations. (Hill, 1991, p. 127)

> When introspecting our mental states, we do not take canonical evidence to be an intermediary between properties introspected and our own conception of them. We take evidence *to be* properties introspected. (Sturgeon, 2000, p. 48)

On this conception, our introspective grasp of qualia does not involve any mode of presentation distinct from the qualia themselves. This means that there is no intermediary to *limit* our introspective grasp of qualia. But we still need to show that this introspective grasp is adequate to determining whether the introspected properties could be present in the absence of physical properties. To make this case, the proponent of the disembodiment argument claims that the essential features of qualia are exhausted by the features in principle available to introspection (together with rational reflection on those features). Moreover, this is a *conceptual* truth about qualia: e.g., by the quale I might express with the term "burnt orange," I mean *this* property, where the property is that to which I am introspectively attending.[8] The idea that qualia concepts allow for this sort of exhaustive grasp of essential properties, a grasp sufficient to allow the subject to determine the possibility of counterfactual scenarios, was argued by Kripke (1980). As Kripke notes, this feature of qualia concepts, like "pain," provides a stark contrast with physical concepts like "water." For conceptual reflection does not reveal the scientific essence of water – whether it is H_2O or XYZ, for instance. And so the apparent conceivability of water that is not H_2O does not provide reason to deny that water is (reducible to) H_2O. By contrast, the nature of our qualia concepts means that the apparent conceivability of *this* (introspectively attended to) property (pain, say) being present in the absence of any physical properties, *does* warrant denying that pain is reducible to any physical property.

There is much more to be said about the operation of qualia concepts. But the basic point is just this: while our concept of a physical property like *being water* is tied to causal intermediaries (its characteristic look, feel, etc.) that constitute a mode of presentation distinct from the property that constitutes its scientific essence (being

H_2O), our concept of pain is not tied to causal intermediaries. Instead, our concepts of pain and other qualia derive from *the qualia themselves*, grasped introspectively. So the *essence* of qualia is not a matter for empirical scientists to determine, but is instead available, at least in principle, to anyone who attentively considers her own qualia (though of course there is plenty of room for ignorance about various features of qualia, including their causal relations). Hence, conceivability intuitions rooted in these qualia concepts can reveal what is genuinely possible.

The zombie argument

The zombie argument, given by Chalmers (1996), is a direct attack on the necessary supervenience thesis. The argument is simple: zombies are conceivable; whatever is conceivable is possible; so zombies are possible. But if zombies are possible, then there can be a difference in qualia (I have them, while my zombie twin does not) with no corresponding physical difference (my zombie twin is physically, functionally, and computationally identical to me). So the reductionist must deny the possibility of zombies.

Objections and replies

Reductionists will either (i) deny that zombies are conceivable, or (ii) claim that while zombies are conceivable, their conceivability does not warrant belief in their possibility. Because my space here is limited, I will focus on (ii), the more popular reductionist position.[9]

Here is a more technical way of putting this objection. Reduction requires that qualia *metaphysically* supervene on physical properties. But the conceivability of zombies shows only that qualia don't *conceptually* supervene. Now Kripke showed that metaphysical necessity doesn't require conceptual necessity: for instance, the identity statement "water = H_2O" is metaphysically necessary but conceptually contingent, since we can imagine discovering that the actual clear liquid in the lakes and rivers is not H_2O. The conceivability of that scenario does not show that water isn't identical to H_2O. So a failure of conceptual supervenience is consistent with identity and, hence, with reducibility.

I will not go into the details of Chalmers' (1999) response to this objection, which employs the framework of two-dimensional semantics. But the key point is this. The necessity of a metaphysically necessary statement like "water = H_2O" is explained by conceptually necessary statements, such as (roughly) "water = the actual clear liquid in the lakes and rivers." This statement relates water to a description whose referent – viz., H_2O – must be determined empirically.[10] Now if qualia supervene, with metaphysical necessity, on physical properties, then – if this is indeed similar to the "water" case – there should be some conceptually necessary statement relating qualia to a description whose referents are determined empirically (as it is an empirical matter that H_2O is the referent of "the actual clear liquid...."). But it appears there is no such statement. So if qualia supervene on the physical with metaphysical necessity, this necessity is not explained in the usual way, but rather is *brute* (in Chalmers' terms, it is a "strong necessity"). And the existence of brute necessities is at least as troubling as the failure of reductionism.[11]

Brie Gertler

Most reductionists deny that metaphysical necessity must be underwritten by conceptual necessity. For instance, Levine (2001) argues that qualia concepts are "non-ascriptive," in that they are not a priori linked with descriptions that determine their referents. Instead, Levine claims, qualia concepts are related to their referents by virtue of a causal-nomic link, much as the concept "water" is linked to H_2O. So the statement "qualia supervene, with metaphysical necessity, on physical properties" is true but – because there is no conceptual necessity in the neighborhood – not accessible through conceivability considerations. I agree with the Chalmers–Jackson claim that metaphysical necessities must be underwritten by conceptual necessities, and, like Chalmers but unlike Jackson, I think that our concepts of physical properties and our concepts of qualia differ in ways that make zombies not only conceivable but also possible. The former concepts contain placeholders: our concept "water" is conceptually tied to the microstructure of the actual waterish stuff (whatever that microstructure is), or perhaps to the decisions of scientific experts regarding water's essential features (whatever those features are). One way to express this is to say that we *defer*, to microphysical facts or to scientific authorities, as to the (scientific) essence of water. By contrast, qualia concepts, at their most basic, contain no such placeholders: we individuals are the authorities about what satisfies these concepts, and while empirical discoveries may reveal what sorts of physical states are correlated with qualia, we do not defer to empirical facts or authorities as to the essence of qualia.

The fact that we retain authority about the nature of qualia is a fact about our concepts, revealed through conceivability arguments. When I'm told that, in the actual world, the presence of water is perfectly correlated with the presence of H_2O, I'm inclined to say that a world without water is a world without H_2O. But when I'm told that, in the actual world, the occurrence of pain is perfectly correlated with the firing of c-fibers, I'm *not* inclined to say that a world without pain is a world without firing c-fibers. And the protest that I *should* be thus inclined carries no weight. For since the lack of deference to empirical facts or authorities is a conceptual fact about pain, a proposed account of pain that requires such deference simply changes the subject, from pain to, perhaps, its physical substrate.[12]

Of course, reductionists have also appealed to the special features of qualia concepts. I've invoked these special features to explain the intuitions that fuel arguments against reduction, whereas reductionists invoke these features to explain *away* those intuitions. I will address some of these reductionist moves as they appear in objections to the knowledge argument.

The knowledge argument

The knowledge argument proceeds as follows. Mary, a neuroscientist of the future, knows all of the physical facts about color experience, but has seen only objects that are black, white, or shades of gray. Upon her release, she sees a fire engine and, knowing that fire engines are red, says, "Aha! So *this* is what it's like to see something red!" There are two principal objections to the knowledge argument: the ability analysis and what Lycan calls the "perspectivalist reply."

The Ability Analysis. What Mary gains upon leaving the room is a new ability, but not a new piece of propositional knowledge (Lewis, 1988; Nemirow, 1990). Compare:

a physics professor may have exhaustive propositional knowledge about how to hit a home run – he might know the speed and the angle at which one should swing the bat – but yet be unable to perform this action. This analysis defuses Jackson's argument, since his conclusion requires that Mary learns a new *fact*.

Reply. The ability in question must be construed narrowly, for as Conee (1994) has shown, the ability to imagine or to remember seeing red isn't perfectly correlated with knowing what it's like to see red. The ability that is, plausibly, conferred on Mary's release is just the ability to *recognize* "seeing red" experiences by their phenomenal features. (She was already able to recognize them by their neurophysiological features.)

But does this ability *constitute* what Mary gains? While it's true that acquiring a piece of propositional knowledge doesn't always suffice for acquiring the associated ability, there are lots of cases in which it does. For instance, given my background knowledge and abilities, I can gain the ability to find your house simply by learning that you live at 123 Main Street. This seems to me a much more accurate model of what Mary gains upon release: she acquires propositional knowledge that "seeing red" experiences are like *this* (where the "this" is filled out by a quale to which one introspectively attends); and this propositional knowledge *explains* her subsequent ability to recognize such experiences by their phenomenal quality. But if her propositional knowledge explains this ability, then the ability doesn't exhaust what she gains upon release. (I develop this argument in Gertler, 1999.)

I want to mention an aspect of the knowledge argument that is often missed. Although Jackson stipulates that Mary hasn't had color sensations before her release, it seems to me that the argument doesn't depend on this. The basis of the argument is simply Mary's inability to link color sensations with the physical, including their neurophysiological bases and their standard causes (such as seeing a fire engine). Her lack of color experience simply blocks one way of making such links. For suppose that Mary, before her release, has hallucinations involving the quale *red*. She might later be able to recall those hallucinations, and she might even give the phenomenal character a name. Still, she couldn't correlate it with neurophysiological states or standard causes, and so she couldn't recognize it as "red." The key point is that these correlations, however they are effected, remain *brute*. And brute correlations are as troublesome as strong necessities.

The Perspectivalist reply. What Mary gains isn't knowledge of a new fact, but just a new way to grasp a fact she already knew. That is, she learns a new, phenomenal mode of presentation of the fact that she previously grasped only under its neurophysiological mode of presentation. The special nature of qualia concepts explains why knowledge of qualia can't be derived from full knowledge of physical (functional, computational) properties. Reductionists have provided a variety of candidates for what is special about qualia. concepts; most involve the idea that qualia concepts pick out their referents *directly*, e.g., "via a species of simulation, without invoking any descriptions" (Papineau, 1998); or "without the use of any descriptive, reference-fixing intermediaries" (Tye, 1999). The lack of a descriptive component would explain why physicalist descriptions of reality won't yield phenomenal knowledge: for such phenomenal knowledge must take descriptive form if it is to be inferred from physical knowledge.

Brie Gertler

Reply. It seems to me that these proposals face two threats. First, they seem to simply relocate the mystery at the heart of the Mary case. If the non-descriptive nature of phenomenal concepts is what prevents Mary from knowing her subjects' qualia on the basis of their neurophysiological states, her epistemic situation upon leaving the room seems little better. While she can now know which qualia are associated with which neurophysiological states, this is simply knowledge of a *correlation*. Hence, this analysis of the case doesn't escape the charge that reductionism about qualia is committed to brute necessities.

In a recent article, Lycan acknowledges that this analysis of the knowledge argument leaves intact the "explanatory gap" (Levine, 1983) between qualia and the physical. But, he claims, this gap derives from the fact that phenomenal information is "intrinsically perspectival," and the gap is as "metaphysically harmless" as the gap between non-indexical information contained on a map, and the indexical knowledge "I am here" that cannot be inferred from simply reading the map (Lycan, 2003, p. 391, n. 8). The assumption is that the latter gap does not tempt us to introduce a new ontological category, *the perspectival*, for my location necessarily supervenes on the non-perspectival.

While this line of reasoning raises a host of issues that I cannot address here, I do want to suggest one anti-reductionist objection to it. Arguably, perspectival facts require consciousness. For imagine: if there were no conscious beings in the world, then while there would be facts such as "the largest elm tree is at location x," there wouldn't be any *perspectival* facts.[13] Now *if* perspectival facts somehow derive from consciousness, then an anti-reductionism about consciousness would provide an elegant explanation of the gap between perspectival and non-perspectival facts. Anti-reductionists can appeal to the ontological difference between qualia and the physical to explain the special operation of qualia concepts. For instance, they can say that qualia are grasped *directly* because there are no *metaphysical* intermediaries between the qualia concept and the qualia themselves. And if my above suggestion is on the right track, this explanation may also yield a satisfyingly unified explanation of the gap between the perspectival and the non-perspectival. In any case, the perspectivalist reply seems, at best, to shift our focus from one gap to another.[14]

The second threat faced by the perspectivalist reply is that reductionist accounts of what is special about qualia concepts don't do justice to our knowledge of our own qualia. For they use the claim that qualia concepts are non-descriptive to *limit* our introspective knowledge of qualia, including their descriptive physical features. But I think that what is so epistemically striking about qualia concepts is that they allow for an *exhaustive* introspective grasp of qualia, as explained in defense of the disembodiment argument above. And I think that this fact cannot be accommodated by the perspectivalist reply, which claims that introspection allows us to grasp qualia only through a non-exhaustive mode of presentation (in Lycan's view, a second-order property of the qualia).

Representationalism

Before closing, let me briefly comment on representationalism, the view that qualitative features of experience are reducible to intentional features. Grant, for the moment, that the representationalist succeeds in blocking purported counterexamples to representationalism, by showing that any phenomenal difference will be accompanied by an appropriate intentional difference. Still, the representationalist faces two obstacles. First, he must provide reason to favor representationalism over other possible diagnoses of the correlation between qualia and intentional features. One competing diagnosis, which is part of a view now gaining prominence, claims that the representationalist has things backwards: intentional features at least depend on, and may even reduce to, qualia (Siewert, 1998; Horgan and Tienson, 2002; Pitt, 2004).

Second, and more importantly, the representationalist must show that the relation between qualia and intentional features is *necessary*. Consider Lycan's representationalist claim that the phenomenal character of a veridical visual experience of a banana "is just the actual color of the banana itself." On pain of circularity, the "actual color" here must be an *objective* property of the banana, rather than, e.g., a disposition to cause a particular quale in a normal viewer. Now the anti-reductionist will deny that phenomenal yellowness is identical to any such objective property of the banana. It is at least perplexing to see how a phenomenal feature, with its characteristic feel, can be identical to some objective – e.g., microstructural – property of the banana, such as its microstructure of spectral reflectance properties grounded in that microstructure, etc. Again, the link seems to be mere correlation or, at best, some sort of nomic relation. This perplexity again calls to mind the "explanatory gap" between the physical and the phenomenal (Levine, 1983). Just as we cannot understand how there could be a necessary link between qualia and physical (functional, computational) states or processes of the brain, we cannot understand how phenomenological experience could be constituted by objective properties of physical objects, like the microstructural properties of the banana. Unless the representationalist can resolve this perplexity, he is forced to posit brute necessities, and thereby to introduce something that is, as I have said, spookier than irreducible qualia.

Conclusion

Anti-reductionists are not opposed to naturalism, or to the scientific method of inquiry. The choice between reductionism and anti-reductionism depends on which data one finds most in need of explanation. Anti-reductionists, myself included, believe that the costs of reductionism – commitment to brute necessities, and disloyalty to intuitions and introspective evidence – cancel out much of its benefits, and outweigh those that remain.

Notes

1 Chalmers (1996) discusses this possibility.
2 Shapiro (2004) argues that the phenomenon of multiple realizability is much less pervasive than usually believed.
3 What I'm calling the disembodiment argument differs from Descartes's *Meditations* argument in that (i) it specifically targets qualia, whereas Descartes' argument targets

Brie Gertler

thought generally; and (ii) Descartes uses God's abilities to show that what is conceivable is possible, whereas I'm presenting a secular version.

4   On some views of concepts, concepts may be revised. I myself find the notion of genuine conceptual change problematic; on my view, most alleged cases of concept change are better described as either abandoning a concept for a closely related one, or of realizing that one misunderstood one's own concept all along. A good example of the latter is the reaction to Gettier's argument (Gettier, 1963) against analyzing "knowledge" as "justified true belief" ("JTB"). Those who were previously inclined to accept that analysis, but were persuaded by Gettier to reject it, were in effect correcting a prior misconstrual of their own concept. The compellingness of Gettier's argument lay in the fact that the cases he described so obviously failed to be knowledge, though they met the JTB condition.

5   If "conceivability" is used in a factive sense, what I term "conceivability" here is better expressed as "apparent conceivability." I will continue to use "conceivability" in a non-factive sense.

6   At the point in the *Meditations* where Descartes's version of the disembodiment argument occurs, the meditator has not yet ruled out the possibility that his mental states were produced by the machinations of a malicious genius.

7   This is a version of what Stoljar (2002) calls the "object-based conception" of the physical. On that conception, "a physical property is a property which *either* is the sort of property required by a complete account of the intrinsic nature of paradigmatic physical objects and their constituents *or* else is a property which metaphysically (or logically) supervenes on" that sort of property (Stoljar, 2002, p. 313).

8   In fact, a term like "burnt orange" will likely underdetermine the quale I'm referring to, for qualia individuation may be very fine-grained.

9   Suitably altered, this sort of objection may be made to the disembodiment argument as well: even if it's conceivable that I lose my physical properties and become a disembodied seat of qualia, this doesn't mean that it's possible that I do so. My reply can be modified to defend the disembodiment argument.

10 This description expresses what Chalmers calls the *primary intension*; Jackson (1998) calls it the *A-intension*.

11 Interestingly, while Jackson (1998) propounds the view that metaphysical necessities must be explained by conceptual necessities, his current position, in that book and elsewhere, is reductionist. This marks a turnabout from his 1982 position.

12 Compare Jackson: "Only in that way [through conceptual analysis] do we define our subject as the subject we folk suppose is up for discussion" (Jackson, 1998, p. 42).

13 We might describe such a world by using indexicals, but of course that doesn't mean that the facts in that world are perspectival.

14 Strikingly, Searle (1992) is a thoroughgoing physicalist, but claims that there is an ontological distinction between the perspectival and the non-perspectival. On his view, some biological properties are "ontologically subjective."

References and further reading

Arnauld, A. (1641/1984). Fourth set of objections. In J. Cottingham, R. Stoothoff, and D. Murdoch (eds.), *The Philosophical Writings of Descartes*, vol. 2. Cambridge: Cambridge University Press.

Chalmers, D. J. (1996). *The Conscious Mind*. Oxford: Oxford University Press.

— (1999). Materialism and the metaphysics of modality. *Philosophy and Phenomenological Research*, 59, 473–96.

Consciousness and Qualia Cannot Be Reduced   215

— (2003). The content and epistemology of phenomenal belief. In Q. Smith and A. Jokic (eds.), *Consciousness: New Philosophical Perspectives*. Oxford: Oxford University Press.

Conee, E. (1994). Phenomenal knowledge. *Australasian Journal of Philosophy*, 72, 136–50.

Descartes, R. (1641/1984). *Meditations on First Philosophy*. In J. Cottingham, R. Stoothoff, and D. Murdoch (eds.), *The Philosophical Writings of Descartes*, vol. 2. Cambridge: Cambridge University Press.

Gertler, B. (1999). A defense of the knowledge argument. *Philosophical Studies*, 93, 317–36.

— (2001a). Introspecting phenomenal states. *Philosophy and Phenomenological Research*, 63, 305–28.

— (2001b). The explanatory gap is not an illusion. *Mind*, 110, 689–94.

Gettier, E. (1963). Is justified true belief knowledge? *Analysis*, 23, 121–3.

Hill, C. (1991). *Sensations: A Defense of Type Materialism*. Cambridge: Cambridge University Press.

Horgan, T. and Tienson, J. (2002). The intentionality of phenomenology and the phenomenology of intentionality. In D. Chalmers (ed.), *Philosophy of Mind: Classical and Contemporary Readings*. Oxford: Oxford University Press.

Jackson, F. (1982). Epiphenomenal qualia. *The Philosophical Quarterly*, 32, 127–36.

— (1998). *From Metaphysics to Ethics: A Defense of Conceptual Analysis*. Oxford: Oxford University Press.

Kirk, R. (1974). Zombies vs. materialists. *Aristotelian Society Supplement*, 48, 135–52.

Kripke, S. (1980). *Naming and Necessity*. Cambridge, MA: Harvard University Press.

Levine, J. (1983). Materialism and qualia: The explanatory gap. *Pacific Philosophical Quarterly*, 64, 345–61.

— (2001). *Purple Haze*. Oxford: Oxford University Press.

Lewis, D. (1988). What experience teaches. *Proceedings of the Russellian Society*. Sydney: University of Sydney. (Reprinted in W. G. Lycan, *Mind and Cognition*. Oxford: Blackwell, 1990.)

Lycan, W. G. (1996). *Consciousness and Experience*, Cambridge, MA: Bradford Books/MIT Press.

— (2003). Perspectival representation and the knowledge argument. In Q. Smith and A. Jokic (eds.), *Consciousness: New Philosophical Perspectives*. Oxford: Oxford University Press.

Nagel, T. (1974). What is it like to be a bat? *Philosophical Review*, 82, 435–56.

Nemirow, L. (1990). Physicalism and the cognitive role of acquaintance. In W. G. Lycan (ed.), *Mind and Cognition*. Oxford: Blackwell.

Papineau, D. (1998). Mind the gap. *Philosophical Perspectives*, 12, 373–88.

Pitt, D. (2004). The phenomenology of cognition; or what is it like to think that *p*? *Philosophy and Phenomenological Research*, 69, 1–36.

Searle, J. (1992). *The Rediscovery of the Mind*. Cambridge, MA: MIT Press.

Shapiro, L. (2004). *The Mind Incarnate*. Cambridge, MA: MIT Press.

Siewert, C. (1998). *The Significance of Consciousness*. Princeton, NJ: Princeton University Press.

Stoljar, D. (2002). Two conceptions of the physical. In D. J. Chalmers (ed.), *The Philosophy of Mind: Classical and Contemporary Readings*. Oxford: Oxford University Press. (Originally published 2001 in *Philosophy and Phenomenological Research*, 62, 253–81.)

Sturgeon, S. (2000). *Matters of Mind: Consciousness, Reason, and Nature*. London: Routledge.

Tye, M. (1999). Phenomenal consciousness: The explanatory gap as a cognitive illusion. *Mind*, 108, 705–25.

DOES COGNITIVE SCIENCE NEED EXTERNAL CONTENT AT ALL?

Locating Meaning in the Mind (Where it Belongs)

Ray Jackendoff

1 Premises of Conceptualist Semantics

This chapter is drawn from a larger project, *Foundations of Language* (Jackendoff, 2002), whose goal is to reconstruct linguistic theory in a way that permits a better integration of linguistics with psychology, neuroscience, and evolutionary theory – and a better integration of the parts of linguistics with each other. In particular, unlike recent mainstream generative linguistics (e.g., Chomsky, 1995), it is intended to include all of language, not just an artificially stipulated core. The reader is referred especially to chapters 9 and 10 for more detail of the material discussed here.

The most basic aspect of generative grammar, the tradition of linguistics within which I work, is that it is *mentalistic*: it takes linguistic theory to be modeling the structural organization in the brain of a language user. It is this ground rule that places interesting constraints on the theory of grammar: First, language must be stored and processed in the brain. Hence theoretical elegance equals not mathematical elegance but rather "brain elegance," however that may come to be characterized. Second, language must be learned. Hence we need a theory of the human language capacity, or Universal Grammar, and how it interacts with experience to create adult language competence. Third, the language capacity must have evolved since humans diverged from chimpanzees about 5 million years ago, which places constraints on what can be attributed to Universal Grammar.

One missing part in standard generative grammar and most of its offshoots is a good compatible theory of meaning, one that is comparably mentalistic. To take the two most influential approaches to meaning within linguistics, Cognitive Grammar (Lakoff, 1987; Langacker, 1987) is mentalistic but mostly isn't made to be compatible with generative grammar; and formal semantics (Chierchia and McConnell-Ginet, 1990) is mostly apsychological, so that it certainly doesn't connect with psycholinguistics and language acquisition. I've been trying to work out a more satisfactory approach for about 30 years. Here I want to go through some aspects of it. Some date back to older work (Jackendoff, 1976, 1983, 1987); some are new to *Foundations of Language*.

I take the basic problem of a mentalistic semantic theory to be:

How can we characterize the messages/thoughts/concepts that speakers express/convey by means of using language?
How does language express/convey these messages?

I leave the terms "messages/thoughts/concepts" and "express/convey" deliberately vague for the moment. Part of our job is to sharpen them. In particular, we have to ask:

What makes these mental entities function the way meanings intuitively should?

Unfortunately, the intellectual politics begins right here: this is not the way everyone construes the term "semantics." Rather than engage in arguments based on terminological imperialism, I will use *conceptualist semantics* as a term of art for this enterprise. (My own particular set of proposals, which I have called Conceptual Semantics (Jackendoff, 1990), is an exemplar of the approach but not the only possible one.) Above all, I don't want to get trapped in the question: Is this enterprise really a kind of semantics or not? The relevant questions are: Is this enterprise a worthwhile way of studying meaning? To what extent can it incorporate intuitions and insights from other approaches, and to what extent can it offer insights unavailable in other approaches? It is important to see that the messages/thoughts/concepts conveyed by language serve other purposes as well. At the very least, they are involved in the cognitive processes illustrated in figure 13.1.

Linguists spend a lot of time accounting for the combinatoriality of phonology and syntax. But it is assumed (although rarely articulated) that these systems serve the purpose of transmitting messages constructed from an equally combinatorial system of thoughts: a sentence conveys a meaning built combinatorially out of the meanings of its words. This combinatorial system is represented in figure 13.1 by the component "formation rules for thoughts," which defines the class of possible thoughts or conceptual structures. (An important terminological point: one use of the term *syntax*

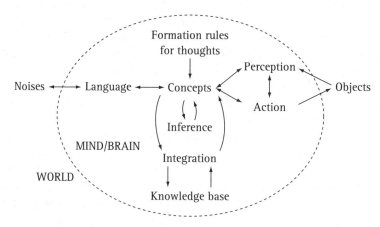

Figure 13.1 The place of conceptualist semantics in the architecture of mind.

Ray Jackendoff

pertains to any sort of combinatorial system. In this sense phonology has a syntax, music has a syntax, chess has a syntax, and of course thought has a syntax. In the use favored by linguists, however, *syntax* refers specifically to the combinatorial organization made up of such units as noun phrase and verb phrase. In this sense thought is definitely *not* syntax.)

In the framework of *Foundations of Language* (Jackendoff, 2002), the combinatorial structures for thought are related to the purely linguistic structures of syntax and phonology by so-called *interface rules* (double arrows in figure 13.1). In particular, different languages have different interfaces, so that the same thought can be mapped into expressions of different languages, within tolerances, allowing for the possibility of reasonably good translation among languages. An important part of the interface rules is the collection of *words* of the language. A word is a long-term memory association of a piece of phonology (its pronunciation), a set of syntactic features (its part of speech and contextual properties such as subcategorization), and a piece of conceptual structure (its meaning). Thus each word in an utterance establishes a part of the utterance's sound-grammar-meaning correspondence; other parts of the correspondence are mediated by interface rules that map between syntactic structure and combinatorial structure in semantics.

These two parts of figure 13.1 – the combinatorial system of meaning and its interfaces to linguistic expression – are closest to what is often called "linguistic semantics." Now consider the other interfaces. The use of thoughts/concepts to produce further thoughts/concepts is what is typically called "inference" or "reasoning." Since we are interested in the study of real people and not just ideals, this interface must include not only logical reasoning but also making plans and forming intentions to act, so-called "practical reasoning" (Kahneman et al., 1982; Bratman, 1987; Gigerenzer, 2000) and "social reasoning" (Fiske, 1991; Tooby and Cosmides, 1992).

We also must account for the integration of thoughts conveyed by language with previous knowledge or beliefs. Part of previous knowledge is one's sense of the communicative context, including one's interlocutor's intentions. Thus the work of this interface is closest to what is often called "pragmatics."

The interfaces to the perceptual systems are what permit one to form thoughts based on observing the world. In turn, by using such thoughts as the input to language production, we can talk about what we see, hear, taste, and feel. These interfaces operate in the other direction as well: language can be used to direct attention to some particular part of the perceptual field. The interface with the action system is what permits one to carry out intentions – including carrying out intentions formed in response to a command or request.

In order to make possible the kinds of interactions just enumerated, all these interfaces need to converge on a common cognitive structure. If we look at thought through the lens of language alone, we don't have enough constraints on possible theories. A richer, more demanding set of boundary conditions emerges from insisting that thought must also make contact with inference, background knowledge, perception, and action.

In fact, this view of thought permits us to make contact immediately with evolutionary considerations as well. Suppose we erase the interface to language from figure 13.1. We then have an architecture equally suitable – at some level of approximation – for nonlinguistic organisms such as apes. They too display complex integration of perception, action, inference, and background knowledge, in both physical and social domains (Köhler, 1927; Goodall, 1971; Byrne and Whiten, 1988; Hauser, 2000). They just can't talk about it. It makes evolutionary sense to suppose that some of the fundamental parts of human thought are a heritage of our primate ancestry (Hauser et al., 2002; Pinker and Jackendoff, 2005).

To presume that we can invoke evolutionary considerations, of course, is also to presume that some of the overall character of thought is determined by the genome. I see at least three major domains of thought that suggest an innate genetic basis. The first is the understanding of the physical world: the identification of objects, their spatial configurations with respect to each other, the events in which they take part and interact, and the opportunities they offer for action on and with them. The second is the understanding of the social world: the identification of persons, characterization of the beliefs and motivations of other persons (so-called "theory of mind"), and the ability to understand the social roles of oneself and others, including such issues as kinship, dominance, group membership, obligations, entitlements, and morals (not as a universal system, but as the underpinning for all cultural variation in social understanding) (Jackendoff, forthcoming). The third domain that I think must be innate is a basic algebra of individuation, categorization, grouping, and decomposition that undergirds both the two systems just mentioned as well as many others.

In short, conceptualist semantics should aspire to offer a common meeting ground for multiple traditions in studying cognition, including not only linguistic semantics but also pragmatics, perceptual understanding, embodied cognition, reasoning and planning, social/cultural understanding, primate cognition, and evolutionary psychology. A high aspiration, but certainly one worth pursuing.

2 Attempts to Integrate the Commonsense View of Reference with Mentalist Linguistics

A crucial part of semantic theory is to explain how reference and truth-value are attached to linguistic expressions. Common sense tells us that linguistic expressions say things about the world. When I say *Russell was a great philosopher*, I am referring to Russell, a real person in the real world. Likewise, sentences intuitively have truth-values by virtue of how they relate to the world. *Snow is green* is false because snow isn't green.

The predominant traditions in Anglo-American semantics and philosophy of language take this commonsense position for granted. They therefore consider it the task of semantic/pragmatic theory to explain how linguistic expressions say things about the world and have truth-values based on their relation to the world. But it is not so easy to fit this commonsense position on reference and truth into a mentalistic theory of language.

Let us first think about how to understand the term "language." Frege and much of the tradition following him take language to be independent of its human users: it relates directly to the world. This combines with the commonsense view of reference to create a view like figure 13.2. More recent variants on this position (e.g., Kripke, 1972; Lewis, 1972; Montague, 1973; Stalnaker, 1984) substitute "possible worlds" and/or "the model" for "world," leaving the basic story unchanged. Language doesn't really

Ray Jackendoff

Figure 13.2 An "objectivist" or "realist" view of language.

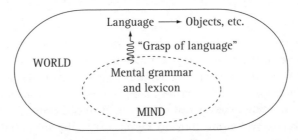

Figure 13.3 The mind grasping "language in the world."

have much to do with the mind. Some in formal semantics, such as David Lewis, are very explicit about this, others are more or less agnostic.

How can this realist view of language to be reconciled with the mentalist approach of generative grammar? One approach would be to jettison the mentalism of generative linguistics, but retain the formal mechanisms: to take the position that there is an objective "language out there in the world," and that this is in fact what generative grammar is studying. Some people have indeed taken this tack (e.g., Katz, 1981). But it disconnects generative linguistics from all sources of evidence based on processing, acquisition, genetics, and brain damage. And it forces us to give up the fundamental motivation for positing Universal Grammar and for exploring its character. I personally think that's too high a price to pay.

An alternative tack might be Frege's (1892): language is indeed "out in the world" and it refers to "objects in the world"; but people *use* language by virtue of their grasp of it, where "grasp" is a transparent metaphor for "the mind holding/understanding/making contact with" something in the world. Figure 13.3 might schematize such an approach. Generative linguistics, it might then be said, is the study of what is in the mind when it grasps a language. This way we could incorporate all the mentalistic methodology into linguistics while preserving a realist semantics.

But what sense are we to make of the notion of "grasping" an abstract object? We know in principle how the mind "grasps" concrete objects: it constructs cognitive structures in response to inputs from the senses. This is a physical process: the sense organs respond to impinging light, vibration, pressure, and so forth by emitting nerve impulses that enter the brain. But what inputs give rise to the "grasp" of an abstract object? An abstract object by definition has no physical manifestations that can impinge on the nervous system. So how does the nervous system "grasp" them? Without a careful exegesis of the term – which no one provides – we are ineluctably led toward a quasimystical interpretation of "grasping," a scientific dead end.

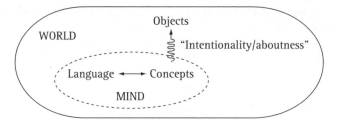

Figure 13.4 Concepts in the mind that are "about" objects in the world.

One way to eliminate the problem of how the mind grasps language is to push language entirely into the mind – as generative grammar does. We might then arrive at a semantic theory structured like figure 13.4. This is Jerry Fodor's position, I think (Fodor, 1975, 1983, 1990, 1998): for him, language is a mental faculty that accesses combinatorially structured concepts (expressions in the "Language of Thought"). In turn, concepts have a semantics: they are connected to the world by virtue of being "intentional." The problem for Fodor is to make naturalistic sense of intentionality. But intentionality suffers from precisely the same difficulty as "grasping" language in figure 13.3: there is no physically realizable causal connection between concepts and objects.

The upshot of these explorations is that there seems to be no way to combine a realist semantics with a mentalist view of language, without invoking some sort of transcendental connection between the mind and the world. The key to a solution, I suggest, lies in examining the realist's notion of "objects in the world."

3 Problems with the Commonsense View: "Objects"

Of course, "objects," "states of affairs," and "things out in the world" have an entirely intuitive construal. "Objects" invites us to think of Bertrand Russell, Noam Chomsky, trees, refrigerators, and so on. You can see them and touch them; you can count them, tell two of them apart, and in some cases move them around. "States of affairs" invites us to think of snow being white, dogs being animals, Russell's having been a philosopher, and so on: observable facts about observable objects.

But consider: we refer routinely to all sorts of "objects" that are not so simple to put our hands on. A wide range of examples appears in (1)–(6). I leave it to the reader to see the difficulties each of them raises.

Figure 13.5a   Figure 13.5b

Ray Jackendoff

1 Fictional and mythical characters
   (a) Sherlock Holmes
   (b) the unicorn in my dream last night
2 Geographical objects
   (a) Wyoming
   (b) the Mississippi River
   (c) the distance between New York and Boston
3 Virtual objects
   (a) the square formed by the four dots in figure 13.5a
   (b) the horizontal rectangle that goes behind the vertical one in figure 13.5b
4 Social entities
   (a) the value of my watch
   (b) the first dollar I ever earned
   (c) Morris Halle's PhD degree
   (d) your reputation
   (e) General Motors
   (f) the score of tomorrow's Red Sox game
5 Auditorily perceived objects
   (a) Beethoven's Seventh Symphony
   (b) the words *banana* and *despite*
6 Other
   (a) the set of all possible worlds
   (b) the best of all possible worlds

Here is the point of these examples: the commonsense view of reference asserts that we refer to "objects in the world" as if this is completely self-evident. It *is* self-evident, if we think only of reference to middle-sized perceivable physical objects like tables and refrigerators. But as soon as we explore the full range of entities to which we *actually* refer, "the world" suddenly begins to be populated with all sorts of curious beasts whose ontological status is far less clear. For each of the types of entities cited above, some more or less elaborate story can be constructed, and some of them have indeed evoked an extensive philosophical literature. But the effect in each case is to distance the notions of reference and "the world" from direct intuition. The cumulative effect of considering all of them together is a "world" in which direct intuition applies only to a very limited class of instances.

4 Pushing "the World" into the Mind

To sum up so far: The commonsense position on reference, which standard approaches to semantics take as their starting point, suffers from two complementary problems. First, if language is in the minds of language users, it is necessary to invoke some mystical connection from the mind to the world, either at the level of language, as in figure 13.3, or at the level of the concepts the language expresses, as in figure 13.4. Second, the notion of "objects in the world" is itself a serious problem.

I propose to deal with these problems by abandoning the unexamined notion of "objects in the world," and, for purposes of the theory of reference, pushing "the world" into the mind of the language user too, right along with language.

What does it mean to "push the world into the mind"? The change is in how we're supposed to understand statements about reference. (7)–(8) give the two opposing alternatives.

7 Commonsense realist theory of reference:
Phrase P of language L, uttered in context C, refers to entity E in the world (or possible worlds).

8 Conceptualist theory of reference:
A speaker S of language L judges phrase P, uttered in context C, to refer to entity E in [the world as conceptualized by S].

That is, in the conceptualist theory, the speaker's judgment and conceptualization play a critical role.

As initial motivation for exploring the conceptualist position, let's observe that a language user cannot refer to an entity without having some conceptualization of it. Consider an example like (9).

9 I don't know what that was, but here it comes again!

In order to utter (9) (and mean it), the speaker must have conceptualized some relevant entity, though certainly without a full characterization. That is, conceptualization of a referent is a necessary condition for a speaker to refer. However, being in the *real* world is not a necessary condition: speakers can refer without difficulty to entities like *Sherlock Holmes* and *the unicorn in my dream last night*. Furthermore, an entity's being in the real world is not *sufficient* for reference either: one has to conceptualize it in at least some minimal way. In short, an entity's being in the real world is neither a necessary nor a sufficient condition for a speaker's being able to refer to it. Rather, the crucial factor is having conceptualized an entity of the proper sort.

Still, I would not blame the reader for being a bit suspicious of this expression "the world as conceptualized by the language user." It smacks of a certain solipsism or even deconstructionism, as though language users get to make up the world any way they want, as though one is referring to one's mental representations rather than to the things represented. And indeed, there seems little choice. Figure 13.1, the conceptualist position, has no direct connection between the form of concepts and the outside world. On this picture our thoughts seem to be trapped in our own brains.

This outcome, needless to say, has come in for harsh criticism, from many different quarters, for example:

But how can mapping a representation onto another representation explain what a representation means? . . . [E]ven if our interaction with the world is always mediated by representation systems, understanding such systems will eventually involve considering

Ray Jackendoff

what the systems are about, what they are representations of. (Chierchia and McConnell-Ginet, 1990, p. 47)

... words can't have their meanings *just* because their users undertake to pursue some or other linguistic policies; or, indeed, just because of any purely *mental* phenomenon, anything that happens purely "in your head." For "John" to be John's name, there must be some sort of real relation between the name and its bearer ... something has to happen *in the world*. (Fodor, 1990, pp. 98–9)

But we can know the Markerese translation of an English sentence [i.e. its conceptual structure] without knowing the first thing about the meaning of the English sentence: namely, the conditions under which it would be true. (Lewis, 1972, p. 169)

How is it possible to escape this attack? I think the only way is to go deeper into psychology, and to deal even more carefully with the notion of thought. Think about it from the standpoint of neuropsychology: the neural assemblies responsible for storing and processing conceptual structures indeed *are* trapped in our brains. They have no direct access to the outside world. A position like Fodor's says that the "Language of Thought" is made of symbols that have meaning with respect to the outside world. I would rather say that conceptual structures are *not* made of symbols – they don't *symbolize* anything – and they don't *have* meanings. Rather, I want to say that they *are* meaning: they do exactly the things meaning is supposed to do, such as support inference and judgment. Language is meaningful, then, because it connects to conceptual structures. Such a statement is of course anathema to many semanticists and philosophers, not to mention to common sense. Still, let's persist and see how far we can go with it.

5 A Simple Act of Deictic Reference

Consider about the simplest act of using language to refer to a "middle-sized object": a use of referential deixis such as (10).

10   Hey, look at that! [pointing]

The deictic pronoun *that* has almost no intrinsic descriptive content; its semantics is almost purely referential. In order to understand (10), the hearer not only has to process the sentence but also has to determine what referent the speaker intends by *that*. This requires going out of the language faculty and making use of the visual system.

Within the visual system, the hearer must process the visual field and visually establish an individual in it that can serve as referent of *that*. The retinal image alone cannot do the job of establishing such an individual. The retina is sensitive only to distinctions like "dark point in bright surround at such-and-such a location on retina." The retina's "ontology" contains no objects and no external location. Nor is the situation much better in the parts of the brain most directly fed by the retina: here we find things like local line and edge detectors in various orientations, all in retinotopic format (Hubel and Wiesel, 1968) – but still no objects, no external world. And this is all the contact the brain has with the outside world; inboard from here it's all computation.

However this computation works, it eventually has to construct a cognitive structure that might be called a "percept." The principles and neural mechanisms that construct percepts are subjects of intensive research in psychology and neuroscience, and are far from understood. The outcome, however, has to be a neurally instantiated cognitive structure that distinguishes individuals in the perceived environment and that permits one to attend to one or another of them. This cognitive structure that gives rise to perceived individuals is nonlinguistic: human infants and various animals can be shown experimentally to identify and track individuals more or less the way we do, so the best hypothesis is that they have percepts more or less like ours.

Of course percepts are trapped inside the brain too. There is no magical direct route between the world and the percept – only the complex and indirect route via the retina and the lower visual areas. Hence all the arguments that are directed against conceptualist semantics apply equally to percepts. This may bother some philosophers, but most psychologists and neuroscientists take a more practical approach: they see the visual system as creating a cognitive structure which constitutes part of the organism's understanding of reality, and which helps the organism act successfully in its environment (Marr, 1982; Koch, 2004). If there is any sense to the notion of "grasping" the world perceptually, this wildly complex computation is it; it is far from a simple unmediated operation.

And of course a visual percept is what is linked to the deictic *that* in (9) and (10), through the interfaces between conceptual structure and the "upper end" of the visual system. Thus language has indeed made contact with the outside world – but through the complex mediation of the visual system rather than through some mysterious mind-world relation of intentionality. Everything is scientifically kosher.

A skeptic may still be left grumbling that something is missing: "We don't perceive our percepts in our heads, we perceive objects out in the world." Absolutely correct. However, as generations of research in visual perception have shown, the visual system populates "the world" with all sorts of "objects" that have no physical reality, for instance the things in example (3): the square subtended by four dots and the "amodally completed" horizontal rectangle. So we should properly think of "the perceptual world" (or "phenomenal world" in the sense of Koffka, 1935) not as absolute reality but as the "reality" constructed by our perceptual systems in response to whatever is "really out there."

Naturally, the perceptual world isn't totally out of synch with the "real world." The perceptual systems have evolved in order that organisms may act reliably in the real world. They are not concerned with a "true model of the world" in the logical sense, but with a "world model" that is good enough to support the planning of actions that in the long run lead to better propagation of the genes. Like other products of evolution, the perceptual systems are full of "cheap tricks," which is *why* we see virtual objects: these tricks *work* in the organism's normal environment. It is only in the context of the laboratory that their artificiality is detected.

Thus *the perceptual world* is *reality for us*. Apart from the sensory inputs, percepts are entirely "trapped in the brain"; they are nothing but formal structures instantiated in neurons. But the perceptual systems give us the sense, the feeling, the affect, of objects being out there. We experience objects in the world, not percepts in our heads. That's the way we're built (Dennett, 1991; Koch, 2004).

In short, the problem of reference for the intuitively clear cases is not at bottom a problem for linguistic theory, it is a problem for perceptual theory: how do the mechanisms of perception create for us the experience of a world "out there"?

I suspect some readers may find this stance disquieting. My late friend John Macnamara, with whom I agreed on so much, used to accuse me of not believing there is a real world. But I think the proper way I should have replied to him is that we are ultimately concerned with *reality for us*, the world in which we lead our lives. Isn't that enough? (Or at least, isn't that enough for linguistic semantics?) If you want to go beyond that and demand a "more ultimate reality," independent of human cognition, well, you are welcome to, but that doesn't exactly render my enterprise pointless.

6 Indexical Features

Let's continue in this direction a bit and see where it leads. A basic characteristic of a percept is that it constitutes a figure distinguished from the background on which it is located and in which it moves. Suppose you hear me say *Hey, look at that!* You stare at the patterned rug and see nothing; then suddenly a bug "pops out" in experience ("Oh god, there it is! Eeuww!"). Nothing has changed in "the physical world" or in your retinal image. All that has changed is the organization of percepts "trapped" in your brain: the bug-percept has emerged as figural. Let us call this figural characteristic the *indexical* feature of the percept. It gives the mind a 'something' to which perceptual features can be bound. A speaker who utters (9) (*I don't know what that was, but here it comes again!*) is reporting a percept with an indexical feature but minimal identifiable perceptual features.

The mind establishes indexical features, among other things, in response to perceptual input. But once established, they need not go away in the absence of perceptual input: we intuitively sense that objects continue to exist when we're not seeing them. Indexical features can undergo "splitting," for instance when we break a lump of clay in half to form two distinct individuals. They can also undergo "merger," as when we mold two lumps of clay into an undifferentiated mass.

The indexical feature of a percept is the crucial feature for linguistic reference. If there is no indexical feature to which perceptual features can be bound, there is nothing that a deictic or other referring linguistic expression can be attached to either: there is no "*that*" there.

We can see how this account extends to some of the problematic entities mentioned earlier. Consider again virtual objects such as the square subtended by four dots. Although there is no square "actually out there," the visual system constructs a percept with all the right features for a "square out there." Hence there *is* something "out there" in the perceived world, and we can refer to it.

Returning to the standard literature on reference: Frege (1892) made the distinction between the sense and the reference of an expression by citing the well-known example *The morning star is the evening star.* In his analysis, two senses are attached to the same reference. We can understand Frege's example in present terms as reporting the merger of indexicals associated with different perceptual features, on the basis of some discovery. So Frege's problem is not a uniquely linguistic problem; rather it lies in a more general theory of how the mind keeps track of individuated entities.

The reverse, indexical splitting, can also occur. I used to think there was one literary/cultural theorist named Bloom, until one day I saw a new book by Bloom and was surprised because I had thought he had been dead for several years. It suddenly dawned on me, to my embarrassment, that there were *two* Blooms, Allan and Harold – so my indexical came to be split into two. Think also of discovering that someone you have seen around the neighborhood is actually twins.

More generally, indexical features play a role altogether parallel to the discourse referents in various approaches within formal semantics such as Discourse Representation Theory (Kamp and Reyle, 1993), File Change Semantics (Heim, 1989), and Dynamic Semantics (Groenendijk et al., 1996). Hence many of the insights of these approaches can be taken over here, with the proviso that the "model" over which reference is defined should be a psychologically motivated one.

7 Entities Other Than Objects

Let's go a bit more into what a psychologically motivated model would include. Let's start by observing that indexical features do not always identify individual objects: these are just one sort of entity that can be identified by an indexical.

For instance, consider uttering *Hey, look at THAT!* in reaction to muddy water pouring out of a pipe. Here the intended reference may well be the *substance* rather than any particular bounded quantity of it. Moreover, various deictics can be used to refer to a wide range of nonmaterial entities, as seen in (11).

11 (a) Goodness! Did you hear *that*?   [Sound]
   (b) [Dentist:] Did *that* hurt?   [Tactile sensation]
   (c) Pro-prepositional phrase:
        Please put your coat *here* [pointing] and put your hat
           there [pointing].   [Location]
        He went *thataway* [pointing].   [Direction]
   (d) Pro-verb phrase:
        Can you do *that* [pointing]?   [Action]
        Can you do *this* [demonstrating]?   [Action]
   (e) that . . . happen:
        If *that* [pointing] happens again, I'm leaving.   [Event/Activity]
   (f) Pro-manner adverbial:
        You shuffle cards *thus/so/like this/this way*
           [demonstrating].   [Manner]
        I used to walk *that way/like that* [pointing to someone
           walking in a funny fashion].   [Manner]

(g) Pro-measure expression:

The fish that got away was *this* long [demonstrating].   [Distance]

There were about *this* many people at Joe's party too.

[gesturing toward the assembled throng].   [Amount]

(h) Pro-time-PP:

You may start . . . right . . . *now*! [clapping]   [Time]

The deictic expressions here refer to entities in the conceptualized world that can be picked out with the aid of the accompanying gesture. But the entities referred to are not objects, they are sounds, sensations, locations, directions, and so on.

In order to accommodate these possibilities for reference, it is useful to introduce a kind of "ur-feature" that classifies the entity being referred to into an *ontological type*. Each of the ontological types – objects, sounds, actions, locations, and so forth – has its own characteristic conditions of identity and individuation. It is a task both for natural language semantics and for cognitive psychology/neuroscience to work out the logic and the characteristic perceptual manifestations of each type.

Are all the sorts of entities in (11) "in the world"? They are certainly not like refrigerators – you can't touch them or move them. In fact, it is odd to say they all *exist* in the way that refrigerators exist ("the length of the fish exists"??). Yet (11) shows that we can pick them out of the perceptual field and use them as the referents of deictic expressions. So we must accord them some dignified status in the perceived world – the "model" that serves as the basis for linguistic reference.

Now notice what has just happened. Up to a moment ago I was concerned with reference to objects, and I used perceptual theory to ground the theory of reference. Now all of a sudden I have turned the argument on its head: If this is the way reference relates to perception, perception must be providing a far richer range of entities than had previously been suspected. It is now a challenge for perceptual theory to describe how the perceptual systems accomplish this. In other words, examples like (11) open the door for fruitful cooperation between linguistic semantics and research in perception.

This repertoire of ontological types seems to me a good candidate for a very skeletal unlearned element of cognition. Again, because it is central not just to language but to perception and action, we need not call it part of Universal Grammar, the human specialization for learning language. But we do have to call it part of the innate human cognitive endowment.

So far, I've only talked about perceivable entities. What makes them perceivable is that they have features that connect to the perceptual interfaces in figure 13.1. Now suppose that conceptual structure contains other features that do not pertain to a perceptual modality, but which connect instead to the inferential system in figure 13.1. Such features would provide "bridges" to other concepts but no direct connection to perception. That is, they are used in *reasoning* rather than in identification. Let's call these *inferential* features by contrast with *perceptual* features.

What would be candidates for inferential features? Consider an object's value. This is certainly not perceivable, but it influences the way one reasons about the object, including one's goals and desires concerning the object. Value can be established by all sorts of means, mostly very indirect. Thus value seems like a prime candidate for a type of inferential feature. Another candidate is high-level taxonomic category such as *natural kind* or *artifact*. The classification of a particular object (a fork, a refrigerator, a book, etc.) as an artifact predicts only that people typically use this object for something. But it does not predict what the object looks like, how it works, or what one does with it. Rather, beyond the ontological feature "physical object," which does have perceptual consequences, *artifact* is not on the whole a collection of perceptual features; rather it bridges to all sorts of inferences that can in turn potentially engage perceptual features.

Now suppose there were a concept that had only inferential features. This then would be an abstract concept such as those expressed by *the value of my watch* and *the meaning of this word*. From the point of view of language, abstract objects are not distinguished from concrete objects: all that is necessary for reference is an indexical feature. The interfaces to language can't "see" whether a concept's descriptive features are perceptual or inferential. So as far as language is concerned, reference proceeds in the same fashion whether or not there is a physical object out there in the world – or even a conceptualized physical object.

8 Satisfaction and Truth

An important piece has been left out of the story so far. Linguistic expressions used in isolation cannot refer: they can only *purport* to refer. For example, suppose I'm talking to you on the phone and say *Hey, will you look at THAT!* You understand that I intend to refer to something; but you can't establish the reference and therefore can't establish the contextualized meaning of the utterance.

A referential expression *succeeds* in referring for the hearer if it is *satisfied* by something that can serve as its referent. Remember: in realist semantics, satisfaction is a relation between a linguistic expression and an entity in the world; but in conceptualist semantics, the entity is in [the world as conceptualized by the language user]. It is this latter notion of satisfaction that we have to work out here.

To work out a conceptualist notion of satisfaction, we invoke one component in figure 13.1 that I haven't yet discussed: the integration of concepts with the knowledge base. Suppose I say to you: *I talked to Henk Verkuyl today in the supermarket*. In isolation, the proper name *Henk Verkuyl* purports to refer; you assume that I intended it actually to refer. If you know Henk Verkuyl (i.e. he is part of your knowledge base), you can establish the intended reference in your own construal of the world. If you do not know him, the proper name is unsatisfied for you.

More generally, four different situations can arise.

12 (a) The purported referent of my utterance is present in your knowledge base or the readily available context, and it satisfies the referential expression.

    (b) The purported referent is not present in your knowledge base or the readily available context, and so you add a new character into your knowledge base to satisfy the referential expression. If I anticipate this situation for you, I'll use a specific indefinite expression like *a friend of mine* or *this friend of mine, Henk Verkuyl* instead of a definite description or an unadorned proper name.

(c)   The purported referent is in conflict with your knowledge base, as in Russell's famous example *the present king of France*. Or it is in conflict with the readily available context, for example in a situation where I speak of *the apple on the table* and you see either no apples or two apples on the table. In this case you have to fall back on some repertoire of repair strategies: guessing what I intend, asking me for clarification, deciding to ignore me altogether, and so on.

(d)   The purported referent contains features that inherently conflict with each other, so that nothing can possibly satisfy the expression. In such a case, for instance *the square circle*, you'll find the expression anomalous, and you'll again have to fall back on repair strategies.

This is all clear with the reference of noun phrases. Next let's look at the reference of sentences. The standard custom in the formal semantics tradition, going back to Frege, is that the intended referent of a (declarative) sentence is a truth-value. I must confess I have never understood the argument for this position (e.g., Chierchia and McConnell-Ginet, 1990, ch. 2). I am going to explore instead the alternative position (proposed in Jackendoff, 1972) that the intended reference of a declarative sentence is a situation (an event or a state of affairs). Traditionalists should not worry: truth-values will get their due shortly.

The view that sentences refer to situations is motivated largely by linguistic parallels to referentiality in noun phrases. This is a kind of evidence not frequently cited in the literatures of philosophy of language and formal semantics – although Situation Semantics (Barwise and Perry, 1984) made a good deal of it. First notice how noun phrases and sentences are parallel in the way they can be used to accompany deictic reference:

13   (a)   Will you look at that! A blimp!
     (b)   Will you look at that! The baby's walking!

(13)(a) draws your attention to an object in the environment; (13)(b) to an event – not to a truth-value. Next, notice that discourse pronouns can co-refer with sentences as well as with noun phrases.

14   (a)   A blimp appeared in the sky. It was huge.
     (b)   Suddenly the baby started walking. It astounded her parents.

The antecedent of *it* in (14)(b) is the whole preceding sentence, so it presumably has the same referent. But *it* certainly does not refer to a truth-value: *it astounded her parents* does not assert that the parents are astounded by the truth of the proposition expressed by *the baby started walking*; they are astounded by the *event* of the baby walking. Hence this event must be the referent of the preceding sentence as well.

Next consider embedded *that*-clauses in a context where they alternate with noun phrases.

15 (a) The apple on the table astounded Max.
   (b) That the Red Sox won today astounded Max.

What astounded Max wasn't a truth-value, it was an event.

Parallel to the four possible situations in (12) for satisfaction of a noun phrase's purported referent, we find four possible situations for the referent of *the Red Sox won today* in (15)(b).

16 (a) Your knowledge base includes the event of the Red Sox winning, and this satisfies the intended referent of the clause.
   (b) Your knowledge base does not include the event of the Red Sox winning, so you add this to your knowledge base as the referent of the clause.
   (c) Your knowledge base includes something in conflict with the purported event of the Red Sox winning (say, your take on the world is that the Red Sox didn't play). Then you have to engage in some repair strategy.
   (d) The features of the purported event are inherently in conflict, so that there is no possible referent. In such a case, for instance *That the square is a circle astounded Max*, the clause is judged anomalous, and you again have to resort to repair.

There are of course, other cases of *that*-clauses that don't come out this way, notably in so-called intensional (with an s) contexts such as the complement of *believe*. However, noun phrases in this position are subject to the same distortions of referentiality:

17 (a) Max believes that there is a tooth fairy/the square is a circle.
   (b) Max believes in the tooth fairy/in square circles.

In both of these, the speaker makes no commitment to the existence of the tooth fairy or square circles.

So far, then, I've tried to convince you that it makes sense to regard a clause as referentially satisfied by a conceptualized situation. What about truth-values, then? The judgment of a declarative sentence's truth-value follows from how it is referentially satisfied.

18 (a) In case (16)(a), where the intended referent of the sentence is present in your knowledge base (or can be deduced from it), you judge the sentence true.
   (b) In case (16)(b), where there is no conflict with your knowledge base, you normally take the sentence to be informative and presumed true.
   (c) In case (16)(c), you judge the sentence false.
   (d) In case (16)(d), you judge it analytically false.

Thus truth is defined in terms of reference and satisfaction, just as proposed by Tarski (1936/1983).

In short, the parallelism in the reference of noun phrases and sentences lies in the parallelism between conceptualized objects and conceptualized situations. The notion of satisfaction applies identically to both. However, sentences have an additional layer of evaluation, in which they are characterized as true or false on the basis of how they are referentially satisfied.

In this approach, then, the problem of characterizing the conditions under which a sentence is judged true does not go away. It is just demoted from the paramount problem of semantic theory to one among many problems. What seems more basic here is the conditions of satisfaction for referential constituents and how they interact with the knowledge base. In fact, a great deal of research in "truth-conditional" semantics can easily be reconstrued as addressing this issue. For instance, the question of whether sentence S_1 entails sentence S_2 has nothing to do with their truth-values – sentences may describe thoroughly fictional or hypothetical situations. Rather, S_1 entails S_2 if adding the situation referred to by S_1 to an otherwise blank knowledge base enables the situation referred to by S_2 to be satisfied. The factors involved in such satisfaction, and the form of the rules of inference, may remain essentially unchanged from a truth-conditional account.

Above all, the conceptualist approach shifts the focus of semantics from the question "What makes sentences true?" to what I take to be the more ecologically sound question, "How do we humans understand language?" – where I mean "ecologically sound" in the sense that it permits us to integrate semantics with the other human sciences. I take this to be a positive step.

There are obviously many further problems in establishing a mentalistic semantics and in particular a mentalistic theory of reference and truth. *Foundations of Language* (Jackendoff, 2002) addresses some of these and not others. But here is where we are so far. We have not ended up with the rock-solid rigid notion of truth that the realists apparently want. Rather, I think we have begun to envision something that has the promise of explaining our human sense of truth and reference – and why philosophical and commonsensical disputes about truth and reference so often proceed the way they do. I have no illusions that this work is over, but it strikes me as a path well worth exploring.

References

Barwise, J. and Perry, J. (1984). *Situations and Attitudes*. Cambridge, MA: MIT Press.

Bratman, M. (1987). *Intention, Plans, and Practical Reason*. Cambridge, MA: Harvard University Press.

Byrne, R. W. and Whiten, A. (eds.) (1988). *Machiavellian Intelligence: Social Expertise and the Evolution of Intellect in Monkeys, Apes, and Humans*. Oxford: Clarendon Press.

Chierchia, G. and McConnell-Ginet, S. (1990). *Meaning and Grammar: An Introduction to Semantics*. Cambridge, MA: MIT Press.

Chomsky, N. (1995). *The Minimalist Program*. Cambridge, MA: MIT Press.

Dennett, D. (1991). *Consciousness Explained*. New York: Little, Brown.

Fiske, A. (1991). *Structures of Social Life*. New York: Free Press.

Fodor, J. A. (1975). *The Language of Thought*. Cambridge, MA: Harvard University Press.

—— (1983). *The Modularity of Mind*. Cambridge, MA: MIT Press.

— (1990). *A Theory of Content and Other Essays*. Cambridge, MA: MIT Press.

— (1998). *Concepts: Where Cognitive Science Went Wrong*. Oxford: Oxford University Press.

Frege, G. (1892). Über Sinn und Bedeutung. *Zeitschrift für Philosophie und Philosophische Kritik*, 100, 25–50. (English translation in P. Geach and M. Black (eds.), *Translations from the Philosophical Writings of Gottlob Frege*. Oxford: Blackwell, 1952.)

Gigerenzer, G. (2000). *Adaptive Thinking: Rationality in the Real World*. New York: Oxford University Press.

Goodall, J. van L. (1971). *In the Shadow of Man*. New York: Dell.

Groenendijk, J., Stokhof, M., and Veltman, F. (1996). Coreference and Modality. In S. Lappin (ed.), *The Handbook of Contemporary Semantic Theory*. Oxford: Blackwell.

Hauser, M. D. (2000). *Wild Minds: What Animals Really Think*. New York: Henry Holt.

Hauser, M. D., Chomsky, N., and Fitch, W. T. (2002). The faculty of language: What is it, who has it, and how did it evolve? *Science*, 298, 1569–79.

Heim, I. (1989). *The Semantics of Definite and Indefinite Noun Phrases in English*. New York: Garland.

Hubel, D. and Wiesel, T. (1968). Receptive fields and functional architecture of monkey striate cortex. *Journal of Physiology* (London), 195, 215–43.

Jackendoff, R. (1972). *Semantic Interpretation in Generative Grammar*. Cambridge, MA: MIT Press.

— (1976). Toward an explanatory semantic representation. *Linguistic Inquiry*, 7, 89–150.

— (1983). *Semantics and Cognition*. Cambridge, MA: MIT Press.

— (1987). *Consciousness and the Computational Mind*. Cambridge, MA: MIT Press.

— (1990). *Semantic Structures*. Cambridge, MA: MIT Press.

— (2002). *Foundations of Language*. Oxford: Oxford University Press.

— (forthcoming). *Language, Culture, Consciousness: Essays on Mental Structure*. Cambridge, MA: MIT Press.

Kahneman, D., Slovic, P., and Tversky, A. (eds.) (1982). *Judgment under Uncertainty: Heuristics and Biases*. Cambridge: Cambridge University Press.

Kamp, H. and Reyle, U. (1993). *From Discourse to Logic*. Dordrecht: Kluwer.

Katz, J. J. (1981). *Language and other Abstract Objects*. Totowa, NJ: Rowman & Littlefield.

Koch, C. (2004). *The Quest for Consciousness: A Neurobiological Approach*. Englewood, CO: Roberts and Company.

Koffka, K. (1935). *Principles of Gestalt Psychology*. New York: Harcourt, Brace & World.

Köhler, W. (1927). *The Mentality of Apes*. London: Routledge & Kegan Paul.

Kripke, S. (1972). Naming and Necessity. In D. Davidson and G. Harman (eds.), *Semantics for Natural Language*. Dordrecht: Reidel.

Lakoff, G. (1987). *Women, Fire, and Dangerous Things*. Chicago: University of Chicago Press.

Langacker, R. (1987). *Foundations of Cognitive Grammar*, vol. 1. Stanford, CA: Stanford University Press.

Lewis, D. (1972). General Semantics. In D. Davidson and G. Harman (eds.), *Semantics for Natural Language*. Dordrecht: Reidel.

Marr, D. (1982). *Vision*. San Francisco: Freeman.

Montague, R. (1973). The proper treatment of quantification in ordinary English. In J. Hintikka, J. Moravcsik, and P. Suppes (eds.), *Approaches to Natural Language*. Dordrecht: Reidel.

Pinker, S. and Jackendoff, R. (2005). The faculty of language: What's special about it? *Cognition*, 95, 201–36.

Stalnaker, R. (1984). *Inquiry*. Cambridge, MA: MIT Press.

Tarski, A. (1936/1983). The establishment of scientific semantics. In A. Tarski, *Logic, Semantics, Metamathematics* (J. H. Woodger, trans; 2nd edn., ed. J. Corcoran). Indianapolis: Hackett.

Tooby, J. and Cosmides, L. (1992). The psychological foundations of culture. In J. H. Barkow, Leda Cosmides, and John Tooby (eds.), *The Adapted Mind*. Oxford: Oxford University Press.

The Intentional Inexistence
of Language – But Not Cars

Georges Rey

In the short space here, I want to address an issue about the reality of language and the ordinary external world that Jackendoff raises in his chapter of the present volume (chapter 13, LOCATING MEANING IN THE MIND, WHERE IT BELONGS),[1] and that has been a persistent theme in his work for the last 20 years.

It would seem to be a commonplace that people, when they talk, produce tokens of such things as words, sentences, morphemes, phonemes, and phones – I'll call tokens of all such types, "standard linguistic entities" ("SLEs"). Part and parcel of this commonplace would be the presumption ("physical tokenism," hereafter abbreviated to "PT") that these entities can be identified with some sorts of *acoustic* phenomena, e.g., wave patterns in space and time. For instance, Devitt and Sterelny write:[2]

> [PT] Tokens are datable, placable parts of the physical world . . . Inscription types and sound types are identifiable by their overt physical characteristics and so we might call them "physical types." (Devitt and Sterelny, 1987, p. 59)

Over the years, however, this latter presumption has been repeatedly challenged by linguists, such as Saussure (1916/1966), Sapir (1933/1963), Chomsky and Halle (1968), Jackendoff (1983, 1987), and Chomsky (2000). In his textbook on phonetics, for example, John Laver writes:

> The stream of speech within a single utterance is a continuum. There are only a few points in this stream which constitute natural breaks, or which show an articulatory, auditorily or acoustically steady state being momentarily preserved, and which could therefore serve as the basis for analytical segmentation of the continuum into "real" phonetic units. . . . The view that such segmentation is mostly an imposed analysis, and not the outcome of discovering natural time-boundaries in the speech continuum, is a view that deserves the strongest insistence. (Laver, 1993, p. 101)

This view about language has sometimes led these linguists to deny the existence not only of SLEs, but, by a kind of parity of reasoning, many of the ordinary non-linguistic things we take ourselves to perceive and discuss. In a number of places, for example, Chomsky (2000, pp. 129ff., pp. 180ff.) has suggested that the ontology for semantics be modeled on that of phonology, and has even gone so far as to consider "naming as a kind of 'world-making,' in something like Nelson Goodman's sense" (2000, p. 181), expressing sympathy with various forms of seventeenth- and eighteenth-century idealism, according to which "The world as known is the world of ideas," which he (2000, p. 182) quotes approvingly from Yolton's (1994) account of that period.

The linguist who has most explicitly endorsed this sort of idealism is Ray Jackendoff. In Jackendoff (1983) he reasonably argues that "musical and linguistic structure must be thought of ultimately as products of the mind; they do not exist in the absence of human creators" (1983, pp. 27–8). But he then rapidly generalizes the view to a familiar form of idealism:

> We have conscious access only to the projected world – the world as unconsciously organized by the mind; and we can talk about things only insofar as they have achieved mental representation through these processes of organization. Hence *the information conveyed by language must be about the projected world.* (Jackendoff, 1983, p. 29)

The view persists in his contribution to the present volume, where he proposes "abandoning the unexamined notion of 'objects in the world,' and, for purposes of the theory of reference, pushing 'the world' into the mind of the language user too, right along with language." He does worry that his proposal

> smacks of a certain solipsism or even deconstructionism, as though language users get to make up the world any way they want, as though one is referring to one's mental representations rather than to the things represented.

But, he claims, "there seems little choice . . . On this picture our thoughts seem to be trapped in our own brains." Indeed "*the perceptual world is reality for us*" (emphasis his). But he thinks this is not so bad, since

> [W]e are ultimately concerned with *reality for us*, the world in which we lead our lives. Isn't that enough? (Or at least, isn't that enough for linguistic semantics?) If you want to go beyond that and demand a "more ultimate reality," independent of human cognition, well, you are welcome to, but that doesn't exactly render my enterprise pointless.

Now, I certainly don't think Jackendoff's enterprise of trying to characterize human conceptions of the world is pointless. I'm actually sympathetic to his trying to do this in a way that is independent of any presumption about whether those conceptions are correct. However, I don't see that that enterprise has to embrace the traditional idealist conclusions he draws. Leave aside the problems of explaining just what an "experiential world" might be (were dinosaurs composed of flesh and blood – *and* our ideas?), as well as the difficulty of reconciling such claims with natural science (*pace* paleontology, did their existence really depend upon our coming recently to think about them?); leave aside the well-known paradoxes raised by claiming that

Georges Rey

we have conscious access and can convey information "*only*" about them, not about the *real* one (Isn't Jackendoff purporting to tell us about *real* people? If not, why should we pay any attention to him?[3]). What I want to address here is whether any of his or other linguists' arguments actually drive us to such extravagant views. Along with Devitt and Sterelny (1987), I think they don't. However, unlike Devitt and Sterelny, I think the linguists are quite right to be skeptical about the existence of, specifically, SLEs. The project of this chapter is to try to sort these issues out.

In section 1 of what follows, I'll set out some distinctions that I hope will help clarify the discussion. Within the broadly intentionalist commitments of contemporary cognitive science (section 1.1), I want to call attention to "existential" versus "(purely) intentional" uses of our intentional vocabulary, particularly of the crucial terms "represent" and "representation" (section 1.2), as well to the related distinction between "internalist" and "externalist" theories of intentional content (section 1.3).

These distinctions will help sharpen the linguist's argument in section 2 for denying PT. Externalism in particular provides a useful condition for serious "existence," which I'll argue is not met by at least the representative SLEs I'll consider – sentences (section 2.1) and phones (section 2.3). Unlike, for example, the structural properties of cars (section 2.2), the structural properties of SLEs are not and need not be realized in space or time. At best, they are "psychologically real," but this kind of reality is no reality at all – at any rate, not the kind of serious "independent" reality that would be required for content externalism (section 2.4).

In section 3 I consider Jackendoff's idealist proposal, showing how it can't easily be restricted merely to SLEs, and that it leads to a general idealism that is problematic in familiar ways. These and other philosophical proposals are, to use a term Chomsky uses in this connection, "wheel-spinning," completely inessential to the theoretical tasks of linguistics. Unlike Chomsky, I just think this is true of *all* the proposals, including the idealist one he himself sometimes endorses. And this is because it seems to me that the sensible thing is not to try to find some peculiar ontological status for SLEs, but simply deny that they exist at all.

But how could anyone sensibly deny the existence of, e.g., utterances of words, sentences, poems, speeches, and the like? What do I think is going on when people talk? The hypothesis that I find implicit in at least much phonological research is what I will call the "*folie à deux*" view: the human ability to speak natural languages is based on the existence of a special faculty that includes a system for the intended production and recovery of SLEs. To a first approximation, instructions issue from speakers' phonological systems to produce certain SLEs, and these instructions cause various motions in their articulatory systems, which in turn produce various wave-forms in the air. These wave-forms turn out, however, not to reliably correspond to the SLEs specified in the instructions. All that seems to be true is that when they impinge on the auditory system of an appropriate hearer, this hearer's phonological system will be able to make an extremely good guess about *the intentional content* of the speaker's instructions, not about any actual SLEs, which, *ex hypothesi*, never actually got uttered. Indeed, this sort of guessing in general is so good, and the resulting perceptual illusion so vivid, that it goes largely unnoticed, and speakers and hearers alike take themselves to be producing and hearing the SLEs themselves. It is in this way that it's a kind of *folie à deux* (or *à n*, for the *n* speakers of a common language): the speaker has the illusion of producing an SLE that the hearer has the illusion of hearing, with however the happy result that the hearer is usually able to determine precisely what the speaker intended to utter. Indeed, were SLE tokens actually to exist, it would be something of an accident. Their existence is completely inessential to the success of normal communication and to the needs of linguistic theory.

But what of the way we and linguists all the time talk of SLEs? How are we to understand such claims as that, for example, a certain *sentence* is ambiguous, is pronounced differently by different people, that "*rhyme*" rhymes with "*slime*," or that *a pronoun* is co-indexed with a certain *NP*? I recognize the temptation to provide for them a kind of nonphysical "psychological reality," of the sort that Jackendoff proposes. However, I conclude in section 4, this temptation – and the problems and paradoxes it invites – can easily be resisted simply by not treating SLEs as having *any kind of being at all* – not in the actual world, nor any possible world, nor in any sort of "experiential," "phenomenal," or "perceptual" world either. To be sure, there are *stable intentional contents*, which facilitate the kind of *folies à n* that play important roles in our lives. But the apparent objects projected from these *folies* are best regarded as (in Franz Brentano's 1874/1973 phrase) "intentional inexistents": "things" that we *think about*, but that (we often know very well) don't actually exist, such as Santa Claus and Zeus. Just how systematically to understand talk about such "things" is a topic of some interest generally. Along lines that parallel some of Jackendoff's, I think such talk is useful – maybe indispensable – to a great deal of psychology, for example, in the case of "mental images," "mental models," even qualia and consciousness (see Rey, 1981; 1997, chapter 11; and forthcoming.).

Unlike Jackendoff, however, I don't think such talk needs to be invoked for *everything*. In particular, for all the importance of intentional inexistents in our lives, I also think we sometimes happily succeed in seeing and referring to real things: e.g., space, time, material objects, people, probably some abstractions, like numbers and sets – not to mention a case that I will take as representative, my automobile, a most reliable Honda Accord.

1 Intentionalism

1.1 Intentional content

I join Jackendoff in taking for granted the (surprisingly controversial) claim that people have minds, that some of their states are the subject matter of cognitive science, and that we may take cognitive scientists at their word when they propose to characterize those states in terms of *internal representations*, as they nearly ubiquitously do. Thus, linguists regularly discuss the character of the language faculty's representations of SLEs; vision theorists, the visual system's representations of, e.g., edges, surfaces, and shapes; and animal psychologists, birds' and bees' representations of, e.g., time, distance, and stars (see Gallistel, 1990). And, of course, anyone interested in the full mental life of human beings will be concerned with representations of anything they can perceive, think about, and discuss. Representation goes hand in hand with the phenomenon of *intentionality*, or the phenomenon by virtue of which a representation is *about* what it *represents*, be it times, places, objects, animals, directions, stars, numbers – and sometimes even non-existent things, such as ghosts, angels, or Sherlock Holmes (cases we'll discuss shortly).

Providing a theory of intentionality, and in particular a theory that explains how specific intentional states arise from physical processes, is one of the hardest problems in philosophy and cognitive science. Jackendoff rightly wonders what it is for someone to think, or "grasp," a content. But he wrongly supposes that this problem doesn't arise as much for (mentally) "grasping" concrete objects as for abstract ones. It is simply not true that

> We know in principle how the mind "grasps" concrete objects: it constructs cognitive structures in response to inputs from the senses. This is a physical process. (Chapter 13, p. 223)

Physical process it undoubtedly is, but it by no means follows that anyone knows how to explain it in physical terms; and this in part is due to the difficulty of specifying in such terms the *intentional content* of a cognitive or perceptual structure – i.e., a representation – or even deciding just what that content is – whether, for example, the content of a certain state of the visual system concerns edges, surfaces, objects, (Euclidean?) lines and distance, or merely mathematics.[4] But this lack of an account in either the abstract or concrete case is no cause for panic. It's just not true that

> without a careful exegesis of the term – which no one provides – we are ineluctably led toward a quasi-mystical interpretation of "grasping," a scientific dead end. (ibid.)

The history of science is replete with uses of terms at one time that had to await theoretical clarification much later. In any case, Jackendoff is certainly wrong to suggest that "no one provides" any efforts in this direction. Intentionality has received considerable philosophical attention in the last hundred years (see, e.g., the recent work discussed in section 1.2), and, although providing an adequate account of it has turned out to be surprisingly difficult, I see no reason to despair and regard the phenomenon as "quasi-mystical."

1.2 Existential versus purely intentional representation

Amazingly enough, one of the hotly contested issues is whether we can even correctly speak, as I casually did, of representations of non-existent things, such as ghosts, angels, and Sherlock Holmes. Some of the contest rests, however, on a vexing ambiguity in our use of "represent." For consider the multiple ways of understanding the phrase:

x represents nothing

This could mean that the (purported) representation, x, is *meaningless*, as in

"uhurhgr" represents nothing

or it could mean that x fails to represent *anything real*, as in

"Zeus" represents nothing

that is, there is no *real* thing that "Zeus" represents – there being no Zeus. Now obviously an expression like "Zeus," could represent something in the first usage – "Zeus" is not a *meaningless* expression – without representing anything in the second. For reasons that will emerge, I shall call the first usage the "(purely) intentional" use, the second the "existential."

However, on the assumption that "Zeus" is meaningful, a problem arises about just *what* in that case it *does* represent on the intentional usage. Notice that the two uses involve different direct objects. If a speaker is talking about things whose existence she expects she and her audience take for granted, she can say:

1 The word "Bush" represents Bush

where she is using the right-hand "Bush" as her way of talking about the very real man *George Bush*. But if she is talking about something whose existence she does not expect her or her audience to take for granted, then she will (ordinarily) still say, e.g.,

2 The word "Zeus" represents Zeus

but she will simply *not* take the right-hand "Zeus" to be a way of talking about any *real* god, Zeus.

So how are we to understand (2)? Well, some people (e.g., Millikan, 2000, pp. 175–6) might balk at it, but it seems to me perfectly OK; it's just that we have to be careful about what we say. One apparently very tempting thing to say is that, in (2), "Zeus is an idea in your head" (cf. Quine, 1953/1980). But, literally understood, this can't be true. Whatever else is in your head, there is no bearded god there; Zeus is certainly not supposed to be a mere idea, and, moreover, if he *were*, well, then, he'd exist after all, since (let us assume) surely the idea exists! The tempting thing to say is absurd.

But it is revealing. I submit that what happens without our ordinarily noticing is that, when we say things like (2), where we know we aren't referring to any actual thing, we resort to the intentional use of "represent," shifting our concern from any actual referent to the mere idea of it. That is, when we use "represent" purely intentionally all that seems to be involved in our use is something like the "sense" not the "reference" of the terms (although, *pace* Frege, we don't thereby *refer* to the sense, or an idea, since, again, someone thinking about Zeus is not thinking about a sense or an idea).

With these distinctions in hand, we can now (provisionally) define the (*intentional*) *content* of a representation in terms of the intentional use, roughly as follows:

An (intentional) content is *whatever we understand x to be when we use the idiom "represent(ation of) x" purely intentionally.*

i.e.:

An (intentional) content is *whatever we understand x to be when we use the idiom "represent(ation of) x" but there is no real x*

Georges Rey

I use the purposefully vague "what we understand x to be" in order to be as neutral as possible about any serious theory about what contents might be, i.e., about precisely *how* we are to understand purely intentional uses (see Rey, 1997, ch. 10, for a survey of recent proposals). Thus, an intentional content is however we are to understand "Zeus" in "That's a representation of Zeus, although there is no real Zeus." Where it is important to distinguish an intentional content from the actual object whose existence is being denied, I will place the words for that content in square brackets. Thus, *Zeus* is one thing, *the content,* [*Zeus*], quite another (for starters, the latter can exist when the former doesn't).

How does all this bear on our discussion of SLEs? Well, I'd like to be able at least to discuss the *possibility* of the unreality of SLEs without calling into question a representational theory of the mind of the sort that I (and Jackendoff) are presupposing. If the purely intentional is not distinguished from the existential use of "represent," this possibility is denied. Indeed, it is important to call attention to the fact that, insofar as theorists do use "represent" in the purely intentional way, they are committed at least to some or other account of intentional content as I've defined it.[5] Insofar as this usage is central to psychological explanation (as I join Jackendoff in taking it to be), the central coin of the realm is intentional content, *not* any actual phenomena in the real world that may be mentioned in that content. Thus, I believe the coin of the linguistic realm involves not SLEs themselves, but the intentional contents of SLEs – e.g., [noun], [NP], [trace], [sentence], not *nouns, NPs, traces, sentences,* themselves (considered as real phenomena in the external world) – even though it would be enormously cumbersome not to talk about those "things" in both ordinary and theoretical talk. The purely intentional use of "represent" has the odd property of directing our attention to "things" that we often know full well don't exist; i.e., "intentional inexistents" (to which I'll return in section 4).

1.3 Internalism versus strong and weak externalism

The foregoing, one would have hoped, "purely verbal" issue, is intimately connected to a more substantive one. For the last century or so, along lines that roughly parallel the distinction between existential and intentional usage, there have been two approaches to intentionality. "(Content) Internalism" is the view that the intentional content of an agent (animal, machine) depends only upon facts internal to the system, e.g., not to facts outside of the agent's brain. Although it was a popular view traditionally, it has come in for sustained criticism in the last 25 years, mostly due to some important families of counterexamples of Kripke (1972), Putnam (1975), and Burge (1979).[6] In its place, philosophers have proposed "Externalist" (sometimes called "direct reference") theories according to which contents (and/or their ascriptions) depend upon the external environment of the agent. This dependence, however, may be spelt out in any, or no, number of ways. What I will call "Weak Externalism" is merely the claim that *some* attitude contents depend in *some way or other* upon some external facts. I shall not be concerned here with this weak and (to my mind) perfectly plausible view. Rather, I shall be concerned here only with "Strong Externalism," or the view that the content of a (non-logical) representation is determined by the *real* phenomenon in the external world to which it bears some specific *causal* relation.

On some views, e.g., Devitt (1996), Millikan (2000), the causal relation is an *actual* historical, causal relation to a *real* phenomenon (the mental representation was actually caused by the phenomenon); on other views, e.g., Dretske (1988), Fodor (1990), it is merely counterfactually co-variant with it (the representation *would* co-vary with the phenomenon under certain counterfactual circumstances). In either case, there is a commitment to the actual or counterfactual reality of the phenomenon that provides the intentional content of the non-logical components of propositional attitudes. It is this commitment that I will argue is brought into question in the case of SLEs.

One might think that Strong Externalism is vulnerable to plenty of commonplace examples of contents that at least do not seem to involve any actual external phenomena: ghosts, spirits, gods, characters in dreams and fiction. But there are many moves externalists make to deal with such cases, the main strategy being to claim that purely intentional usage of "represent" involves only logically complex representations, not any atomic ones – indeed, for some, any apparently atomic cases (e.g., "angel") have *no* genuine content at all (see, e.g., Fodor, 1990, 1998; Millikan, 2000, pp. 175–6; 2004; and Taylor, 2003, pp. 207–12)! What interests me about the examples of SLEs is that these moves seem particularly implausible in their case, a case that may involve expressions that, as components of a dedicated language module, may well be conceptually or contentfully *atomic*, and one, moreover, in which the issues are motivated by serious theoretical considerations and not merely ordinary talk.

Indeed, a benefit of this debate between these different theories of content is that it provides a way to sharpen the discussion about the existence of SLEs. As Jackendoff (Chapter 13) and Chomsky (2000, pp. 177–8) rightly emphasize, ordinary talk of "existence" and "objects" is pretty wild, involving a kind of existential promiscuity: we refer to "things" like "rainbows," "the sky," "the wind," "a person's reputation," but would be hard put to specify just what these "things" might be. I am not, however, concerned here with ordinary talk. Rather, I want to press the purely theoretical issue about the existence of SLEs as serious *explanatory posits*: do such real entities play any essential explanatory role in any linguistic or psychological theory? In order to give a certain bite to the discussion, I will defend the denial of the existence of SLEs in the context of these Strong Externalist theories of mental content. I do this partly because of the widespread influence of such theories of content, which I think needs to be checked, but also in part because the claims such theories make provide a useful constraint on the ordinary promiscuity regarding existence. In particular, if the Strong Externalist theory is to provide an explanatorily adequate account of content, then the external phenomena to which it appeals had better be specifiable independently of the state whose content it purports to provide. This latter constraint is what I believe linguists have given us reason to think cannot be satisfied by SLEs, which is why it is plausible to suppose they don't exist.

2 SLEs versus Cars

2.1 Sentences

One of the linguist's arguments for the nonexistence of SLEs is in a way extremely short. Consider some ordinary English sentences that we orthographically represent as:

Georges Rey

(U1) John seems to Bill to want to help himself.

In standard generative grammars this sentence bears *at least* something like the accompanying analysis.

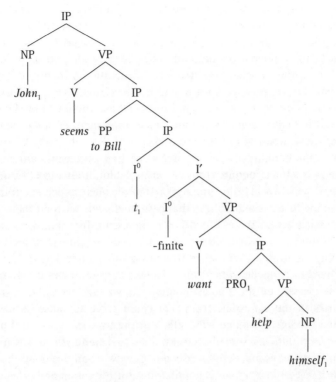

Thus, not only is there an elaborate tree structure in (U1), there are also "empty" categories: trace (t_1) and PRO that indicate a node in the tree that for one reason or another has no SLE attached to it, for example, because an SLE has been "moved" to a different node in some "transformation" of the sentence, and/or needs to be co-indexed with elements at other nodes: thus t_1 is co-indexed with *John*, PRO, and with *himself*, capturing the fact that the subject of *want* and *help* are both *John*, and not *Bill*.

Now *what actual thing in the world possesses this structure?* For example, does the utterance that is purportedly named by "(U1)" above possess this structure? Well, what is that (purported) utterance? A token of an English sentence. According to PT, this is something in space/time. But does anything I actually produced in *space and time* have the above structure? I think not.

2.2 Cars

A useful contrast here is my automobile, as I said, a most reliable Honda Accord. Cars, like (purported) linguistic entities, are artifacts, arguably tokens of types, produced by human beings with certain specific intentions. It seems to me very probably true that, had there been no people, there would have been no cars. But, of course, this doesn't for a moment imply that my Honda isn't real – e.g., that it doesn't exist in the garage when no one's looking or thinking about it (I expect that, hardy car that it is, it might well persist long after all of us are gone). Indeed, I submit it's absolutely crucial to the *explanation* of why my Honda *is* so reliable that it in fact has (or realizes) a certain causal structure: the pistons fit snugly into the cylinders, so that when the gas is ignited by the sparks from the plugs, they are pushed down with sufficient force to turn the crankshaft, which, through the transmission, turns the axles and the tires, which, in contact with the road, allow it to scoot from here to there.

Now, does anything in space/time have the structure ascribed to (U1) in the way that my car has the structure of my Honda? It would seem not. Whereas examining the spatiotemporal region of my car clearly reveals the existence of the intended structure, examining the spatiotemporal region of my utterance reveals nothing remotely like the linguistic structure that I presumably intended. And, if my *folie* view is correct, nothing in the explanation of the success of linguistic communication depends upon there being such a structure. One can *imagine* building a kind of Rube-Goldberg tree structure, replete with little ornamental morphemes suspended from each terminal node, and with wires and pulleys that permitted some movements or connections here and prevented others there. But it is an interesting fact that the noises we produce when we intend to utter sentences are nothing like this, and don't need to be. There is nothing we ordinarily produce that has a tree structure with items that have in fact been "moved" or even in fact "cross-indexed" from one node to another, leaving a nevertheless still existing node "empty." As we will see shortly, there are not even boundaries in the acoustic stream that could serve to causally distinguish the physical parts of *words*, let alone NPs, VPs and the like. In "uttering (U1)," I simply didn't succeed in producing something with an actual linguistic structure in the way that the technicians at Honda produced something with an automotive one.

Someone (e.g., Ned Block) might claim that the structure of an SLE is "more abstract," in the way that, for example, a computer can have an abstract computational structure not easily visible in the array of transistors and the pieces of metal and plastic of which it's made. However, there is an important difference between the two cases: in the case of the computer and for at least *some* of the algorithms it can be literally be said to be running (e.g., the operating system), *there are all sorts of causal claims and true dispositional counterfactuals about what would happen if you were to apply a certain current to certain points in the network, and it's these causal claims and counterfactuals that make it true, if it is true, that the computer is executing a certain algorithm.* Indeed, the steps in the algorithm can, if the computer is actually executing it, be clearly mapped in an explanatorily illuminating way to specific physical states of the machine. Nothing analogous seems to be true of an SLE – at least not independently of human perceivers (to whom we shall return shortly).

2.3 Phonetics versus acoustics

Still, someone might insist that, although the *structure* of SLEs might be regarded as something of an illusion, the *entities* upon which this structure is imposed are real enough, *à la* PT. However, phones, too, seem to be pretty much as illusory as sentence structures, along the lines of the quote from Laver (1993) with which we

Georges Rey

began. There is not space to explain here the variety of reasons for discrepancies between the linguistic and acoustic streams (see also Fodor et al., 1972, pp. 279–313; and Jackendoff, 1987, pp. 57ff.). Suffice it to note a particularly interesting phenomenon for my *folie* view: *cue displacement*. Consider:

(U2) Proust was a great writer of prose but a poor rider of horses.

A typical speaker of American English will issue a command to produce a /t/ in the course of trying to produce "writer" and a /d/ in the course of trying to produce "rider," however, the command will in both cases produce exactly the same acoustic wave front, or "formant," at the supposed point of the /t/ and the /d/. But this seems a little surprising, since most hearers of (U2) wouldn't notice the indistinguishability of the /t/ and /d/ here until their attention was explicitly drawn to it. How do they manage to keep things straight? What happens is that the effect of the command to produce a /t/ in the context of the other intended phones of /writer/ is to shorten the duration of sound associated with the immediately preceding vowel /i/. So the speaker did not in fact succeed in produce the /t/ that he commanded; nor did the hearer hear an actual /t/. But both speaker and hearer may have thought that a token of the word /writer/ was produced (a similar dislocation occurs in the case of "latter" and "ladder"; see Fodor et al., 1972, pp. 292–3 and Jackendoff, 1987, pp. 61–2).

In a useful analogy, Fodor et al. (1972) compare the formants to the clues left by a criminal: the hearer is in the position of a detective, inferring the identity of the criminal *from* the clues – but not by *identifying* the criminal *with the clues*:

> The acoustic representative of a phone turns out to be quite unlike a fingerprint. It is more like the array of disparate data from which Sherlock Holmes deduces the identity of the criminal. (Fodor et al., 1972, p. 301; see also Laver, 1993, p. 106)

Note that what "clues" and "signals" a speaker provides a hearer will vary according to the speaker's estimation of what the hearer in a particular context will need: articulating slowly and distinctly for children, foreigners, and noisy telephones; speeding up and employing copious contractions with familiar friends and colleagues; and proceeding to a breakneck pace in the highly stylized speech of an auctioneer. And, of course, clues and evidence would seem to be the order of the day when we consider the tactile "Tadoma" language developed for the deaf and blind (whereby SLEs are detected, to some 80 percent accuracy, by merely touching the face and neck of a speaker!). According to the *folie à deux* I am urging, we're all, as it were, acoustic Tadomists.

2.4 "Psychological reality"

As I said at the end of section 2.2, one might, of course, appeal to *perceivers* and claim that the boundaries and categories are "*psychologically* real." Certainly, standard linguistic data regarding which strings of phonemes are and which are not "acceptable," which things "co-refer" (as "John" and "himself" do in (U1)), present pretty impressive evidence for the reality of how the mind *represents* those strings.

But is something's being "psychological real" sufficient for its being real *tout court*? Consider an example very different in this regard from the examples of Hondas and computers: Kanizsa figures.

Human beings standardly seem to see the figure above as a triangle – so vividly in fact that novices often have to put their fingers over the apexes to see that it's an *illusion*. That is to say, despite the figures being "psychologically real," there is in fact no triangle there, nothing with the standard three-sided structures of these things. Indeed, Kanizsa figures are only particularly dramatic examples illustrating the point familiar since Plato, that, strictly speaking, no one has seen or could ever really *see* a genuine triangle, since all the proffered examples are manifestly defective (the sides aren't perfectly straight, much less one-dimensional). In any case, "psychologically real" needs to be understood along the lines of "suspected criminal." The burden is on those who would claim that something that is "psychologically real" is genuinely real – real *tout court*.

A number of people (e.g., Sue Carey, Zenon Pylyshyn) have replied to me at this point that there *is* a triangle even in this Kanizsa case, for isn't there a triangular *region of space* (defined perhaps in terms of distances between point locations) where the triangle appears to be? Well, no, strictly speaking there probably is not, since it is likely that our ordinary conceptions of geometrical phenomena are Euclidean, and real space is Riemannian. But, putting that difficulty aside, on such a view space would be chock full of *continuum many* squares, diamonds, triangles, etc., every-where one looks – it's just that one *perceives* (at best) very few, if any, of them. This seems to me a desperate and needlessly profligate move, and, in any case, would ill serve the purposes of the Strong Externalist, since it would only be *perceptible triangles* (if such exist) that would be the cause of certain representations, which would then seem to have their content restricted accordingly.

Moreover, it's important to bear in mind the threat of circularity here: if contents of representations are to be substantially identified with the causes of them, those causes had better be *identifiable independently* of that content, i.e., independently of what people *take to be* a triangle – or an SLE. But this is precisely what seems difficult in the case of Kanizsa figures: as figure (a) nicely illustrates, the types of figure that might be defined by the apexes depends entirely how it is oriented to the perceiver, who is caused to "take" it as a triangle.

Georges Rey

Orthographic SLEs are at least as badly off as Kanizsa figures, since there are entire Kanizsa "alphabets" consisting of them (see Ninio, 1998/2001, p. 90), and one can imagine a group of people recording information and communicating quite effectively by the use of them. But acoustic SLEs are even worse, for here one doesn't even have recourse to anything like the background geometry of space. The "heard boundaries" – not to mention the tree structure and empty nodes – of the sentences one takes oneself to utter and hear are even more obviously "imposed" by the perceiver. One would certainly be hard put to identify an SLE as a cause of an SLE representation independently of what a subject "took" something to be one.

"But," someone (e.g., Louise Antony) might remind us, "Isn't it crucial to Chomskyan theories that the sentences a child hears are in fact *structured* along the lines he suggests?" To be sure, a person's *understanding* of a language does involve, *inter alia*, being able automatically to *hear* an acoustic blast *as manifesting* an *intended structure*. However, manifestation of an intentional content is one thing; instantiation of it quite another. As many would-be novelists can attest, one can manifest an intention to produce something without actually ever producing it. Evidently language acquisition does depend upon there being some fairly systematic manifestation of linguistic structure, but this does not entail that the acoustic blast in fact possess or display that structure: it may be enough that it provides merely sufficient *clues* to it, enough bells and whistles to serve as *indicators* of the *intended structure*, along the lines of the *folie* view I am recommending.[7]

3 SLE Idealism

Many philosophers make a living providing ingenious analyses of problematic entities that render their existence unproblematic. Since Jackendoff does not defend any of them, I won't consider them here (but see Rey, forthcoming). I will simply comment on the idealist proposal that he does defend, viz., that SLEs – like all the things we can conceive – don't exist in the real world, but rather in a "phenomenal," "experiential" world that is somehow partly constituted by our thought.

The chief problem is, of course, to make sense of exactly what such "objects" are supposed to be, and how any of the things we believe to be true of SLEs could be true of them. For starters, it's hard to see how they could be *uttered* or be otherwise *produced* and then *heard* by an audience if they don't exist in real space/time. And if they exist only in a phenomenal space/time, is, e.g., the c-command structure causally efficacious in *it*? How does that work, in such a way that other, actual people are caused to hear it? Or are "other people" also only phenomenal, not actual? Do *they* only exist insofar as we conceptualize or experience them? And their bodies? ... It would appear that idealism about SLEs soon threatens to engulf the world, and we are left with the usual paradoxes that I mentioned in passing earlier: why we should take Jackendoff's account seriously, since, by its own lights, none of it is about the actual world.

Note that Jackendoff offends here not only against these sorts of standard philosophical reflections, but also against the reflections of an ordinary "us" for whom he claims to speak: it is simply not the case that "*the perceptual world is reality for us*" (emphasis his), or that "[W]e are ultimately concerned with *reality for us*, the world in which we lead our lives." Speaking at least for myself (but surely many others), it is precisely when I concern myself with "ultimately" what's real that I abstract from the odd *errors* of my perceptual and cognitive system and acknowledge that there *really are* no Kanisza figures (indeed, no genuine Euclidean figures at all) – nor any SLEs. It's only when I don't care how things *ultimately* are – which, to be fair to Jackendoff, is a very good deal of the time – that I acquiesce in ordinary talk and "refer" to things that I fully believe don't exist.

In any case, if one looks at the theoretical work SLEs are supposed to perform in a theory, their actual existence is entirely *needless* and extraneous to linguistic theory. For recall how linguistics discusses SLEs. Outside of explicitly acoustic phonetics, linguists almost never discuss acoustic phenomena. Rather, they discuss how SLEs enter into complex sequences: phones into phonemes, phonemes into morphemes, morphemes into words and syllables, words into phrases and sentences, and sentences into discourse. There are abundant theories and disputes about the specific structures, rules, principles, and parameters for these structures, which provide the substance of linguistics about which I wish to remain as neutral as possible. The only issue that concerns me is what the structures and/or sequences are structures and sequences *of*, if, at the basic level of them, phones can't be identified with particular acoustic phenomena. The structures would seem to be enormous and intricate buildings resting on – nothing. Or, if there turned out to be something, this would be entirely accidental. As Chomsky (2000, p. 129) says of various proposals to identify SLEs with acoustic phenomena, they are all needless "wheel-spinning."[8]

A proposal that I've found many people inclined to make at this point is to claim that SLEs should be regarded as merely "abstract" objects like numbers. Without entering into in-house controversies in this regard that I said I would avoid (n. 2), let me just note the following crucial difference between the two cases: our best theories of the nonpsychological world seem to be committed to numbers, e.g. as the magnitudes of various parameters like mass or energy, quite independently of whether anyone has represented them: the magnitude of the mass of the moon causes a certain magnitude of tides whether anyone ever thinks about it. But in "psychological" domains such as linguistics, I submit that the entities *have no role to play independently of our representations of them*. As Cartwright nicely put it with reference to purely "fictional objects":

> Must not dragons have some *mode of being*, exist in *some universe of discourse*? To [such] rhetorical questions, it is sufficient to reply with another: What, *beyond the fact that it can be referred to*, is said of something when it is said to have some mode of being or to exist in a universe of discourse? The alleged universes are so admirably suited to perform their function that they are not above suspicion of having been invented for the purpose. (Cartwright, 1960/1987, p. 30)

This seems to me precisely the suspicion I think one ought to have about SLEs and many other what might be called "representation-dependent" entities: there's no reason to believe in them over and above the reasons one has for believing that there are simply representations with the corresponding content.

250 **Georges Rey**

4 Conclusion

In sum, what I take to be the linguistic argument for the nonexistence of SLEs consists of noting that nothing in the external world has the properties that linguistic theory plausibly identifies as the properties of SLEs. Those properties are specified by the language faculty, not as a result of any causal interaction with those properties in the world, but as a result of categories the faculty itself provides and, so to say, "imposes" upon the physical input. As philosophers and psychologists at least since Kant have been reminding us, our understanding of the world is as much a product of our minds as of any input from it. Moreover, in *some* cases, for example, SLEs and (Kanizsa) triangles, there turns out on examination to be nothing corresponding to the mind's categories: nothing in the external world has the properties that these categories require.

However – and this is the first point at which I depart from Jackendoff's generalization of the Kantian point – in other cases, notably my car, things do manage to have the required properties. And at least one distinctive reason to believe this is that the properties of cars play crucial causal-explanatory roles in an account of how things work in the world, in a way that the properties of SLEs do not. The *folie à n* that might work for SLEs pretty clearly won't work for cars.

What leads Jackendoff to think otherwise is, I suspect, his rightly noting that the same mechanisms of mind, whereby concepts are imposed upon input, are likely at work in *all* our categorizations of the world. But he wrongly concludes from this that *the world itself* depends upon our categorization. One can see the temptation to such a view in the case of SLEs, and I'll return to that temptation in a moment. But there's no reason to yield to this temptation when our efforts at categorization turn out to *succeed*. From the fact that our *concepts* might be constituted in part by material provided by our minds, it doesn't follow that *the things themselves* picked out by those concepts are constituted in part by that structure. Surely it's *possible* that what our minds impose corresponds to what's actually there, as, I've argued, it does in the case of cars. But cars are constituted of metal and plastic, not ideas. Moreover, if cars do exist, then we're entitled to switch from the purely intentional to the existential use of "represent" and say that our representations relate us not to mere to ideas of cars, but to the cars themselves.[9]

However, the second point at which I depart from Jackendoff and Chomsky is in seriously thinking of the "experiential world" or "world of ideas" as a *world* even in the case of nonexistent things like SLEs. There's of course *something* right about the thought: especially in such cases as SLEs and Kanizsa figures, the illusions are so wonderfully stable, not only across time, but across people, that it's easy to proceed "as if" the things existed, and even "discuss" them socially: most people would surely spontaneously agree (as they might put it) "*those* Kanizsa figures reproduced above are astonishingly vivid, *their* surfaces seeming more luminous than *their* surrounds." But the thought of a separate world is over-thought if it invites claims about a rival world in addition to (and even superceding) the actual one. A better thought is that it's like being in a play, and knowing we are, but being unable to completely disengage ourselves from it: we keep "referring to Polonius," with smashing social success, even though we know that "he" is a fiction. If you'll pardon my French, my *folie à n* is a kind of *façon de parler*, or, more accurately, a *façon de penser*, since it's surprisingly difficult even to *think* such stable contents without engaging in this odd sort of "projection" of the nonexistent things to which they seem to refer.

It's here that I think Brentano's talk of "intentional inexistents" may be of help. When there is a *sufficiently stable* system of representations with a content [x], it is useful – almost ineluctable – to talk about *x*'s, even when (we know) there are none, and this stability licenses talking of them as "intentional inexistents." Thus, Hamlet, Polonius, Zeus, and the other gods, as well as Kanizsa triangles and SLEs, all would qualify – but not, as Cartwright (1960/1987) notes, carnivorous cows, since (so far) there's no such stable system with [carnivorous cow] as its content. This sort of talk seems harmless enough, a piece of the "existential promiscuity" noted earlier; who would be so philosophically puritanical to object, if it can be paraphrased away in terms of stable representations with certain content?

The only error would be to suppose that we have to accord such things some kind of genuine *being*, distinct from actual existence, one that, moreover, threatens to usurp our references to actual existent things in ways that Jackendoff and Chomsky suggest. Indeed, I'll end here as Cartwright did: "unreality is just that: it is not another reality" (Cartwright, 1960/1987, p. 30).

Acknowledgments

I am indebted to Ray Jackendoff, who graciously made available to me the manuscript of his chapter in the present volume. I am also indebted to discussions with too many people to mention here; I will just express particular gratitude to Paul Pietroski and Dan Blair for discussions of the linguistic material.

Notes

1   This chapter is a portion of a much longer work-in-progress, Rey (forthcoming), on the role of intentional inexistence in cognitive science generally. At the request of the editor of the present volume, I have focused on those issues that overlap Jackendoff's chapter in this volume. Hereafter, unless otherwise stated, all quotations are from Jackendoff's chapter in the present volume.

2   The label "PT" (for "physical tokenism") is mine. Note that, aside from a brief remark in section 3, I will not be concerned here with issues surrounding the existence of the *types* themselves, as abstractions, since this raises special issues in metaphysics, epistemology, and about the understanding of linguistics that there's neither need nor space to discuss adequately here. See section 3.4 for some brief remarks, and, e.g., Katz, 1981; Bromberger and Halle, 2000, and Rey (forthcoming) for fuller discussion. For simplicity, I shall also be concerned only with oral, not Sign or written language, although most of what I shall say would apply to them.

3   Jackendoff (1983) worries in passing about this difficulty, but thinks he can evade it by claiming he is "assuming tacitly that we, as hypothetically omniscient observers, are not so limited [to speaking only of the projected world]" (pp. 31–2). However, Jackendoff is

presumably consciously thinking the things he writes, and those things appear to be expressed in *English* and so will surely be subject to the constraints of English. If he thinks English can't express x, then he'd better not try to express x in English! In any case, I would have thought that one of the constraints on any language is at least a disquotational principle, that, e.g., "tables" is about tables. Whatever one might think about the ontological status of *tables*, it can't even be *tempting* to think in one's use of "table" "one is referring to one's mental representations [of tables] *rather than* to the things [the *tables*] represented."

4 Jackendoff seems more certain than I think he is entitled to be about our understanding of early vision and its contents: see Burge, 1986; Segal, 1991; Davies, 1991; and Egan, 1992 for interesting controversy. It is for resolving these sorts of controversies that a theory of the "mysterious mind-world relation of intentionality" is required.

5 A case in point is Chomsky (2000), who claims that, as he understands them, "[internal] representations are postulated entities, to be understood in the manner of the mental image of a rotating cube, whether it be the result of . . . a real rotating cube . . . or imagined" (2000, pp. 159–60), but then proceeds to deny that his own use of representations commits him to any intentionality (2000, pp. 22–3, 105; 2003, p. 279). I suspect a similar denial in Jackendoff when he writes, "language has . . . made contact with the outside world – but through the complex mediation of the visual system rather than through some mysterious mind-world relation of intentionality." As I argue in Rey, 2003, these denials are incompatible both with the claims of practicing linguists (including Chomsky and Jackendoff themselves!), and with making sense of their explanatory project.

6 These are the examples of beings that are physical duplicates, but whose thought contents seem to depend upon which environment they inhabit. For example, two internally identical people might be referring to different individuals in their use of a proper name, in part because they are living in different worlds. Note that all that such examples themselves support is *Weak*, not *Strong* Externalism.

7 Note that, apart from occasional deliberate (and untypical) standardizations, written language presents many of the same problems. Note also that mechanical speech recognizers do not function by responding to well-defined SLEs in the input, but by elaborate statistical inferences, exploiting "Hidden Markov Models" ("HMMs") by means of which unobserved sequences of probabilistically related states are "inferred" as the statistically "best explanation" of observed acoustic events (see Rabiner, 1989). Leaving aside the degree to which the success of these machines depends upon humans setting many of their parameters, such "prototypical" SLEs have no more reality than "the average face" – which nevertheless may provide a perfectly good way of identifying faces.

8 Chomsky (2000, 2003), himself, seems to identify at least some SLEs with items "in the head," whose nature he expects to be spelled out by some future biology. I consider and reject this option in Rey (2003, sections 5–6). To make that long story short: the explanatory force of at least the kind of computational/representational theory of thought that seems everywhere presupposed in cognitive science derives from Turing's brilliant strategy for reducing all computation to operations defined in terms of *local physical properties*. SLEs are manifestly not such properties. Therefore a computational theory of language processing will need to proceed *via* computations on representations of SLEs. See Rey (1997, section 3.4) for general discussion.

9 Note that Jackendoff sometimes recognizes this point, surprisingly agreeing with his "skeptic" that "we don't perceive percepts in our heads, we perceive objects out in the world," indeed, that "the perceptual world isn't totally out of synch with the 'real world'." One aim of the present chapter is to provide Jackendoff a way of avoiding this embarrassed use of quotation marks around "real world" – and the inconsistency (noted in n. 3) between these claims and the idealism he otherwise espouses.

The Intentional Inexistence of Language | 253

References and further reading

Brentano, F. (1874/1973). *Psychology from an Empirical Standpoint* (A. Rancurello, D. Terrell, and L. McAlister, trans.). London: Routledge & Kegan Paul.

Bromberger, S. and Halle, M. (2000). The ontology of phonology (revised). In N. Burton-Roberts, P. Carr, and G. Docherty (eds.), *Phonological Knowledge: Conceptual and Empirical Approaches.* Oxford: Oxford University Press.

Burge, T. (1979). Individualism and the mental. *Midwest Studies in Philosophy*, 4, 73–121.

— (1986). Individualism and psychology. *Philosophical Review*, 95/1, 3–46.

Cartwright, R. (1960/1987). Negative existentials. In R. Cartwright, *Philosophical Essays*, Cambridge, MA: MIT Press.

Chomsky, N. (2000). *New Horizons in the Study of Language.* Cambridge: Cambridge University Press.

— (2003). Reply [to Rey]. In L. Antony and N. Hornstein (eds.), *Chomksy and His Critics.* Oxford: Blackwell.

Chomsky, N. and Halle, M. (1968). *The Sound Pattern of English.* New York: Harper & Row.

Davies, M. (1991). Individualism and perceptual content. *Mind*, 100/4, 461–84.

Devitt, M. (1996). *Coming to Our Senses: A Naturalistic Program for Semantic Localism.* Cambridge: Cambridge University Press.

Devitt, M. and Sterelny, K. (1987). *Language and Reality: An Introduction to the Philosophy of Language*, Cambridge: MIT Press.

Dretske, F. (1988). *Explaining Behavior: Reasons in a World of Causes.* Cambridge, MA: MIT Press.

Egan, F. (1992). Individualism, computation and perceptual content. *Mind*, 101, 445–59.

Evans, G. (1982). *Varieties of Reference*, ed. J. McDowell. Oxford: Oxford University Press.

Fodor, J. (1990). *A Theory of Content and Other Essays.* Cambridge, MA: MIT Press.

— (1998). *Concepts: Where Cognitive Science Went Wrong.* Cambridge: MIT Press.

Fodor, J., Bever, T., and Garrett, M. (1972). *The Psychology of Language.* New York: McGraw Hill.

Frege, G. (1892/1980). On sense and reference. In P. Geach and M. Black (eds.), *Translations from the Philosophical Writings of Gottlob Frege.* Oxford: Blackwell.

Gallistel, C. (1990). *The Organization of Learning*, Cambridge, MA: MIT Press.

Hardcastle, W. and Laver, J. (1993). *The Handbook of Phonetic Sciences.* Oxford: Blackwell.

Heim, H. (1982). The semantics of definite and indefinite noun phrases. PhD dissertation, University of Massachusetts, Amherst.

Jackendoff, R. (1983). *Semantics and Cognition.* Cambridge, MA: MIT Press.

— (1987). *Consciousness and the Computational Mind.* Cambridge, MA: MIT Press.

Katz, J. (1981). *Language and Other Abstract Objects.* Totowa, NJ: Rowman & Littlefield.

Kripke, S. (1972). Naming and necessity. In D. Davidson and G. Harman, *Semantics of Natural Language.* Dordrecht: Reidel.

Laver, J. (1993). *Principles of Phonetics.* Cambridge: Cambridge University Press.

Millikan, R. (2000). *On Clear and Confused Ideas.* Cambridge: Cambridge University Press.

— (2004). Existence proof for a viable externalism. In R. Schantz (ed.), *The Externalist Challenge: New Studies on Cognition and Intentionality*, New York: de Gruyter.

Ninio, J. (1998/2001). *The Science of Illusions* (F. Philip, trans.). Ithaca, NY: Cornell University Press.

Putnam, H. (1975). The meaning of "meaning." In H. Putnam, *Philosophical Papers*, vol. 2. Cambridge: Cambridge University Press.

Quine, W. (1953/1980). On what there is. In *From a Logical Point of View and Other Essays* (2nd edn., revised). Cambridge, MA: Harvard University Press.

Rabiner, L. (1989). A tutorial on hidden Markov models. *Proceedings of the IEEE*, 77, 257–86.

Rey, G. (1981). What are mental images? In N. Block (ed.), *Readings in the Philosophy of Psychology*, vol. 2. Cambridge, MA: Harvard University Press.

— (1997). *Contemporary Philosophy of Mind: A Contentiously Classical Approach*. Oxford: Blackwell.

— (2003). Intentionality and a Chomskyan linguistics. In A. Barber (ed.), *Epistemology of Linguistics*, Oxford: Oxford University Press.

— (2004). Millikan's (un?)compromised externalism. In R. Schantz (ed.), *The Externalist Challenge: New Studies on Cognition and Intentionality*. New York: de Gruyter.

— (forthcoming). *Representing Nothing: Phones, Feels and Other Intentional Inexistents*. Oxford: Oxford University Press.

Sapir, E. (1933/1963). The psychological reality of the phoneme. In D. Mandelbaum (ed.), *The Selected Writings of Edward Sapir*. Berkeley: University of California Press.

Saussure, F. (1916/1966). *Course in General Linguistics*. New York: McGraw Hill.

Segal, G. (1991). Defense of a Reasonable Individualism. *Mind*, 100/4, 485–93.

— (2000). *A Slim Book About Narrow Content*. Cambridge: MIT Press.

Taylor, K. (2003). *Reference and the Rational Mind*, Stanford: CSLI Publications.

Yolton, J. (1994). *Perceptual Acquaintance*, Minneapolis: University of Minnesota Press.

IS THE AIM OF PERCEPTION TO PROVIDE ACCURATE REPRESENTATIONS?

CHAPTER FIFTEEN

Is the Aim of Perception to Provide Accurate Representations?

Kirk Ludwig

> Ears in the turrets hear
> Hands grumble on the door
> Eyes in the gables see
> The fingers at the locks.
> (Dylan Thomas)

I take the title question to be the question whether the instrumental or biological function of perceptual systems is to provide us with perceptual experiences that are by and large accurate representations of our environments. I will argue that the answer to this question is "yes."

The assumption that perception yields experiences that represent the world around us by and large accurately is deeply embedded in the tradition in the philosophy and psychology of perception. This is the representational theory of perception. On this view, when we perceive objects, we have perceptual experiences, which represent our environments, differently in different modes, but typically through a field medium, as in the paradigmatic case of visual experience, which represents a spatial field filled in in various ways. We form perceptual beliefs on this basis, and our beliefs are accurate, since they in effect abstract from the richer representational medium of experience, just insofar as our experiences are accurate.

This traditional view has been challenged on the basis of recent experimental work in psychology on "change blindness"[1] and "inattentional blindness"[2] among other phenomena, and the accumulating body of knowledge about neurophysiology of vision, which is taken to suggest at the least that our ordinary views about the degree of accuracy and completeness of our visual representations of the world before our eyes are vastly exaggerated, and, perhaps, indeed, that some even more radical overhaul of our traditional picture of perception is required. It has been suggested, in particular, that

Research in this area calls into question whether we really enjoy perceptual experiences which represent the environment in rich detail. If we do not enjoy experiences of this sort, then we need to rethink the idea that perception is a process aiming at the production of such experiences. (Noë, 2002b, preface)

In recent discussions this has come to be called "the grand illusion," though it is not clear that all participants in the debate express the same view with this phrase.[3]

There are, in this challenge to the traditional view, two different strains to be distinguished. The first and more radical, hinted at in the above passage, raises the question whether perception involves representations at all. If it does not, then the question of their accuracy, and whether they aim at accuracy, does not even come up. The second admits that perception involves representations, but argues that they are largely non-veridical or largely inaccurate. We will take up both sorts of objection in the following.

I will begin by sketching the view that is taken to be under attack, and then sketch some of the evidence that has been advanced against it. Then I take up the radical view, motivated in part by these empirical findings, that denies that perception involves representations at all. I will then return to the question of whether the traditional view and the view under attack are the same, whether we have been in any interesting sense subject to a grand illusion, and whether the empirical findings undermine the view that perceptual experiences are by and large accurate representations of our environment. Finally, I will address in the light of the discussion whether perception aims at accurate representation.

According to many psychologists and philosophers of perception, and even ordinary people – it is said – visual perceptual experience in particular represents the visual scene in uniform, rich detail. This conception of visual experience has been called "the snapshot conception of experience," according to which "you open your eyes and – presto – you enjoy a richly detailed picture-like experience of the world, one that represents the world in sharp focus, uniform detail, and high resolution from the center out to the periphery" (Noë, 2002a, p. 2). Attention ranges over this present rich detail, which is stored in some sense as an internal representation of the environment. It is because of this richly detailed internal representation of the visual scene that we have the impression of a complete and detailed field of vision and a richly detailed world.

On closer examination, however, the snapshot conception of experience begins to look more like a myth. Phenomenologically, it is clear that the visual field (how things are subjectively presented to us in visual experience) is not uniformly detailed and in sharp focus from the center right out to the periphery. Our representation of the scene before us fades as it were toward the edges of the visual field, with far less detail being represented at the periphery than at the center. This is what we should expect given that the sensory receptors on the retina are sparser toward the edge than in the foveal region. We get much less information[4] about what goes on in the regions around us by way of signals generated by light falling on the portions of the retina which are at the periphery. This is strikingly illustrated in a famous experiment, in which subjects were seated before a computer screen and asked to read a page of text while their eye movements were tracked. They had the impression of a

Kirk Ludwig

stable page of intelligible text. But outside the area their eyes were focused on, about 18 characters in width, only junk characters were displayed. That is, the intelligible text was shifted with their eye movements, and everywhere else junk characters were displayed.[5] In addition, it is well known that the eye saccades three to four times a second, and during movement there is no information transmitted to the brain. Yet this seems not to be represented in visual experience. We likewise fail to notice the blind spot in the visual field corresponding to the location of the optic nerve on the retina where there are no rods or cones. The information the brain gets, therefore, is sparse over much of the scene before us, intermittent, and gappy. How could experience be any better? And surely the fact that these things do not come to our attention without investigation shows that we had thought experience provided a richer and more accurate representation of our surroundings that in fact it does.

In addition, the recently investigated phenomena of change blindness[6] and inattentional blindness,[7] among others, has been cited as showing that we are radically mistaken about our experience representing everything that goes on in our field of vision. In experiments on change blindness, many subjects fail to notice quite significant changes in the visual scene they are looking at (for example, in the color of flowers and cars or the structure of a house or position of a rail in the background) if the changes are made during eye saccades or during the simultaneous display of visual distractions.[8] More specifically, many subjects fail to report noticing any changes when asked. Subjects thus appear to be blind to changes that occur during such events. Inattentional blindness is a related phenomenon. Subjects fail to notice what seem to be quite significant features of the visual scene if their attention is directed elsewhere. In one study subjects were asked to concentrate on a cross in the middle of a screen presented briefly, then masked, and presented again. They were asked to estimate which arm of the cross was longer. On the third or fourth trial they were presented with a new stimulus, a colored square or moving bar. When the stimulus was presented close to the fixation point, 75 percent of the subjects failed to report it when asked if they noticed anything different. In another widely discussed experiment, subjects were shown a video of two basketball teams, one in black and one in white, each passing basketballs.[9] They were to count the number of passes for one team. They were asked afterwards if they noticed anything unusual. Forty-five seconds into the video an intruder walks through the players, a woman holding an umbrella or a man in a gorilla suit. In some trials the intruder was semi-transparent, and in some fully opaque. Seventy-three percent of the subjects reported nothing unusual in the semi-transparent trials, and 23 percent in the fully opaque trials. The conclusion we are invited to draw is that subjects may fail to see or perhaps visually represent what they don't pay attention to.

I will return to what these phenomena show about the traditional view and their relevance to our question in a moment. I first consider a radical alternative to the traditional view motivated by them, the sensorimotor view of perception advocated by Noë and O'Regan (Noë and O'Regan, 2001). Officially, this view holds that perception does not involve representations at all, and seeks to exhibit it as a matter of a pattern of engagement with the environment. We will be concerned with how tenable it is, and whether it really represents as radical an alternative as is suggested.

The sensorimotor theory holds that "Visual experience [for example] . . . does not consist in the occurrence of 'qualia' or such like. Rather it is a kind of give-and-take between you and the environment" (Noë and O'Regan, 2001, p. 80). "[P]erceivers have sensations in a particular sense modality, when they *exercise their mastery of the sensorimotor laws* that govern the relation between possible actions and the resulting changes in incoming information in that sense modality" (p. 82). It is "in this sense to be 'attuned' to the ways in which one's movements will affect the character of input" (p. 84). It is a "form of practical knowledge" (p. 84). According to the sensorimotor view of perception, then, visual experience is not to be understood in terms of representational states at all, but rather in terms of patterns of behavior and their connection with sensory influx embodied in "the whole neurally enlivened body" (p. 85). This point of view is expressed clearly in the following passage:

> both the representationalist and sensationalist [about visual experience], make a . . . fundamental error. Each relies on a conception of visual experience according to which experiences are internal items of which we become conscious when we undergo them . . . momentarily occurring, internal states of consciousness. . . . As against this conception, I have proposed that perceptual experiences are not internal, momentarily occurring states of this sort. I advocate that we think of experience rather as a form of active engagement with the environment. Perceptual experience is a form of integration with the environment as governed by patterns of sensorimotor contingency. (Noë, 2002c, p. 74)

Sometimes the thesis is put as if it were actual behavior that was crucial – "it is a give and take between you and the environment" ((Noë and O'Regan, 2001, p. 80); "experience is not something that happens in us but something that we do" (p. 99); "sensation occurs when a person *exercises* mastery of those sensorimotor contingencies" (p. 99; emphasis added). I will call this the activity theory. Sometimes the view is put in a way that suggests it is not actual activity that is required, but a disposition of a certain sort. I will call this the dispositional theory. Saying that visual experience is a form of practical knowledge suggests the dispositional, rather than the activity view. And at one point exercising one's mastery of sensorimotor contingencies is characterized as consisting itself in "our practical understanding that if we *were* to move our eyes or bodies" (p. 84) there would be appropriate resulting changes of such things as "the influx from monochromatically tuned rod photoreceptors taking over as compared to influx from the three different cone types present in central vision" (p. 83). Thus, in visual experience, there is a characteristic change in neural influx when we step toward an object and away from it, when we turn our heads to the right or left, or when we close our eyes, or blink. On this view, the sum of all these sensorimotor contingencies and our attunement to them associated with a particular sensation, e.g., of red or yellow, *is* the visual experience or sensation of red or yellow.

The activity interpretation is untenable, as Noë and O'Regan recognize. One may perceive a surface as red so briefly that one has no time to move. Actually engaging in activity cannot be a requirement on perception. Moreover, it seems clearly to be a category mistake to talk of perceptual experience, when we have in mind

Kirk Ludwig

something like my visual or auditory experience at a given moment in time, as "something that is performed – enacted – by a living animal engaged in a pattern of exploration of its world" (Noë, 2001, p. 53), or "a form of active engagement with the environment" or "integration with the environment as governed by patterns of sensorimotor contingency" (Noë and O'Regan, 2001, p. 74).[10] A perceptual experience, in the target sense, is a state, not an event. Perceptual experiences change, of course, but these are changes in states. We might as well speak of being red as something that is performed by an object in its response to the various conditions of changing light that affect what it reflects.

The dispositional interpretation appears to be the one intended by Noë and O'Regan, even though their rhetoric often suggests the activity view. However, the retreat from the activity to the dispositional theory robs us of a reason to deny that perceptual experience involves representational states, and so leaves us without a radical alternative to the traditional view. For the dispositional view takes perceiving to be a matter of being in certain states, albeit dispositional states. We can call these experiences if we like, and provide standards of correctness. If one's practical knowledge of sensorimotor contingencies, summed up in one's expectations, is appropriate for one's environment, then the experience is veridical, and otherwise not. Standards of accuracy could be defined similarly.

Apart from not being an alternative to the view that perception involves representations, the dispositional theory has a number of flaws. A disposition has one or more manifestation properties and corresponding manifestation conditions. The manifestation property is exhibited in the appropriate manifestation condition. Salt is water-soluble. The manifestation condition is being put in water. The manifestation property is dissolving. Is having a perceptual experience being in a dispositional state? This is not tenable for a number of reasons. First, it leaves out the phenomenal character of perceptual experiences, which is an occurrent, rather than dispositional feature of us – a manifest property rather than a dispositional one. Second, it is not clear that this view can accommodate hallucinations which we know to be hallucinations. When we have a hallucination which we know to be one, we do not expect any of the usual changes to sensory input given the various possible movements we can make. We may, indeed, have no expectations, implicit or explicit, about what changes in sensory input will occur given various possible movements. Yet, on the sensorimotor view, the consequence would be that we did not have any experience at all. For having the experience is having the practical knowledge of what changes would occur if we were to move in such and such a way. And in this case, we have no such practical knowledge. Third, if we characterize the relevant dispositions in terms of detailed facts about actual human and animal perceptual systems, then it is doubtful that they could be conceptually necessary for perceptual experience. There is no apparent conceptual barrier to creatures constructed quite differently from us having perceptual experiences like ours (Clark, 2002, p. 193ff.). It looks as if the practical knowledge concerned, to meet this challenge, would have to abstract altogether from physical realization. The relevant dispositions would have to be dispositions involving expectations about changing sensory input characterized in terms of its content. But this presupposes an independent characterization of the content of the experiences. Finally, it is not clear that perceptual experience requires even such dispositions. Consider Galen Strawson's thought experiment involving the weather watchers (Strawson, 1994, ch. 9). The weather watchers are sessile beings. They are unable to move, but we are invited to conceive of them as having perceptual experiences, visual experiences in particular. They watch the passing show, the clouds moving across the sky, the rain, the wind across the grass, the fall of leaves and snow, and so on. The weather watchers are prima facie possible. If the thought experiment is coherent, then it deals a fatal blow to the view that dispositions of the sort that Noë and O'Regan have in mind are necessary for perceptual experience.[11]

I turn to the various considerations which prompted this radical alternative to the traditional view to ask whether they give us any reason to think that though perceptual experiences are representations, they are so misleading or inaccurate that we must call into question whether they could be treated as having the aim of providing us with accurate representations of our environments.

The question whether perceptual experience involves in some way a grand illusion has received starkly different answers in the literature. One author writes, "If [consciousness] seems to be a continuous stream of rich and detailed experiences, happening one after the other to a conscious person, this is the illusion" (Blackmore, 2002, p. 17). The title of another article is "Our perception of the world has to be an illusion" (Ballard, 2002). Another writes: "Is visual consciousness a Grand Illusion? In one sense, the answer must be 'Of course'" (Durgin, 2002, p. 88). But others write just as confidently, "The simplest and most straightforward answer to this question taken literally is no, since, after all, we do see" (Mack, 2002, p. 103). Or, again, "I conclude that once we take care to formulate accurately what we believe, on a first-person basis, about the richness of our ordinary visual experience, efforts to expose this as erroneous on a grand scale collapse" (Siewert, 2002, p. 140). And another calls the affirmative answer to the question "The Grand Grand Illusion Illusion," and concludes that "while [change blindness] and [inattentional blindness] raise a number of interesting empirical questions, the view that they show up a widespread grand illusion concerning perception is itself something of a grand illusion" (Cohen, 2002, p. 141).

There are two different interpretations of the grand illusion hypothesis in the literature. The first – the "world illusion" interpretation – is that perceptual experience does not represent the environment as being the way it is. The second – the "perception illusion" interpretation – locates the illusion not between perceptual experience and the world but between us and perceptual experience. Maybe our perceptual experiences do correctly represent the world around us, but we misrepresent the extent and nature of that representation. Most discussants have in mind the second, but some seem to have in mind at least in part the first (Ballard, 2002; Bridgeman, 2002; Durgin, 2002).

In response to the world illusion interpretation, we can offer a transcendental argument to show that there must be limits to the degree to which our perceptual experiences fail to represent correctly the nature of our environments. It is a condition on the possibility of discovering how our perceptual systems work and the extent to which they do not represent our environment correctly that we come to know quite a lot about our environments. It is a condition on the possibility of our coming to know quite a lot about our environments that, in many cases that we can identify, our representations of our environment are veridical. Our perceptual beliefs, being abstractions from the contents of our perceptual representations, are correct only to the extent to which our perceptual experiences are veridical. Our perceptual beliefs in turn form the basis for our empirical investigations into the world, our inductive practices, the formation and testing of empirical theories about physical law and the neurophysiology of perception. Any empirical argument to the effect that our experiences did not represent the world by and large correctly, at least with respect to those features that form the basis for our scientific theorizing, would be self-defeating, because its premises would be established by the very perceptual mechanisms it called into question. If it were sound, then there could be no reason to accept its premises.

We could at most be justified empirically in thinking that in some circumscribed respects our perceptual experiences did not correctly represent the nature of the world around us. For any argument in favor of that would presuppose that in other respects, determined by the standpoint from which the skeptical argument was given, our perceptual experiences were largely veridical. One traditional example of this kind of circumscribed skepticism is skepticism about the reality of color, and other so-called secondary qualities. Recently, very general considerations have been advanced to show that the conditions necessary for the success of such a skeptical argument cannot be met (Stroud, 2000, esp. ch. 7). The difficulty is that to identify a general illusion about color, we must simultaneously be able to attribute color experiences and beliefs to people, and to establish that nothing is colored. But the practices which make sense of attributing color experiences and beliefs to people depend upon identifying what they believe relative to the objective features of objects in their environments to which they generally respond. If we can make sense of attributing color experiences and beliefs to people only if we can find those beliefs and experiences to be generally responsive in the right way to colored objects in the environment, then there would be no way coherently and simultaneously to identify color experiences and beliefs and to deny the reality of color. The line of thought here is connected with the application of the Principle of Charity in interpretation, which enjoins one, as a condition on the possibility of finding another person interpretable as a speaker at all, to find him to have beliefs which are about the conditions in the environment that prompt them (Davidson, 2001; Rawling, 2003). If this line of argument can be sustained, then we would have established the stronger conclusion that we cannot show we are mistaken in there being things falling in fundamental categories we represent. The world illusion interpretation of the grand illusion hypothesis, according to which the world that perceptual experience represents to us is largely illusory, or illusory in certain fundamental respects, would be shown to be fundamentally in error.

I turn now to the perception illusion interpretation of the grand illusion hypothesis, according to which the illusion lies in our misrepresentations not of the world but of the character of our perceptual experiences. The perception illusion interpretation is directly relevant to our overall question only to the extent to which the evidence cited calls into question the general *accuracy* of perceptual representations. Let us take up first the challenges to the snapshot model of visual experience. The falsity of the snapshot model, at least if the representations we are interested in are those embodied in conscious visual experience, is obvious from a moment's reflection. Visual experience does not represent the world in sharp focus, uniform detail, and high resolution from the center out to the periphery. The detail represented in visual experience is not uniform from the center out to the periphery. Even for objects close to one, outside the center of one's visual field the level of detail falls off quite significantly. Even in the center of the visual field not everything is represented in the same degree of detail. Objects nearer or further off than what we focus on are not in sharp focus. Some, like one's nose, are too close to focus on at all. Some are too far (recall Descartes' example of the square tower that looks round in the distance). Things that are in focus for us at a given distance can be brought into sharper focus, up to a limit, by moving closer to them.

Precisely because it is so obvious that the snapshot model does not correspond to the phenomenology of visual perception, however, it seems doubtful that ordinary people have been suffering under an illusion about this. We certainly *behave* as if we think that our visual experience does not represent the world in "sharp focus, uniform detail and high resolution from the center out to the periphery" of our visual fields. If we have an interest in seeing what something is like, *we turn our heads or eyes toward it*, even if it is already visible, and *focus on it*, and *approach it* if necessary in order *to examine it more closely*. If we suffered from a grand illusion because we embraced the snapshot view of perception, we would expect it to show up in our behavior, but it does not. There is no grand illusion we suffer from to the effect that visual experience conforms to the snapshot view of experience.[12]

Does the fact that the visual field is not uniformly detailed, in high resolution, and in sharp focus, over its entire extent, and through its entire depth, show that visual experience does not accurately represent the environment?

In discussing the accuracy or inaccuracy of a representation it is important to keep in mind both the subject and degree of definiteness of the representation. Consider an analogy with maps. An interstate highway map does not misrepresent by failing to represent state routes. Moreover, it has a certain standard of resolution. It is responsible only for features which rise to a certain level of significance. Not every curve in a highway is represented. Therefore, certain actual differences in what is being represented will not be represented by any feature on the map. In this sense, the map fails to represent something that is present, even though it is part of the job of the map to represent things of that sort. But this does not count as a misrepresentation because it is not the map's job to represent to that degree of definiteness. This is shown in our handling of the information which maps give to us. We use them for purposes that do not require greater resolution than they provide. We do not take a topographical map of the United States that represents differences in elevation in 500-foot increments to tell us whether there are any small hills in Florida, and we do not protest that it is inaccurate or non-veridical when we learn that Florida is not completely flat. The lesson carries over to perceptual experience, which has a field-like character.

It is their designers who decide what maps are to represent and what degree of resolution they are to be held to. What determines what visual experience is supposed to represent and what standard of resolution it is to be held to? One might here appeal to the evolutionary function of features of perceptual experience. Yet we would be convinced that perceptual experience represents our environment even if evolutionary theory were false. The correctness of our judgments about what experience represents and its accuracy is not hostage to our understanding of its biological function. The content of our perceptual representations is given to us by the experience itself. This is largely autonomous from what we believe, as is shown by the possibility of illusions persisting though we realize that they are illusions. An object may still look as if there is a window in it even though we learn that it is the effect of a *trompe l'oeil* painting.

The relevant degree of resolution of perceptual experience for the purposes of assessing it for accuracy is determined by the uses we make of perceptual experience in standard conditions. This includes what beliefs we form on its basis and what we think we need to do to find out more about the scene before us when we have a certain visual experience. To see this, consider a thought experiment. Suppose there were certain plants whose leaves had markings on them, which we discovered by accident could be used as maps of their root systems. What would show what degree of resolution we took them to have? It would be our use of them after some experience with how well features of the markings corresponded with their root systems. The resolution we took them to have would be shown by the limits on the judgments we formed on their basis, what we did and did not take them to show us about the root systems of the plants whose leaves they were. We have of course a great deal of practical knowledge of how well and to what degree of resolution our perceptual experience represents our environments. At a given distance, we know quite a bit about how much detail is visually represented, and how much more we can expect to uncover through closer examination. In addition we deploy a framework of concepts which tells us that even at the greatest resolution we can achieve in optimum conditions in, say, visual experience, there is much detail that escapes our view. In a field of grass, we can see blades of grass at our feet if we look down, but this detail disappears as we look out across the field. This is not to represent the grass fusing into a textured and then smooth green plane as the field recedes from our position. We understand that if we walk across the field, we will see more detail than we did initially. We do not take our visual experience of the field in the distance to be a misrepresentation because it fails to resolve individual blades of grass. We know that at that distance visual experience does not represent to that degree of resolution. If, however, when we started walking we were to find that what we were looking at was not green but brown, then we would conclude that our visual experience had misrepresented what was there. We also understand that the standards of resolution will be attuned to what we focus on, and what portion of the visual field is concerned. The less sharply detailed and focused regions of the visual field away from its center are not more inaccurate representations of those portions of the scene before us, but rather representations that have a lower degree of resolution.[13] At night, when colors are washed out or absent because of the low level of light, we do not take our visual experience to represent objects as colored in shades of black and white, but to fail to be resolving their colors under the illumination conditions. This attunement of our standards of resolution for experience to our practical knowledge guarantees that by and large our perceptual representations do not represent beyond their capacities for resolving detail.

What about the suggestion that visual experience misrepresents because while signals to the brain are interrupted by saccades, our visual experience does not appear to be intermittent, and we do not represent a hole in the visual field where there is a blind spot?

The fact that the signal to the brain is interrupted during saccades does not show that visual experience of objects in the environment is non-veridical or inaccurate any more than the fact that a film of a current event has a maximum frame rate, and so could not be said to be capturing changes in what is being filmed continuously, shows that it is non-veridical or inaccurate. The visual experience is representing the environment, not the mechanisms which implement it. Like a film, it has a maximum sensitivity to change. Changes that fall below the threshold are not represented. That perceptual experience has a limit to its temporal resolution is a matter of everyday experience. If I snap my fingers while watching, I do not see the movement of thumb and finger, only their starting position and end positions. But this does not mean that we misrepresent what happens when things move faster than we can see. When the movement falls below the resolution of visual perception, we fail to represent it, but this is not to misrepresent it.

In the case of the blind spot, there is no question of a misrepresentation with binocular vision, because for each eye the other covers the portion of the visual field it receives no signals from. In the case of monocular vision, the question whether a misrepresentation is involved depends on whether the visual field is filled in in the portion corresponding to the optic nerve or not. If it is, then it is at least sometimes a misrepresentation; if not, it is the absence of representation.[14] Neither case looks to show something significant about whether visual experience generally provides accurate representations of the visual scene. In binocular vision, there is no representational deficit due to the blind spot. At most, in monocular vision, there is a lack of representation of a small area in the visual scene or sometimes a misrepresentation.

Let me turn to evidence for the grand illusion hypothesis drawn from studies of change and inattentional blindness, both of which, I will suggest, are rather ordinary phenomena, and do little to support either the grand illusion hypothesis or the thesis that perceptual experience is inaccurate.

Inattentional blindness, that is, failure to notice or recall things that one was not paying attention to, though these things did clearly physically affect our sensory organs, both intermodally and intramodally, is familiar from ordinary experience. When we concentrate on a visual task – reading, or writing, or painting a design on a cup, we often fail to notice even quite significant aural events in our environment. Similarly, when listening to the radio, or a conversational partner at a cocktail party, we may miss most of what goes on in front of our eyes. And it is a commonplace that one often fails to notice somatic sensation when engaged in a difficult task or one's attention is directed elsewhere – as pickpockets are well aware – even to the extent of not noticing that one has cut or bruised oneself or any sensations associated with that. Likewise, intramodally, one may, in concentrating on what one person is saying, fail to notice what her companion is saying though it is at the same volume. Or one may in keeping track of a sprinter not notice or be able to recall the color of the jersey of the runner next to her or much else about the visual scene. Change blindness too is a pervasive feature of everyday life. We often fail to notice all the changes in scenes in front of us even as we look at them. Some movie-goers I know have failed to notice that in Luis Buñuel's film *That Obscure Object of Desire* the female protagonist is played by two different actresses. Many card tricks are based on our failure to be able to recall in detail facts about cards we see. Prepare a deck of cards by placing the seven of diamonds and the eight of hearts on the top of a deck of cards, and the seven of hearts and the eight of diamonds on the bottom of the deck. Shuffle the deck in front of the subject without disturbing the two cards on the top and bottom. Ask the subject to take two cards off the top, look at them so that he can recall them, and then place them anywhere in the middle of the deck. Shuffle the cards a number of times, without disturbing the two bottom cards. Place the deck on the table, tap it twice, and then deal the two bottom cards onto the table face up. The subject of the trick will take the two cards dealt out to be those which he had memorized. In this case, clearly it is not a matter of failing to pay attention to the cards which explains why one fails to see that they are not the cards one initially looked at. In drawing attention to these things I do not mean to disparage systematic study of the phenomenon of inattentional blindness and change blindness, but only to point out that it is systematic study of a phenomenon we are already familiar with. If there were a case to be made for a grand illusion involving inattentional or change blindness, it is a case that could be made independently of psychological studies.

What do these phenomena show, first of all, about the extent to which we are subject to an illusion about the completeness of experience? Second, what do they show about the veridicality or accuracy of perception?

In the case of inattentional blindness, it has been claimed that the evidence shows that "there is no conscious perception at all in the absence of attention and therefore no perceptual object can exist preattentively" (Mack and Rock, 1998, p. 227). If this were true, then I think it would be fair to say that we were subject to a kind of illusion that we were conscious of things in our visual or auditory fields about which later we cannot report in much detail. But is it true? Is paying visual attention to something phenomenally like having tunnel vision? Does the rest of the visual field disappear or shrink, so that, except for what you are paying attention to, phenomenally the scene in front of you is just like the scene behind your head? This is an experiment which one can perform without a laboratory, and for my part I can report that it is just not so. I am paying attention at the moment to the words that are appearing on my computer screen as I type. But I do not experience a sudden shrinking of the visual field even if I would not be able to tell you much about the detail of the visual scene outside the area of my attention.[15] Similarly for the intermodal case. In paying attention to the words, my body does not suddenly go numb, I do not suddenly go deaf, etc. It is quite easy to imagine how one's whole experience would be different if in paying visual attention to something one simply ceased to have somatic or proprioceptive or auditory experience. A restricted ability to report on things one is not paying attention to does not impugn the view that if they affect one's sensory organs in a way that usually leads to some effect on the phenomenal character of one's visual or auditory experience, etc., then they have a similar effect on the phenomenal character of the appropriate portion of the visual or auditory

Perception and Accurate Representations

field even when one is not paying attention. For the ability to recall or report that one was in a certain complex phenomenal state and one's being in that state are not the same thing, and it is no surprise that we are better able to recall matters involving, and experiences of, things we are paying attention to than things we are not paying attention to.

Why would anyone suggest attention was necessary for consciousness? Mack and Rock reach their conclusion by identifying being able to recall or report something later with having at the time been conscious of it: "A perception is . . . conscious if subjects can recall or recognize it" (Mack and Rock, 1998, p. 233). However, while this is plausibly a sufficient condition for having been conscious of it, it is not a necessary condition, at least if we mean conscious or phenomenal experience. One could defend Mack and Rock's conclusion by introducing an operational definition of "conscious," which does not aim to capture the ordinary meaning, and is tailored to their experimental results. But the air of excitement goes out of the announcement when we take "no conscious perception" to be shorthand for "no or limited ability to recall in the experimental conditions."

This point applies equally to change blindness. Change blindness does not directly show that we do not at time t and at time $t + \varepsilon$, after the change, represent correctly features which have changed. What is shown at most is that one may have limited ability to notice a change in the scene, and by extension in the representation.[16] For change in the world is represented in experience by a corresponding change in what the experience represents, and so in the experience itself. If an object is blue at one time, then red, one's experience represents that change if before the change it represented the object as blue and after the change it represented it as red. To notice that one's experience has represented a change requires taking note of a difference between one representation and another. The results of change blindness experiments do not suggest that before and after the change one's experience does not correctly represent. So they do not suggest that one's experience does not represent a change. The experimental results suggest only that we may fail to notice changes in our experience when they occur during saccades, or blinks, or when there are simultaneous distracting events in the visual scene. Given this, it is a mistake to suppose that people thinking that they would notice such changes shows that they are subject to an illusion about the accuracy or veridicality of their experience.[17] Rather, they overestimate the extent to which they are able to attend to changes in their experience, and remember the character of their experiences at later times.

It is easy enough to explain why we take ourselves to be better at noticing changes in the special situations that elicit change blindness. As Jonathan Cohen has noted, "all the inductive evidence available to perceivers supports their belief in their ordinary capacity to notice ambient events" (Cohen, 2002, p. 152). We typically do notice changes in our environments that are important to us. It is natural then that we should be surprised when we fail to notice some changes that in retrospect seem obvious in circumstances that we do not know are rigged to test the limits of our abilities.[18] But as Cohen remarks, this should no more incline us to say we are subject to a grand illusion than the fact that we are surprised that we are mistaken in the Müller-Lyer or Ponzo or Ebbinghaus illusions. The "grand illusion"

Kirk Ludwig

is an instance of a very general phenomenon: ordinary subjects are ignorant about the limitations on their cognitive and perceptual capacities, and when controlled experimental conditions make these limitations apparent, they (and we) learn something new. (Cohen, 2002, p. 155)

Given that perceptual experience does by and large provide accurate representations of the environment, the question whether that is its aim is straightforward. Experience has the instrumental function of providing accurate representations if its doing so helps us achieve our aims. It is clear that knowing about the environment is important to our achieving many of our aims. This requires correct perceptual beliefs about the environment. And since these abstract from our perceptual experiences, this requires accurate perceptual experiences. Accurate perceptual experience therefore helps us achieve our aims. Perception therefore has the instrumental function of providing accurate representations. Any answer to the question of whether the biological function of perceptual experience is to provide accurate representations is more speculative, since it is an empirical question whose confirmation depends upon historical facts we have only indirect evidence about. Yet it seems overwhelmingly plausible that accurate representations of the environment tailored to an organism's needs provides a selectional advantage. Given this, we may safely conclude that it is also a biological function of perceptual experience to provide accurate representations.

Notes

1 See O'Regan et al., 1996, 1999; Simmons, 2000; Simmons and Levine, 1997.
2 Mack and Rock, 1998.
3 The phrase was introduced into the literature in Noë et al., 2000. A recent issue of *The Journal of Consciousness Studies* (Noë, 2002b) has been devoted to it.
4 There is a dangerous ambiguity in "information" which it would be well to note here. In the text, I use "information" in the sense of a physical signal which together with appropriate laws and background conditions enables one who knows the laws, background conditions, and signal, to infer something about its cause. In this sense, rings in the trunk of a tree carry information about its age. This does not mean that they carry information in the sense in which a newspaper does. A newspaper carries information in two senses, in the signal sense, and in the sense that it represents that certain things have occurred, that is, it contains representations that have intentional content and are true or false. Tree rings are not intentional and are not true or false.
5 O'Regan, 1990.
6 See Simmons, 2000 for a recent review.
7 See Mack and Rock, 1998.
8 O'Regan, 1992; O'Regan et al., 1996.
9 Neisser, 1979; Simons and Chabris, 1999.
10 "Experience" has an event as well as a state reading. However, it is the state reading which is at issue in the question whether the sensorimotor view provides an adequate analysis of perceptual experience in the sense in which we speak of my visual or auditory experience at a given moment in time.
11 The same point can be made by the more traditional thought experiments of the brain in a vat, and the disembodied mind all of whose experiences are determined by an evil demon.

12   Consider in this respect Daniel Dennett's example of walking into a room and seeing wallpaper, in his example, of identical photographic portraits of Marilyn Monroe. Dennett says that "you would see in a fraction of a second that there were 'lots and lots of identical, detailed, focused portraits of Marilyn Monroe'", but that since "your eyes saccade four or five times a second at most, you could foveate only on one or two Marilyns in the time it takes you to jump to the conclusion *and thereupon to see* hundreds of identical Marilyns" (Dennett, 1991, p. 354). Dennett says rightly that we do not represent in detail more than we actually foveate on. But then he goes on to say: "Of course it does not seem that way to you. It seems to you as if you are actually seeing hundreds of identical Marilyns" (Dennett, 1991, p. 355). But this needs to be handled carefully. You do see a wall on which there are hundreds of portraits of Marilyn Monroe which are detailed. And it seems to you as if you do. But does it or would it seem to you that your *visual experience represented all of that detail*? I don't think that anyone would be under the illusion that it did. It is just that we know that wallpaper involves repetition of a pattern, and if we see the pattern, we know we are seeing a wall on which the pattern is repeated in all its detail. There is no illusion, and no surprise, in any of this.

13   Space constraints prevent a detailed discussion of Kathleen Akins's interesting argument that the peripheral thermoreceptor system does not provide veridical representations (Akins, 1996). The argument is based on an observation and an assumption. The observation is that the warm and cold spots that respond to temperature and temperature change are distributed unevenly over the skin, and have both static and dynamic responses that are nonlinear. The assumption is that intensity of felt sensation represents surface skin temperature if anything. It is the assumption that I would question. We treat sensations of heat and cold as providing information about distal objects and objects we are in contact with, not our skins, and, as in the case of visual experience, the relation between the subjective features of experience and the representation of objectively unvarying properties in the environment may be quite complex. The angle subtended by an object on the retina is not directly correlated either with its represented size or shape, which depends in addition on the represented distance and viewing angle. We may look for a similar interplay between what is represented and a variety of different sorts of information, including cross temporal information, in the case of sensations of heat and cold. For example, when we step into a hot bath, we know that the intensity of the sensation of heat will diminish after a moment. But we do not take this to be a representation of the bath water cooling down – we do not suddenly plunge the rest of the body in after the feet have ceased to complain.

14   Dennett claims there is no filling in Dennett, 1991, but see Pessoa et al., 1998 for discussion and some contrary evidence.

15   Fortunately, drivers do not go blind when they are talking on a mobile phone, though they are apt to do very poorly in reporting on the visual scene before them.

16   See Simons et al., 2002 for some recent experimental work that suggests under probing subjects often can recover information about a scene that it seemed initially that they had not taken note of. This suggests that "change blindness" as defined operationally in these experiments does not correspond to failure to be able to recall and report on the change at all, but failure in response to open-ended questions to make comparisons that would have called the change to mind.

17   See Levine, 2002 for studies of the extent to which people overestimate their ability to detect change.

18   In an informal survey I have found that people have difficulty picking out the difference between the pair of photographs reproduced in Blackmore et al. 1995 when viewing them at the same time, though they pick out the difference easily on being told what to look

Kirk Ludwig

for. No wonder subjects can fail to notice a change when they are presented one after another with an intervening eye movement.

References

Akins, K. (1996). Of sensory systems and the "aboutness" of mental states. *Journal of Philosophy*, 937, 337–72.

Ballard, D. H. (2002). Our perception of the world has to be an illusion. *Journal of Consciousness Studies*, 9/5–6, 54–71.

Blackmore, S. J. (2002). There is no stream of consciousness. *Journal of Consciousness Studies*, 9/5–6, 17–28.

Blackmore, S. J., Brelstaff, G., Nelson, K., and Troscianko, T. (1995). Is the richness of our visual world an illusion? Transsaccadic memory for complex scenes. *Perception*, 24, 1075–81.

Bridgeman, B. (2002). The grand illusion and petit illusions: interactions of perception and sensory coding. *Journal of Consciousness Studies*, 9/5–6, 29–34.

Clark, A. (2002). Is seeing all it seems? Action, reason and the grand illusion. *Journal of Consciousness Studies*, 9/5–6, 181–202.

Cohen, J. (2002). The grand grand illusion illusion. *Journal of Consciousness Studies*, 9/5–6, 141–57.

Davidson, D. (2001). Radical Interpretation. In D. Davidson, *Inquiries into Truth and Interpretation* (2nd edn.). New York: Clarendon Press.

Dennett, D. (1991). *Consciousness Explained*. Boston: Little, Brown.

Durgin, F. H. (2002). The Tinkerbell effect: Motion perception and illusion. *Journal of Consciousness Studies*, 9/5–6, 88–101.

Levine, D. T. (2002). Change blindness as visual metacognition. *Journal of Consciousness Studies*, 9/5–6, 111–30.

Mack, A. (2002). Is the visual world a grand illusion? *Journal of Consciousness Studies*, 9/5–6, 102–10.

Mack, A. and Rock, I. (1998). *Inattentional Blindness*. Cambridge, MA: MIT Press.

Neisser, U. (1979). The control of information pickup in selective looking. In A. Pick (ed.), *Perception and its Development*. Hillfield, NJ: Erlbaum.

Noë, A. (2001). Experience and the active mind. *Synthese*, 129/1, 41–60.

— (2002a). Is the visual world a grand illusion? *Journal of Consciousness Studies*, 9/5–6, 1–12.

— (ed.) (2002b). *Is the Visual World a Grand Illusion?* Special issue of *Journal of Consciousness Studies*, 9/5–6. Charlottesville, VA: Imprint Academic.

— (2002c). On what we see. *Pacific Philosophical Quarterly*, 83/1, 57–80.

Noë, A. and O'Regan, J. K. (2001). What it is like to see: A sensorimotor theory of perceptual experience. *Synthese*, 129/1, 79–103.

Noë, A., Thompson, E., and Pessoa, L. (2000). Beyond the grand illusion: What change blindness really teaches us about vision. *Visual Cognition*, 7/1–3, 93–106.

O'Regan, J. K. (1990). Eye movements and reading. In E. Kowler (ed.), *Eye Movements and Their Role in Visual and Cognitive Processes*. Amsterdam: Elsevier.

— (1992). Solving the "real" mysteries of visual perception: The world as an outside memory. *Canadian Journal of Psychology*, 3/46, 461–88.

O'Regan, J. K., Rensink, J. A., and Clark, J. J. (1996). "Mud splashes" render picture changes invisible. *Investigative Ophthalmology and Visual Science*, 37, 213.

—, —, and — (1999). Change-blindness as a Result of "Mud splashes." *Nature*, 398, 34.

Pessoa, L., Thompson, E., and Noë, A. (1998). Finding out about filling in: a guide to perceptual completion for visual science and the philosophy of perception. *Behavioral and Brain Sciences*, 216, 723–802.

Rawling, P. (2003). Radical interpretation. In K. Ludwig (ed.), *Donald Davidson*. New York: Cambridge University Press.

Siewert, C. (2002). Is visual experience rich or poor? *Journal of Consciousness Studies*, 9/5–6, 131–40.

Simmons, D. J. (2000). Current approaches to change blindness. *Visual Cognition*, 7/1–3, 1–15.

Simons, D. and Chabris, C. (1999). Gorillas in our midst: Sustained inattentional blindness for dynamic events. *Perception*, 28, 1059–74.

Simmons, D. J. and Levine, D. T. (1997). Change blindness. *Trends in Cognitive Sciences*, 1/7, 261–7.

Simons, D., Chabris, C., Schnur, T., and Levine, D. T. (2002). Evidence for preserved representations in change blindness. *Consciousness and Cognition*, 11/1, 78–97.

Strawson, G. (1994). *Mental Reality*. Cambridge, MA: MIT Press.

Stroud, B. (2000). The Quest for Reality: Subjectivism and the Metaphysics of Colour. New York: Oxford University Press.

CHAPTER
SIXTEEN

Is the Aim of Perception to Provide Accurate Representations? A Case for the "No" Side

Christopher Viger

1 Introduction

Is the aim of perception to provide accurate representations? My view is that the multiple modes of perception and their varied roles in guiding behavior are so diverse that there is no univocal answer to this question. The aim of perception is to help guide action via planning and directly responding to a dynamic and often hostile environment; sometimes that requires accurate representations and, I shall argue, sometimes it does not. So in many circumstances the appropriate answer to our question is "no" and understanding the conditions in which it is not the aim of perception to provide accurate representations is an important development in cognitive science.

First I present cases in which our perceptual systems do not provide accurate representations and argue that their usefulness derives from their *in*accuracy. In these cases, we represent the world as being different from how it actually is to make important environmental differences more salient. I then show that there is an ambiguity in the notion of representation and argue that on the more natural reading there are cases in which it is not the aim of perception to provide representations at all. Moreover, the ambiguity does not arise from careless use of language but from the structure of perception itself, as shown by Melvyn Goodale and David Milner's dual route model. This empirically well-supported model reveals another class of cases in which perceptual representations are not accurate, nor is it their aim to be so. In the final section, I discuss how our question is related to a very similar but importantly different question, namely, "Is the visual world a grand illusion?"

2 Cases of Inaccurate Perception

What would it mean to say that perception does not provide accurate representations? One possibility is that we perceive the world to be fundamentally different from the way it is, such as in the case of hallucinations. The representations perception provides us with are not representations of things in the world, at least nothing with which we are in direct sensory contact at the time of perception. If such perceptions were relatively infrequent, as hallucinations surely are, then we would not on these grounds claim that perception provides inaccurate representations; we would merely concede that on occasion perception is inaccurate. To support a negative response to our title question the error would have to be pervasive and this immediately raises an epistemological worry about how we could ever know of our systematic misperception. Kirk Ludwig (chapter 15, IS THE AIM OF PERCEPTION TO PROVIDE ACCURATE REPRESENTATIONS?) cogently argues that reasons for thinking that our perceptions are fundamentally in error in this way would at least in part be perceptual themselves, so that in accepting the conclusion of such reasoning we would have to reject the very premises that lead to the conclusion. As with many other variations of skepticism, this brand is self-refuting. Radical skepticism is not the route to denying that the aim of perception is to provide accurate representations.

Another way in which it could be the case that perception does not provide accurate representations is if perception represents the structure of properties we perceive differently from the actual structure of those properties in the world. The difference between this case and radical skepticism is that it does not commit us to pervasive misrepresentations. Provided the perceptual means for determining the structure of some property, typically via some instrument we create for that purpose, is independent of our ordinary perception of that property, we avoid Ludwig's critique. That is to say, what we require is for enough of our perceptions to be accurate so as to make possible an assessment of a particular way of perceiving using reliable independent criteria. Color perception is a case in point. In this case the reality of color is not denied as in the radical interpretation. What makes detecting error possible is that we have developed means for determining the wavelengths of light that give rise to our color vision that are independent of color vision. We have also learned a great deal about the physiology of color vision. Putting together what we know about color vision and the stimuli that give rise to it, the conclusion to draw is that color perception does not provide accurate representations. Let's consider the case in more detail.

Color discrimination requires at least two types of photoreceptors with different spectral sensitivities. In our case we have three such photoreceptors, or cones, that respond preferentially to different ranges of the visible band of electromagnetic radiation (between 400 and 700 nm). Some cones respond best to blue light, others green, and others red. Responses are preferential but not exclusive to particular wavelengths of light because the activation of a cone is caused by a quantum interaction between photons and the pigment in the cone. There is only a statistical chance that an interaction will occur, so cones do not always respond even to the light they are most sensitive to, and any kind of cone can respond to any wavelength of light. Colors

Christopher Viger

are determined by the brain based on the differential responses between the clusters of cone types. The details of cell organization to effect this processing are beyond the scope of this chapter, but the system is organized so as to maximize contrast between green/red and blue/yellow stimuli (Kandel et al., 1995, pp. 453–68). The upshot for our discussion is that phenomenologically we do see the biggest contrasts between red/green and blue/yellow, consistent with, indeed caused by, our physiological organization.[1] This is not the actual structure of the electromagnetic radiation we visibly detect, however. The wavelengths of the light we see as red are much closer to those of green than blue, even though red and blue seem more similar to us. In fact, our red and green cones are maximally sensitized to wavelengths less than 30 nm apart (Kandel et al., 1995, p. 456).

Not only does our color perception fail to provide accurate representations, it may be adaptive that it does not. Austen Clark (2000, p. 245) and Gonzalo Munevar (forthcoming, ch. 9) both make the claim that color perception is like "false color" used in satellite telemetry. Arbitrary physical features that have nothing more in common than that they affect some of the satellite's detectors in the same way are represented as having the same color. From the vantage point of the satellite, we would not perceive the scene as it is represented, but the representation makes real physical differences more salient.

I think that all colours are, in this sense, false colours. Colour similarities may not represent any resemblance of physical properties other than the propensity of disparate classes of objects to affect our receptors in the same way. Nonetheless, colour differences – borders – can be informative about real physical differences in the scene. (Clark, 2000, p. 245)

A plausible selective advantage conferred by color perception is a heightened sensitivity to difference. To effect this sensitivity, the color system exaggerates differences, thereby misrepresenting the visible array of electromagnetic radiation. "Useful contrast is the key to perceptual success, not faithful resemblance" (Munevar, forthcoming, ch. 9).

Clark applies the lesson from color perception to perceptual systems more generally.

Nervous systems in general seem much more keyed to spatial and temporal changes and discontinuities than to spatial or temporal similarities. To sameness the neurons in every modality eventually adapt, accommodate, and grow quiet; but hit an edge, or make a change, and the alarms go off. Spatial and temporal edges are enhanced in every modality. (Clark, 2000, p. 238)

Motion is a typical way of bringing about change in our environment and, not surprisingly, it is something to which we are sensitively attuned. However, we are so sensitive to motion that in some cases we perceive motion even when there is none. The advantage here is simple; it is far better to make a false positive identification than a false negative one, since failing to notice motion can be fatal. A simple experiment demonstrates how false motion is perceived when similar items are seen in quick succession. When a red spot is flashed briefly on a blank computer screen anywhere on the perimeter of a circle followed quickly by flashing a green spot at the centre of the circle, what we see is the red spot moving toward the centre and changing color mid-trajectory from red to green. This effect is known as the color phi phenomenon (Kolers and von Grünau, 1976, reported in Dennett, 1991). Similar effects are created by many billboard designers to create the illusion of motion through patterns of light.[2] Unlike color perception, this effect occurs near the limits of motion detection only, but it serves to highlight that what is useful is not always what is accurate and our perceptual systems favor usefulness.

A non-visual instance of false motion detection is created in the cutaneous rabbit experiment. Mechanical tappers are placed on a subject's wrist, elbow, and upper arm. When the subject is given a series of taps only on the wrist no illusion occurs. However when several quick taps at the wrist are followed by taps at the elbow and upper arm the subject experiences the taps at intermediate positions equidistantly spaced along the arm, where no tappers are placed. The experience is as of a rabbit hopping up one's arm, hence the name. Again, motion is detected where there is none (Geldard and Sherrick, 1972, reported in Dennett, 1991).

Phonology provides an example in which our auditory perception exaggerates differences by providing inaccurate representations. As with the case of color vision, we have designed special instruments to reveal the structure of acoustic stimuli against which our auditory perceptions can be compared. What we find is that there are many phonological illusions in which we hear consonants that are not pronounced or hear consonant sounds that are pronounced identically as being different. To offer just one example, in many American English dialects the words *writer* and *rider* are thought to be distinguished in pronunciation by the medial consonants *t* and *d*.

> The pronunciations of *writer* and *rider* are indeed different. But phonetic study reveals that the medial dental consonants are in fact pronounced identically . . . The difference instead resides in the vowel – it is longer in *rider* than in *writer*. Unless one has had phonetic training, however, this vowel length difference is ignored because it is below the level of consciousness. (Kenstowicz, 1994, p. 6)

The actual difference in this case is the length of the vowel, but the difference is exaggerated in auditory perception by our hearing distinct consonants – to the extent that our orthography reflects the illusion. A curious feature of such phonological illusions is that they are language specific. This suggests that in lexical acquisition the auditory system is trained to alter what we hear, thereby making differences more salient, and interpretation easier. Again, accuracy is not the aim, discrimination is.[3]

The final case I consider in this section is our perception of temperature. There is some real property of the world, the mean kinetic energy of molecules, which we can determine independently of our perceptual access to temperature through our thermoreceptors by using thermometers. As with color vision and hearing, we know enough about temperature and how our thermoreceptors work to conclude that our thermoreceptors do not provide accurate representations. Thermoreceptors sensitive to colder temperatures, so called "cold spots," respond with exactly the same firing rate for different skin temperatures. That is, the firing rate of a cold spot as a function of temperature is a many-one function. In providing exactly the same representation

Christopher Viger

for different stimuli, the representations cannot be said to be accurate. Warm spots – thermoreceptors sensitive to warmer temperatures – though not many-one in their response rates, nonetheless do not respond in a linear fashion to linear changes in temperature either. So neither type of thermoreceptor preserves the structure of the external stimuli. Furthermore, how a thermoreceptor responds to a change in temperature depends on the starting temperature. Our thermal requirements are such that a fixed temperature change within a moderate range is less relevant than the same change near the extremes of tolerance. Warm spots give a dynamic response only to increases in temperature, cold spots only to decreases, and in both cases the strength of the response is determined by the starting temperature; changes from moderate starting temperatures yield small responses, whereas increases from hot starting temperatures and decreases from cold starting temperatures yield very strong responses, thereby meeting our thermal needs. We are better served with information that our left hand is getting too hot than we are by the information that the external temperature has increased by ten degrees. Thermoreceptors are not thermometers.[4]

The cases of perception just considered are not intended to be exhaustive, nor are they offered as the general case from which our understanding of the nature of perception should be drawn. They simply serve as examples in which perception does not provide accurate representations. And careful consideration reveals that this is not just a failing of the perceptual systems to get things right in these cases. It is advantageous to creatures to distort what they perceive in these ways. So in such cases the aim of perception is not to provide *accurate* representations because they are less useful than systematically distorted representations. "Evolutionary fitness rests upon cognitive functions that are useful, and usefulness does not necessarily track the truth" (Bermudez, 1999, p. 80). When usefulness and truth come apart, as they do in the perceptual cases discussed above, it is not the aim of perception to provide accurate representations.

The lesson we can take from the examples presented above is that it is not precise enough to ask whether the aim of perception, *tout court*, is to provide accurate representations. Even restricted to a single modality the question is not precise enough. Sometimes perception is accurate, but when the usefulness of perception relies on a distortion of the underlying structure being perceived, such as in the case of color vision or language parsing, it is not. The question, "Is the aim of perception to provide accurate representations?" must be answered on a case-by-case basis as we learn enough about our world, using specially developed tools, to understand its properties and how they are related, and enough about our perceptual systems to understand how they represent those relations. And in many cases the question will be answered negatively because in those cases our perceptual systems do not provide accurate representations.

Before switching gears let's take stock of where we are. So far I have presented cases in which we know enough about our own perceptual systems and independently we know enough about the properties we perceive to conclude that our perceptions are not accurate. In these cases it is not an accident that our perceptions are not accurate; by being inaccurate our perceptual systems make salient important environmental differences, thereby sacrificing accuracy for usefulness. As a result, our question must be considered on a case-by-case basis and since we already know of cases favoring positive and negative responses no univocal answer can be forthcoming; the issues our question raises are too complex to yield a single answer.

As complex as the question is based on what we have considered so far, answering it in full is even more complex because the question itself is ambiguous. There are two notions of representation and how the question is answered will depend on how we interpret it. In the next section, I present the two notions of representation at play and argue that on the more natural reading there are cases in which it is not the aim of perception to provide representations at all. Moreover, this ambiguity is not a simple matter of careless use of terminology. There is an impressive amount of empirical evidence for a dual model of perception, which predicts that there are distinct kinds of representations produced within the visual system. So we cannot stipulate a use of language to decide our question. And the situation is even more complex still because the dual route model of perception reveals yet another class of cases in which perception is not accurate, nor is it the aim of perception to be so. I turn now to discussing these issues.

3 Two Notions of Representation

In its weakest sense, having a representation is nothing more than being able to respond to something in the environment. In this sense thermostats represent room temperature and behave in virtue of their representational states. In our case, such representations are manifest in various instinctive responses such as ducking, being startled, etc. We can duck to avoid something without having any idea of what it is. Zenon Pylyshyn's (2001, 2003) visual index theory explains how such minimal representation is possible. According to Pylyshyn, we have a small number (four to six) of visual indexes that grab on to or index salient features or objects of the environment. These visual indexes act as nonconceptual demonstratives – the visual system's version of "this" and "that." They operate very early in the visual system and very quickly. In extreme cases, when time is short, we can even track objects without representing *any* of their features. This would be the case in ducking without knowing what is coming at us. To function under the real-time constraints of our world, this type of representation is ready made for use by the motor system, so I refer to them as sensorimotor representations.

In contrast to sensorimotor representations, which may not result in any conscious experience at all, are the representations appealed to in the representational theory of mind, mental particulars – words, images, symbols in the language of thought – whose tokenings give content to our thoughts. It is these representations that make us aware of things and of which we are aware when introspecting on our experiences. Since these representations are ready made for cognitive systems, I refer to them as conceptual representations.

Now while it is possible to interpret our question as being about either kind of representation, or both, in the absence of any specification I think it is more natural to interpret "representation" as meaning conceptual representations. It is conceptual representations, after all, that determine the content of our experiences. Moreover,

Christopher Viger

on the visual index theory there are some cases in which it wouldn't even make sense to ask if the sensorimotor representation were accurate because no property is represented. It is merely a demonstrative representation. And in these very cases, when immediate real-time action is required – in such circumstances as ducking, blocking, catching, etc. – it is not only *not* the aim of perception to provide accurate representations, their production is detrimental to acting. Processing conceptual representations is too slow in these cases to produce real-time responses. In the context of immediate real-time responses our question only makes sense if we interpret it as asking about conceptual representations, in which case the answer is that in these cases the aim of perception is not to provide a (conceptual) representation at all.

As I mentioned above, the ambiguity in the notion of representation is not a simple consequence of sloppy usage. There is significant and compelling empirical data supporting David Milner and Melvyn Goodale's (1995, 1998) dual route model of perception. This model reveals the source of the ambiguity, showing that our term is locked on to two distinct processes in perception. Let's look at the details of the model.

4 Vision for Action, Vision for Perception: The Dual Route Model of Perception

Generalizing from research done on macaque monkeys and from behavioural evidence in humans with brain damage, Milner and Goodale propose that "the visual projections from primary visual cortex to the temporal and parietal lobes in the human brain may involve a separation into ventral and dorsal streams similar to that seen in the monkey" (Milner and Goodale, 1998). What is important about the two streams they postulate is that each has a quite different function. The dorsal stream guides immediately responsive action – visuomotor skills – whereas the ventral stream is responsible for visual recognition. For example, human subjects with brain damage to the dorsal stream suffer from optic ataxia, a visuomotor disorder in which reaching to pick up objects and grasping them are difficult. Surprisingly, these subjects can accurately report the location and orientation of the objects they fail to grasp. In other cases, subjects with ventral stream damage suffer visual form agnosia. They are unable to determine the relative size between objects, though they can grasp quite accurately, adjusting their handgrip to the appropriate size while reaching for the object. One subject, D. F., could not report on the orientation of a slot but could orient her hand or a hand-held card to place it in the slot. Milner and Goodale conclude that the dorsal stream, which evolved first, is for fast acting visuomotor response, whereas the ventral stream is for object recognition.

In summary, there is a wealth of psychophysical evidence that is consistent with the general view that in specific situations, particularly where rapid responses to visible targets are required, visuomotor control engages processing mechanisms that are quite different from those that underlie our conscious visual experience of the world. (Goodale and Westwood, 2004, p. 5)

If some sort of dual route model is correct – and evidence from "neuroimaging experiments, human neuropsychology, monkey neurophysiology, and human psychophysical experiments" (Goodale and Westwood, 2004, abstract, p. 1) in its favor is impressive – then the two streams of visual processing are the source of our two notions of representation. "According to the Goodale and Milner model, the dorsal and ventral streams both process information about the structure of objects and about their spatial locations, but they transform this information into quite different outputs" (Goodale and Westwood, 2004, p. 2). That is to say, the representations produced by each stream are quite different. The dorsal stream produces sensorimotor representations for immediate responses, whereas the ventral stream produces conceptual representations in which objects are recognized as such.

The difference in function between the two streams is extremely important to determining the accuracy of the representations each produces. The dorsal stream must produce representations ready for use by the motor system. Its representations are egocentric in providing relational information about how our effectors are positioned relative to a target object and often[5] highly accurate to the point of "seeing through" visual illusions. For example, in the "Tichener circles" illusion we judge a disk surrounded by smaller circles to be larger than the same size disk surrounded by larger circles. However, when we grasp for the disks we open our hands to the same size, showing that the dorsal stream is insensitive to the illusion (Aglioti et al., 1995, reported in Goodale and Westwood, 2004, p. 3). On the other hand, ventral stream processing is the source of the illusion since it "has no such requirement for absolute metrics, or egocentric coding. Indeed, object recognition depends on the ability to see beyond the absolute metrics of a particular visual scene; for example, one must be able to recognise an object independent of its size and its momentary orientation and position" (Goodale and Westwood, 2004, p. 3). Object recognition requires abstracting away from the egocentric particulars of our perceptual circumstances, and so is often inaccurate, as evidenced in various illusions.[6] But giving up accuracy has the benefit of making the representations available to more central[7] cognitive systems. The payoff for giving up accuracy in the ventral stream is that "we can intentionally act in the very world we experience" (Clark, 2002, p. 201). Yet again, we have cases in which (conceptual) representations are useful in being inaccurate.

Before concluding, it is worth distinguishing our question from a closely related one: Is the visual world a grand illusion?

5 The Grand Illusion Hypothesis

Recently, the phenomena of change blindness and inattentional blindness have led people to the view that the visual world is a grand illusion. The phenomena in question are as follows. Change blindness is the name given to the phenomenon that during saccades or events of visual distraction large and salient features of a scene can be changed without our noticing. Inattentional blindness refers to our inability to notice quite significant and central events in our visual field when we are not attending to them. In a quite extreme case, many subjects given the task of counting the number of passes made by basketball players warming up for a game fail to notice a man in a gorilla suit that walks into the middle of the scene (Simons and Chabris, 1999).

Ludwig (this volume, chapter 15) characterizes the grand illusion hypothesis as having two interpretations: the "world illusion" and the "perception illusion."[8] According to the world illusion interpretation, the world is different in some respect from how we represent it. On this interpretation the visual world being a grand illusion amounts to vision being inaccurate. Since I have discussed this at length in section 2, I won't say more about it here. The perception illusion interpretation is the claim that there is a mismatch between our perceptual experiences and our judgments of those experiences.[9] Note that this is not the same as our question because it is possible that we judge our perceptions to be inaccurate even though they are accurate.

The arguments for a perception illusion are based on an assumption, known as the snapshot conception of experience, that we – lay observers – judge our visual experience to be like a photograph in being richly and uniformly detailed, with equally high resolution from center to periphery. The arguments proceed by producing evidence that undermines the snapshot conception of experience. The phenomena of change blindness and inattentional blindness are offered as evidence, being taken to demonstrate that we are profoundly mistaken about the nature of our visual experiences. Experience is gappy; color and resolution diminish outside the fovea; our eye position changes approximately three times a second; and, during each saccade no information is transmitted. The rich, detailed, evenly colored experience we seem to have is an illusion; the snapshot conception of experience is badly in error.

In response to the line of reasoning above, many writers, including Alva Noë and Kirk Ludwig reject the first premise, namely that ordinary observers hold the snapshot conception of experience.

> We peer, squint, lean forward, adjust lighting, put on glasses, and we do so automatically. The fact that we are not surprised by our lack of immediate possession of detailed information about the environment shows that we don't take ourselves to have all that information in consciousness all at once. (Noë, 2002a, p. 7)

> Precisely because it is so obvious that the snapshot model does not correspond to the phenomenology of visual perception, however, it seems doubtful that ordinary people have been suffering under an illusion about this ... If we have an interest in seeing what something is like, *we turn our heads or eyes toward it*, even if it is already visible, and *focus on it*, and *approach it* if necessary *to examine it more closely*. If we suffered from a grand illusion because we embraced the snapshot view of perception, we would expect it show up in our behavior, but it does not. (Chapter 15, p. 266; emphasis in original)

Indeed, conventional wisdom seems to reject the snapshot model of perception as expressed in the old adage: Blink and you'll miss it.

Despite rejecting the snapshot view of perception, Noë and Ludwig accept that we are confused about conscious experience as demonstrated by change blindness and inattentional blindness, though only in a very modest way. It turns out that ordinary perceivers are surprised that changes can occur *right before their eyes* without them noticing. This surprise betrays their expectations to the contrary, but for Noë and Ludwig, that our attention is more limited than we take it to be hardly merits the title "grand illusion." After all, on a moment's reflection, we would never be aware of what we are not attending to and so in ordinary experience would never notice that we missed something. To have what we missed pointed out to us is therefore surprising, but "the grand illusion is more aptly regarded as a sort of banal surprise" (Cohen, 2002, p. 151).

However banal the surprise of failing to notice salient aspects of our environment, we are surprised. And the source of our surprise is a tension in our phenomenology. We *do* have some sense of things to which we are not attending. For example, we may habituate to the ticking of a clock and so not seem to hear it, yet we notice if it stops. Similarly, the periphery of a visual scene is not invisible even if much of the detail is lost. As I read the page in front of me I still see the wall behind it. Curiously, we experience the world as richly detailed even though we do not take in the detail all at once.[10] "O'Regan and Noë . . . are right that it need not seem to people that they have a detailed picture of the world in their heads. But typically it does" (Dennett, 2002, p. 16). How can it be that we experience the world as richly detailed even as we move to get a better look? Noë refers to this tension as the problem of perceptual presence.

With the dual route model in hand, the resolution to the problem of perceptual presence is clear. Distinct representations with distinct functions are simultaneously produced. As a result of dorsal stream processing, we make adjustments such as moving to get a better look, squinting, etc. to improve our impoverished perceptual input; our sensorimotor knowledge is in the dorsal stream. Ventral stream processing, on the other hand, leads to object recognition, so that when we so much as glimpse a wall, we often recognize it *qua* wall; i.e., as the sort of thing that is not made of cream cheese, the sort of thing we can't walk through, etc. In particular, in recognizing a wall we recognize it as being a richly detailed object, of which we are familiar with many of the details, and thereby experience it as such, even though we are not taking in all that detail at once, as evidenced by dorsal stream guided movements.

Noë takes a different approach to resolving the problem of perceptual presence, which is important for, besides being an interesting theory of perception, if correct it forces a "no" answer to our question because perception *never* involves conceptual representations. Developing on the skill theory presented in O'Regan and Noë (2001), Noë (2002a, 2004), offers the enactive model of perception in place of the snapshot model as a solution to the problem of perceptual presence. On this view, "perceiving is a way of acting. Perception is not something that happens to us, or in us. It is something we do. Think of a blind person tap-tapping his or her way around a cluttered space, perceiving that space by touch, not all at once, but through time, by skillful probing and movement. That is, or at least ought to be, our paradigm of what perceiving is" (Noë, 2004, p. 1). According to Noë, perceivers do not experience the rich detail of the world; they have access to that detail because of the sensorimotor knowledge they possess. For example, if we see a cat partly occluded by a fence, it does not seem to us as if we see an entire cat, since some of it is obscured. However, it does not seem to us that we see detached cat parts, either.

Christopher Viger

Rather, it seems as if we have access to an entire cat; i.e., it seems that there is an entire cat that is partly occluded. We know from being embodied observers that if we move slightly, hidden parts will come into view and other parts will cease to be visible (Noë, 2002a, p. 10).

Naturally, Ludwig sees insurmountable difficulties with Noë's view. First he argues that it is a category mistake to suppose that actual activity constitutes perception, since "[a] perceptual experience . . . is a state, not an event" (chapter 15, p. 263). Ludwig concludes that Noë's position requires a dispositional reading. On this interpretation, possessing sensorimotor skills and practical knowledge are constitutive of being a perceiver. But Ludwig offers several reasons for why having a perceptual experience cannot be being in a dispositional state, two of which are relevant to our question. First, he argues that Noë's account leaves out the phenomenal character of perceptual experiences, which is occurrent rather than dispositional. Second, he points out that the view cannot accommodate our having hallucinations that we know are hallucinations. The reason is that in such a case we would not have the usual expectations derived from our practical knowledge about how our own movement would alter the sensory input. Knowing something to be a hallucination, we wouldn't expect sensorimotor knowledge to be relevant. But without such expectations we would fail to have an experience.[11]

What is of interest to us in these objections is that something is missing from a purely dispositional account. Something occurrent must accompany whatever dispositional state we are in to explain why we are having the perceptions we are experiencing when they are experienced. In short, what's missing is a conceptual representation.[12] Noë's model leaves out ventral stream processing. Just as perception is too varied and complex for a univocal "yes" answer to our question, it is also too complex for a simple "no" as suggested by Noë's model. Nonetheless, in developing our understanding of sensorimotor representation, Noë's view may well yield new cases in which it is not the aim of perception to provide (conceptual) representations at all, accurate or otherwise.

6 Conclusion

I have argued that there are circumscribed cases in which our sensory systems do not provide accurate representations, and that those representations are useful because they are not accurate, highlighting and making salient subtle but important differences in our environment. I have also pointed out an ambiguity in the notion of representation and shown that on the more natural reading of representation as conceptual representation – more natural since those are the representations of which we are aware – there are cases in which it is not the aim of perception to provide representations at all. Finally, there are at least some cases in which abstracting away from the particular perceptual circumstances to produce conceptual representations that can be used by more central cognitive processes results in inaccurate representations. So there are many circumstances in which it is not the aim of perception to provide accurate representations. In sum, perception is too complex and varied to yield a univocal answer to our question.

Acknowledgments

Thanks to Dan Blair, Kirk Ludwig, Gonzalo Munevar, John Nicholas, Robert Stainton, and Catherine Wearing for helpful feedback on these issues.

Notes

1 Our phenomenology regarding color similarity is represented in the color solid. A clear description of the color solid is given by Palmer (1999).
2 Durgin (2002) gives another example of perceived visual motion where there is none.
3 My thanks to Dan Blair for bringing these phonological examples to my attention.
4 The content of this discussion of thermoreceptors is based on Akins, 1996.
5 Cases in which sensorimotor representations are not accurate, such as those produced by the thermoreceptors, were presented in section 2.
6 It need not be the case that abstraction leads to inaccuracy since the process may produce accurate but less detailed representations. However, empirical results in the form of illusions such as the Tichener circles or the Müller-Lyre lines show that in many cases the representations are, in fact, inaccurate.
7 Central in Fodor's sense of being non-modular as opposed to the homuncular sense of central that Dennett (1991) rejects.
8 Schwitzgebel (2002, p. 35) makes the same distinction.
9 Many of the papers in Noë, 2002b address this issue.
10 Dennett (1991, p. 354) invites us to imagine entering a room covered with pictures of Marilyn Monroe. We sense being in a room full of Marilyns despite only attending to a very few. Yet having the impression we might continue to scan the room.
11 My view is that Noë can respond to Ludwig's objections by augmenting his view along the lines suggested in the text or those in Andy Clark, 2002. Ludwig also objects that the relevant dispositions cannot be conceptually necessary for perceptual experiences, but surely that was never Noë's claim. He is making an empirical claim not a conceptual one. This makes the relevant notion of possibility physical and not conceptual and takes much of the sting out of Ludwig's "fatal blow" to the sensorimotor model of perception. A full discussion of these issues is beyond the scope of this chapter.
12 Note that in characterizing Noë's view as not involving representations, Ludwig (chapter 15, IS THE AIM OF PERCEPTION TO PROVIDE ACCURATE REPRESENTATIONS?) is committed to taking our question to be about conceptual representations.

References and further reading

Aglioti, S., DeSouza, J. F., and Goodale, M. (1995). Size-contrast illusions deceive the eye but not the hand. *Current Biology*, 5/6, 679–85.
Akins, K. (1996). Of sensory systems and the "aboutness" of mental states. *Journal of Philosophy*, 93/7, 337–72.
Ballard, D. H. (2002). Our perception of the world has to be an illusion. *Journal of Consciousness Studies*, 9/5–6, 54–71.
Bridgeman, B. (2002). The grand illusion and petit illusions: Interactions of perception and sensory coding. *Journal of Consciousness Studies*, 9/5–6, 29–34.

Christopher Viger

Bermudez, J. L. (1999). Naturalism and conceptual norms. *Philosophical Quarterly*, 49/194, 77–85.

Clark, Andy (1997). *Being There: Putting Brain, Body, and World Together Again*. Cambridge, MA: Bradford/MIT Press.

— (2002). Is seeing all it seems? Action, reason and the grand illusion. *Journal of Consciousness Studies*, 9/5–6, 181–202.

Clark, Austen (2000). *A Theory of Sentience*. New York: Oxford University Press.

Cohen, J. (2002). The grand grand illusion illusion. *Journal of Consciousness Studies*, 9/5–6, 141–57.

Dennett, D. (1991). *Consciousness Explained*. Boston: Little, Brown.

— (2002). How could I be wrong? How wrong could I be? *Journal of Consciousness Studies*, 9/5–6, 13–16.

Durgin, F. H. (2002). The Tinkerbell effect: Motion perception and illusion. *Journal of Consciousness Studies*, 9/5–6, 88–101.

Geldard, F. A. and Sherrick, C. E. (1972). The cutaneous "rabbit": A perceptual illusion. *Science*, 178, 178–9.

Goodale, M. and Westwood, D. (2004). An evolving view of duplex vision: Separate but interacting cortical pathways for perception and action. *Current Opinion in Neurobiology*, 14, 1–9.

Kandel, E., Schwartz, J., and Jessell, T. (1995). *Essentials of Neural Science and Behavior*. Stamford, CT: Appleton & Lange.

Kenstowicz, M. (1994). *Phonology in Generative Grammar*. Malden, MA: Blackwell.

Kolers, P. A. and von Grünau, M. (1976). Shape and color in apparent motion. *Vision Research*, 16, 329–35.

Levine, D. T. (2002). Change blindness as visual metacognition. *Journal of Consciousness Studies*, 9/5–6, 111–30.

Mack, A. (2002). Is the visual world a grand illusion? A response. *Journal of Consciousness Studies*, 9/5–6, 102–10.

Mack, A. and Rock, I. (1998). *Inattentional Blindness*. Cambridge, MA: MIT Press.

Milner, A. D. and Goodale, M. (1995). *The Visual Brain in Action*. Oxford: Oxford University Press.

— and — (1998). The visual brain in action (precis). *Psyche*, 4, 1–12.

Munevar, G. (forthcoming). *A Theory of Wonder*.

Noë, A. (2001). Experience and the active mind. *Synthese*, 129/1, 41–60.

— (2002a). Is the visual world a grand illusion? *Journal of Consciousness Studies*, 9/5–6, 1–12.

— (ed.) (2002b). *Is the Visual World a Grand Illusion?* Special issue of *Journal of Consciousness Studies*, 9/5–6. Charlottesville, VA: Imprint Academic.

— (2002c). On what we see. *Pacific Philosophical Quarterly*, 83/1, 57–80.

— (2004). *Action in Perception*. Cambridge, MA: MIT Press.

Noë, A., Thompson, E., and Pessoa, L. (2000). Beyond the grand illusion: What change blindness really teaches us about vision. *Visual Cognition*, 7/1–3, 93–106.

O'Regan, J. K. and Noë, A. (2001). What it is like to see: A sensorimotor theory of perceptual experience. *Synthese*, 129/1, 79–103.

Palmer, S. (1999). Color, consciousness, and the isomorphism constraint. *Behavioral and Brain Sciences*, 22/6, 923–43.

Pylyshyn, Z. (2001). Visual indexes, preconceptual objects, and situated vision. *Cognition*, 80/1–2, 127–58.

— (2003). *Seeing and visualizing: It's not what you think*. Cambridge, MA: MIT Press.

The Case Against Accurate Representations

Schwitzgebel, E. (2002). How well do we know our own conscious experience? The case of visual imagery. *Journal of Consciousness Studies*, 9/5–6, 35–53.

Siewert, C. (2002). Is visual experience rich or poor? *Journal of Consciousness Studies*, 9/5–6, 131–40.

Simons, D. and Chabris, C. (1999). Gorillas in our midst: Sustained inattentional blindness for dynamic events. *Perception*, 28, 1059–74.

CAN MENTAL STATES, KNOWLEDGE IN PARTICULAR, BE DIVIDED INTO A NARROW COMPONENT AND A BROAD COMPONENT?

Can Cognition be Factorized into Internal and External Components?

Timothy Williamson

Platitudinously, cognitive science is the science of cognition. Cognition is usually defined as something like the process of acquiring, retaining, and applying knowledge. To a first approximation, therefore, cognitive science is the science of knowing. Knowing is a relation between the knower and the known. Typically, although not always, what is known involves the environment external to the knower. Thus knowing typically involves a relation between the agent and the external environment. It is not internal to the agent, for the internal may be the same whether or not it is related to the external in a way that constitutes knowing. Cognition enables agents to achieve their goals by adjusting their actions appropriately to the environment. Such adjustment requires what is internal to the agent to be in some sense in line with what is external; that matching depends on both internal and external sides. Thus if cognitive science were restricted to what is internal to the agent, it would lose sight of its primary object of study.

Although cognition depends on both the internal and the external, one can try to analyze it into internal and external factors. Call a state S *narrow* if and only if whether an agent is in S at a time t depends only on the total internal qualitative state of the agent at t, so that if one agent in one possible situation is internally an exact duplicate of another agent in another possible situation, then the first agent is in S in the first situation if and only if the second agent is in S in the second situation.[1] Call S *broad* if and only if it is not narrow. A state is *environmental* if and only if it depends only on the total state of the environment external to the given agent (as it were, the total internal state of the external environment) at the relevant time. The factorizing strategy attempts to analyze cognitive states into combinations of narrow states and environmental states (likewise for cognitive processes). If the strategy succeeds, it may be tempting to regard the narrow states that emerge from that analysis as the only strictly mental or psychological states, at least for the purposes of cognitive science. If the strategy fails, it will be tempting to regard some broad cognitive states as themselves strictly mental for the purposes of cognitive science. *Internalism* is here the view that (for the purposes of cognitive science) all mental states are narrow. *Externalism* is the negation of internalism. Of course, what matters is not so much how we use the word "mental" as whether the factorizing strategy succeeds at all.

For present purposes let us not worry about exactly what counts as internal: (internal to the brain or merely to the body, and "internal" in what sense?). A radical view is that there is no natural boundary between the internal and the external: they somehow flow into each other. That would be bad news for internalism rather than externalism, since only the former attributes a central significance to the internal-external boundary with respect to the mental. Thus it is legitimate to assume a natural internal-external boundary for the sake of an argument *against* internalism.[2] But given that plausible assumption, internalism may seem an obviously attractive or even compelling view. Isn't the aim of cognitive science precisely to identify the internal mechanisms that are the contribution of mind, and to understand how their inter-action with the external environment produces knowledge?

The aim of this chapter is to sketch an argument that the internalist program of factorization rests on a myopic view of what it would take to understand the role of cognition in guiding action. The cognitive states that explain action at an appropriate level of generality are not merely broad; they are broad in a way that makes their factorization into narrow and environmental constituents impossible in principle.

The internalism-externalism debate has ramified in many directions over recent decades. It would be hopeless to attempt here to survey all the arguments that have been advanced in favour of internalism. Instead, one central line of externalist thought will be developed. That should give the reader a sufficient clue as to where the internalist arguments go wrong.[3]

Section 1 considers two main ways in which the intentional states of folk psychology as delineated by natural language predicates are broad. Internalists may respond by denying that those folk psychological states are strictly mental in the sense relevant to cognitive science and attempting to factorize them into narrow and environmental components. Section 2 sketches some abstract structural considerations, to explain why the factorizing strategy is problematic in principle. Section 3 develops that argument in more detail by reference to some examples. Section 4 suggests a more general moral about cognition.

1 Broad Attitudes and Broad Contents

Knowing is central to the subject matter of cognitive science; it is also a central source of broad intentional states. Consider, for instance, the state of knowing that one is holding a glass of water, the state such that, necessarily, one is in it if and only if one knows that one is holding a glass of water. Two agents in different possible situations may be exact internal duplicates even though one of them knows that she is holding a glass of water while the other merely has a false belief that she

Timothy Williamson

is holding a glass of water (actually it is gin). One cannot know something false, although one can believe falsely that one knows it. Thus the state of knowing that one is holding a glass of water is broad.

Knowing is a *factive* attitude, in the sense that, necessarily, one has it only to truths. Other factive attitudes include seeing and remembering (in the usual senses of those terms). Unless the glass contains water, you cannot see that it contains water; if you are misperceiving, you only think that you can see that it contains water. Unless you drank water yesterday, you cannot remember that you drank water yesterday; if you are misremembering, you only think that you remember that you drank water yesterday. By contrast, the attitude of believing is non-factive; false belief is possible, indeed actual and widespread. Arguably, knowing is the most general factive attitude, the one that subsumes all others: any factive attitude is a form of knowing.

In unfavorable circumstances, for instance when they are being hoaxed, agents falsely believe that P, and believe that they know that P, without being in a position to know that they do not know that P. Thus agents are not always in a position to know which knowledge states they are in; such states lack first-person transparency. If first-person transparency were a necessary condition for being a mental state, know-ledge states would not be mental. But why impose any such condition on mentality? There is no obvious inconsistency in the hypothesis that someone has dark desires without being in a position to know that he has them: for example, the opportunity to put them into effect may not arise. It is a commonplace of cognitive science that agents' beliefs as to their mental states are sometimes badly mistaken. That is not to deny that we often know without observation whether we are in a given mental state: but then we often know without observation whether we are in a given know-ledge state. The partial transparency of knowing is consistent with its being a mental state.

Do non-factive attitudes such as believing yield narrow mental states? Whatever the glass contains, one can *believe* that it contains water. Nevertheless, famous extern-alist arguments show that the content of intentional states can yield a broad mental state even when the attitude to that content is non-factive. Indeed, the current debate between internalism and externalism in the philosophy of mind originally arose with respect to the contents of the attitudes rather than the attitudes themselves.

We can adapt Hilary Putnam's classic example to argue that even the state of believing that one is holding a glass of water is broad.[4] Imagine a planet Twin-Earth exactly like Earth except that the liquid observed in rivers, seas, and so on is not H_2O but XYZ, which has the same easily observable properties as H_2O but an utterly different chemical composition. Thus XYZ is not water. However, the thought experi-ment is set in 1750, before the chemical composition of water was known. Oscar on Earth and Twin-Oscar on Twin-Earth are internal duplicates of each other; they are in exactly the same narrow states. Oscar is holding a glass of H_2O; Twin-Oscar is holding a glass of XYZ. Since H_2O is water and XYZ is not:

1 Oscar is holding a glass of water.
2 Twin-Oscar is not holding a glass of water.

They both express a belief by saying "I am holding a glass of water." Since Oscar uses the word "water" to refer to water, we can report his belief thus:

3   Oscar believes that he [Oscar] is holding a glass of water.

Suppose (for a *reductio ad absurdum*) that believing that one is holding a glass of water is a narrow state. By (3), Oscar is in that state. By hypothesis, Oscar and Twin-Oscar are in exactly the same narrow states. Therefore Twin-Oscar is also in that state:

4   Twin-Oscar believes that he [Twin-Oscar] is holding a glass of water.

Now consider elementary schemas governing true and false belief:

T   If S believes that P, S believes truly that P if and only if P.
F   If S believes that P, S believes falsely that P if and only if not P.

Here is an instance of (T):

5   If Oscar believes that he [Oscar] is holding a glass of water, Oscar believes truly that he [Oscar] is holding a glass of water if and only if he [Oscar] is holding a glass of water.

Here is an instance of (F):

6   If Twin-Oscar believes that he [Twin-Oscar] is holding a glass of water, Twin-Oscar believes falsely that he [Twin-Oscar] is holding a glass of water if and only if he [Twin-Oscar] is not holding a glass of water.

From (1), (3), and (5) we easily conclude:

7   Oscar believes truly that he [Oscar] is holding a glass of water.

By the same token, from (2), (4), and (6) we conclude:

8   Twin-Oscar believes falsely that he [Twin-Oscar] is holding a glass of water.

But (7) and (8) imply an implausible asymmetry between Oscar and Twin-Oscar. There is no more reason to impute error to Twin-Oscar than to Oscar. They manage equally well in their home environments. Since (1), (2), (3), (5), and (6) are clearly true, the culprit must be (4). Since (4) follows from (3) and the assumption that believing that one is holding a glass of water is a narrow state, we conclude that believing that one is holding a glass of water is a broad state, not a narrow one.

The Putnam-inspired argument generalizes from believing to all sorts of other propositional attitudes, such as wondering, desiring, and intending. It also generalizes beyond natural kind concepts like *water* to a huge array of contents that turn out to depend on the agent's natural or social environment, or simply on the identity of the agent.

For example, the qualitatively identical twins Tweedledum and Tweedledee both speak truly when they simultaneously utter the words "Only I believe that *I* won"; each correctly self-attributes a belief the other lacks. Similarly with perceptual demonstratives: both twins speak truly when they point at each other and simultaneously utter the words "Only he believes that *he* won." Intentional content as attributed in natural languages depends on reference, which in turn depends on causal and other relations of the agent that are left undetermined by all internal qualities. The broadness of reference extends further to folk psychological relational states such as seeing Vienna, thinking about Vienna, and loving or hating Vienna. If intentionality (aboutness) is the mark of the mental, and our thoughts are typically about the external environment, then our mental states are typically broad.

Thus both the contents of folk psychological intentional states and the attitudes to those contents make the states broad. Of course, that does not prevent internalists from postulating a core of narrow mental states for the purposes of cognitive science and trying to identify them by more theoretical means. But it is not obvious that such a core exists. Granted, when human agents are in an intentional state they are also in some underlying narrow physical state or other, but it does not follow that the latter is intentional in any useful sense. We can clarify the issue by considering the role of cognitive states in the causal explanation of action.

2 Explaining and Capturing Significant Generalizations

Suppose that we are trying to explain an agent's action in terms of the state of the world at a prior time *t*. A first internalist hypothesis is that all we really need consider is the agent's internal state at *t*. If causation is local, that will determine what she does (insofar as quantum mechanics allows it to be determined in advance at all); other aspects of the state of the world make a difference only to whether what she does gets her what she wants.

That internalist hypothesis raises a question about the individuation of actions. Suppose that the agent's action was *drinking from this stream here*. That action was not determined purely by her total internal state. She could have been in that state even if she had seen a numerically distinct but qualitatively identical stream, or been the victim of an illusion with no stream nearby. In the former case the same internal state would not have led to her drinking from *this* stream; in the latter it would not have led to her drinking from any stream at all. Many actions are individuated broadly and are consequently not determined by preceding narrow mental states (Evans, 1982, p. 203). Of course, the internalist will now insist on individuating the action to be explained in narrow terms, for instance as *making as if to drink from a stream of this qualitative appearance*. There is a danger of a stand-off here, with the internalist accusing the externalist of begging the question by individuating the action to be explained broadly and the externalist in turn accusing the internalist of begging the question by individuating the action to be explained narrowly. The externalist can point out that the content of the agent's intention typically corresponds to the broad individuation of the action in terms of the external objects that it involves; if we are trying to explain an intentional action, don't we need to explain the action as specified in the intention? The internalist may reply that the factorizing strategy must be applied to the agent's intention too. Alternatively, the internalist explanation may be restricted to a class of basic actions more primitive than either *drinking from this stream here* or *making as if to drink from a stream of this qualitative appearance*.

Even if actions are narrowly individuated, other problems arise for the attempt to explain them on the basis of the agent's prior internal state. Action is typically not instantaneous, and not merely because there is no such moment as the one immediately preceding the moment of action if time is dense. It takes time even to bend one's head until one's lips touch the water and more time to drink. That is enough time to spot piranha fish in the water and withdraw before completing the action. Thus the internal state of the agent at t does not even determine whether she will go through the sequence of internal states corresponding to drinking in some brief interval shortly after t. Again, the internalist may respond by attempting to analyze extended actions such as bending and drinking into sequences of more basic actions, each to be explained in terms of an "immediately" preceding internal state of the agent.

To restrict ourselves to concatenating explanations of basic actions would drastically curtail our explanatory ambitions. Consider a tourist in a strange town whose camera and passport have just been stolen. We may be able to explain on general grounds why he will sooner or later get to the local police station, whose location he does not yet know, without assuming anything specific about the layout of the town, his current position in it, or his beliefs about those things. By contrast, if we concatenate explanations of the basic actions by which, step by step, he actually gets to the local police station in terms of "immediately" preceding internal states, we shall need to invoke a mass of detailed extra assumptions about the sequence of his mental states (for example, his perceptions of the streets around him and of the responses to his questions about the way to the nearest police station) far beyond anything that the more general explanation need assume. Thus by moving down to the level of basic actions we lose significant generalizations that are available at the higher level. If the layout of the town, his position in it or the responses to his questions had been different, he would have gone through a different sequence of basic actions, but he would still have got to the police station in the end. To understand cognition at an appropriate level of generality, we often need to understand non-basic actions themselves, not merely the sequences of basic actions that realize them on particular occasions. Since the performance of non-basic actions depends on the environment as well as the agent, they are not to be explained solely in terms of the agent's internal states.

Appeals to the locality of causation do not motivate the idea that only narrow states of the agent at t are causally relevant to effects that are not complete until some time after t, for environmental states at t are also causally relevant to those effects. Rather, the issue is whether the causally relevant states at t can be factorized into narrow states and environmental states.

We should therefore assume that when we are trying to explain the agent's action in terms of the state of the world at t, both the state of the agent at t and the state of the external environment at t are potentially relevant. Nevertheless, it might be argued, the factorization strategy is bound to succeed, for the *total* (maximally specific) narrow state of the agent at t and the *total* environmental state (state of the external

Timothy Williamson

environment) at t together determine the total state of the whole world at t (no difference in the latter without a difference in one of the former), which in turn determines the action (insofar as it is determined at t at all). Let us grant the determination claim, although it is not completely uncontentious – in principle there might be global states of the whole world not determined by the combination of states local to the agent and states local to the external environment. Even so, when we explain an action we do not assume a particular maximally specific state of the world at t. It is not just that we cannot know exactly what the state of the world was at t. Even if we did know, it would be methodologically undesirable to build all that knowledge into our explanation of the action, because the maximal specificity of the assumption implies the minimal generality of the explanation. It would not apply to any of those alternative states of the world that would have led to the same action. A significant generalization would again have been missed. Compare Putnam's example:

> A peg (1 inch square) goes through a 1 inch square hole and not through a 1 inch round hole. Explanation: (?) The peg consists of such-and-such elementary particles in such-and-such a lattice arrangement. By computing all the trajectories we can get applying forces to the peg (subject to the constraint that the forces must not be so great as to distort the peg or the holes) in the fashion of the famous Laplacian super-mind, we determine that some trajectory takes the peg through the square hole, and no trajectories take it through the round hole. (Covering laws: the laws of physics.) (Putnam, 1978, p. 42)

In our cases of interest, what matters is whether an explanation that assumes an unspecific state of the world at t (very roughly, the one necessary and sufficient for the action to be taken) can be analyzed into an explanation that assumes a narrow state of the agent at t and an environmental state at t, not both of them maximally specific.[5]

Some but not all states of the world can be analyzed in the way that internalists require. To see this, consider a very simple model with just three possible maximally specific narrow states of the agent, I1, I2, and I3, and three possible maximally specific environmental states, E1, E2, and E3. Any possible narrow state is compatible with any possible environmental state, so there are just nine possible maximally specific combined internal-external states of the whole world, each of the form Ii&Ej. An example that can be analyzed as the conjunction of a narrow and an environmental state is the unspecific disjunctive state (I1&E1) $\vee$ (I1&E2) $\vee$ (I2&E1) $\vee$ (I2&E2), which the world is in when and only when it is in one of the specific states I1&E1, I1&E2, I2&E1, and I2&E2. That unspecific state is equivalent to the state (I1 $\vee$ I2) & (E1 $\vee$ E2), which the world is in when and only when the agent is in the unspecific narrow state I1 $\vee$ I2 and the external environment is in the unspecific state E1 $\vee$ E2. Contrast that with the unspecific state of the world (I1&E1) $\vee$ (I2&E2) $\vee$ (I3&E3), which cannot be analyzed in the required way. To see that, suppose the opposite. Then (I1&E1) $\vee$ (I2&E2) $\vee$ (I3&E3) is equivalent to some conjunction I&E, where I is a narrow state and E is an environmental state. I must be equivalent to a disjunction of some subset of I1, I2, and I3. If I1 is not in the subset then I1 excludes I, so I1&E1 excludes I&E; but I1&E1 cannot exclude I&E, for I1&E1 is possible and is a disjunct of the disjunction that is equivalent by hypothesis to I&E. Thus I1 is in the disjunction that is equivalent to I, so I1 implies I. By a parallel argument, E2 implies E. Therefore I1&E2 implies I&E; but I1&E2 cannot imply I&E, for I1&E2 is possible and excluded by each disjunct of the disjunction that is equivalent by hypothesis to I&E. So the original supposition leads to a contradiction. Hence (I1&E1) ∨ (I2&E2) ∨ (I3&E3) is not equivalent to the conjunction of a narrow state and an environmental state. Thus whether a state of the world is equivalent to the conjunction of a narrow state and an environmental state depends on whether that state of the world is like (I1&E1) ∨ (I1&E2) ∨ (I2&E1) ∨ (I2&E2) or like (I1&E1) ∨ (I2&E2) ∨ (I3&E3).

Call a state *composite* if and only if it is equivalent to the conjunction of a narrow state and an environmental state. All narrow states trivially count as composite, because they are equivalent to the conjunction of themselves and the maximally unspecific environmental state that always obtains; but not all composite states are narrow. For example, I1&E1 is composite but not narrow. Call a state *prime* if and only if it is not composite. Trivially, all prime states are broad; but not all broad states are prime. I1&E1 is broad but not prime. In the toy model, with nine possible maximally specific states of the world, there are 512 states altogether, of which 8 are narrow and 504 broad, 50 composite and 462 prime.[6]

We already have a very general reason to expect that many cognitive states will be prime. For we noted that cognition is supposed to help agents achieve their goals by interacting more successfully with the environment, which typically requires their narrow states to be in some sense in line with environmental states. That idea is vague, but it implies at least this much: in the relevant respect, a specific narrow state I1 may be in line with a specific environmental state E1 but not with a specific alternative environmental state E2, while a specific alternative narrow state I2 is in line with E2 but not with E1. Now consider the cognitive state C that the agent is in when and only when her specific internal state is in line with the specific environmental state in the given way. Thus the conjunctive states I1&E1 and I2&E2 imply C, while the conjunctive states I1&E2 and I2&E1 exclude C. But then an argument just like that two paragraphs back shows that C must be prime. On purely structural grounds, the state of being in some total narrow state or other that matches the total environmental state in some given way cannot be equivalent to the conjunction of a narrow state and an environmental state, however unspecific. We will see later how to apply this abstract point to particular cases.

Could an internalist object that although a state such as (I1&E1) ∨ (I2&E2) ∨ (I3&E3) is prime, it has still been analyzed into a disjunction of conjunctions of narrow states and environmental states, so the factorizing strategy remains viable? That objection trivializes the factorizing strategy in several ways:

First, the relevant disjunctions will in practice have infinitely many disjuncts, or at least vastly more than we can list. It is unlikely that such analyses will be available to cognitive science in usable form.

Second, the possibility of such analyses was not derived from any distinctive feature of the internal-external boundary, but merely from the quite general idea that for any boundary whatsoever, the total global state of the world is fixed by the conjunction of the total local state on one side of the boundary and the total local state on the other side. That holds even for utterly *ad hoc*, arbitrary, unnatural

Timothy Williamson

boundaries. Thus the mere possibility of such analyses is uninformative. That a cognitive state is equivalent to a disjunction of conjunctions of states tailored to any one of those gerrymandered or irrelevant boundaries shows nothing interesting about its underlying nature.

Third, and most important, if a prime state C is equivalent to a disjunction of conjunctions of narrow states and environmental states, it does not follow that an explanation that postulates C can be reduced to an explanation that postulates a narrow state and an environmental state. That would follow only on the further assumption that C is equivalent to the conjunction of those states, in which case C is composite, contrary to hypothesis. Of course, on any particular occasion on which C obtains, so too does some specific conjunction Ii&Ej that implies C (but not vice versa), where Ii is narrow and Ej environmental. But it would be a mistake to conclude that the "real explanation" invokes Ii&Ej rather than C. For the explanation that invokes Ii&Ej typically involves a drastic loss of generality. It applies only to one specific type of case, whereas the explanation that invoked C covered a greater variety of cases. As already emphasized, significant generality is a crucial virtue in scientific explanations. The moral is that when an explanation assumes a given prime state, there need be no pair of a narrow state and an environmental state by assuming which one can do the same explanatory work.

Some explanations that invoke a composite state achieve generality on one side of the internal-external boundary by sacrificing generality on the other side. For example, let I be the disjunction of all total narrow states that, conjoined with the total environmental state Ei, yield the outcome of interest. I has some generality, since a range of internal states in that environment yield that outcome. Since I too is narrow, the state I&Ei is composite, and yields the outcome to be explained. But even this explanation involves an undesirable loss of generality: most obviously concerning the environmental state, but also concerning the agent's internal state, since I excludes internal states that yield the outcome only in combination with environmental states other than Ei. Similarly, let E be the disjunction of all total environmental states that, conjoined with the total internal state Ii, yield the outcome of interest. E has some generality, since Ii yields the outcome in a range of environmental states. The composite state Ii&E also yields the outcome to be explained. But this explanation too involves an undesirable loss of generality: most obviously concerning the internal state, but also concerning the environmental state, since E excludes environmental states in which only another internal state yields the outcome.

Whichever way we turn, we attain the requisite level of generality in explaining action only if our explanations cite prime states of agents.

3 Examples of Prime States

To argue that a cognitive state is composite, we need only find a narrow state and an environmental state of which it is the conjunction. But how can we argue that a cognitive state is prime? We cannot go through all possible conjunctions of narrow states and environmental states and argue case by case that it is not equivalent to any of them. A more useful criterion is this:

PRIME A state S is prime if and only if some narrow state I and some environmental state E are separately compatible with S but I&E is incompatible with S.[7]

Suppose that we can find possible combinations of narrow states I1 and I2 and environmental states E1 and E2 such that I1&E1 and I2&E2 imply the cognitive state C while I1&E2 excludes C. Then I1 and E2 are compatible with C while I1&E2 is incompatible with C. Consequently, by PRIME, C is prime. Furthermore, PRIME implies that for each prime state there is a pair like I1 and E2.

For a simple example, let C be the unspecific state of *knowing which direction home is in* (in egocentric space). Consider two possible scenarios. In scenario 1, you know which direction home is in by knowing that home is straight in front of you. Thus home *is* straight in front of you, and you believe that it is. Call your narrow and environmental states in scenario 1, I1 and E1 respectively. In scenario 2, you know which direction home is in by knowing that home is straight behind you. Thus home *is* straight behind you, and you believe that it is. Call your narrow and environmental states in scenario 2, I2 and E2 respectively. Narrow state I1 is compatible with C because you are simultaneously in I1 and C in scenario 1. Environmental state E2 is compatible with C because you are simultaneously in E2 and C in scenario 2. But the conjunctive state I1&E2 is incompatible with C, because if I1&E2 obtains you do not know which direction home is in; rather, you believe that home is straight in front of you (by I1) while in fact it is straight behind you (by E2); you have a mere false belief as to which direction home is in. Consequently, by PRIME, C is prime. Knowing which direction home is in is not equivalent to the conjunction of a narrow state and an environmental state.

For another example, let C* be the state of *consciously thinking about Rover* (not necessarily under the verbal mode of presentation "Rover"). Again, consider two possible scenarios. In scenario 1*, you can see two very similar dogs, Rover on your right and Mover on your left. You are consciously thinking about Rover, visually presented as "that dog on my right" and in no other way; you are not consciously thinking about Mover at all. Call your narrow and environmental states in scenario 1*, I1* and E1* respectively. In scenario 2*, you can see Rover on your left and Mover on your right. You are consciously thinking about Rover, visually presented as "that dog on my left" and in no other way; you are not consciously thinking about Mover at all. Call your narrow state and environmental states in scenario 2*, I2* and E2* respectively. Narrow state I1* is compatible with C* because you are simultaneously in I1* and C* in scenario 1*. Environmental state E2* is compatible with C* because you are simultaneously in E2* and C* in scenario 2*. But the conjunctive state I1*&E2* is incompatible with C*, because if I1*&E2* obtains you are not consciously thinking about Rover; rather, you are consciously thinking about Mover, visually presented as "that dog on my right." Consequently, by PRIME, C* is prime. Consciously thinking about Rover is not equivalent to the conjunction of a narrow state and an environmental state.

It is not difficult to multiply such examples. In general, the folk psychological intentional states individuated by natural language predicates tend to be prime. But do those states matter for purposes of cognitive science?

Timothy Williamson

Much depends on whether we are interested in short-term or long-term effects. The short-term effects of merely believing that home is straight in front of you may be the same as the short-term effects of knowing that home is straight in front of you. For example, if you want to go home, you take a step forward. Thus what the internalist may conceive as the narrow state of believing that home is straight in front of you may be more relevant in the short term than the broad state of knowing that home is in front of you. But the long-term effects are likely to be quite different. If you believe falsely that home is straight in front of you, you will not get there by going forward. Nor are the long-term differences confined to your broad states when you get home; even your internal states are likely to be different if you do not get home. It may be a matter of life and death.

Of course, internalists can appeal to the composite state (as they may see it) of believing truly that home is straight in front of you, the supposedly narrow conjunct being the state of believing that home is straight in front of you and the environmental conjunct the state of home's being straight in front of you. But even if you believe truly that home is straight in front of you without knowing that it is, for example because that true belief is based on a false belief about where you are, and home is many miles further on through the forest than you think, then you are liable subsequently to discover the falsity of the belief on which your true belief is based and abandon the latter.[8] Thus the long-term effects even of believing truly without knowing are not generally the same as the long-term effects of knowing. If we are interested in whether the agent actually gets home, the state of knowing which direction home is in has a significance that cannot be subsumed under the significance of having a belief as to which direction home is in, or even of having a true such belief. Of course, if the agent maintains a true belief as to which direction home is in all the way home, that trivially suffices to get home, but appealing to the maintenance of that true belief throughout the journey fails to address the original challenge, which was to understand the long-term effects of the agent's cognitive state at a fixed time t. Whether the agent's true beliefs at t are likely to be maintained after t is part of what we are trying to understand in terms of the agent's cognitive state at t; merely assuming that they are maintained does not help us answer that question.

The externalist can produce a more general explanation by invoking the state of knowing which direction home is in, as opposed to the more specific state of knowing that home is straight ahead. It would not help the internalist to match that generality by invoking the state of having a true belief as to which direction home is in, as opposed to the more specific state of believing truly that home is straight ahead. For the state of having a true belief as to which direction home is in is itself prime, as one can show by using scenarios 1 and 2 above. Invoking that prime state does not yield an explanation that reduces to one that just invokes a narrow state and an environmental state. As usual, the explanatory work is done by the prime state itself. Moreover, we have already seen that the substitution of true belief for knowledge involves explanatory loss.

Similar considerations apply to the state of consciously thinking about Rover. The short-term effects of consciously thinking "that dog on my right" may be the same whether doing so constitutes consciously thinking about Rover, about Mover, or about nothing at all (in case of hallucination). For example, you may move to the right. That may differ from what you do if you realize the state of consciously thinking about Rover (in scenario 2*) by thinking "that dog on my left." Thus what internalists conceive as the narrow state of consciously thinking with that visual mode of presentation may be more relevant to short-term effects than is the broad state of consciously thinking about Rover. But the long-term effects of consciously thinking with that visual mode of presentation may depend critically on whether doing so constitutes thinking about Rover. In one case, the effect may be that you buy Rover; in the other, that you buy Mover, a dog of similar visual appearance but totally different personality, or discover that you were hallucinating. From then onwards, further developments are liable to diverge increasingly, even with respect to your narrow states. Similarly, the long-term effects of consciously thinking about Rover may be the same whether you think of him as "that dog on my right" or "that dog on my left." You may be more likely to buy him either way.

Obviously, the long-term effects under discussion are highly sensitive to the agent's other mental states, such as desires. Nevertheless, a pattern emerges. The more short term the effects we consider, the greater the explanatory relevance of narrow states. As we consider longer-term effects, narrow states tend to lose that explanatory advantage and the intentional states of folk psychology come into their own. Those states are typically not just broad but prime. We have already seen that if we ignore long-term effects we fail to capture significant general patterns in cognition. Thus prime cognitive states are no mere curiosity of folk psychology: they are central to the understanding of long-term cognitive effects.

When we investigate cognitive effects that depend on continuous feedback from a complex environment, we cannot expect to lay down strict laws. We can hope to identify probabilistic tendencies, perhaps comparable to those of evolutionary biology at species level. For example, we might want to investigate the general cognitive effects of literacy (as a means of public communication and not just of private note taking). In doing so, we seek generalizations that hold across different languages and scripts. But literacy is itself a prime cognitive state, for it involves a kind of match between the individual's dispositions to produce and respond to written marks and those prevalent in the appropriate social environment. The narrow states that go with mastery of written communication in English-speaking countries today did not go with mastery of written communication in Babylon 3000 years ago, and vice versa. Knowing how to read is not a narrow or even composite state; it is prime and broad.[9] Perhaps recent developments in cognitive science in the study of embodied, situated, and distributed cognition, particularly cognition that relies on continuous feedback loops into the external environment, can be interpreted as investigations of prime cognitive states.[10]

4 Success-Oriented and Success-Neutral Explanatory Strategies

We have seen that the two main sources of broadness in the intentional states of folk psychology – factive attitudes and environmentally determined contents – are

Timothy Williamson

also sources of primeness, in ways that make those states especially fit to explain long-term effects at an appropriate level of generality.[11] In particular, such states as knowing, seeing, remembering, and referring play key roles in those explanations. The appeal to such states in understanding cognition raises a general question about the nature of the theoretical enterprise. For words like "know," "see," "remember," and "refer" are *success terms*. They describe what happens when cognition goes well. Even if we replace the ordinary language terms by more theoretical ones for the purposes of cognitive science, the argument of previous sections suggests that some of those more theoretical terms will need to have a relevantly similar character. To give success terms a central role in our theorizing about cognition is to understand it in relation to its successes. That is not to ignore the failures; rather, we understand them *as* failures, deviations from success. For example, to a first approximation, we can treat merely believing that P as merely being in a state with the content that P that the agent cannot distinguish from knowing that P; having it merely visually appear to one that P as merely being in a state with the content that P that one cannot distinguish from seeing that P; and misremembering that P as merely being in a state with the content that P that one cannot distinguish from remembering that P.[12] Again, we might understand cases of reference failure as cases merely indistinguishable by the agent from cases of reference. That is to employ a sort of teleological strategy for understanding cognition. The internalist follows the opposite strategy, starting from states that are neutral between success and failure, and then trying to distinguish the two classes by adding environmental conditions.

The externalist's point is emphatically not to deny that the successes and the failures have something in common. Indeed, the failures were all described as merely indistinguishable by the agent from successes; since everything is indistinguishable from itself, it follows that both successes and failures are indistinguishable by the agent from successes. The point is rather that the failures differ internally among themselves, and that what unifies them into a theoretically useful category with the successes is only their relation to those successes. For example, many different total internal states are compatible with its perceptually appearing to an agent that there is food ahead; what they have in common, on this view, is their relation to cases in which the agent perceives that there is food ahead ("perceive" is factive).

To use a traditional analogy, consider the relation between real and counterfeit money. Uncontroversially, a counterfeit banknote can in principle be an exact internal duplicate of a real banknote. The internalist strategy corresponds to taking as theoretically fundamental not the category of (real) money but the category that contains both real money and all internal duplicates of it.[13] One would then have to circumscribe the real money by further constraints (presumably concerning origin and economic role). But that strategy seems quite perverse, for being real money cannot usefully be analyzed as having a certain intrinsic property and in addition satisfying some further constraints: those further constraints do all the theoretical work. Indeed, the property of being money is prime, in the sense that by a criterion like PRIME it is not the conjunction of a purely intrinsic property and a purely extrinsic one, for being money is compatible with being gold, and it is compatible with being in a social environment in which only silver counts as money, but it is incompatible with the conjunction of those two properties. It is no use complaining that real money and its internal duplicates have the same causal powers. For purposes of economic theory, the category of real money is primary, the category of counterfeit money must be understood as parasitic on it, and the category of all internal duplicates of real money is of no interest whatsoever.[14]

Of course, the analogy is not decisive. But it does show that the factorizing strategy is not always compelling or even attractive. Each application of it must be argued on its individual merits. The argument of this chapter has been that, for the study of cognition, the factorizing strategy is often inappropriate. Sometimes, we need to use concepts like *knowledge* and *reference* (or *money*) in our explanations, and we cannot replace them without loss of valuable generality by conjunctions of purely internal and purely external constituents.

Acknowledgments

Thanks to Rob Stainton for helpful comments on an earlier draft.

Notes

1   On some alternative definitions, a state S is "narrow" if and only if S has no existential implications outside the subject of S (Putnam influentially defined "methodological solipsism" as "the assumption that no psychological state presupposes the existence of any individual other than the subject to whom that state is ascribed," 1975, p. 220). Even when clarified, such definitions awkwardly deprive the class of "narrow" states of closure properties required by the conception of such states as forming a self-enclosed domain. In particular, they permit the conjunction of two "narrow" states not to be "narrow": if N1 and N2 are two incompatible "narrow" states, and B a non-"narrow" state, then the disjunctive states N1 ∨ B and N2 ∨ B are also "narrow" by such definitions, since N1 and N2 imply any existential implication of N1 ∨ B and N2 ∨ B respectively; but (N1 ∨ B) & (N2 ∨ B) is not "narrow," for it is equivalent to B. By contrast, definitions like that in the text, on which the narrow is whatever supervenes on the internal, automatically make conjunctions of narrow states narrow.

2   In the same spirit, the text treats both narrow states and environmental states as synchronic. That is a significant over-simplification. Whether one is in a given folk psychological intentional state is typically sensitive to causal origins. Although reference cannot be defined in causal terms, reference to particulars and kinds in the environment is still normally carried by causal connections to them through memory and perception. Similarly, although knowledge cannot be defined in causal terms, the difference between knowing and merely believing is often partly constituted by the presence or absence of an appropriate causal connection. In applying the internal-external distinction, we must therefore decide how to classify the agent's past internal history. Since the rationale for drawing the distinction depends on the assumed locality of causation, which is both spatial and temporal, the natural ruling is that the past history of both agent and environment counts as external for purposes of distinguishing broad from narrow. This makes the conception of the internal and the external as independent dimensions harder to maintain, since the external includes all the causal antecedents of the internal. That complication is consistent with the conclusions in the text.

Timothy Williamson

3   Williamson, 2000 develops the argument of this chapter in greater detail with reference to epistemology, and responds to some internalist challenges.

4   Compare Putnam, 1975, where the argument (formulated rather differently) is directed only against internalism about linguistic meaning, and takes internalism about psychological states for granted. Burge, 1979 made the natural generalization to psychological states, which Putnam later accepted. See Pessin et al., 1996 for more on the debate.

5   The gloss "necessary and sufficient for the action to be taken" is indeed very rough, for we do not expect an explanation of an outcome to generalize to cases in which the same outcome occurred for completely different reasons. Satisfying explanations have a certain unity and naturalness; they do not rope together essentially disparate cases. Nevertheless, subject to this vague constraint, the point stands that generality is an explanatory virtue. For more on the importance of generality in causally relevant properties and the trade-off between generality and naturalness see Yablo, 1992, 1997, 2005.

6   More generally, if there are m possible maximally specific narrow states and n possible maximally specific environmental states, and the possible maximally specific states of the world correspond to all pairs of the former and the latter, then there are 2^m narrow states, 2^n environmental states and 2^{mn} states of the word altogether. For simplicity, the calculation includes both the universal state (which always obtains) and the null state (which never obtains); they are the only states that are both narrow and environmental. The null state is composite; every non-null composite state corresponds to a unique combination of a non-null narrow state and a non-null environmental state, so there are $1 + (2^m-1)(2^n-1)$ composite states altogether. In the toy model in the text, $m = n = 3$.

7   To establish PRIME, we assume *Free Recombination*, the principle that any possible narrow state is compatible with any possible environmental state. Although this principle is contentious, it is natural for the internalist to assume it, since it reflects the internalist analysis of the state of the world into two logically independent dimensions, the internal state of the agent and the external state of the environment. Thus it is fair to the internalist to assume Free Recombination. Moreover, it is independently plausible that Free Recombination holds at least to a first approximation. We can now argue for PRIME. ($\Leftarrow$) Suppose that some narrow state I and environmental state E are separately compatible with S but I&E is not, yet S is not prime. Thus for some narrow state I* and environmental state E*, S is equivalent to I*&E*. Hence I is compatible with I*&E*, so I&I* is a possible narrow state. Similarly, since E is compatible with I*&E*, E&E* is a possible environmental state. Therefore, by Free Recombination, I&I* is compatible with E&E*, so I&E is compatible with I*&E*, and so with S, contrary to hypothesis. ($\Rightarrow$) Suppose that for every narrow state I and environmental state E, if I and E are separately compatible with S, so is I&E. Consider all conjunctions of the form I&E that imply S, where I and E are possible maximally specific narrow and environmental states respectively. Let I* be the (infinite) disjunction of all first conjuncts of such conjunctions and E* the (infinite) disjunction of all second conjuncts. Thus I* is narrow and E* environmental. S implies I*&E*, for if S obtains so does some conjunction I&E that implies S, where I and E are possible maximally specific narrow and environmental states respectively; hence I implies I* and E implies E*, so I&E implies I*&E*, so I*&E* obtains. Conversely, I*&E* implies S, for if I*&E* obtains then for some possible maximally specific narrow states I and I** and environmental states E and E**, I&E also obtains and both I&E** and I**&E entail S; both I&E** and I**&E are possible by Free Recombination, so I and E are both compatible with S; therefore, by hypothesis, I&E is compatible with S; since I and E are maximally specific, I&E entails S, so S obtains. Thus S is equivalent to I*&E* and so is not prime.

8   Gettier, 1963 has classic examples of true beliefs that fail to constitute knowledge because they are essentially based on false premises.

9   See Stanley and Williamson, 2001 for a general argument that knowing how is a species of knowing that. If so, the discussion of propositional knowledge applies to knowledge how as a topic for cognitive science.

10 See Clark, 1997; Hurley, 1998; and Gigerenzer et al., 1999. For example, "smart" as used in Gigerenzer's title presumably refers to a prime state, one that depends on the appropriateness of the agent's simple heuristics to the nature of the environment.

11 Factiveness and reference need not be independent sources of broadness, for knowledge-based constraints may play a constitutive role in the determination of reference (Williamson, 2004).

12 This idea is arguably the core of the so-called Disjunctive Theory of Perception. For recent discussion see Martin, 2004 and other papers in the same volume. See Williamson, 2000, pp. 45–8 for necessary qualifications.

13 The internalist category contains much beyond real and counterfeit money: for instance, if some distant society uses internal duplicates of my paperclips as money, my own paperclips fall into the category, without being either real or counterfeit money.

14 One cannot even assume that counterfeit money that is an exact internal duplicate of real money is undetectable; it may be detected by extrinsic properties like location.

References and further reading

Burge, T. (1979). Individualism and the mental. *Midwest Studies in Philosophy*, 4, 73–121.

Clark, A. (1997). *Being There: Putting Brain, Body, and World Together Again.* Cambridge, MA: MIT Press.

Evans, G. (1982). *The Varieties of Reference.* Oxford: Clarendon Press.

Gettier, E. (1963). Is justified true belief knowledge? *Analysis*, 23, 121–3.

Gigerenzer, G., Todd, P., and the ABC Research Group (1999). *Simple Heuristics that Make Us Smart.* Oxford: Oxford University Press.

Hurley, S. (1998). *Consciousness in Action.* Cambridge, MA: Harvard University Press.

Martin, M. G. F. (2004). The limits of self-awareness. *Philosophical Studies*, 120, 37–89.

McDowell, J. (1977). On the sense and reference of a proper name. *Mind*, 86, 159–85.

Pessin, A., Goldberg, S., and Putnam, H. (1996). *The Twin Earth Chronicles: Twenty Years of Reflection on Hilary Putnam's "The Meaning of 'Meaning'."* Armonk, NY: M. E. Sharpe.

Putnam, H. (1975). The meaning of "meaning." In *Mind, Language and Reality.* Cambridge: Cambridge University Press.

— (1978). *Meaning and the Moral Sciences.* London: Routledge & Kegan Paul.

Stanley, J. and Williamson, T. (2001). Knowing how. *Journal of Philosophy*, 98, 411–44.

Williamson, T. (2000). *Knowledge and its Limits.* Oxford: Oxford University Press.

— (2004). Philosophical "intuitions" and scepticism about judgement. *Dialectica*, 58: 109–53.

Yablo, S. (1992). Mental causation. *Philosophical Review*, 101: 245–80.

— (1997). Wide causation. *Philosophical Perspectives*, 11: 251–81.

— (2005). Prime causation. *Philosophy and Phenomenological Research*, 70, 459–67.

CHAPTER EIGHTEEN

The Internal and External Components of Cognition

Ralph Wedgwood

In his chapter in this volume, Timothy Williamson presents several arguments that seek to cast doubt on the idea that cognition can be factorized into internal and external components. In the first section of my chapter, I shall attempt to evaluate these arguments. My conclusion will be that these arguments establish several highly important points, but in the end these arguments fail to cast any doubt either on the idea that cognitive science should be largely concerned with internal mental processes, or on the idea that cognition can be analyzed in terms of the existence of a suitable connection between internal and external components.

In the second and third sections of the chapter, I shall present an argument for the conclusion that cognition involves certain causal processes that are entirely internal – processes in which certain purely internal states and events cause certain other purely internal states and events. There is every reason to think that at least a large part of cognitive science will consist in the study of these purely internal causal processes.

1 An Assessment of Williamson's Arguments

Williamson starts out by assuming, purely for the sake of argument, that there is some distinction that can be drawn between "internal" states of an agent, and "environmental" states. (Environmental states are states that are entirely independent of the intrinsic state of the agent and depend purely on the agent's external environment.) It does not matter for Williamson's purposes exactly how this distinction is drawn, only that some such distinction can be drawn. (I shall have to return to this point, because it *will* matter for my purposes how exactly this distinction is drawn.)

On the basis of this notion of an "internal" state, Williamson then defines the notions of "broad" and "narrow" states. A state S is "narrow" if and only if "whether an agent is in S at a time *t* depends only on the total internal qualitative state of [the agent] at *t*, so that if one agent in one possible situation is internally an exact duplicate of another agent in another possible situation, the first agent is in S in the first situation if and only if the second agent is in S in the second situation." A state is "broad" if and only if it is not "narrow."

In section 1 of his chapter, Williamson rehearses some familiar arguments for the conclusion that practically all the mental states that we ascribe in ordinary folk-psychological discourse are in fact broad. It seems to me that these arguments are eminently plausible. It would be a rash philosopher indeed who sought to challenge Williamson's arguments at this point.

As Williamson points out, there are two main sources of the broadness of these mental states. Many mental states consist in having a certain type of *attitude* towards a certain *content*. Thus, one mental state consists in having the attitude of *belief* towards the content *that Tashkent is the capital of Uzbekistan*; another mental state consists in having the attitude of *hope* towards the content *that Turkey will join the European Union before 2015*; and so on.

In some cases, the broadness of these mental states is guaranteed by the type of *attitude* that they involve. This is the case with the so-called *factive* attitudes, such as the attitude of *knowing*. One cannot know that Tashkent is the capital of Uzbekistan unless Tashkent really is the capital of Uzbekistan: the content of the attitude of knowledge is always a content that is true. (This is why some philosophers have claimed that the object of knowledge is a fact, rather than merely a true proposition.) Suppose that someone in another possible situation is internally an exact duplicate of me, but in that possible situation the capital of Uzbekistan is not in fact Tashkent at all, but Samarkand instead. In that case, even though in the actual situation, I count as *knowing* that Tashkent is the capital of Uzbekistan, the person in the other possible situation does *not* count as knowing this. Thus, the state of knowing that Tashkent is the capital of Uzbekistan is a broad state, not a narrow state.

The other reason why so many mental states are broad rather than narrow has to do with the *content* of those states. This point can be illustrated by means of the following example. Suppose that Twin-Earth is a planet far away from Earth that is qualitatively extraordinarily similar to Earth in all respects. Consider again my belief that Tashkent is the capital of Uzbekistan. There could surely be someone who is internally an exact duplicate of me but who lives not on Earth, but on Twin-Earth. On this person's lips, the name "Tashkent" refers not to Tashkent, but to Twin-Tashkent (the corresponding city on Twin-Earth). So the content of the beliefs that that person expresses by utterances of sentences that involve the name "Tashkent" cannot be the same as the content of the thoughts that I express by using the name. My beliefs are about Tashkent, and the other person's beliefs are about Twin-Tashkent, even though internally we are duplicates of each other. Thus the state of believing or thinking that Tashkent is the capital of Uzbekistan is a broad state, not a narrow state. The considerations that led to this conclusion will generalize to practically all the mental states that we ascribe in ordinary folk-psychological discourse. So it seems that practically all of these ordinary mental states are broad.

In sections 2 and 3 of his chapter, Williamson recapitulates some of the most original arguments that he developed in a groundbreaking book (Williamson, 2000). Here he argues for two main points. First, broad mental states play an important explanatory role (especially in explaining the "long-term effects" of our mental states). Second, many of the mental states that play this important explanatory role are not just broad but *prime*: that is, they are not equivalent to any conjunction of a narrow state and an environmental state.

As I shall argue, Williamson's arguments for these points are entirely sound. Their conclusions are both important and true. Nonetheless, the conclusions of these arguments in fact imply much less than one might at first think. They are quite compatible both with a fairly robust version of "internalism" or "methodological solipsism" (see Fodor, 1980) about cognitive science, and with the view that broad mental states can be illuminatingly analyzed in terms of the existence of an appropriate sort of connection between internal and external elements. The internalist or methodological solipsist about cognitive science can happily accept all of the arguments that Williamson makes here.

I shall focus on Williamson's arguments for the claim that the factive attitudes (like the attitude of knowing) play a crucial role in certain causal explanations. If these arguments are sound, then it should be relatively straightforward to see how to adapt them into arguments for the claim that broad mental states of other kinds play a crucial role in causal explanations. The clearest sort of case in which such broad factive attitudes play an important explanatory role is in the explanation of actions that last a significant amount of time and involve the agent's interacting with his environment. To take one of Williamson's examples (1995), suppose that a burglar spends the whole night ransacking a certain house, even though by ransacking the house so thoroughly he runs a higher risk of being caught. Offhand, it seems quite possible that the explanation of the burglar's acting in this way might have been that he *knew* that the house contained a certain extraordinarily valuable diamond.[1]

As Williamson points out, we would not get such a good explanation of the burglar's behavior by appealing merely to the fact that he *believed* that the house contained the diamond. This is because one crucial difference between knowing something and believing something is that knowledge involves a *robust* connection to the truth. If you know a proposition p, then it is not only the case that p is true and you believe p, but it is also *not* the case that you might easily encounter some (misleadingly) defeating evidence that would lead you to abandon your belief in p.[2] Thus, if the burglar had merely believed that the house contained the diamond, he might easily have discovered evidence in the house that would have led him to abandon his belief that the diamond was there. For example, he might have believed that the diamond was in the house because he believed (i) that if the diamond had not yet fallen into his arch-rival's possession, then it could only be in a certain sugar bowl in the house, and (ii) that the diamond had not yet fallen into his rival's possession. Then he would not have ransacked the house at all: he would have fled the house as soon as he found that the diamond was not in the sugar bowl. Thus, the probability of the burglar's ransacking the house for the whole night given that he knew that it contained the diamond is greater than the probability of his doing so given only that he believed that it contained the diamond.[3]

A second alternative explanation of the burglar's behavior might appeal, not just to the burglar's belief that the house contained the diamond, but to *all* of the burglar's background beliefs and all of his perceptual experiences during the course of his ransacking the house. It may well be that the probability of the burglar's ransacking the house given that he knew that it contained the diamond is no higher than the probability of his ransacking the house given that he had all those background beliefs and perceptual experiences. But as Williamson points out, this second alternative explanation has a different defect. It is vastly *less general* than the original explanation. Even if the burglar had had a slightly different set of background beliefs or a slightly different sequence of perceptual experiences, so long as he had still known that the house contained the diamond, he would still have ransacked the house. This second alternative explanation is overloaded with too many specific details; these details are not really necessary to explain why the burglar ransacked the house. Thus, the original explanation, which appealed to the burglar's knowing that the house contained the diamond, seems preferable to this second alternative explanation as well.

It seems to me that this point will in fact generalize to most cases where we are interested in explaining *actions*. According to a plausible philosophy of action, which is due to Al Mele (2000), actions typically involve a causal feedback loop between (i) the agent's perception of what she is doing and (ii) her intentions to move her limbs in such a way as to realize her goals. Typically, the agent is perceptually monitoring her behavior and its immediate environmental effects, and continually adjusting her behavior so that its effects are in line with her goals. Moreover, practically all the actions that we are interested in explaining take more than an instant to be performed. (Think of such actions as cooking a meal, washing one's laundry, writing an email message, paying one's bills, and so on.) So the fact that one performs such an action is itself a fact about a complicated interaction between one's desires and perceptions, one's bodily movements, and one's environment. It is only to be expected that if the effect or *explanandum* involves this sort of interaction between an agent and her environment, the cause or *explanans* will also involve the agent's relation to her environment. Thus, it is not surprising that broad mental states (such as the agent's perceptual knowledge of her immediate environment) will feature in the explanation of most actions.

For these reasons, then, Williamson's main point seems to be correct: an agent's factive attitudes, like the burglar's knowing that the house contains the diamond, may indeed play a crucial role in causally explaining the agent's behavior. As I mentioned above, there seems to be no reason why this point should not also hold of other broad mental states as well, like my belief that this glass contains water, or that Tashkent is the capital of Uzbekistan. Broad mental states play a crucial explanatory role.

Although this central point seems to me correct, it does not entail the conclusion that Williamson seems to be seeking to support – namely, the conclusion that the "internalist" position that the only mental states that are important *for the purposes of cognitive science* are narrow states is false. Admittedly, once we accept that broad mental states play a crucial role in explaining behavior, it certainly becomes plausible that these broad mental states will play an important role in certain branches of psychology and social theory. It certainly seems plausible that social psychology and the social sciences (including various forms of anthropology, sociology, economics, and political science) will find it useful to appeal to such broad mental states.[4] It also seems overwhelmingly plausible that historians will invoke broad mental states in explaining historical events. But it is not clear that the same point will apply to cognitive science as it is usually understood.

Williamson says at the beginning of his chapter that cognitive science is "the science of cognition," and suggests that cognition is the "process of acquiring, retaining and applying knowledge." But this is too specific to do justice to the broad array of inquiries that are pursued by cognitive scientists. A better statement of the goal of cognitive science would just be to say that it is to "understand how the mind works."

There are many sorts of ways in which one interpret this goal of "understanding how the mind works." But one sort of understanding that cognitive scientists are often interested in achieving is analogous to the understanding that one would have of a clock if one could identify each of its functional parts (its springs and cogwheels, its pendulum, and so on), and the way in which all these parts interact to bring it about that the clock has a reliable disposition to tell the correct time. As Hobbes put it:

> For everything is best understood by its constitutive causes. For as in a watch, or some such small engine, the matter, figure and motion of the wheels cannot well be known, except it be taken insunder and viewed in parts; so to make a more curious search into the rights of states and duties of subjects, it is necessary, (I say, not to take them insunder, but yet that) they be so considered as if they were dissolved . . . (Hobbes, 1651, preface, section 3)

This sort of understanding of how clocks work is quite different from the understanding of clocks that one would have if one studied the impact of clocks on human society, or the economics of clock production, or the stylistic properties of ornamental clocks (from the standpoint of art history). An analogous understanding of how a computer works would involve an understanding of the structure of its electrical circuits and of the logical structure of its programming code. If this is the sort of understanding that cognitive science is particularly interested in, that would help to explain why cognitive scientists are so interested in actually trying to *build* machines that can do some of the things that minds can do.

Thus, at least one of the goals of cognitive science will be to explain the *micro-level processes* that are characteristic of the mind. These are processes in which one mental event or state is caused by another mental event or state that precedes it as closely as one mental event can precede another. None of the examples of psychological explanations that Williamson focuses on are explanations of processes of this sort. These micro-level processes are precisely not processes in which one mental state causes "long-term effects" by a complicated and extensive interaction between the thinker's mind and his environment. Thus, it is not clear that Williamson's arguments cast much doubt on the idea that the mental states that cognitive science is interested in will very often be narrow states.

Still, someone might think that Williamson's argument that these explanatorily important broad states are typically "prime" states (that is, they are not equivalent to any conjunction of narrow states and environmental states) establishes that broad states cannot be analyzed in terms of any relation between narrow mental states and other non-mental factors. (Williamson himself does not claim that his argument establishes that broad states are unanalyzable in this way, but some of his readers might think that his argument does show this.) If broad states cannot be analyzed in this way, then given the importance of broad mental states to the explanation of action, any science of the mind that ignores these broad mental states will, as Williamson puts it, "lose sight of the primary object of its study."

In fact, however, even if broad states are prime, they could still very well be analyzable in terms of some relation between narrow states and non-mental factors. This is because a state is prime just in case it is not equivalent to any *conjunction* of narrow states and environmental states. But obviously there could be an analysis of broad states that does not take the form of a conjunction.

In fact, many of the most promising attempts that philosophers have made on the project of analyzing knowledge (to take just the most prominent example of a broad mental state that philosophers have sought to analyze) have not taken the form of conjunctions at all. Instead, they have taken the form of *existential quantifications*.

Thus, for example, at first glance it might seem that Nozick's (1981, ch. 3) analysis of what it is for an agent to know *p* is just a conjunction of a number of conditions. That is, it might seem that Nozick's analysis is this:

An agent knows a proposition *p* if and only if
1 *p* is true,
2 the agent believes *p*,
3 if *p* were not true, the agent would not believe *p*, and
4 if things were slightly different but *p* were still true, the agent would still believe *p*.

Conditions (3) and (4) are summed up by saying that the agent's belief in *p* "tracks the truth."

On closer inspection, it is clear, however, that when Nozick comes to present the most carefully considered version of his analysis, these four conditions fall within the scope of an existential quantifier. In the final version of his account, Nozick (1981, p. 179) offers first an analysis of what it is for an agent to know *p via method (or way of believing) M*:

An agent knows *p* via method M if and only if
1 *p* is true,
2 the agent believes *p* via M,
3 if *p* were not true, and the agent still used M to arrive at a belief about whether (or not) *p* is true, the agent would not believe *p* via M, and
4 if things were slightly different, but *p* were still true, and the agent still used M to arrive at a belief about whether *p* is true, the agent would still believe *p* via M.

Then Nozick (1981, p. 182) uses this notion of knowing *p* via method M to define what it is for an agent to know *p simpliciter*:

Ralph Wedgwood

An agent knows *p* if and only if *there is some method M* such that (a) the agent knows *p* via M, and (b) if there are any other methods M₁ via which the agent believes *p* but does not know *p*, then these methods are "outweighed" by M.

Ignoring some of these complications, we may say that according to Nozick's analysis, for an agent to know *p* is just for there to be some method M such that M tracks the truth, and the agent believes *p* via M.

What has this to do with Williamson's claim that knowing *p* is a "prime" state? Let us assume – just for the sake of argument – that the state of believing *p* via a particular method M is a narrow state; and let us also assume that the state of being in a situation in which method M tracks the truth is an environmental state. Still, Nozick's analysis will guarantee that the state of knowing *p* is not equivalent to the *conjunction* of any pair of narrow and environmental states of this sort. The reason for this is that there are usually many methods that one could use to arrive at a belief about whether (or not) *p* is true, and for almost all such methods, there are possible situations in which they track the truth, and other possible situations in which they do not.

Consider a simple model in which there are just two relevant methods, M_1 and M_2, and two relevant possible situations S_1 and S_2. Suppose that in both situations, S_1 and S_2, both method M_1 and method M_2 will lead one to believe *p*. However, in situation S_1, method M_1 tracks the truth while method M_2 does not; and in situation S_2, method M_2 tracks the truth while method M_1 does not.

Then, given Nozick's analysis, knowing *p* will not be equivalent to the conjunction of believing *p* via M_1 and M_1's tracking the truth – since one might know *p* even if one were not in this conjunctive state, if one believed *p* via M_2 in situation S_2, in which M_2 tracks the truth. Similarly, knowing *p* is also not equivalent to the conjunction of believing *p* via M_2 and M_2's tracking the truth – for one might know *p* even if one were not in that conjunctive state, if one believed *p* via M_1 in situation S_1, in which M_1 tracks the truth. Moreover, knowing *p* is not equivalent to the conjunction of believing *p* via either M_1 or M_2 in a situation in which either M_1 or M_2 tracks the truth, since one might be in that conjunctive state even if one did *not* know *p* – if one believed *p* via M_1 in S_2, in which M_1 does not track the truth (or if one believed *p* via M_2 in S_1, in which M_2 does not track the truth). And finally, knowing *p* is obviously not equivalent to the conjunction of believing *p* via either M_1 or M_2 in a situation in which *both* M_1 and M_2 track the truth, or to the conjunction of believing *p* via *both* M_1 and M_2 in a situation in which both M_1 and M_2 track the truth.

So it seems that Nozick's analysis of knowledge implies that knowing *p* is not equivalent to any such conjunction at all. At best, it is equivalent to an open-ended disjunction of conjunctions "Either: believing *p* via M_1 while M_1 tracks the truth; or believing *p* via M_2 while M_2 tracks the truth; or ..." But we are assuming here, for the sake of argument, that the state of believing *p* via method M is a narrow state, and being in a situation in which M tracks the truth is an environmental state. According to Nozick's analysis, it is states of this sort that determine whether or not one knows *p*. So, if knowing *p* were a "composite" state according to Nozick's analysis, then knowing p would surely be equivalent to a conjunction of a narrow state and an environmental state of this sort. Since, as we have seen, according to Nozick's analysis, knowing p is not equivalent to any such conjunction, we should conclude that according to this analysis, knowing p is prime, rather than composite. But of course, if Nozick's analysis of knowledge is correct,[5] then knowledge *can* be analyzed by using such notions as "tracking the truth" and "believing p via method M" and the like.

Thus, Williamson's plausible claim that many broad mental states are prime, rather than composite, does not by itself show that the broad state of knowing p cannot be analyzed along Nozick's lines (even if we assume that the state of believing p via method M is an entirely narrow state). So the claim that these broad states are prime does not show that these broad states cannot be analyzed in terms of the existence of narrow states of certain kinds connected in appropriate ways to various non-mental environmental factors. If broad mental states could be analyzed in this way, then it would not be justified to complain that an approach to cognitive science that did not explicitly mention these broad mental states would "lose sight of the primary object of its study." Thus, the claim that these broad mental states are prime does not support this complaint.

2 The Argument from Hallucination

Even if the implications of Williamson's arguments are limited in the ways that I outlined in the previous section, this is hardly yet an argument in favor of any sort of internalism. In particular, it has not even been shown that there are any narrow mental states at all. Some readers may doubt whether there are any narrow mental states, given that – as Williamson argues, and as I have conceded – almost all (if not absolutely all) of the mental states that we ascribe in ordinary folk-psychological discourse are broad. In this section, I shall argue for the existence of narrow mental states. I shall do this by deploying a generalized version of the well-known "argument from hallucination" (see for example Johnston, 2004).

As I shall argue, the argument from hallucination is in effect a general type of argument; there are many specific arguments that are examples of this general type. I shall give two examples of the argument later in this section. The characteristic structure of these arguments is as follows. First, each of these arguments describes a pair of cases, which are externally highly dissimilar, but internally very similar. (For example, such a pair might consist of: (i) a case in which one genuinely perceives one's immediate environment, and (ii) a case in which one has a hallucination that one would not be able to distinguish from such a genuine perception of one's environment.) Then, the argument will try to make it plausible that there must be a mental state that is present in both cases. Since this mental state is present in both cases despite the enormous difference in the external features of the two cases, this makes it plausible that this mental state is a narrow state.

Many philosophers have tried to criticize such arguments from hallucination.[6] But it seems to me that such criticisms at best undermine certain incautious formulations of these arguments. For example, some incautious formulations of the argument try

Ralph Wedgwood

to conclude, not just that there is a mental state that is present in both of the two cases that the argument focuses on, but that this is a mental state of a very special kind, with a very special object (such as a "sense datum") or a special sort of content (such as a special "narrow content" different from the sort of content that ordinary mental states have). As I shall formulate it, the argument from hallucination does not itself try to establish any of these further claims: its conclusion is simply that there is a mental state that is present in both of the two cases, neither more nor less.

Of course, if there is a mental state that is present in both of these two cases, it is natural to ask further questions about this mental state: What sort of mental state is this? And what is the relation between this mental state, which is present in both these two cases, and those mental states that are present in one but not the other of these two cases? However, there is a wide range of answers that could be given to these further questions. While it would indeed be an objection to the argument from hallucination if there were *no* plausible answer that could be given to those further questions, the argument itself is not tied to any specific answer to those further questions.

The first of the two examples of the argument from hallucination that I shall present here starts with a pair of cases that consists of (i) a genuine perception and (ii) a hallucination. (One of the differences between these two cases is that a perception is a factive state: if one perceives that *p* is the case, then *p* is the case: for example, if you see that the window is broken, then the window must indeed be broken.) Let us take the pair of cases that Mark Johnston (2004) invokes in his statement of the argument from hallucination. You are undergoing brain surgery, while quite conscious, under local anesthetic. The surgeon

> applies electrical stimulation to a well-chosen point on your visual cortex. As a result, you hallucinate dimly illuminated spotlights in a ceiling above you.... As it happens, there really are spotlights in the ceiling at precisely the places where you hallucinate lights.

Then:

> the surgeon stops stimulating your brain. You now genuinely see the dimly lit spotlights in the ceiling. From your vantage point there on the operating table these dim lights are indistinguishable from the dim lights you were hallucinating. The transition from ... hallucination to ... veridical perception could be experientially seamless. Try as you might, you would not notice any difference, however closely you attend to your visual experience.[7] (Johnston, 2004, p. 122)

What does it mean to say that "from your vantage point," the dim lights that you see in the ceiling are "indistinguishable from the dim lights you were hallucinating"? It seems to mean this: you lack any reliable ability to respond to the hallucination by forming different beliefs and judgments from the beliefs and judgments that you would form in response to the genuine perception. And the reason why this is the case seems to be that in each of these two cases, you are disposed to form almost exactly the same beliefs and judgments – that is, the same beliefs (and the same doubts and uncertainties) about what is going on in your environment, about your own mental states, and so on.[8]

What can explain this remarkable fact that these two cases are so extraordinarily similar with respect to the beliefs and judgments that you are disposed to form in those cases? One plausible explanation is that there is a mental state that is present in both of these two cases, and it is this common mental state that disposes you to form those beliefs and judgments. As I noted above, I do not have to take a definite stand on the further question of what exactly this common mental state is. Many different answers to this further question are possible. For example, one possible answer is that in this pair of cases, the mental state that is common to both cases might be an *experience as of there being dimly illuminated lights in a ceiling above you*.

Some philosophers deny that there is any common mental state. According to these philosophers the two cases involve fundamentally different mental states – in the one case a hallucination, and in the other a genuine perception; all that these cases have in common is that both cases involve the *disjunction* of these two mental states – that is, they both involve the disjunctive state of *either* hallucinating spotlights in a ceiling *or* seeing spotlights in the ceiling.[9] However, this "disjunctivist" response clearly fails to provide any explanation of something that surely cries out for explanation – namely, how it can be that these two cases are so similar with respect to the beliefs and judgments that one is disposed to form in those cases. After all, *any* two cases in an agent's mental life, no matter how dissimilar these cases may be from each other, will both involve the disjunction of some mental state involved in the first case and some mental state involved in the second. For example, consider one case in which I am in excruciating agony, and another in which I am listening to some beautiful music. These two cases have in common that they both involve the disjunctive state of *either* being in excruciating agony *or* listening to some beautiful music. But that the two cases have this much in common would hardly explain any other similarity that they might have (such as a striking similarity in the beliefs and judgments that one is disposed to form in those cases). Disjunctivism does not begin to engage seriously with the explanatory problem that is raised by the argument from hallucination.

The argument from hallucination can be generalized to other cases as well. In particular, it can also be applied to two cases where your mental states differ in content. There are several different theories about what determines the reference of terms like our term "water" and of the concepts that they express. According to most of these theories, such terms refer to the natural kind that actually causes the thinker (or members of the thinker's community) to use the term in the thinker's normal environment. Now suppose that you are transported from Earth to Twin-Earth in your sleep, and that you then remain on Twin-Earth for the rest of your life. At some point, it will be Twin-Earth, rather than Earth, that counts as your normal environment, and it will be a community on Twin-Earth, rather than any community on Earth, that counts as your community. At that point, then, your terms and concepts switch from referring to the objects and kinds of Earth to referring to the objects and kinds of Twin-Earth. But it is striking that you do not notice any switch in the content of your thoughts. This change seems to leave everything else about your mental states and dispositions unchanged. But that is an extraordinary fact. How can

Ralph Wedgwood

the contents of all your thoughts change so thoroughly and yet leave so much intact? You might even move back and forth between Earth and Twin-Earth several times, in which case the contents of your thoughts might change back and forth several times. How is it possible for such repeated cognitive revolutions to escape your attention?

The best explanation of this, it seems to me, is that there is a mental state that is common to both the Earth case and the Twin-Earth case. In saying that there is a "mental state" present in both cases, I just mean that there is a mental *property* that you have in both cases. I am not requiring that this mental property should take the form of standing in a definite mental relation to a particular content. Again, I do not need to take a definite stand on the further question of what exactly this common mental property is. But one plausible answer to this further question may be that the common mental state is a state such as that of *believing a content of such-and-such a type*. Even if there is no such thing as "narrow content" – that is, even if all intentional contents depend on the thinker's relations to her environment – there may still be narrow *types* of content. That is, it may be that purely internal facts about the thinker are enough to determine that she is indeed believing a content *of such-and-such a type*, even though it is not enough to determine precisely *which* content of this type she is believing. (For example, for a content to be of such a narrow type might be for the content to be composed in such-and-such a way out of *concepts* of such-and-such types – such as concepts that have such-and-such basic conceptual roles. But it does not matter for my purposes exactly how these narrow types of content are defined – only that there are such narrow types of content.)

I shall suppose then that the argument from hallucination succeeds in showing that there is a mental state that is common to both cases in all these pairs of cases. But does it really show that these common mental states are *narrow* states? As I noted at the beginning of section 1, there is some initial unclarity about how exactly we should draw the boundary between internal states and external states. I suggest that we can use these pairs of cases that the argument from hallucination appeals to – the pair consisting of the case of genuine perception and the case of hallucination, the pair consisting of the case on Earth and the case on Twin-Earth, and so on – in order to clarify where this boundary between the internal and the external should be drawn. Admittedly, I have not given a precise account of what all these pairs of cases have in common. Giving such an account, it seems to me, would require much further investigation (possibly including empirical psychological investigation); and I shall not try to anticipate the results of such an investigation here. But to fix ideas, here is a suggestion that seems plausible, at least on first inspection: in each of these pairs of cases, the broad states are uncontroversially different between the two cases, but if the thinker shifts from one case to the other and back again, she will not notice any change; and the reason for this seems to be because all the thinker's mental dispositions are unaffected by the difference between the two cases (except of course the thinker's dispositions with respect to the broad mental states that differ between the two cases).

At all events, once we have a grasp on what these pairs of cases have in common, then we can just *stipulate* that the states that are present in both cases in all these pairs of cases all count as "internal states."[10] If a state is present in all these cases, despite the enormous difference of environmental states between all these cases, this makes it reasonable to call these states "internal states"; and a state that supervenes on these internal states is what I am calling a "narrow state."

At least when the notion of a "narrow state" is understood in this way, it seems to me that it is indeed plausible that the argument from hallucination provides a strong reason to accept the conclusion that there are indeed narrow mental states. As I noted above, this conclusion does not depend on the correctness of any particular answers to the further questions about what sort of states these narrow mental states are, or what their relation is to the broad mental states that are also present in these cases. But to fix ideas, it may be helpful for me to suggest some possible answers to these further questions. In answer to the first of these further questions, I have already suggested that these narrow states consist in standing in *non-factive mental relations* towards certain *narrow types of content*. For example, such narrow states would include: having an experience with a content of such-and-such a type; having a belief with a content of such-and-such a type; and so on.

What about the second of these further questions? What is the relation between broad states and narrow states? For example, what is the relationship between the broad state of knowing p and the narrow state of believing a content of such-and-such a type (where the content p is in fact of such-and-such a type)? It seems plausible that the relationship is one of one-way strict implication: necessarily, if one is in the broad state of knowing p, then one is in the narrow state of believing a content of such-and-such a type; but the converse does not hold. This makes it plausible that the relationship is that of a *determinate* to a *determinable*, as the property of being scarlet is a determinate of the determinable property of being red, and the property of being an equilateral triangle is a determinate of the determinable property of being a triangle. Thus, for example, the relation of knowing is a determinate of the determinable relation of believing; the content p is a determinate of such-and-such a determinable narrow type of content; and the state of knowing p is a determinate of the determinable property of believing a content of such-and-such a narrow type.

3 Internal Causal Processes

Even if there are indeed narrow mental states, as I argued in the previous section, perhaps we cannot expect that the causal explanation of such narrow mental states will themselves appeal only to such narrow mental states. Perhaps broad states will always be needed to explain such narrow states. If so, then there does not seem to be much prospect for a form of cognitive science that focuses exclusively on narrow states. In this section, I shall argue that this is not so. There is a large class of narrow mental states, and a certain sort of causal explanation of these narrow states, such that causal explanations of this sort will explain narrow states purely on the basis of other narrow mental states. The causal processes that are described by these explanations are what I shall call "internal causal processes."

First, the explanations that I am concerned with are explanations of cases in which someone forms or revises their attitudes for a reason. For example, these would include

Ralph Wedgwood

explanations of why a certain agent forms a certain new belief or intention, or revises an old belief or intention, on an occasion on which the agent forms or revises her attitudes in this way for a reason. In a very broad sense, then, these are all explanations of pieces of *reasoning*. The piece of reasoning in question may be either theoretical reasoning (the upshot of which is that the agent forms or revises her beliefs), or practical reasoning (the upshot of which is that the agent forms or revises her intentions about what to do), or any other kind of reasoning that there may be. What this class of explanations excludes, then, are explanations of cases where an agent comes to have a mental state, but not for any reason – such as cases where an agent comes to feel thirsty, or to have a certain sensory experience (on the assumption that these are not mental states that the agent comes to have for a reason).

Second, the explanations that I am concerned with are explanations that seek to break down a process of reasoning into its *basic steps*. (As Hobbes would say, we are trying to understand the mental process's "constitutive causes.") A basic step of this sort would be a mental process that cannot itself be analyzed, at the relevant level of psychological explanation, into any other mental sub-processes at all. Thus, suppose that there is a basic step that leads from one's having a sensory experience as of p's being the case to one's coming to believe p. Then one's having this experience is (at least part of) the *proximate psychological explanation* of one's coming to hold this belief. There are *no intervening steps*, between the experience and the belief, that can be captured at the relevant level of psychological explanation.

In this section, I shall argue that in a case of this kind, if the *explanandum* consists of the fact that the agent acquires (or ceases to have) a narrow mental state, then the proximate explanation will always also consist in some fact about the agent's narrow mental states.[11] I shall argue for this in two stages. First, I shall argue that in any case of this kind, the proximate psychological explanation of an agent's acquiring a *mental* state is always some fact about that agent's *mental* states. Then I shall argue that when the mental state in question is a *narrow* state, then the proximate explanation of the agent's acquiring that state is always a *narrow* mental state of the agent.

In arguing for the first point, I am not denying that it is *ever* correct to explain the fact that an agent acquires a mental state through reasoning on the basis of something other than a fact about the agent's mental states. For example, the fact that I come to believe that Fermat's last theorem is true could surely be explained by the fact that I have been *told by a reliable informant* that Fermat's last theorem is true – even though the fact that I have been told by a reliable informant that Fermat's last theorem is true is not a fact about my mental states. This explanation may be quite correct. It just does not identify the *proximate psychological explanation* of my coming to believe that Fermat's last theorem is true.

Intuitively, it seems, if this is a correct explanation, there must also be a more detailed correct explanation, in which my coming to believe that the theorem is true is not directly explained by my being told by a reliable informant that Fermat's last theorem is true, but is instead explained by some intervening fact about my mental states. For example, perhaps my coming to believe that Fermat's last theorem is true is explained by my having the *belief* that I have been told by a reliable informant that the theorem is true; and my having this belief (that I have been told by a reliable informant that the theorem is true) is itself explained by my having an *experience* as of someone (whom I take to be a reliable informant) telling me that the theorem is true.

Suppose that I claim that an agent's acquiring a certain belief is explained by a certain external fact that is not a fact about that agent's mental states; and suppose that the context does nothing to make it clear how there could be any more detailed correct explanation in which the link between that external fact and the acquisition of that belief is mediated by any intervening facts about the thinker's mental states. For example, suppose that I say, "I once lived in Edinburgh, so George W. Bush believes that I once lived in Edinburgh." It would be natural for you to reply, "But how does Bush know anything about you at all? Did you meet him and talk about your life? Did he have you investigated by the CIA? Or what?" In asking these questions, you seem to reveal that you would not accept this explanation unless it is plausible to you that this link, between the fact that I once lived in Edinburgh and Bush's believing that I once lived in Edinburgh, is mediated by intervening facts about Bush's mental states.

In general, then, if an agent acquires a mental state through reasoning, the proximate psychological explanation of her acquiring this mental state on this occasion will be some fact about her mental states. In fact, it is plausible that this is one of the distinctive features of reasoning – the process of forming or revising one's mental states for a reason – in contrast to mental processes of other kinds: reasoning involves some change in a thinker's beliefs or intentions or other attitudes the proximate explanation of which is some other fact about the thinker's mental states.

So far, I have only argued that the proximate explanation of an agent's acquiring a mental state through reasoning must involve some fact about the agent's *mental states*. I have not yet argued that if the *explanandum* consists in the fact that the agent acquires a certain *narrow* mental state through reasoning, the *explanans* must also consist in a fact about the agent's narrow mental states as well. Ironically, my argument will rely on the very same principle that Williamson relied on to defend the causal efficacy of the state of knowing *p*: if the *explanandum* consists of the fact that the agent acquired a certain narrow mental state, we will achieve a *more general* explanation by appealing to another fact about the agent's narrow mental states than by appealing to a fact about the agent's broad states.

In this second stage of the argument of this section, I shall rely on the idea that I suggested at the end of the previous section, that the relation between a broad mental state and the corresponding narrow state is the relation of a *determinate* to a *determinable*. Thus, for example, the broad state of knowing *p* is a determinate of the determinable narrow state of believing a content of such-and-such a type (where *p* is a content of the relevant type).

If narrow states are related to broad states as determinables to determinates, then it is plausible that whenever one is in a narrow state, one is also in some more determinate broad state. For example, whenever one believes a content of narrow type T, one either knows *p* or falsely believes *q* (where *p* and *q* are both contents of type T) or has some other broad state of this kind. Suppose that in fact one knows *p*. Thus, the event of one's coming to believe a content of type T occurs at exactly

Ralph Wedgwood

the same place and time as the event of one's coming to know p. Some philosophers will want to conclude that these events are in fact identical. But I have been assuming that entities that enter into explanatory relations, either as the thing that gets explained (the *explanandum*) or as the thing that does the explaining (the *explanans*), are *facts* rather than events. It surely is plausible that even if the event of one's coming to believe a content of type T occurs at exactly the same time and place as the event of one's coming to know p, the fact that one comes to believe a content of type T is not the *same fact* as the fact that one comes to know p. After all, even though in fact both of these facts obtain, it could easily happen that the first fact obtains (you come to believe a content of type T) but the second fact does not (this belief does not count as a case of knowing p). Since they are distinct facts, I shall assume that they may have distinct explanations.

So, consider a case in which the *explanandum* – the fact that we are trying to explain – is the fact that an agent acquires a certain narrow mental state through reasoning. Specifically, suppose that this *explanandum* is the fact that the agent acquires a belief in a content of a certain narrow type T_1. Now consider two rival explanations of this fact. According to the first of these explanations, the agent acquires this narrow mental state because she is in a certain antecedent *broad* mental state – say, the state of knowing a certain propositional content p. According to the second explanation, she acquires this narrow mental state because she is in certain antecedent narrow state – where this narrow state is in fact a *determinable* narrow state of which the broad state cited in the first explanation is a determinate. Thus, if the broad state cited in the first explanation is the state of knowing p, the narrow state cited in the second explanation might be the state of believing a content of type T_2 – where the propositional content p is a content of type T_2, and knowing is a type of believing.

Now it seems quite possible that the fact that the agent is in the narrow mental state that is cited in the second explanation will be just as close to being causally sufficient for the *explanandum* as the fact that she is in the broad mental state that is cited in the first explanation. The probability that the agent will acquire a belief in a content of type T_1 is just as high given that she is in the antecedent narrow state of believing a content of type T_2 as the probability that she will acquire such a belief given that she is in the antecedent broad state of knowing p.

However, the second explanation will obviously be *more general* than the first. Consider a case in which you are *not* in the broad state that is cited in the first explanation, but you are still in the narrow state that is cited in the second explanation (which is a determinable of which the broad state cited in the first explanation is a determinate). Surely you would still acquire the narrow mental state (such as the belief in a content of type T_1), which is the fact that both explanations sought to explain. After all, the argument for postulating such narrow states in the first place – the argument from hallucination – was precisely that such narrow states were needed to explain certain striking similarities in the short-term mental effects of certain pairs of cases. Thus, I argued that there must be a narrow mental state present both in the case of hallucination and in the case of genuine perception because both cases had such similar short-term mental effects (so that it was possible for an agent to shift from the case of hallucination to the case of genuine perception without noticing any difference at all). Similarly, I argued that there must be a narrow mental state present both in the Earth case and in the Twin-Earth case to explain the striking similarities in the mental causal effects of the two cases (and to explain why one would not notice the contents of one's thoughts change as one is transported back and forth between Earth and Twin-Earth in one's sleep).

It is plausible that other things being equal, we should prefer the more general of two explanations that otherwise count as equally good explanations of the same effect, from the same temporal distance. This point is especially plausible if the fact cited as the *explanans* in the more general explanation is a determinable of which the fact cited as the *explanans* in the less general explanation is a determinate. Here is a simple illustration of this point. Suppose that we want to explain why a certain code-protected door opened for the heroine. One explanation that we could give would be to say that the door opened because the heroine drew an equilateral triangle with each side measuring three inches, using her right index finger. A second explanation that we could give would be to say that the door opened because she drew a triangle. Now suppose that in fact *any* triangle drawn on the code-pad would have succeeded in opening the door. In that case, the second explanation is a better explanation, because it is more general than the first.[12]

For these reasons, then, it seems highly plausible that the proximate psychological explanation of these cases in which an agent acquires a narrow mental state through reasoning is itself always a fact about the agent's narrow mental states. This is not to say that broad states *never* play a role in psychological explanations. As we saw when I endorsed Williamson's arguments in section 1, knowledge does seem to play such a role in the explanation of certain *actions*. Here, however, the *explanandum* – such as the burglar's ransacking the house that contains the diamond – consists in an agent's interacting with his environment in a certain way. It is only to be expected that the *explanans* – the burglar's knowing that the house contains the diamond – will also consist in the agent's standing in a certain relation to his environment. This does not show that such broad states will figure in the explanation of the fact that the agent acquires a *narrow* mental state (such as the fact that a thinker comes to believe a content of type T_1 at time t). A narrow mental fact of this sort is surely more likely to have a correspondingly narrow mental explanation. In general, the overall effect of the principle about explanation that I am appealing to here is that in any correct explanation there must be a certain sort of *proportionality* between the *explanandum* and the *explanans*. The *explanans* must be sufficient in the circumstances to produce the *explanandum*; but it also must not contain any irrelevant elements that could be stripped away without making it any less sufficient to produce the *explanandum*. This proportionality principle makes it plausible that narrow mental states will be particularly well placed to explain other narrow mental states, and broad mental states will be particularly well placed to explain other broad mental states (as well as actions, which like broad mental states also depend, in part, on the agent's relations to her environment).

For these reasons, then, it seems plausible to me that there are correct explanations in which both the fact that is explained (the *explanandum*) and the fact that does the explaining (the *explanans*) are facts about the agent's narrow mental states. At least one branch of cognitive science could be devoted to ascertaining precisely which explanations of this sort are correct. This branch of cognitive science would

Ralph Wedgwood

be a theory of the nature of internal mental processes of this kind, which would be largely independent of the agent's relationship to her wider environment.

Moreover, as we saw in considering Nozick's definition of knowledge, Williamson's arguments do not show that broad states, like the state of knowing *p*, cannot be analyzed in terms of the existence of appropriate connections between narrow states and the non-mental objects, properties, and kinds in the agent's environment. It may be that some such analysis can be given of all such broad mental states.[13] If that is the case, then a correct account of all the causal relations, actual and counter-factual, among both the agent's narrow states and the non-mental objects, propert-ies, and kinds in the agent's environment, will in fact state all the same facts as a correct account that overtly appeals to broad mental states. In that case, a form of cognitive science that focused purely on explaining narrow mental states in terms of other narrow states (when supplemented by an account of the causal relations between these narrow mental states and various non-mental features in the agent's environment) would be able to capture everything that can be stated in terms of such broad states; and a cognitive science of this kind could not fairly be accused of "losing sight of the primary object of its study."

I cannot undertake to settle the question here of whether all broad mental states can be analyzed in such terms. Even if broad mental states cannot be analyzed in this way, a form of cognitive science that restricts itself to studying purely internal cognitive processes would still be investigating some pervasive and genuinely cognitive phenomena. But if broad mental states can be analyzed in this way, then such a form of cognitive science could truly claim to be seeking the answer to the question of "how the mind works."

Acknowledgments

This chapter was written with the support of a Research Leave award from the UK Arts and Humanities Research Board, for which I should like to express my gratitude. I should also like to thank Alex Byrne, Timothy Williamson, and Rob Stainton, the editor of this volume, for very helpful comments on an earlier draft.

Notes

1   See also Williamson (2000, pp. 60–4, 75–88). Of course, if we can give a noncircular definition of knowledge in terms of other folk-psychological notions – for example, if knowledge can be defined as a rational belief that is in a certain sense "reliable," as I believe – then knowledge would not play an *indispensable* role in any of these explanations. I shall touch on this question in the last section.

2   This point is due to Harman (1973, pp. 143–4); for further discussion, see Wedgwood, 2002a.

3   We would also not get such a good explanation of the burglar's behavior by appealing to the fact that the burglar *truly believed* that the diamond was in the house. Even if the diamond was in the house (say, hidden inside the grand piano), the burglar might have believed that it was in the house only because he believed that it was in the sugar bowl, in which case he would still not have ransacked the house for the whole night.

4 For example, see Diamond (1997, p. 143): "an entire field of science, termed ethnobiology, studies people's knowledge of the wild plants and animals in their environment."

5 Of course, this is a big "if." Almost no one thinks that Nozick's analysis is exactly right as it stands. But I actually think that an analysis that is at least a little like Nozick's does succeed; see Wedgwood, 2002a.

6 For such criticisms, see McDowell, 1994 and Dancy, 1995.

7 Johnston actually focuses on three cases: a hallucination whose content is false or non-veridical, a veridical hallucination, and a genuine perception. It seems to me however that this additional sophistication is not strictly necessary for the argument.

8 I say "*almost* exactly the same beliefs and judgments" because strictly speaking demonstrative judgments (such as the judgment that *those lights there* are dim) will be different in the two cases, as we can see from the fact that such demonstrative judgments will have different truth conditions in the two cases.

9 This is the view of a school of thought known as "disjunctivism." For some canonical statements of this disjunctivist view, see Hinton, 1973; Snowdon, 1981; and McDowell, 1994. For criticism of some of the arguments that are used to support this disjunctive view, see Millar, 1996.

10 One question that requires further investigation is whether these "internal" states supervene on intrinsic features of the agent's brain or whether their supervenience base must include something about the wider environment. It may be, for example, that a brain in a vat that had *never* been connected to a body that was capable of acting in a normal environment could not have any mental states at all. If so, then these "internal" states will not supervene on intrinsic features of the agent's brain, but only on a *slightly* wider supervenience basis, which might include certain highly general and unspecific features of the agent's environment. Nonetheless, the supervenience basis for these internal states would presumably be much narrower than the broad states that Williamson focuses on.

11 The argument that I give here is a generalization of an argument that I gave elsewhere (Wedgwood, 2002b).

12 I owe this example to the editor of this volume. For some further discussion of this principle about why we should under certain circumstances prefer the more general causal explanations, see Yablo, 1992a, pp. 413–23; 1992b; 1997.

13 Indeed, I believe that it can be argued that there would be something wildly puzzling and mysterious about broad mental states if they were not analyzable in some such way. But there is not enough space to present this argument here.

References and further reading

Dancy, J. (1995). Arguments from Illusion. *Philosophical Quarterly*, 45, 421–38.
Diamond, J. (1997). *Guns, Germs and Steel: The Fates of Human Societies.* New York: Norton.
Fodor, J. (1980). Methodological solipsism considered as a research strategy in cognitive science. *Behavioral and Brain Sciences*, 3, 63–109.
Harman, G. (1973). *Thought.* Princeton, NJ: Princeton University Press.
Hinton, J. M. (1973). *Experiences.* Oxford: Clarendon Press.
Hobbes, T. (1651). *De Cive.* (English edn., *Philosophical Rudiments concerning Government and Society*). London: R. Royston.
Johnston, M. (2004). The obscure object of hallucination. *Philosophical Studies*, 120, 113–83.
McDowell, J. (1994). *Mind and World.* Cambridge, MA: Harvard University Press.
— (1995). Knowledge and the internal. *Philosophy and Phenomenological Research*, 55, 877–93.

Mele, A. (2000). Goal-directed action: Teleological explanations, causal theories, and deviance. *Philosophical Perspectives*, 14, 279–300.

Millar, A. (1996). The idea of experience. *Proceedings of the Aristotelian Society*, 96, 75–90.

Nozick, R. (1981). *Philosophical Explanations*. Cambridge, MA: Harvard University Press.

Putnam, H. (1975). The meaning of "meaning." In H. Putnam, *Mind, Language and Reality: Philosophical Papers*, vol. 2. Cambridge: Cambridge University Press.

Snowdon, P. F. (1981). Perception, vision and causation. *Proceedings of the Aristotelian Society*, 81, 175–92.

Wedgwood, R. (2002a). The aim of belief. *Philosophical Perspectives*, 16, 267–97.

— (2002b). Internalism explained. *Philosophy and Phenomenological Research*, 65, 349–69.

Williamson, T. (1995). Is knowing a state of mind? *Mind*, 104, 533–65.

— (2000). *Knowledge and Its Limits* Oxford: Clarendon Press.

Yablo, S. (1992a). Cause and essence. *Synthese*, 93, 403–49.

— (1992b). Mental causation. *Philosophical Review*, 101, 245–80.

— (1997). Wide causation. *Philosophical Perspectives*, 11, 251–81.

Index

Page numbers in italics refer to figures

innateness, 66
judgments, 315–16
knowledge, 215 n. 4, 292–3, 301–2,
   305 n. 8, 308, 323 n. 1
location, 148–9
mental states, 293
modules, 16
perceptual, 265, 309–10
philosophical, 148–9
Quechua speakers, 26
representation, 134–5
theory confirmation, 158 n. 7
Berkeley, G., 83
Bermudez, J. L., 279
Bernoulli, D., 116
Big Computer view, 4, 41–2
binocular vision, 268
biological approach, 8–11, 41, 42–3, 162
biophysical machinery approach, 97–8, 100,
   101, 102–3, 109
Blackmore, S. J., 272–3 n. 18
blind spot, 261, 268
blindness, 4, 26, 29, 247
   see also change blindness; inattentional
      blindness
Block, N. J., 189–90, 195, 196–7, 246
bounded rationality
   Enlightenment Picture, 136–42
   Gigerenzer, G., 135–6, 137, 139, 142
   optimization, 118
   probability calculus, 141–2
Boyd, R. N., 62
Boyle-Charles law, 161, 170
brain damage, people with, 281
brain surgery example, 315
Brentano, F., 240, 252
Broca's area, 23, 24, 29
Bruner, J., 52
Buñuel, L., 269
Burge, T., 243
burglary example, 309–10, 322, 323 n. 3
Bush, R. R., 171
Buss, D., 46

Cab Problem example, 137–8, 139
camel concept, 28
car example, 245–6
carbohydrate metabolism, 162
card tricks, 269
Carey, S., 248

Carruthers, P.
   encapsulation, 30, 33, 45
   massive mental modularity, 48
   modularity, xiii, 22, 37, 40
   practical reasoning, 16
   qualia, 190
Cartwright, R., 250, 252
central systems, 37, 41–2
ceteris paribus generalizations, 155–6
Chalmers, D. J., 207, 210
change blindness, 270
   examples, 268–9
   experiments, 259–60, 272 n. 16
   illusion, 264, 283
   visual field, 261
Chierchia, G., 227
children
   antibiotics prescriptions, 126
   environment for learning, 92
   I-language, 98
children's language acquisition
   American Sign Language, 168
   Chomsky, N., 72, 84, 86
   deafness, 73–4
   domain specific knowledge, 93
   errors, 107
   Gold, E. M., 69–70
   innateness, 65, 83–4
   internalist reasoning, 99–100
   interrogatives, 86–7, 110 n. 4
   past-tense formation, 166
   sentence constructions, 101
   unacquired linguistic universals, 71–2
Chomsky, N.
   Cartesian Linguistics, 106
   children's language acquisition, 72, 84, 86
   core language, 75 n. 4
   creative aspect of language use, 106–7
   E-languages, 98–9
   existence of objects, 244
   experiential world, 251
   factors of language growth, 102
   generative grammar, 159
   I-language, 98
   language acquisition, 62, 75 n. 1, 84,
      94 n. 6
   linguistic nativism, 90
   natural languages, 92, 105
   phonetics, 237
   poverty of the stimulus, 111 n. 13

proportionality principle, 322
psychological explanation, 319
psychological primitive structures, 64
psychological states, 305 n. 4
psychophysics, 170, 182
psychosemantics, 195-6
Pullum, G., xiii, 72, 88, 97, 101, 103
Putnam, H., 68, 94 n. 15, 243, 293-5, 297,
    304 n. 1
Pylyshyn, Z., 248, 280

qualia, 189-90
    experiences, 199 n. 4
    introspection, 209
    Lycan, W. G., 190, 197
    narrow, 196-7
    natural languages, 190
    non-physical, 207
    phenomenal character, 193-8
    reductionism, 202-3
quasi-representationism, 195
Quechua speakers, 26
Quilian, M. R., 169
Quine, W. V. O., 139, 242
Quinlan, J. R., 126

Ramachandran, V. S., 32
rationalism, 83, 109 n. 1
rationalist research program, 97
rationality
    arguments about, 115-16
    ecological, 116, 119-21
    Enlightenment, 115
    external form, 123
    Homo sapiens, 128-9
    innate knowledge, 82-3
    uncertainty, 137-8, 141-2
    see also bounded rationality; unbounded
        rationality
Reali, F., 72
realism, 117-18, 226
reality
    color, 265
    Jackendoff, R., 240, 244, 249-51,
        252-3 n. 3, 253 n. 9
    language, 237
    perceivers, 247-8
    psychological, 240, 247-9
    standard linguistic entities, 250

reasoning
    explanation, 319
    internalist, 99-100, 128, 239
    mental states, 320, 322
    modularity, 41-2
    practical, 16, 221
    social, 221
reciprocity, 122-3
recognition, visual, 25
    see also face recognition
recognition heuristic, 124-5
reduction, type/token, 190-1, 203
reductionism
    conceivability argument, 203-5
    natural science, 206-7
    physicalist, 207
    qualia, 202-3
reductivism, 61-2
reference
    conceptualist theory, 226-7
    deictic, 227-9, 233-4
    intended, 233
    perception, 231-2
    purported, 232-5
    realist theory, 226
    truth, 235
    truth-value, 222-3
relevance module, 48
representation, 118
    accuracy, 266, 276-80
    beliefs, 134-5
    causes, 248
    Chomsky, N., 253 n. 5
    conceptual, 280-1
    contentful/architectural, 103-6
    existential, 241-3
    Higher Order, 191-2, 193, 195, 196, 199
    intentionality, 239, 241-3
    internal, 240-1
    Lycan, W. G., 195, 196, 214
    mental systems, 53 n. 1
    non-existent things, 241-2
    noun phrase, 104
    perception, 275
    perceptual systems, 259-60
    psychosemantics, 195-6
    sensorimotor, 280-1
    standard linguistic entities, 240-1
    thermoreceptors, 278-9
    visual experiences, 260

representation-world relations, 104
representationalism, 193, 197, 213-14
retina, 25, 227-8
Rey, G., xiv, 192, 197, 252 n. 1
Rips, L., 123
Rock, I., 269-70
Rosenblatt, F., 163
Rosenthal, D., 190, 191
rules
    application of, 163
    exceptionless, 147-8, 154-5, 157
    language processing, 159
    programmable, 155
Rumelhart, D. E., 166

Saffran, J. R., 63
Sampson, G., 72
Samuels, R., xiii, 12, 64, 65, 129
Sapir, E., 237
satisfaction, 232-5
satisficing, 15
Saussure, F. de, 237
Saussurean arbitrariness, 102
Scholz, B. C., xiii, 72, 88, 97, 101, 103
science, laws, 161
scientific approach, 206-7
scope ambiguity, 16
search rules, 32, 125
Searle, J., 215 n. 14
Segal, G., 6
selection processor, 47
selection task, 122
semantics
    Chomsky, N., 238
    conceptualist, 219-22
    dynamic, 230
    priming, 25
    situation, 233
    syntax, 150-1
    truth conditional, 235
SEMs (linguistic meanings), 105
senses, 26, 59, 62, 194
sensorimotor intelligence, 85, 284-5
sensorimotor model, 261-3, 280-1,
        286 n. 11
sensory receptors, 260-1
sentences, 100-1, 233-4, 235, 244-5
shallowness, modularity, 39
Shoemaker, S., 192, 197
Siegler, R., 180

Siewert, C., 264
signing, 73-4, 168, 247
similarity, 300, 301-2, 314
Simon, H., 8, 10, 42-3, 118-19
Simons, D., 272 n. 16
simple recurrent networks (SRNs), 76 n. 11,
        110 n. 5
    auxiliary inversion, 70, 98
    connectionism, 90, 102
    Elman, J. L., 72, 99, 181
    generalization, 72
situatedness heuristics, 121
Skinner, B. F., 61, 74, 106
Smith, B., 189
Smith, L., 178
Smolensky, P., 168
snapshot model, 265-6, 283-4
Sober, E., 65
social exchanges, 24
social heuristics, 126-7
social psychology, 310-11
social reasoning, 41
social skills, 11, 26
Socrates, 82
Solomonoff, R., 68
sound/touch, 32
specificity: see domain specificity
speech continuum, 237
speed, 25, 39
Sperber, D., 50, 53 n. 1
square peg/round hole example, 297
SRNs: see simple recurrent networks
standard linguistic entities
    acoustic, 249, 250
    cars, 245-6
    Chomsky, N., 253 n. 8
    denial of, 238
    non-existence, 251
    orthographic, 249
    reality, 250
    representation, 240-1
    tokens, 237, 240
    unreality, 243
state changes, 169, 173
statistical sampling, 98, 100
steam engine, 175, 176
Sterelny, K., 237, 239
Sternberg, S., 171-2, 173
Stevens, S. S., 170
Stich, S., 64, 66